Machine Learning for Finance

Principles and practice for financial insiders

Jannes Klaas

BIRMINGHAM - MUMBAI

Machine Learning for Finance

Acquisition Editors: Frank Pohlmann, Ben Renow-Clarke

Acquisition Editor – Peer Reviews: Suresh Jain

Project Editor: Tom Jacob

Development Editor: Alex Sorrentino

Technical Editor: Gaurav Gavas

Proofreader: Safis Editing

Indexer: Rekha Nair

Graphics: Sandip Tadge, Tom Scaria

Production Coordinator: Sandip Tadge

First published: May 2019

Production reference: 2170619

Published by Packt Publishing Ltd.
Livery Place
35 Livery Street
Birmingham B3 2PB, UK.

ISBN 978-1-78913-636-4

www.packtpub.com

`mapt.io`

Mapt is an online digital library that gives you full access to over 5,000 books and videos, as well as industry leading tools to help you plan your personal development and advance your career. For more information, please visit our website.

Why subscribe?

- Spend less time learning and more time coding with practical eBooks and Videos from over 4,000 industry professionals
- Learn better with Skill Plans built especially for you
- Get a free eBook or video every month
- Mapt is fully searchable
- Copy and paste, print, and bookmark content

Packt.com

Did you know that Packt offers eBook versions of every book published, with PDF and ePub files available? You can upgrade to the eBook version at `www.Packt.com` and as a print book customer, you are entitled to a discount on the eBook copy. Get in touch with us at `customercare@packtpub.com` for more details.

At `www.Packt.com`, you can also read a collection of free technical articles, sign up for a range of free newsletters, and receive exclusive discounts and offers on Packt books and eBooks.

Contributors

About the author

Jannes Klaas is a quantitative researcher with a background in economics and finance. He taught machine learning for finance as lead developer for machine learning at the Turing Society, Rotterdam. He has led machine learning bootcamps and worked with financial companies on data-driven applications and trading strategies.

Jannes is currently a graduate student at Oxford University with active research interests including systemic risk and large-scale automated knowledge discovery.

About the reviewer

James Le is currently a master's student studying computer science at Rochester Institute of Technology. He is pursuing a research path in computer vision using deep learning. On the side, he is an active freelance data scientist and data journalist, with specialties including machine/deep learning, recommendation systems, and data analysis/visualization.

Table of Contents

Preface

Aided by the availability of vast amounts of data computing resources, **machine learning (ML)** has made big strides. The financial industry, which at its heart is an information processing enterprise, holds an enormous amount of opportunity for the deployment of these new technologies.

This book is a practical guide to modern ML applied in the financial industry. Using a code-first approach, it will teach you how the most useful ML algorithms work, and how to use them to solve real-world problems

Who this book is for

There are three kinds of people who would benefit the most from this book:

- Data scientists who want to break into finance and would like to know about the spectrum of possible applications and relevant problems

- Developers in any FinTech business or quantitative finance professionals who look to upgrade their skill set and want to incorporate advanced ML methods into their modeling process

- Students who would like to prepare themselves for the labor market and learn some practical skills valued by employers

This book assumes you have some working knowledge in linear algebra, statistics, probability theory, and calculus. However, you do not have to be an expert in any of those topics.

To follow the code examples, you should be comfortable with Python and the most common data science libraries, such as pandas, NumPy, and Matplotlib. The book's example code is presented in Jupyter Notebooks.

Explicit knowledge of finance is not required.

What this book covers

Chapter 1, Neural Networks and Gradient-Based Optimization, will explore what kinds of ML there are, and the motivations for using them in different areas of the financial industry. We will then learn how neural networks work and build one from scratch.

Chapter 2, Applying Machine Learning to Structured Data, will deal with data that resides in a fixed field within, for example, a relational database. We will walk through the process of model creation: from forming a heuristic, to building a simple model on engineered features, to a fully learned solution. On the way, we will learn about how to evaluate our models with scikit-learn, how to train tree-based methods such as random forests, and how to use Keras to build a neural network for this task.

Chapter 3, Utilizing Computer Vision, describes how computer vision allows us to perceive and interpret the real world at scale. In this chapter, we will learn the mechanisms with which computers can learn to identify image content. We will learn about convolutional neural networks and the Keras building blocks we need to design and train state-of-the-art computer vision models.

Chapter 4, Understanding Time Series, looks at the large number of tools devoted to the analysis of temporally related data. In this chapter, we will first discuss the "greatest hits" that industry professionals have been using to model time series and how to use them efficiently with Python. We will then discover how modern ML algorithms can find patterns in time series and how they are complemented by classic methods.

Chapter 5, Parsing Textual Data with Natural Language Processing, uses the spaCy library and a large corpus of news to discuss how common tasks such as named entity recognition and sentiment analysis can be performed quickly and efficiently. We will then learn how we can use Keras to build our own custom language models. The chapter introduces the Keras functional API, which allows us to build much more complex models that can, for instance, translate between languages.

Chapter 6, Using Generative Models, explains how generative models generate new data. This is useful when we either do not have enough data or want to analyze our data by learning about how the model perceives it. In this chapter, we will learn about (variational) autoencoders as well as generative adversarial models. We will learn how to make sense of them using the t-SNE algorithm and how to use them for unconventional purposes, such as catching credit card fraud. We will learn about how we can supplement human labeling operations with ML to streamline data collection and labeling. Finally, we will learn how to use active learning to collect the most useful data and greatly reduce data needs.

Chapter 7, Reinforcement Learning for Financial Markets, looks at reinforcement learning, which is an approach that does not require a human-labeled "correct" answer for training, but only a reward signal. In this chapter, we will discuss and implement several reinforcement learning algorithms, from Q-learning to **Advantage Actor-Critic (A2C)**. We will discuss the underlying theory, its connection to economics, and in a practical example, see how reinforcement learning can be used to directly inform portfolio formation.

Chapter 8, Privacy, Debugging, and Launching Your Products, addresses how there is a lot that can go wrong when building and shipping complex models. We will discuss how to debug and test your data, how to keep sensitive data private while training models on it, how to prepare your data for training, and how to disentangle why your model is making the predictions it makes. We will then look at how to automatically tune your model's hyperparameters, how to use the learning rate to reduce overfitting, and how to diagnose and avoid exploding and vanishing gradients. After that, the chapter explains how to monitor and understand the right metrics in production. Finally, it discusses how you can improve the speed of your models.

Chapter 9, Fighting Bias, discusses how ML models can learn unfair policies and even break anti-discrimination laws. It highlights several approaches to improve model fairness, including pivot learning and causal learning. It shows how to inspect models and probe for bias. Finally, we discuss how unfairness can be a failure in the complex system that your model is embedded in and give a checklist that can help you reduce bias.

Chapter 10, Bayesian Inference and Probabilistic Programming, uses PyMC3 to discuss the theory and practical advantages of probabilistic programming. We will implement our own sampler, understand Bayes theorem numerically, and finally learn how we can infer the distribution of volatility from stock prices.

To get the most out of this book

All code examples are hosted on Kaggle. You can use Kaggle for free and get access to a GPU, which will enable you to run the example code much faster. If you do not have a very powerful machine with a GPU, it will be much more comfortable to run the code on Kaggle. You can find links to all notebooks on this book's GitHub page: https://github.com/PacktPublishing/Machine-Learning-for-Finance.

This book assumes some working knowledge of mathematical concepts such as linear algebra, statistics, probability theory, and calculus. You do not have to be an expert, however.

Equally, knowledge of Python and some popular data science libraries such as pandas and Matplotlib is assumed.

Download the example code files

You can download the example code files for this book from your account at http://www.packt.com. If you purchased this book elsewhere, you can visit http://www.packt.com/support and register to have the files emailed directly to you.

You can download the code files by following these steps:

1. Log in or register at http://www.packt.com.
2. Select the **SUPPORT** tab.
3. Click on **Code Downloads & Errata**.
4. Enter the name of the book in the **Search** box and follow the on-screen instructions.

Once the file is downloaded, please make sure that you unzip or extract the folder using the latest version of:

- WinRAR / 7-Zip for Windows
- Zipeg / iZip / UnRarX for Mac
- 7-Zip / PeaZip for Linux

We also have other code bundles from our rich catalog of books and videos available at https://github.com/PacktPublishing/. Check them out!

Download the color images

We also provide a PDF file that has color images of the screenshots/diagrams used in this book. You can download it here: http://www.packtpub.com/sites/default/files/downloads/9781789136364_ColorImages.pdf.

Conventions used

There are a number of text conventions used throughout this book.

CodeInText: Indicates code words in the text, database table names, folder names, filenames, file extensions, pathnames, dummy URLs, user input, and Twitter handles. For example; "Mount the downloaded WebStorm-10*.dmg disk image file as another disk in your system."

A block of code is set as follows:

```
import numpy as np
x_train = np.expand_dims(x_train,-1)
x_test = np.expand_dims(x_test,-1)
x_train.shape
```

When we wish to draw your attention to a particular part of a code block, the relevant lines or items are set in bold:

```
from keras.models import Sequential
img_shape = (28,28,1)
model = Sequential()
model.add(Conv2D(6,3,input_shape=img_shape))
```

Any command-line input or output is written as follows:

```
Train on 60000 samples, validate on 10000 samples

Epoch 1/10

60000/60000 [==============================] - 22s 374us/step - loss:
7707.2773 - acc: 0.6556 - val_loss: 55.7280 - val_acc: 0.7322
```

Bold: Indicates a new term, an important word, or words that you see on the screen, for example, in menus or dialog boxes, also appear in the text like this. For example: "Select **System info** from the **Administration** panel."

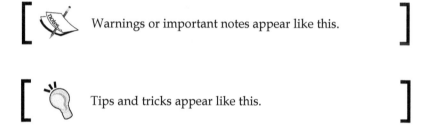

> Warnings or important notes appear like this.

> Tips and tricks appear like this.

Get in touch

Feedback from our readers is always welcome.

General feedback: If you have questions about any aspect of this book, mention the book title in the subject of your message and email us at customercare@packtpub.com.

Errata: Although we have taken every care to ensure the accuracy of our content, mistakes do happen. If you have found a mistake in this book we would be grateful if you would report this to us. Please visit, http://www.packt.com/submit-errata, selecting your book, clicking on the Errata Submission Form link, and entering the details.

Piracy: If you come across any illegal copies of our works in any form on the Internet, we would be grateful if you would provide us with the location address or website name. Please contact us at copyright@packt.com with a link to the material.

If you are interested in becoming an author: If there is a topic that you have expertise in and you are interested in either writing or contributing to a book, please visit http://authors.packtpub.com.

Reviews

Please leave a review. Once you have read and used this book, why not leave a review on the site that you purchased it from? Potential readers can then see and use your unbiased opinion to make purchase decisions, we at Packt can understand what you think about our products, and our authors can see your feedback on their book. Thank you!

For more information about Packt, please visit packt.com.

1

Neural Networks and Gradient-Based Optimization

The financial services industry is fundamentally an information processing industry. An investment fund processes information in order to evaluate investments, an insurance company processes information to price their insurances, while a retail bank will process information in order to decide which products to offer to which customers. It is, therefore, no accident that the financial industry was an early adopter of computers.

The first stock ticker was the printing telegraph, which was invented back in 1867. The first mechanical adding machine, which was directly targeted at the finance industry, was patented in 1885. Then in 1971, the automatic teller banking machine, which allowed customers to withdraw cash using a plastic card, was patented. That same year, the first electronic stock exchange, the NASDAQ, opened its doors, and 11 years later, in 1982, the first Bloomberg Terminal was installed. The reason for the happy marriage between the finance sector and computers is that success in the industry, especially in investing, is often tied to you having an information advantage.

In the early days of Wall Street, the legends of the gilded age made brazen use of private information. Jay Gould, for example, one of the richest men of his time, placed a mole inside the US government. The mole was to give notice of government gold sales and through that, tried to influence President Ulysses S. Grant as well as his secretary. Toward the end of the 1930s, the SEC and CFTC stood between investors and such information advantages.

As information advantages ceased to be a reliable source of above-market performance, clever financial modeling took its place. The term *hedge fund* was coined back in 1949, the Harry Markowitz model was published in 1953, and in 1973, the Black-Scholes formula was first published. Since then, the field has made much progress and has developed a wide range of financial products. However, as knowledge of these models becomes more widespread, the returns on using them diminish.

When we look at the financial industry coupled with modern computing, it's clear that the information advantage is back. This time not in the form of insider information and sleazy deals, but instead is coming from an automated analysis of the vast amount of public information that's out there.

Today's fund managers have access to more information than their forbearers could ever dream of. However, this is not useful on its own. For example, let's look at news reports. You can get them via the internet and they are easy to access, but to make use of them, a computer would have to read, understand, and contextualize them. The computer would have to know which company an article is about, whether it is good news or bad news that's being reported, and whether we can learn something about the relationship between this company and another company mentioned in the article. Those are just a couple of examples of contextualizing the story. Firms that master sourcing such **alternative data,** as it is often called, will often have an advantage.

But it does not stop there. Financial professionals are expensive people who frequently make six- to seven-figure salaries and occupy office space in some of the most expensive real estate in the world. This is justified as many financial professionals are smart, well-educated, and hard-working people that are scarce and for which there is a high demand. Because of this, it's thus in the interest of any company to maximize the productivity of these individuals. By getting more bang for the buck from the best employees, they will allow companies to offer their products cheaper or in greater variety.

Passive investing through exchange-traded funds, for instance, requires little management for large sums of money. Fees for passive investment vehicles, such as funds that just mirror the S&P 500, are often well below one percent. But with the rise of modern computing technology, firms are now able to increase the productivity of their money managers and thus reduce their fees to stay competitive.

Our journey in this book

This book is not only about investing or trading in the finance sector; it's much more as a direct result of the love story between computers and finance. Investment firms have customers, often insurance firms or pension funds, and these firms are financial services companies themselves and, in turn, also have customers, everyday people that have a pension or are insured.

Most bank customers are everyday people as well, and increasingly, the main way people are interacting with their bank, insurer, or pension is through an app on their mobile phone.

In the decades before today, retail banks relied on the fact that people would have to come into the branch, face-to-face, in order to withdraw cash or to make a transaction. While they were in the branch, their advisor could also sell them another product, such as a mortgage or insurance. Today's customers still want to buy mortgages and insurance, but they no longer have to do it in person at the branch. In today's world, banks tend to advise their clients online, whether it's through the app or their website.

This online aspect only works if the bank can understand its customers' needs from their data and provide tailor-made experiences online. Equally, from the customers, perspective, they now expect to be able to submit insurance claims from their phone and to get an instant response. In today's world, insurers need to be able to automatically assess claims and make decisions in order to fulfill their customers' demands.

This book is not about how to write trading algorithms in order to make a quick buck. It is about leveraging the art and craft of building machine learning-driven systems that are useful in the financial industry.

Building anything of value requires a lot of time and effort. Right now, the market for building valuable things, to make an analogy to economics, is highly inefficient. Applications of machine learning will transform the industry over the next few decades, and this book will provide you with a toolbox that allows you to be part of the change.

Many of the examples in this book use data outside the realm of "financial data." Stock market data is used at no time in this book, and this decision was made for three specific reasons.

Firstly, the examples that are shown demonstrate techniques that can usually easily be applied to other datasets. Therefore, datasets were chosen that demonstrate some common challenges that professionals, like yourselves, will face while also remaining computationally tractable.

Secondly, financial data is fundamentally time dependent. To make this book useful over a longer span of time, and to ensure that as machine learning becomes more prominent, this book remains a vital part of your toolkit, we have used some non-financial data so that the data discussed here will still be relevant.

Finally, using alternative and non-classical data aims to inspire you to think about what other data you could use in your processes. Could you use drone footage of plants to augment your grain price models? Could you use web browsing behavior to offer different financial products? Thinking outside of the box is a necessary skill to have if you want to make use of the data that is around you.

What is machine learning?

"Machine learning is the subfield of computer science that gives computers the ability to learn without being explicitly programmed."

- Arthur Samuel, 1959

What do we mean by machine learning? Most computer programs today are handcrafted by humans. Software engineers carefully craft every rule that governs how software behaves and then translate it into computer code.

If you are reading this as an eBook, take a look at your screen right now. Everything that you see appears there because of some rule that a software engineer somewhere crafted. This approach has gotten us quite far, but that's not to say there are no limits to it. Sometimes, there might just be too many rules for humans to write. We might not be able to think of rules since they are too complex for even the smartest developers to come up with.

As a brief exercise, take a minute to come up with a list of rules that describe all dogs, but clearly distinguish dogs from all other animals. Fur? Well, cats have fur, too. What about a dog wearing a jacket? That is still a dog, just in a jacket. Researchers have spent years trying to craft these rules, but they've had very little success.

Humans don't seem to be able to perfectly tell why something is a dog, but they know a dog when they see a dog. As a species, we seem to detect specific, hard-to-describe patterns that, in aggregate, let us classify an animal as a dog. Machine learning attempts to do the same. Instead of handcrafting rules, we let a computer develop its own rules through pattern detection.

There are different ways this can work, and we're now going to look at three different types of learning: supervised, unsupervised, and reinforcement learning.

Supervised learning

Let's go back to our dog classifier. There are in fact many such classifiers currently in use today. If you use Google images, for example, and search for "dog," it will use an image classifier to show you pictures of dogs. These classifiers are trained under a paradigm known as supervised learning.

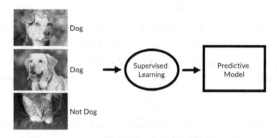

Supervised learning

In supervised learning, we have a large number of training examples, such as images of animals, and labels that describe what the expected outcome for those training examples is. For example, the preceding figure would come with the label "dog," while an image of a cat would come with a label "not a dog."

If we have a high number of these labeled training examples, we can train a classifier on detecting the subtle statistical patterns that differentiate dogs from all other animals.

 Note: The classifier does not know what a dog fundamentally is. It only knows the statistical patterns that linked images to dogs in training.

If a supervised learning classifier encounters something that's very different from the training data, it can often get confused and will just output nonsense.

Unsupervised learning

While supervised learning has made great advances over the last few years, most of this book will focus on working with labeled examples. However, sometimes we may not have labels. In this case, we can still use machine learning to find hidden patterns in data.

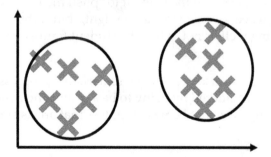

Clustering is a common form of unsupervised learning

Imagine a company that has a number of customers for its products. These customers can probably be grouped into different market segments, but what we don't know is what the different market segments are. We also cannot ask customers which market segment they belong to because they probably don't know. Which market segment of the shampoo market are you? Do you even know how shampoo firms segment their customers?

In this example, we would like an algorithm that looks at a lot of data from customers and groups them into segments. This is an example of unsupervised learning.

This area of machine learning is far less developed than supervised learning, but it still holds great potential.

Reinforcement learning

In reinforcement learning, we train agents who take actions in an environment, such as a self-driving car on the road. While we do not have labels, that is, we cannot tell what the *correct* action is in any situation, we can assign rewards or punishments. For example, we could reward keeping a proper distance from the car in front.

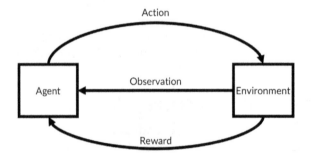

Reinforcement learning

A driving instructor does not tell the student to "push the brake halfway down while moving the steering wheel two degrees to the right," but rather they tell the student whether they are doing well or not, while the student figures out the exact amount of brakes to use.

Reinforcement learning has also made some remarkable progress in the past couple of years and is considered by many to be a promising avenue toward general artificial intelligence, that being computers that are as smart as humans.

The unreasonable effectiveness of data

In 2009, three Google engineers published a landmark paper titled *The unreasonable effectiveness of data*. In the paper, they described how relatively simple machine learning systems that had been around for a long time had exhibited much better performance when fed with the enormous amounts of data Google had on its servers. In fact, they discovered that when fed with more data, these simple systems could master tasks that had been thought to be impossible before.

From there, researchers quickly started revisiting old machine learning technologies and found that artificial neural networks did especially well when trained on massive datasets. This was around the same time that computing power became cheap and plentiful enough to train much bigger networks than before.

These bigger artificial neural networks were so effective that they got a name: deep neural networks, or deep learning. Deep neural networks are especially good at pattern detection. They can find complex patterns, such as the statistical pattern of light and dark that describes a face in a picture, and they can do so automatically given enough data.

Machine learning is, therefore, best understood as a paradigm change in how we program computers. Instead of carefully handcrafting rules, we feed the computer vast amounts of information and train it to craft the rules by itself.

This approach is superior if there is a very large number of rules, or even if these rules are difficult to describe. Modern machine learning is, therefore, the ideal tool for combing through the huge amounts of data the financial industry is confronted with.

All models are wrong

There is a saying in statistics that *all models are wrong, but some are useful*. Machine learning creates incredibly complex statistical models that are often, for example, in deep learning, not interpretable to humans. They sure are useful and have great value, but they are still wrong. This is because they are complex black boxes, and people tend to not question machine learning models, even though they should question them precisely because they are black boxes.

There will come a time when even the most sophisticated deep neural network will make a fundamentally wrong prediction, just as the advanced **Collateralized Debt Obligation (CDO)** models did in the financial crises of 2008. Even worse, black box machine learning models, which will make millions of decisions on loan approval or insurance, impacting everyday people's lives, will eventually make wrong decisions.

Sometimes they will be biased. Machine learning is ever only as good as the data that we feed it, data that can often be biased in what it's showing, something we'll consider later on in this chapter. This is something we must pay a lot of time in addressing, as if we mindlessly deploy these algorithms, we will automate discrimination too, which has the possibility of causing another financial crisis.

This is especially true in the financial industry, where algorithms can often have a severe impact on people's lives while at the same time being kept secret. The unquestionable, secret black boxes that gain their acceptance through the heavy use of math pose a much bigger threat to society than the self-aware artificial intelligence taking over the world that you see in movies.

While this is not an ethics book, it makes sense for any practitioner of the field to get familiar with the ethical implications of his or her work. In addition to recommending that you read Cathy O'Neil's *Weapons of math destruction,* it's also worth asking you to swear *The Modelers Hippocratic Oath.* The oath was developed by Emanuel Derman and Paul Wilmott, two quantitative finance researchers, in 2008 in the wake of the financial crisis:

> *"I will remember that I didn't make the world, and it doesn't satisfy my equations.*
> *Though I will use models boldly to estimate value, I will not be overly impressed*
> *by mathematics. I will never sacrifice reality for elegance without explaining why*
> *I have done so. Nor will I give the people who use my model false comfort about its*
> *accuracy. Instead, I will make explicit its assumptions and oversights. I understand*
> *that my work may have enormous effects on society and the economy, many of them*
> *beyond my comprehension."*

In recent years, machine learning has made a number of great strides, with researchers mastering tasks that were previously seen as unsolvable. From identifying objects in images to transcribing voice and playing complex board games like Go, modern machine learning has matched, and continues to match and even beat, human performance at a dazzling range of tasks.

Interestingly, **deep learning** is the method behind all these advances. In fact, the bulk of advances come from a subfield of deep learning called **deep neural networks**. While many practitioners are familiar with standard econometric models, such as regression, few are familiar with this new breed of modeling.

The bulk of this book is devoted to deep learning. This is because it is one of the most promising techniques for machine learning and will give anyone mastering it the ability to tackle tasks considered impossible before.

In this chapter, we will explore how and why neural networks work in order to give you a fundamental understanding of the topic.

Setting up your workspace

Before we can start, you will need to set up your workspace. The examples in this book are all meant to run in a Jupyter notebook. Jupyter notebooks are an interactive development environment mostly used for data-science applications and are considered the go-to environment to build data-driven applications in.

You can run Jupyter notebooks either on your local machine, on a server in the cloud, or on a website such as Kaggle.

 Note: All code examples for this book can be found here: `https://github.com/PacktPublishing/Machine-Learning-for-Finance` and for chapter 1 refer the following link: `https://www.kaggle.com/jannesklaas/machine-learning-for-finance-chapter-1-code`.

Deep learning is computer intensive, and the data used in the examples throughout this book are frequently over a gigabyte in size. It can be accelerated by the use of **Graphics Processing Units (GPUs)**, which were invented for rendering video and games. If you have a GPU enabled computer, you can run the examples locally. If you do not have such a machine, it is recommended to use a service such as Kaggle kernels.

Learning deep learning used to be an expensive endeavor because GPUs are an expensive piece of hardware. While there are cheaper options available, a powerful GPU can cost up to $10,000 if you buy it and about $0.80 an hour to rent it in the cloud.

If you have many, long-running training jobs, it might be worth considering building a "deep learning" box, a desktop computer with a GPU. There are countless tutorials for this online and a decent box can be assembled for as little as a few hundred dollars all the way to $5,000.

The examples in this book can all be run on Kaggle for free, though. In fact, they have been developed using this site.

Using Kaggle kernels

Kaggle is a popular data-science website owned by Google. It started out with competitions in which participants had to build machine learning models in order to make predictions. However, over the years, it has also had a popular forum, an online learning system and, most importantly for us, a hosted Jupyter service.

To use Kaggle, you can visit their website at `https://www.kaggle.com/`. In order to use the site, you will be required to create an account.

After you've created your account, you can find the **Kernels** page by clicking on **Kernels** located in the main menu, as seen in the following screenshot:

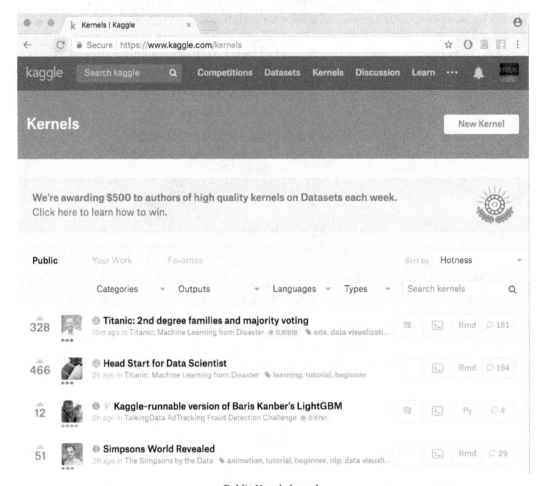

Public Kaggle kernels

In the preceding screenshot, you can see a number of kernels that other people have both written and published. Kernels can be private, but publishing kernels is a good way to show skills and share knowledge.

To start a new kernel, click **New Kernel**. In the dialog that follows, you want to select **Notebook**:

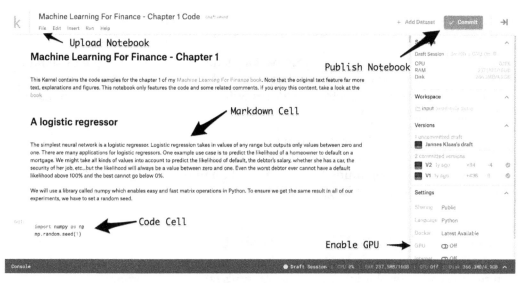

The kernel editor

You will get to the kernel editor, which looks like the preceding screenshot.

Note that Kaggle is actively iterating on the kernel design, and so a few elements might be in different positions, but the basic functionality is the same. The most important piece of a notebook is the code cells. Here you can enter the code and run it by clicking the run button on the bottom left, or alternatively by pressing *Shift + Enter*.

The variables you define in one cell become environment variables, so you can access them in another cell. Markdown cells allow you to write text in markdown format to add a description to what is going on in your code. You can upload and download notebooks with the little cloud buttons featured in the top-right corner.

To publish a notebook from the kernel editor, firstly you must click the **Commit & Run** button and then set the notebook to **Public** in the settings. To enable a GPU on your notebook, make sure to check the **Enable GPU** button located in the bottom right. It's important to remember that this will restart your notebook, so your environment variables will be lost.

Once you run the code, the run button turns into a stop button. If your code ever gets stuck, you can interrupt it by clicking that stop button. If you want to wipe all environment variables and begin anew, simply click the restart button located in the bottom-right corner.

With this system, you can connect a kernel to any dataset hosted on Kaggle, or alternatively you can just upload a new dataset on the fly. The notebooks belonging to this book already come with the data connection.

Kaggle kernels come with the most frequently used packages preinstalled, so for most of the time you do not have to worry about installing packages.

Sometimes this book does use custom packages not installed in Kaggle by default. In this case, you can add custom packages at the bottom of the Settings menu. Instructions for installing custom packages will be provided when they are used in this book.

Kaggle kernels are free to use and can save you a lot of time and money, so it's recommended to run the code samples on Kaggle. To copy a notebook, go to the link provided at the beginning of the code section of each chapter and then click **Fork Notebook**. Note that Kaggle kernels can run for up to six hours.

Running notebooks locally

If you have a machine powerful enough to run deep learning operations, you can run the code samples locally. In that case, it's strongly recommended to install Jupyter through Anaconda.

To install Anaconda, simply visit `https://www.anaconda.com/download` to download the distribution. The graphical installer will guide you through the steps necessary to install Anaconda on your system. When installing Anaconda, you'll also install a range of useful Python libraries such as NumPy and matplotlib, which will be used throughout this book.

After installing Anaconda, you can start a Jupyter server locally by opening your machine's Terminal and typing in the following code:

```
$ jupyter notebook
```

You can then visit the URL displayed in the Terminal. This will take you to your local notebook server.

To start a new notebook, click on **New** in the top-right corner.

All code samples in this book use Python 3, so make sure you are using Python 3 in your local notebooks. If you are running your notebooks locally, you will also need to install both TensorFlow and Keras, the two deep learning libraries used throughout this book.

Installing TensorFlow

Before installing Keras, we need to first install TensorFlow. You can install TensorFlow by opening a Terminal window and entering the following command:

```
$ sudo pip install TensorFlow
```

For instructions on how to install TensorFlow with GPU support, simply click on this link, where you will be provided with the instructions for doing so: `https://www.tensorflow.org/`.

It's worth noting that you will need a CUDA-enabled GPU in order to run TensorFlow with CUDA. For instructions on how to install CUDA, visit `https://docs.nvidia.com/cuda/index.html`.

Installing Keras

After you have installed TensorFlow, you can install Keras in the same way, by running the following command:

```
$ sudo pip install Keras
```

Keras will now automatically use the TensorFlow backend. Note that TensorFlow 1.7 will include Keras built in, which we'll cover this later on in this chapter.

Using data locally

To use the data of the book code samples locally, visit the notebooks on Kaggle and then download the connected datasets from there. Note that the file paths to the data will change depending on where you save the data, so you will need to replace the file paths when running notebooks locally.

Kaggle also offers a command-line interface, which allows you to download the data more easily. Visit `https://github.com/Kaggle/kaggle-api` for instructions on how to achieve this.

Using the AWS deep learning AMI

Amazon Web Services (**AWS**) provides an easy-to-use, preconfigured way to run deep learning in the cloud.

Visit `https://aws.amazon.com/machine-learning/amis/` for instructions on how to set up an **Amazon Machine Image** (**AMI**). While AMIs are paid, they can run longer than Kaggle kernels. So, for big projects, it might be worth using an AMI instead of a kernel.

To run the notebooks for this book on an AMI, first set up the AMI, then download the notebooks from GitHub, and then upload them to your AMI. You will have to download the data from Kaggle as well. See the *Using data locally* section for instructions.

Approximating functions

There are many views on how best to think about neural networks, but perhaps the most useful is to see them as function approximators. Functions in math relate some input, x, to some output, y. We can write it as the following formula:

$$y = f(x)$$

A simple function could be like this:

$$f(x) = 4 * x$$

In this case, we can give the function an input, x, and it would quadruple it:

$$y = f(2) = 8$$

You might have seen functions like this in school, but functions can do more; as an example, they can map an element from a set (the collection of values the function accepts) to another element of a set. These sets can be something other than simple numbers.

A function could, for example, also map an image to an identification of what is in the image:

$$imageContent = f(image)$$

This function would map an image of a cat to the label "cat," as we can see in the following diagram:

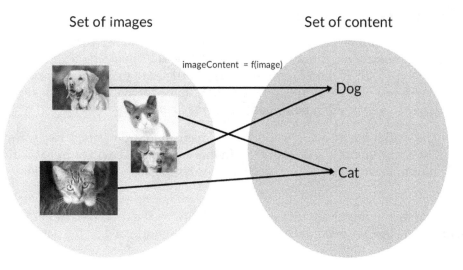

Mapping images to labels

We should note that for a computer, images are matrices full of numbers and any description of an image's content would also be stored as a matrix of numbers.

A neural network, if it is big enough, can approximate any function. It has been mathematically proven that an indefinitely large network could approximate every function. While we don't need to use an indefinitely large network, we are certainly using very large networks.

Modern deep learning architectures can have tens or even hundreds of layers and millions of parameters, so only storing the model already takes up a few gigabytes. This means that a neural network, if it's big enough, could also approximate our function, f, for mapping images to their content.

The condition that the neural network has to be "big enough" explains why deep (big) neural networks have taken off. The fact that "big enough" neural networks can approximate any function means that they are useful for a large number of tasks.

A forward pass

Over the course of this book, we will build powerful neural networks that are able to approximate extremely complex functions. We will be mapping text to named entities, images to their content, and even news articles to their summaries. But for now, we will work with a simple problem that can be solved with logistic regression, a popular technique used in both economics and finance.

We will be working with a simple problem. Given an input matrix, X, we want to output the first column of the matrix, X_1. In this example, we will be approaching the problem from a mathematical perspective in order to gain some intuition for what is going on.

Later on in this chapter, we will implement what we have described in Python. We already know that we need data to train a neural network, and so the data, seen here, will be our dataset for the exercise:

X_1	X_2	X_3	y
0	1	0	0
1	0	0	1
1	1	1	1
0	1	1	0

In the dataset, each row contains an input vector, X, and an output, y.

The data follows the formula:

$$y = X_1$$

The function we want to approximate is as follows:

$$f(X) = X_1$$

In this case, writing down the function is relatively straightforward. However, keep in mind that in most cases it is not possible to write down the function, as functions expressed by deep neural networks can become very complex.

For this simple function, a shallow neural network with only one layer will be enough. Such shallow networks are also called logistic regressors.

A logistic regressor

As we just explained, the simplest neural network is a logistic regressor. A logistic regression takes in values of any range but only outputs values between zero and one.

There is a wide range of applications where logistic regressors are suitable. One such example is to predict the likelihood of a homeowner defaulting on a mortgage.

We might take all kinds of values into account when trying to predict the likelihood of someone defaulting on their payment, such as the debtor's salary, whether they have a car, the security of their job, and so on, but the likelihood will always be a value between zero and one. Even the worst debtor ever cannot have a default likelihood above 100%, and the best cannot go below 0%.

The following diagram shows a logistic regressor. X is our input vector; here it's shown as three components, X_1, X_2, and X_3.

W is a vector of three weights. You can imagine it as the thickness of each of the three lines. W determines how much each of the values of X goes into the next layer. b is the bias, and it can move the output of the layer up or down:

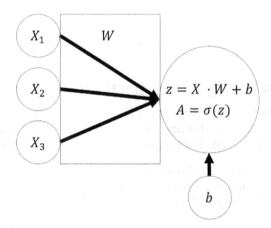

Logistic regressor

To compute the output of the regressor, we must first do a **linear step**. We compute the dot product of the input, X, and the weights, W. This is the same as multiplying each value of X with its weight and then taking the sum. To this number, we then add the bias, b. Afterward, we do a **nonlinear step**.

In the nonlinear step, we run the linear intermediate product, *z*, through an **activation function**; in this case, the sigmoid function. The sigmoid function squishes the input values to outputs between zero and one:

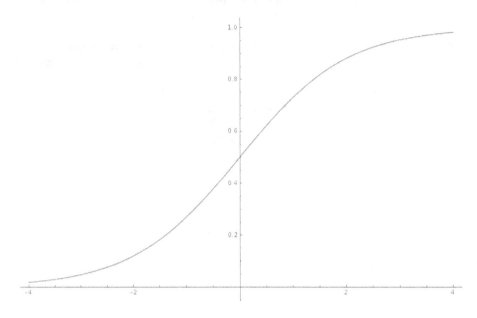

The Sigmoid function

Python version of our logistic regressor

If all the preceding math was a bit too theoretical for you, rejoice! We will now implement the same thing, but this time with Python. In our example, we will be using a library called NumPy, which enables easy and fast matrix operations within Python.

NumPy comes preinstalled with Anaconda and on Kaggle kernels. To ensure we get the same result in all of our experiments, we have to set a random seed. We can do this by running the following code:

```
import numpy as np
np.random.seed(1)
```

Since our dataset is quite small, we'll define it manually as NumPy matrices, as we can see here:

```
X = np.array([[0,1,0],
              [1,0,0],
              [1,1,1],
              [0,1,1]])

y = np.array([[0,1,1,0]]).T
```

We can define the sigmoid, which squishes all the values into values between 0 and 1, through an activation function as a Python function:

```
def sigmoid(x):
    return 1/(1+np.exp(-x))
```

So far, so good. We now need to initialize W. In this case, we actually know already what values W should have. But we cannot know about other problems where we do not know the function yet. So, we need to assign weights randomly.

The weights are usually assigned randomly with a mean of zero, and the bias is usually set to zero by default. NumPy's `random` function expects to receive the shape of the random matrix to be passed on as a tuple, so `random((3,1))` creates a 3x1 matrix. By default, the random values generated are between 0 and 1, with a mean of 0.5 and a standard deviation of 0.5.

We want the random values to have a mean of 0 and a standard deviation of 1, so we first multiply the values generated by 2 and then subtract 1. We can achieve this by running the following code:

```
W = 2*np.random.random((3,1)) - 1
b = 0
```

With that done, all the variables are set. We can now move on to do the linear step, which is achieved with the following:

```
z = X.dot(W) + b
```

Now we can do the nonlinear step, which is run with the following:

```
A = sigmoid(z)
```

Now, if we print out A, we'll get the following output:

```
print(A)
```

out:
```
[[ 0.60841366]
 [ 0.45860596]
 [ 0.3262757 ]
 [ 0.36375058]]
```

But wait! This output looks nothing like our desired output, y, at all! Clearly, our regressor is representing *some* function, but it's quite far away from the function we want.

To better approximate our desired function, we have to tweak the weights, W, and the bias, b. To this end, in the next section, we will optimize the model parameters.

Optimizing model parameters

We've already seen that we need to tweak the weights and biases, collectively called the parameters, of our model in order to arrive at a closer approximation of our desired function.

In other words, we need to look through the space of possible functions that can be represented by our model in order to find a function, $\hat{f}$, that matches our desired function, f, as closely as possible.

But how would we know how close we are? In fact, since we don't know f, we cannot directly know how close our hypothesis, $\hat{f}$, is to f. But what we can do is measure how well $\hat{f}$'s outputs match the output of f. The expected outputs of f given X are the labels, y. So, we can try to approximate f by finding a function, $\hat{f}$, whose outputs are also y given X.

We know that the following is true:

$$f(X) = y$$

We also know that:

$$\hat{f}(X) = \hat{y}$$

We can try to find f by optimizing using the following formula:

$$\underset{\hat{f} \in \mathcal{H}}{minimize} \, D(y, \hat{y})$$

Within this formula, $\mathcal{H}$ is the space of functions that can be represented by our model, also called the hypothesis space, while D is the distance function, which we use to evaluate how close $\hat{y}$ and y are.

 Note: This approach makes a crucial assumption that our data, X, and labels, y, represent our desired function, f. This is not always the case. When our data contains systematic biases, we might gain a function that fits our data well but is different from the one we wanted.

An example of optimizing model parameters comes from human resource management. Imagine you are trying to build a model that predicts the likelihood of a debtor defaulting on their loan, with the intention of using this to decide who should get a loan.

As training data, you can use loan decisions made by human bank managers over the years. However, this presents a problem as these managers might be biased. For instance, minorities, such as black people, have historically had a harder time getting a loan.

With that being said, if we used that training data, our function would also present that bias. You'd end up with a function mirroring or even amplifying human biases, rather than creating a function that is good at predicting who is a good debtor.

It is a commonly made mistake to believe that a neural network will find the intuitive function that we are looking for. It'll actually find the function that best fits the data with no regard for whether that is the desired function or not.

Measuring model loss

We saw earlier how we could optimize parameters by minimizing some distance function, D. This distance function, also called the loss function, is the performance measure by which we evaluate possible functions. In machine learning, a loss function measures how bad the model performs. A high loss function goes hand in hand with low accuracy, whereas if the function is low, then the model is doing well.

In this case, our issue is a binary classification problem. Because of that, we will be using the binary cross-entropy loss, as we can see in the following formula:

$$D_{BCE}(y,\hat{y}) = -\frac{1}{N}\sum_{i=1}^{N}\left[y_i log(\hat{y}_i) + (1-y_i)log(1-\hat{y}_i)\right]$$

Let's go through this formula step by step:

- D_{BCE}: This is the distance function for binary cross entropy loss.
- $\frac{1}{N}\sum_{i=1}^{N}$: The loss over a batch of N examples is the average loss of all examples.
- $y_i * log(\hat{y}_i)$: This part of the loss only comes into play if the true value, y_i is 1. If y_i is 1, we want $\hat{y}_i$ to be as close to 1 as possible, so we can achieve a low loss.
- $(1-y_i)log(1-\hat{y}_i)$: This part of the loss comes into play if $y_{i'}$ is 0. If so, we want $\hat{y}_i$ to be close to 0 as well.

In Python, this loss function is implemented as follows:

```
def bce_loss(y,y_hat):
    N = y.shape[0]
    loss = -1/N * (y*np.log(y_hat) + (1 - y)*np.log(1-y_hat))
    return loss
```

The output, A, of our logistic regressor is equal to $\hat{y}$, so we can calculate the binary cross-entropy loss as follows:

```
loss = bce_loss(y,A)
print(loss)
```

out:

0.82232258208779863

As we can see, this is quite a high loss, so we should now look at seeing how we can improve our model. The goal here is to bring this loss to zero, or at least to get closer to zero.

You can think of losses with respect to different function hypotheses as a surface, sometimes also called the "loss surface." The loss surface is a lot like a mountain range, as we have high points on the mountain tops and low points in valleys.

Our goal is to find the absolute lowest point in the mountain range: the deepest valley, or the "global minimum." A global minimum is a point in the function hypothesis space at which the loss is at the lowest point.

A "local minimum," by contrast, is the point at which the loss is lower than in the immediately surrounding space. Local minima are problematic because while they might seem like a good function to use at face value, there are much better functions available. Keep this in mind as we now walk through gradient descent, a method for finding a minimum in our function space.

Gradient descent

Now that we know what we judge our candidate models, $\hat{f}$, by, how do we tweak the parameters to obtain better models? The most popular optimization algorithm for neural networks is called gradient descent. Within this method, we slowly move along the slope, the derivative, of the loss function.

Imagine you are in a mountain forest on a hike, and you're at a point where you've lost the track and are now in the woods trying to find the bottom of the valley. The problem here is that because there are so many trees, you cannot see the valley's bottom, only the ground under your feet.

Now ask yourself this: how would you find your way down? One sensible approach would be to follow the slope, and where the slope goes downwards, you go. This is the same approach that is taken by a gradient descent algorithm.

To bring it back to our focus, in this forest situation the loss function is the mountain, and to get to a low loss, the algorithm follows the slope, that is, the derivative, of the loss function. When we walk down the mountain, we are updating our location coordinates.

The algorithm updates the parameters of the neural network, as we are seeing in the following diagram:

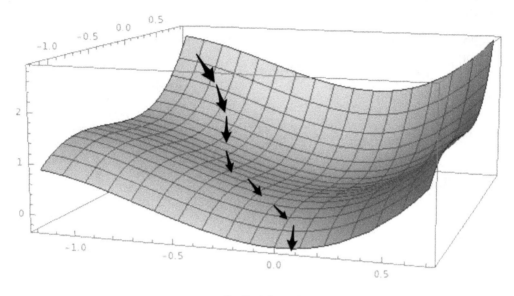

Gradient descent

Gradient descent requires that the loss function has a derivative with respect to the parameters that we want to optimize. This will work well for most supervised learning problems, but things become more difficult when we want to tackle problems for which there is no obvious derivative.

Gradient descent can also only optimize the parameters, weights, and biases of our model. What it cannot do is optimize how many layers our model has or which activation functions it should use, since there is no way to compute the gradient with respect to model topology.

These settings, which cannot be optimized by gradient descent, are called **hyperparameters** and are usually set by humans. You just saw how we gradually scale down the loss function, but how do we update the parameters? To this end, we're going to need another method called backpropagation.

Backpropagation

Backpropagation allows us to apply gradient descent updates to the parameters of a model. To update the parameters, we need to calculate the derivative of the loss function with respect to the weights and biases.

If you imagine the parameters of our models are like the geo-coordinates in our mountain forest analogy, calculating the loss derivative with respect to a parameter is like checking the mountain slope in the direction north to see whether you should go north or south.

The following diagram shows the forward and backward pass through a logistic regressor:

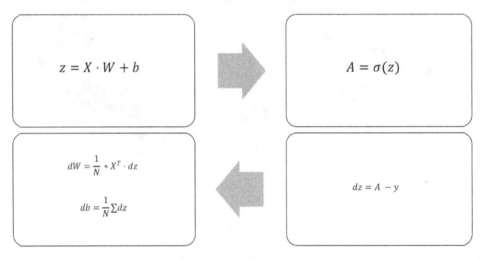

Forward and backward pass through a logistic regressor

To keep things simple, we refer to the derivative of the loss function to any variable as the d variable. For example, we'll write the derivative of the loss function with respect to the weights as dW.

To calculate the gradient with respect to different parameters of our model, we can make use of the chain rule. You might remember the chain rule as the following:

$$\left(f\left(g\left(x\right)\right)\right)' = g\left(x\right)' * f'\left(g\left(x\right)\right)$$

This is also sometimes written as follows:

$$\frac{dy}{dx} = \frac{dy}{du}\frac{du}{dx}$$

The chain rule basically says that if you want to take the derivative through a number of nested functions, you multiply the derivative of the inner function with the derivative of the outer function.

This is useful because neural networks, and our logistic regressor, are nested functions. The input goes through the linear step, a function of input, weights, and biases; and the output of the linear step, z, goes through the activation function.

So, when we compute the loss derivative with respect to weights and biases, we'll first compute the loss derivative with respect to the output of the linear step, z, and use it to compute *dW*. Within the code, it looks like this:

```
dz = (A - y)

dW = 1/N * np.dot(X.T,dz)

db = 1/N * np.sum(dz,axis=0,keepdims=True)
```

Parameter updates

Now we have the gradients, how do we improve our model? Going back to our mountain analogy, now that we know that the mountain goes up in the north and east directions, where do we go? To the south and west, of course!

Mathematically speaking, we go in the opposite direction to the gradient. If the gradient is positive with respect to a parameter, that is, the slope is upward, then we reduce the parameter. If it is negative, that is, downward sloping, we increase it. When our slope is steeper, we move our gradient more.

The update rule for a parameter, *p*, then goes like this:

$$p = p - \alpha * dp$$

Here *p* is a model parameter (either in weight or a bias), *dp* is the loss derivative with respect to *p*, and α is the learning rate.

The learning rate is something akin to the gas pedal within a car. It sets by how much we want to apply the gradient updates. It is one of those hyperparameters that we have to set manually, and something we will discuss in the next chapter.

Within the code, our parameter updates look like this:

```
alpha = 1
W -= alpha * dW
b -= alpha * db
```

Putting it all together

Well done! We've now looked at all the parts that are needed in order to train a neural network. Over the next few steps in this section, we will be training a one-layer neural network, which is also called a logistic regressor.

Firstly, we'll import numpy before we define the data. We can do this by running the following code:

```
import numpy as np
np.random.seed(1)

X = np.array([[0,1,0],
              [1,0,0],
              [1,1,1],
              [0,1,1]])

y = np.array([[0,1,1,0]]).T
```

The next step is for us to define the sigmoid activation function and loss function, which we can do with the following code:

```
def sigmoid(x):
    return 1/(1+np.exp(-x))

def bce_loss(y,y_hat):
    N = y.shape[0]
    loss = -1/N * np.sum((y*np.log(y_hat) + (1 - y)*np.log(1-y_hat)))
    return loss
```

We'll then randomly initialize our model, which we can achieve with the following code:

```
W = 2*np.random.random((3,1)) - 1
b = 0
```

As part of this process, we also need to set some hyperparameters. The first one is alpha, which we will just set to 1 here. Alpha is best understood as the step size. A large alpha means that while our model will train quickly, it might also overshoot the target. A small alpha, in comparison, allows gradient descent to tread more carefully and find small valleys it would otherwise shoot over.

The second one is the number of times we want to run the training process, also called the number of epochs we want to run. We can set the parameters with the following code:

```
alpha = 1
epochs = 20
```

Since it is used in the training loop, it's also useful to define the number of samples in our data. We'll also define an empty array in order to keep track of the model's losses over time. To achieve this, we simply run the following:

```
N = y.shape[0]
losses = []
```

Now we come to the main training loop:

```
for i in range(epochs):
    # Forward pass
    z = X.dot(W) + b
    A = sigmoid(z)

    # Calculate loss
    loss = bce_loss(y,A)
    print('Epoch:',i,'Loss:',loss)
    losses.append(loss)

    # Calculate derivatives
    dz = (A - y)
    dW = 1/N * np.dot(X.T,dz)
    db = 1/N * np.sum(dz,axis=0,keepdims=True)

    # Parameter updates
    W -= alpha * dW
    b -= alpha * db
```

As a result of running the previous code, we would get the following output:

```
out:

Epoch: 0 Loss: 0.822322582088

Epoch: 1 Loss: 0.722897448125

Epoch: 2 Loss: 0.646837651208

Epoch: 3 Loss: 0.584116122241

Epoch: 4 Loss: 0.530908161024

Epoch: 5 Loss: 0.48523717872

Epoch: 6 Loss: 0.445747750118

Epoch: 7 Loss: 0.411391164148

Epoch: 8 Loss: 0.381326093762

Epoch: 9 Loss: 0.354869998127

Epoch: 10 Loss: 0.331466036109

Epoch: 11 Loss: 0.310657702141
```

```
Epoch: 12 Loss: 0.292068863232
Epoch: 13 Loss: 0.275387990352
Epoch: 14 Loss: 0.260355695915
Epoch: 15 Loss: 0.246754868981
Epoch: 16 Loss: 0.234402844624
Epoch: 17 Loss: 0.22314516463
Epoch: 18 Loss: 0.21285058467
Epoch: 19 Loss: 0.203407060401
```

You can see that over the course of the output, the loss steadily decreases, starting at 0.822322582088 and ending at 0.203407060401.

We can plot the loss to a graph in order to give us a better look at it. To do this, we can simply run the following code:

```
import matplotlib.pyplot as plt
plt.plot(losses)
plt.xlabel('epoch')
plt.ylabel('loss')
plt.show()
```

This will then output the following chart:

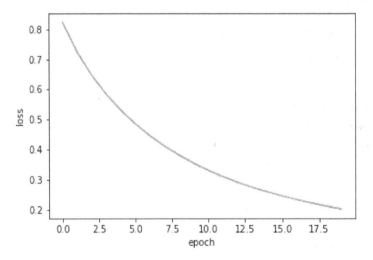

The output of the previous code, showing loss rate improving over time

A deeper network

We established earlier in this chapter that in order to approximate more complex functions, we need bigger and deeper networks. Creating a deeper network works by stacking layers on top of each other.

In this section, we will build a two-layer neural network like the one seen in the following diagram:

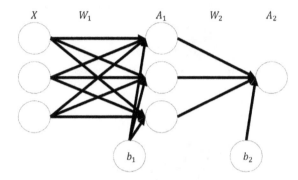

Sketch of a two-layer neural network

The input gets multiplied with the first set of weights, W_1, producing an intermediate product, z_1. This is then run through an activation function, which will produce the first layer's activations, A_1.

These activations then get multiplied with the second layer of weights, W_2, producing an intermediate product, z_2. This gets run through a second activation function, which produces the output, A_2, of our neural network:

```
z1 = X.dot(W1) + b1

a1 = np.tanh(z1)

z2 = a1.dot(W2) + b2

a2 = sigmoid(z2)
```

 Note: The full code for this example can be found in the GitHub repository belonging to this book.

As you can see, the first activation function is not a sigmoid function but is actually a tanh function. Tanh is a popular activation function for hidden layers and works a lot like sigmoid, except that it squishes values in the range between -1 and 1 rather than 0 and 1:

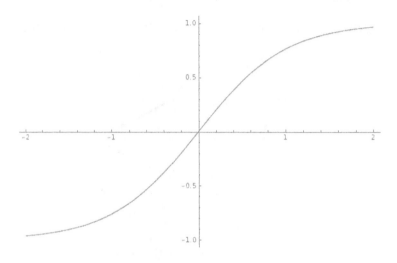

The tanh function

Backpropagation through our deeper network works by the chain rule, too. We go back through the network and multiply the derivatives:

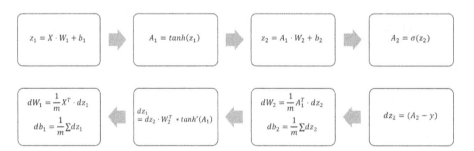

Forward and backward pass through a two-layer neural network

The preceding equations can be expressed as the following Python code:

```
# Calculate loss derivative with respect to the output
dz2 = bce_derivative(y=y,y_hat=a2)

# Calculate loss derivative with respect to second layer weights
dW2 = (a1.T).dot(dz2)
```

```
# Calculate loss derivative with respect to second layer bias
db2 = np.sum(dz2, axis=0, keepdims=True)

# Calculate loss derivative with respect to first layer
dz1 = dz2.dot(W2.T) * tanh_derivative(a1)

# Calculate loss derivative with respect to first layer weights
dW1 = np.dot(X.T, dz1)

# Calculate loss derivative with respect to first layer bias
db1 = np.sum(dz1, axis=0)
```

Note that while the size of the inputs and outputs are determined by your problem, you can freely choose the size of your hidden layer. The hidden layer is another hyperparameter you can tweak. The bigger the hidden layer size, the more complex the function you can approximate. However, the flip side of this is that the model might overfit. That is, it may develop a complex function that fits the noise but not the true relationship in the data.

Take a look at the following chart. What we see here is the two moons dataset that could be clearly separated, but right now there is a lot of noise, which makes the separation hard to see even for humans. You can find the full code for the two-layer neural network as well as for the generation of these samples in the Chapter 1 GitHub repo:

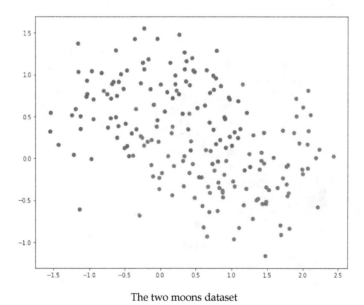

The two moons dataset

The following diagram shows a visualization of the decision boundary, that is, the line at which the model separates the two classes, using a hidden layer size of 1:

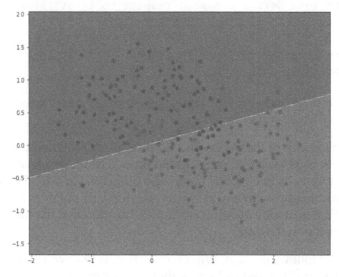

Decision boundary for hidden layer size 1

As you can see, the network does not capture the true relationship of the data. This is because it's too simplistic. In the following diagram, you will see the decision boundary for a network with a hidden layer size of 500:

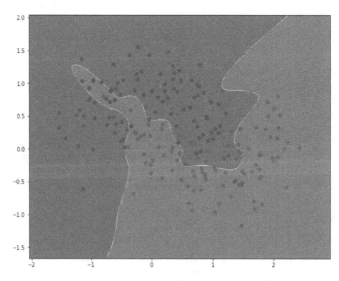

Decision boundary for hidden layer size 500

This model clearly fits the noise, but not the moons. In this case, the right hidden layer size is about 3.

Finding the right size and the right number of hidden layers is a crucial part of designing effective learning models. Building models with NumPy is a bit clumsy and can be very easy to get wrong. Luckily, there is a much faster and easier tool for building neural networks, called Keras.

A brief introduction to Keras

Keras is a high-level neural network API that can run on top of TensorFlow, a library for dataflow programming. What this means is that it can run the operations needed for a neural network in a highly optimized way. Therefore, it's much faster and easier to use than TensorFlow. Because Keras acts as an interface to TensorFlow, it makes it easier to build even more complex neural networks. Throughout the rest of the book, we will be working with the Keras library in order to build our neural networks.

Importing Keras

When importing Keras, we usually just import the modules we will use. In this case, we need two types of layers:

- The `Dense` layer is the plain layer that we have gotten to know in this chapter
- The `Activation` layer allows us to add an activation function

We can import them simply by running the following code:

```
from keras.layers import Dense, Activation
```

Keras offers two ways to build models, through the sequential and the functional APIs. Because the sequential API is easier to use and allows more rapid model building, we will be using it for most of the book. However, in later chapters, we will take a look at the functional API as well.

We can access the sequential API through this code:

```
from keras.models import Sequential
```

A two-layer model in Keras

Building a neural network in the sequential API works as follows.

Stacking layers

Firstly, we create an empty sequential model with no layers:

```
model = Sequential()
```

Then we can add layers to this model, just like stacking a layer cake, with `model.add()`.

For the first layer, we have to specify the input dimensions of the layer. In our case, the data has two features, the coordinates of the point. We can add a hidden layer of size 3 with the following code:

```
model.add(Dense(3,input_dim=2))
```

Note how we nest the functions inside `model.add()`. We specify the `Dense` layer, and the positional argument is the size of the layer. This `Dense` layer now only does the linear step.

To add a `tanh` activation function, we call the following:

```
model.add(Activation('tanh'))
```

Then, we add the linear step and the activation function of the output layer in the same way, by calling up:

```
model.add(Dense(1))
model.add(Activation('sigmoid'))
```

Then to get an overview of all the layers we now have in our model, we can use the following command:

```
model.summary()
```

This yields the following overview of the model:

```
out:
Layer (type)                    Output Shape                Param #
=================================================================
dense_3 (Dense)                 (None, 3)                   9
_____
activation_3 (Activation)       (None, 3)                   0
_____
dense_4 (Dense)                 (None, 1)                   4
_____
activation_4 (Activation)       (None, 1)                   0
=================================================================
```

```
Total params: 13
Trainable params: 13
Non-trainable params: 0
```

You can see the layers listed nicely, including their output shape and the number of parameters the layer has. None, located within the output shape, means that the layer has no fixed input size in that dimension and will accept whatever we feed it. In our case, it means the layer will accept any number of samples.

In pretty much every network, you will see that the input dimension on the first dimension is variable like this in order to accommodate the different amounts of samples.

Compiling the model

Before we can start training the model, we have to specify how exactly we want to train the model; and, more importantly, we need to specify which optimizer and which loss function we want to use.

The simple optimizer we have used so far is called the **Stochastic Gradient Descent**, or **SGD**. To look at more optimizers, see *Chapter 2, Applying Machine Learning to Structured Data*.

The loss function we use for this binary classification problem is called binary cross-entropy. We can also specify what metrics we want to track during training. In our case, accuracy, or just acc to keep it short, would be interesting to track:

```
model.compile(optimizer='sgd',
              loss='binary_crossentropy',
              metrics=['acc'])
```

Training the model

Now we are ready to run the training process, which we can do with the following line:

```
history = model.fit(X,y,epochs=900)
```

This will train the model for 900 iterations, which are also referred to as epochs. The output should look similar to this:

```
Epoch 1/900
200/200 [==============================] - 0s 543us/step -
loss: 0.6840 - acc: 0.5900
Epoch 2/900
```

```
200/200 [==============================] - 0s 60us/step -
loss: 0.6757 - acc: 0.5950
...


Epoch 899/900
200/200 [==============================] - 0s 90us/step -
loss: 0.2900 - acc: 0.8800
Epoch 900/900
200/200 [==============================] - 0s 87us/step -
loss: 0.2901 - acc: 0.8800
```

The full output of the training process has been truncated in the middle, this is to save space in the book, but you can see that the loss goes continuously down while accuracy goes up. In other words, success!

Over the course of this book, we will be adding more bells and whistles to these methods. But at this moment, we have a pretty solid understanding of the theory of deep learning. We are just missing one building block: how does Keras actually work under the hood? What is TensorFlow? And why does deep learning work faster on a GPU?

We will be answering these questions in the next, and final, section of this chapter.

Keras and TensorFlow

Keras is a high-level library and can be used as a simplified interface to TensorFlow. That means Keras does not do any computations by itself; it is just a simple way to interact with TensorFlow, which is running in the background.

TensorFlow is a software library developed by Google and is very popular for deep learning. In this book, we usually try to work with TensorFlow only through Keras, since that is easier than working with TensorFlow directly. However, sometimes we might want to write a bit of TensorFlow code in order to build more advanced models.

The goal of TensorFlow is to run the computations needed for deep learning as quickly as possible. It does so, as the name gives away, by working with tensors in a data flow graph. Starting in version 1.7, Keras is now also a core part of TensorFlow.

So, we could import the Keras layers by running the following:

```
from tensorflow.keras.layers import Dense, Activation
```

This book will treat Keras as a standalone library. However, you might want to use a different backend for Keras one day, as it keeps the code cleaner if we have shorter `import` statements.

Tensors and the computational graph

Tensors are arrays of numbers that transform based on specific rules. The simplest kind of tensor is a single number. This is also called a scalar. Scalars are sometimes referred to as rank-zero tensors.

The next tensor is a vector, also known as a rank-one tensor. The next The next ones up the order are matrices, called rank-two tensors; cube matrices, called rank-three tensors; and so on. You can see the rankings in the following table:

Rank	Name	Expresses
0	Scalar	Magnitude
1	Vector	Magnitude and Direction
2	Matrix	Table of numbers
3	Cube Matrix	Cube of numbers
n	n-dimensional matrix	You get the idea

This book mostly uses the word tensor for rank-three or higher tensors.

TensorFlow and every other deep learning library perform calculations along a computational graph. In a computational graph, operations, such as matrix multiplication or an activation function, are nodes in a network. Tensors get passed along the edges of the graph between the different operations.

A forward pass through our simple neural network has the following graph:

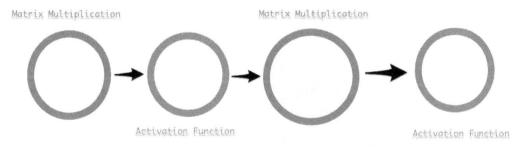

A simple computational graph

The advantage of structuring computations as a graph is that it's easier to run nodes in parallel. Through parallel computation, we do not need one very fast machine; we can also achieve fast computation with many slow computers that split up the tasks.

This is the reason why GPUs are so useful for deep learning. GPUs have many small cores, as opposed to CPUs, which only have a few fast cores. A modern CPU might only have four cores, whereas a modern GPU can have hundreds or even thousands of cores.

The entire graph of just a very simple model can look quite complex, but you can see the components of the dense layer. There is a **matrix multiplication (matmul)**, adding bias and a ReLU activation function:

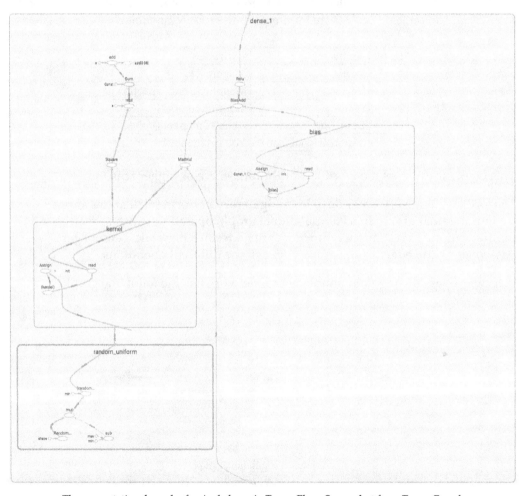

The computational graph of a single layer in TensorFlow. Screenshot from TensorBoard.

Another advantage of using computational graphs such as this is that TensorFlow and other libraries can quickly and automatically calculate derivatives along this graph. As we have explored throughout this chapter, calculating derivatives is key for training neural networks.

Exercises

Now that we have finished the first chapter in this exciting journey, I've got a challenge for you! You'll find some exercises that you can do that are all themed around what we've covered in this chapter!

So, why not try to do the following:

1. Expand the two-layer neural network in Python to three layers.
2. Within the GitHub repository, you will find an Excel file called 1 `Excel Exercise`. The goal is to classify three types of wine by their cultivar data. Build a logistic regressor to this end in Excel.
3. Build a two-layer neural network in Excel.
4. Play around with the hidden layer size and learning rate of the 2-layer neural network. Which options offer the lowest loss? Does the lowest loss also capture the true relationship?

Summary

And that's it! We've learned how neural networks work. Throughout the rest of this book, we'll look at how to build more complex neural networks that can approximate more complex functions.

As it turns out, there are a few tweaks to make to the basic structure for it to work well on specific tasks, such as image recognition. The basic ideas introduced in this chapter, however, stay the same:

*   Neural networks function as approximators
*   We gauge how well our approximated function, $\hat{f}$, performs through a loss function
*   Parameters of the model are optimized by updating them in the opposite direction of the derivative of the loss function with respect to the parameter
*   The derivatives are calculated backward through the model using the chain rule in a process called backpropagation

The key takeaway from this chapter is that while we are looking for function f, we can try and find it by optimizing a function to perform like f on a dataset. A subtle but important distinction is that we do not know whether $\hat{f}$ works like f at all. An often-cited example is a military project that tried to use deep learning to spot tanks within images. The model trained well on the dataset, but once the Pentagon wanted to try out their new tank spotting device, it failed miserably.

In the tank example, it took the Pentagon a while to figure out that in the dataset they used to develop the model, all the pictures of the tanks were taken on a cloudy day and pictures without a tank where taken on a sunny day. Instead of learning to spot tanks, the model had learned to spot grey skies instead.

This is just one example of how your model might work very differently to how you think, or even plan for it to do. Flawed data might seriously throw your model off track, sometimes without you even noticing. However, for every failure, there are plenty of success stories in deep learning. It is one of the high-impact technologies that will reshape the face of finance.

In the next chapter, we will get our hands dirty by jumping in and working with a common type of data in finance, structured tabular data. More specifically, we will tackle the problem of fraud, a problem that many financial institutions sadly have to deal with and for which modern machine learning is a handy tool. We will learn about preparing data and making predictions using Keras, scikit-learn, and XGBoost.

2
Applying Machine Learning to Structured Data

Structured data is a term used for any data that resides in a fixed field within a record or file, two such examples being relational databases and spreadsheets. Usually, structured data is presented in a table in which each column presents a type of value, and each row represents a new entry. Its structured format means that this type of data lends itself to classical statistical analysis, which is also why most data science and analysis work is done on structured data.

In day-to-day life, structured data is also the most common type of data available to businesses, and most machine learning problems that need to be solved in finance deal with structured data in one way or another. The fundamentals of any modern company's day-to-day running is built around structured data, including, transactions, order books, option prices, and suppliers, which are all examples of information usually collected in spreadsheets or databases.

This chapter will walk you through a structured data problem involving credit card fraud, where we will use feature engineering to identify the fraudulent transaction from a dataset successfully. We'll also introduce the basics of an **end-to-end** (E2E) approach so that we can solve common financial problems.

Fraud is an unfortunate reality that all financial institutions have to deal with. It's a constant race between companies trying to protect their systems and fraudsters who are trying to defeat the protection in place. For a long time, fraud detection has relied on simple heuristics. For example, a large transaction made while you're in a country you usually don't live in will likely result in that transaction being flagged.

Yet, as fraudsters continue to understand and circumvent the rules, credit card providers are deploying increasingly sophisticated machine learning systems to counter this.

In this chapter, we'll look at how a real bank might tackle the problem of fraud. It's a real-world exploration of how a team of data scientists starts with a heuristic baseline, then develops an understanding of its features, and from that, builds increasingly sophisticated machine learning models that can detect fraud. While the data we will use is synthetic, the process of development and tools that we'll use to tackle fraud are similar to the tools and processes that are used every day by international retail banks.

So where do you start? To put it in the words of one anonymous fraud detection expert that I spoke to, "*I keep thinking about how I would steal from my employer, and then I create some features that would catch my heist. To catch a fraudster, think like a fraudster.*" Yet, even the most ingenious feature engineers are not able to pick up on all the subtle and sometimes counterintuitive signs of fraud, which is why the industry is slowly shifting toward entirely E2E-trained systems. These systems, in addition to machine learning, are both focuses of this chapter where we will explore several commonly used approaches to flag fraud.

This chapter will act as an important baseline to *Chapter 6, Using Generative Models,* where we will again be revisiting the credit card fraud problem for a full E2E model using auto-encoders.

The data

The dataset we will work with is a synthetic dataset of transactions generated by a payment simulator. The goal of this case study and the focus of this chapter is to find fraudulent transactions within a dataset, a classic machine learning problem many financial institutions deal with.

Note: Before we go further, a digital copy of the code, as well as an interactive notebook for this chapter are accessible online, via the following two links:

An interactive notebook containing the code for this chapter can be found under https://www.kaggle.com/jannesklaas/structured-data-code

The code can also be found on GitHub, in this book's repository: https://github.com/PacktPublishing/Machine-Learning-for-Finance

The dataset we're using stems from the paper *PaySim: A financial mobile money simulator for fraud detection*, by E. A. Lopez-Rojas, A. Elmir, and S. Axelsson. The dataset can be found on Kaggle under this URL: https://www.kaggle.com/ntnu-testimon/paysim1.

Before we break it down on the next page, let's take a minute to look at the dataset that we'll be using in this chapter. Remember, you can download the data with the preceding link.

step	type	amount	nameOrig	oldBalance Orig	newBalance Orig	nameDest	oldBalance Dest	newBalance Dest	isFraud	isFlagged Fraud
1	PAYMENT	9839.64	C1231006815	170136.0	160296.36	M1979787155	0.0	0.0	0	0
1	PAYMENT	1864.28	C1666544295	21249.0	19384.72	M2044282225	0.0	0.0	0	0
1	TRANSFER	181.0	C1305486145	181.0	0.0	C553264065	0.0	0.0	1	0
1	CASH_OUT	181.0	C840083671	181.0	0.0	C38997010	21182.0	0.0	1	0
1	PAYMENT	11668.14	C2048537720	41554.0	29885.86	M1230701703	0.0	0.0	0	0
1	PAYMENT	7817.71	C90045638	53860.0	46042.29	M573487274	0.0	0.0	0	0
1	PAYMENT	7107.77	C154988899	183195.0	176087.23	M408069119	0.0	0.0	0	0
1	PAYMENT	7861.64	C1912850431	176087.23	168225.59	M633326333	0.0	0.0	0	0
1	PAYMENT	4024.36	C1265012928	2671.0	0.0	M1176932104	0.0	0.0	0	0
1	DEBIT	5337.77	C712410124	41720.0	36382.23	C195600860	41898.0	40348.79	0	0

As seen in the first row, the dataset has 11 columns. Let's explain what each one represents before we move on:

- **step**: Maps time, with each step corresponding to one hour.
- **type**: The type of the transaction, which can be CASH_IN, CASH_OUT, DEBIT, PAYMENT, or TRANSFER.
- **amount**: The amount of the transaction.
- **nameOrig**: The origin account that started the transaction. C relates to customer accounts, while M is the account of merchants.
- **oldbalanceOrig**: The old balance of the origin account.
- **newbalanceOrig**: The new balance of the origin account after the transaction amount has been added.
- **nameDest**: The destination account.
- **oldbalanceDest**: The old balance of the destination account. This information is not available for merchant accounts whose names start with M.
- **newbalanceDest**: The new balance of the destination account. This information is not available for merchant accounts.
- **isFraud**: Whether the transaction was fraudulent.
- **isFlaggedFraud**: Whether the old system has flagged the transaction as fraud.

In the preceding table, we can see 10 rows of data. It's worth noting that there are about 6.3 million transactions in our total dataset, so what we've seen is a small fraction of the total amount. As the fraud we're looking at only occurs in transactions marked as either TRANSFER or CASH_OUT, all other transactions can be dropped, leaving us with around 2.8 million examples to work with.

Heuristic, feature-based, and E2E models

Before we dive into developing models to detect fraud, let's take a second to pause and ponder over the different kinds of models we could build.

- A heuristic-based model is a simple "rule of thumb" developed purely by humans. Usually, the heuristic model stems from having an expert knowledge of the problem.

- A feature-based model relies heavily on humans modifying the data to create new and meaningful features, which are then fed into a (simple) machine learning algorithm. This approach mixes expert knowledge with learning from data.

- An E2E model learns purely from raw data. No human expertise is used, and the model learns everything directly from observations.

In our case, a heuristic-based model could be created to mark all transactions with the TRANSFER transaction type and an amount over $200,000 as fraudulent. Heuristic-based models have the advantage that they are both fast to develop and easy to implement; however, this comes with a pay-off, their performance is often poor, and fraudsters can easily play the system. Let's imagine that we went with the preceding heuristic-based model, fraudsters transferring only $199,999, under the fraudulent limit, would evade detection.

An important heuristic in the field of trading is the momentum strategy. Momentum strategies involve betting that a stock that's on the rise will continue to rise, with people then buying that stock. While this strategy sounds too simple to be any good, it is in fact, a reasonably successful strategy that many high-frequency trading and quantitative outlets are using today.

To create features, experts craft indicators that can distinguish fraudulent transactions from those that are genuine. This is often done using statistical data analysis, and when compared to the heuristic-based model that we proposed early on, it will take longer, but with the benefit of better results.

Feature engineering-based models are a midway between data and humans shaping rules, where human knowledge and creativity are exploited to craft good features, and data and machine learning are used to create a model from those features.

E2E models learn purely from collected data without using expert knowledge. As discussed before, this often yields much better results, but at the cost of taking a lot of time to complete. This method also has some additional elements worth considering. For instance, collecting the large amount of data that will be needed is an expensive task, as humans have to label millions of records.

Though for many people in the industry right now, they take the view that shipping a poor model is often better than not shipping anything at all. After all, having some protection against fraud is better than simply having none.

Using a heuristic approach that lets through half of all fraudulent transactions is better than having no fraud detection at all. The graph shows us the performance of the three models we introduced earlier on, against the time taken to implement them.

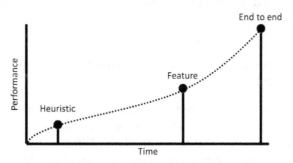

The methods used and the performance of the system during development

The best method is to use a combination of all three. If we deploy a heuristic model that meets the basic requirements of the task that it set out to achieve, then it can be shipped. By employing this method, the heuristic then becomes the baseline that any other approach has to beat. Once your heuristic model is deployed, then all your efforts should then be directed toward building a feature-based model, which as soon as it beats the initially deployed heuristic model, can then be deployed while you continue to refine the model.

As we've discussed before, feature-based models often deliver pretty decent performance on structured data tasks; this gives companies the time to undertake the lengthy and expensive task of building an E2E model, which can be shipped once it beats the feature-based model. Now that we understand the type of models we're going to build, let's look at the software we need to build them.

The machine learning software stack

In this chapter, we will be using a range of different libraries that are commonly used in machine learning. Let's take a minute to look at our stack, which consists of the following software:

- **Keras**: A neural network library that can act as a simplified interface to TensorFlow.

- **NumPy**: Adds support for large, multidimensional arrays as well as an extensive collection of mathematical functions.

- **Pandas**: A library for data manipulation and analysis. It's similar to Microsoft's Excel but in Python, as it offers data structures to handle tables and the tools to manipulate them.

- **Scikit-learn**: A machine learning library offering a wide range of algorithms and utilities.

- **TensorFlow**: A dataflow programming library that facilitates working with neural networks.

- **Matplotlib**: A plotting library.

- **Jupyter**: A development environment. All of the code examples in this book are available in Jupyter Notebooks.

The majority of this book is dedicated to working with the Keras library, while this chapter makes extensive use of the other libraries mentioned. The goal here is less about teaching you all the tips and tricks of all the different libraries, but more about showing you how they are integrated into the process of creating a predictive model.

Note: All of the libraries needed for this chapter are installed on Kaggle kernels by default. If you are running this code locally, please refer to the setup instructions in *Chapter 1, Neural Networks and Gradient-Based Optimization*, and install all of the libraries needed.

The heuristic approach

Earlier in this chapter, we introduced the three models that we will be using to detect fraud, now it's time to explore each of them in more detail. We're going to start with the heuristic approach.

Let's start by defining a simple heuristic model and measuring how well it does at measuring fraud rates.

Making predictions using the heuristic model

We will be making our predictions using the heuristic approach over the entire training data set in order to get an idea of how well this heuristic model does at predicting fraudulent transactions.

The following code will create a new column, `Fraud_Heuristic`, and in turn assigns a value of 1 in rows where the type is `TRANSFER`, and the amount is more than $200,000:

```
df['Fraud_Heuristic '] = np.where(((df['type'] == 'TRANSFER') &
(df['amount'] > 200000)),1,0)
```

With just two lines of code, it's easy to see how such a simple metric can be easy to write, and quick to deploy.

The F1 score

One important thing we must consider is the need for a common metric on which we can evaluate all of our models on. In *Chapter 1, Neural Networks and Gradient-Based Optimization*, we used accuracy as our emulation tool. However, as we've seen, there are far fewer fraudulent transactions than there are genuine ones. Therefore a model that classifies all the transactions as genuine can have a very high level of accuracy.

One such metric that is designed to deal with such a skewed distribution is the F1 score, which considers true and false positives and negatives, as you can see in this chart:

	Predicted Negative	Predicted Positive
Actual Negative	True Negative (TN)	False Positive (FP)
Actual Positive	False Negative (FN)	True Positive (TP)

We can first compute the precision of our model, which specifies the share of predicted positives that were positives, using the following formula:

$$precision = \frac{TP}{TP + FP}$$

Recall measures the share of predicted positives over the actual number of positives, as seen in this formula:

$$recall = \frac{TP}{TP + FN}$$

The F1 score is then calculated from the harmonic mean, an average, of the two measures, which can be seen in the following formula:

$$F_1 = 2 * \frac{precision * recall}{precision + recall}$$

To compute this metric in Python, we can use the `metrics` module of scikit-learn, or sklearn for short:

```
from sklearn.metrics import f1_score
```

Given the predictions we've made, we can now easily compute the F1 score using the following command:

```
f1_score(y_pred=df['Fraud_Heuristic '],y_true=df['isFraud'])
```

out: 0.013131315551742895

You'll see that the preceding command outputs a number–starting 0.013131315…-What this number means exactly is that our heuristic model is not doing too well, as the best possible F1 score is 1, and the worst is 0. In our case, this number represents the harmonic mean of the share of correctly caught frauds over everything labeled as fraud and the share of correctly caught frauds over all frauds.

Evaluating with a confusion matrix

A more qualitative and interpretable way of evaluating a model is with a confusion matrix. As the name suggests, the matrix shows how our classifier confuses classes.

Firstly, let's study the code appendix for the `plot_confusion_matrix` function:

```
from sklearn.metrics import confusion_matrix cm = confusion_matrix(
    y_pred=df['Fraud_Heuristic '],y_true=df['isFraud'])
plot_confusion_matrix(cm, ['Genuine','Fraud'])
```

Which, when we run, produces the following graphic:

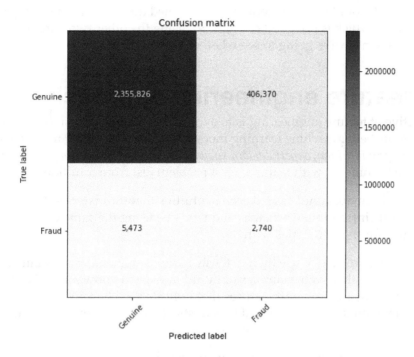

A confusion matrix for a heuristic model

So, just how accurate was that model? As you can see in our confusion matrix, from our dataset of 2,770,409 examples, 2,355,826 were correctly classified as genuine, while 406,370 were falsely classified as fraud. In fact, only 2,740 examples were correctly classified as fraud.

When our heuristic model classified a transaction as fraudulent, it was genuine in 99.3% of those cases. Only 34.2% of the total frauds got caught. All this information is incorporated into the F1 score we formulated. However, as we saw, it is easier to read this from the generated confusion matrix graphic. The reason we used both the heuristic model and the F1 score is that it is good practice to have a single number that tells us which model is better, and also a more graphical insight into how that model is better.

To put it frankly, our heuristic model has performed quite poorly, detecting only 34.2% of fraud, which is not good enough. So, using the other two methods in the following sections, we're going to see whether we can do better.

The feature engineering approach

The objective of feature engineering is to exploit the qualitative insight of humans in order to create better machine learning models. A human engineer usually uses three types of insight: *intuition*, *expert domain knowledge*, and *statistical analysis*. Quite often, it's possible to come up with features for a problem just from intuition.

As an example, in our fraud case, it seems intuitive that fraudsters will create new accounts for their fraudulent schemes and won't be using the same bank account that they pay for their groceries with.

Domain experts are able to use their extensive knowledge of a problem in order to come up with other such examples of intuition. They'll know more about how fraudsters behave and can craft features that indicate such behavior. All of these intuitions are then usually confirmed by statistical analysis, something that can even be used to open the possibilities of discovering new features.

Statistical analysis can sometimes turn up quirks that can be turned into predictive features. However, with this method, engineers must beware of the **data trap**. Predictive features found in the data might only exist in that data because any dataset will spit out a predictive feature if it's wrangled with for long enough.

A data trap refers to engineers digging within the data for features forever, and never questioning whether those features they are searching for are relevant.

Data scientists stuck in to the data trap keep euphorically finding features, only to realize later that their model, with all those features, does not work well. Finding strong predictive features in the training set is like a drug for data science teams. Yes, there's an immediate reward, a quick win that feels like a validation of one's skills. However, as with many drugs, the data trap can lead to an after-effect in which teams find that weeks' or months' worth of work in finding those features was actually, useless.

Take a minute to ask yourself, are you in that position? If you ever find yourself applying analysis after analysis, transforming data in every possible way, chasing correlation values, you might very well be stuck in a data trap.

To avoid the data trap, it is important to establish a **qualitative rationale** as to why this statistical predictive feature exists and should exist outside of the dataset as well. By establishing this rationale, you will keep both yourself and your team alert to avoiding crafting features that represent noise. The data trap is the human form of overfitting and finding patterns in noise, which is a problem for models as well.

Humans can use their qualitative reasoning skills to avoid fitting noise, which is a big advantage humans have over machines. If you're a data scientist, you should use this skill to create more generalizable models.

The goal of this section was not to showcase all the features that feature engineering could perform on this dataset, but just to highlight the three approaches and how they can be turned into features.

A feature from intuition – fraudsters don't sleep

Without knowing much about fraud, we can intuitively describe fraudsters as shady people that operate in the dark. In most cases, genuine transactions happen during the day, as people sleep at night.

The time steps in our dataset represent one hour. Therefore, we can generate the time of the day by simply taking the remainder of a division by 24, as seen in this code:

```
df['hour'] = df['step'] % 24
```

From there, we can then count the number of fraudulent and genuine transactions at different times. To calculate this, we must run the following code:

```
frauds = []
genuine = []
for i in range(24):
    f = len(df[(df['hour'] == i) & (df['isFraud'] == 1)])
    g = len(df[(df['hour'] == i) & (df['isFraud'] == 0)])
    frauds.append(f)
    genuine.append(g)
```

Then finally, we can plot the share of genuine and fraudulent transactions over the course of the day into a chart. To do this, we must run the following code:

```
fig, ax = plt.subplots(figsize=(10,6))
ax.plot(genuine/np.sum(genuine), label='Genuine')
ax.plot(frauds/np.sum(frauds),dashes=[5, 2], label='Fraud')
plt.xticks(np.arange(24))
legend = ax.legend(loc='upper center', shadow=True)
```

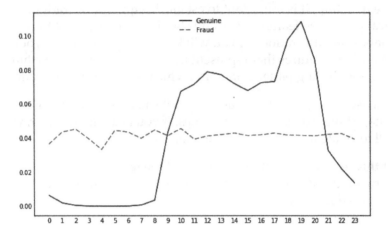

The share of fraudulent and genuine transactions conducted throughout each hour of the day

As we can see in the preceding chart, there are much fewer genuine transactions at night, while fraudulent behavior continues over the day. To be sure that night is a time when we can hope to catch fraud, we can also plot the number of fraudulent transactions as a share of all transactions. To do this, we must run the following command:

```
fig, ax = plt.subplots(figsize=(10,6))
ax.plot(np.divide(frauds,np.add(genuine,frauds)), label='Share of
fraud')
plt.xticks(np.arange(24))
legend = ax.legend(loc='upper center', shadow=True)
```

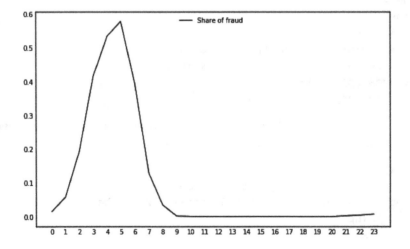

The share of transactions that are fraudulent per hour of the day

Once we run that code, we can see that at around 5 AM, over 60% of all transactions seem to be fraudulent, which appears to make this a great time of the day to catch fraud.

Expert insight – transfer, then cash out

The description of the dataset came with another description that explained the expected behavior of fraudsters. First, they transfer money to a bank account they control. Then, they cash out that money from an ATM.

We can check whether there are fraudulent transfer destination accounts that are the origin of the fraudulent cash outs by running the following code:

```
dfFraudTransfer = df[(df.isFraud == 1) & (df.type == 'TRANSFER')]
dfFraudCashOut = df[(df.isFraud == 1) & (df.type == 'CASH_OUT')]
dfFraudTransfer.nameDest.isin(dfFraudCashOut.nameOrig).any()
```

out: **False**

According to the output, there seems to be no fraudulent transfers that are the origin of fraudulent cash outs. The behavior expected by the experts is not visible in our data. This could mean two things: firstly, it could mean that the fraudsters behave differently now, or secondly that our data does not capture their behavior. Either way, we cannot use this insight for predictive modeling here.

Statistical quirks – errors in balances

A closer examination of the data shows that there are some transactions where the old and new balances of the destination account is zero, although the transaction amount is not zero. This is odd, or more so a quirk, and so we want to investigate whether this type of oddity yields predictive power.

To begin with, we can calculate the share of fraudulent transactions with this property by running the following code:

```
dfOdd = df[(df.oldBalanceDest == 0) &
           (df.newBalanceDest == 0) &
           (df.amount)]
len(dfOdd[(df.isFraud == 1)]) / len(dfOdd)
```

out: **0.7046398891966759**

As you can see, the share of fraudulent transactions stands at 70%, so this quirk seems to be a good feature at detecting fraud in transactions. However, it is important to ask ourselves how this quirk got into our data in the first place. One possibility could be that the transactions never come through.

This could happen for a number of reasons including that there might be another fraud prevention system in place that blocks the transactions, or that the origin account for the transaction has insufficient funds.

While we have no way of verifying if there's another fraud prevention system in place, we can check to see if the origin accounts have insufficient funds. To do this, we have to run the following code:

```
len(dfOdd[(dfOdd.oldBalanceOrig <= dfOdd.amount)]) / len(dfOdd)
```

out: 0.8966412742382271

As we can see in the output, close to 90% of the odd transactions have insufficient funds in their origin accounts. From this, we can now construct a rationale in which fraudsters try to drain a bank account of all its funds more often than regular people do.

We need this rationale to avoid the data trap. Once established, the rationale must be constantly scrutinized. In our case, it has failed to explain 10% of the odd transactions, and if this number rises, it could end up hurting the performance of our model in production.

Preparing the data for the Keras library

In *Chapter 1, Neural Networks and Gradient-Based Optimization*, we saw that neural networks would only take numbers as inputs. The issue for us in our dataset is that not all of the information in our table is numbers, some of it is presented as characters.

Therefore, in this section, we're going to work on preparing the data for Keras so that we can meaningfully work with it.

Before we start, let's look at the three types of data, *Nominal*, *Ordinal*, and *Numerical*:

- **Nominal data**: This comes in discrete categories that cannot be ordered. In our case, the type of transfer is a nominal variable. There are four discrete types, but it does not make sense to put them in any order. For instance, TRANSFER cannot be more than CASH_OUT, so instead, they are just separate categories.
- **Ordinal data**: This also comes in discrete categories, but unlike nominal data, it can be ordered. For example, if coffee comes in large, medium, and small sizes, those are distinct categories because they can be compared. The large size contains more coffee than the small size.
- **Numerical data**: This can be ordered, but we can also perform mathematical operations on it. An example in our data is the number of funds, as we can both compare the amounts, and also subtract or add them up.

Both nominal and ordinal data are **categorical data**, as they describe discrete categories. While numerical data works fine with neural networks, only out of the box, categorical data needs special treatment.

One-hot encoding

The most commonly used method to encode categorical data is called **one-hot encoding**. In one-hot encoding, we create a new variable, a so-called **dummy variable** for each category. We then set the dummy variable to 1 if the transaction is a member of a certain category and to zero otherwise.

An example of how we could apply this to our data set can be seen as follows:

So, this is what the categorical data would look like before one-hot encoding:

Transaction	Type
1	TRANSFER
2	CASH_OUT
3	TRANSFER

This is what the data would look like after one-hot encoding:

Transaction	Type_TRANSFER	Type_CASH_OUT
1	1	0
2	0	1
3	1	0

The Pandas software library offers a function that allows us to create dummy variables out of the box. Before doing so, however, it makes sense to add `Type_` in front of all actual transaction types. The dummy variables will be named after the category. By adding `Type_` to the beginning, we know that these dummy variables indicate the type.

The following line of code does three things. Firstly, `df['type'].astype(str)` converts all the entries in the **Type** column to strings. Secondly, the `Type_` prefix is added as a result of combining the strings. Thirdly, the new column of combined strings then replaces the original **Type** column:

```
df['type'] = 'Type_' + df['type'].astype(str)
```

We can now get the dummy variables by running the following code:

```
dummies = pd.get_dummies(df['type'])
```

We should note that the `get_dummies()` function creates a new data frame. Next we attach this data frame to the main data frame, which can be done by running:

```
df = pd.concat([df,dummies],axis=1)
```

The `concat()` method, as seen in the preceding code, concatenates two data frames. We concatenate along axis 1 to add the data frame as new columns. Now that the dummy variables are in our main data frame, we can remove the original column by running this:

```
del df['type']
```

And, voilà! We have turned our categorical variable into something a neural network will be able to work with.

Entity embeddings

In this section, we're going to walk through making use of both embeddings and the Keras functional API, showing you the general workflow. Both of these topics get introduced and explored fully in *Chapter 5, Parsing Textual Data with Natural Language Processing*, where we will go beyond the general ideas presented here and where we'll begin discussing topics like implementation.

It's fine if you do not understand everything that is going on just now; this is an advanced section after all. If you want to use both of these techniques, you will be well prepared after reading this book, as we explain different elements of both methods throughout the book.

In this section, we will be creating embedding vectors for categorical data. Before we start, we need to understand that embedding vectors are vectors representing categorical values. We use embedding vectors as inputs for neural networks. We train embeddings together with a neural network, so that we can, over time, obtain more useful embeddings. Embeddings are an extremely useful tool to have at our disposal.

Why are embeddings so useful? Not only do embeddings reduce the number of dimensions needed for encoding over one-hot encoding and thus decrease memory usage, but they also reduce sparsity in input activations, which helps reduce overfitting, and they can encode semantic meanings as vectors. The same advantages that made embeddings useful for text, *Chapter 5, Parsing Textual Data with Natural Language Processing*, also make them useful for categorical data.

Tokenizing categories

Just as with text, we have to tokenize the inputs before feeding them into the embeddings layer. To do this, we have to create a mapping dictionary that maps categories to a token. We can achieve this by running:

```
map_dict = {}
for token, value in enumerate(df['type'].unique()):
    map_dict[value] = token
```

This code loops over all the unique type categories while counting upward. The first category gets token 0, the second 1, and so on. Our `map_dict` looks like this:

```
{'CASH_IN': 4, 'CASH_OUT': 2, 'DEBIT': 3, 'PAYMENT': 0,
'TRANSFER': 1}
```

We can now apply this mapping to our data frame:

```
df["type"].replace(map_dict, inplace=True)
```

As a result, all types will now be replaced by their tokens.

We have to deal with the non-categorical values in our data frame separately. We can create a list of columns that are not the type and not the target like this:

```
other_cols = [c for c in df.columns if ((c != 'type') and (c !=
'isFraud'))]
```

Creating input models

The model we are creating will have two inputs: one for the types with an embedding layer, and one for all other, non-categorical variables. To combine them with more ease at a later point, we're going to keep track of their inputs and outputs with two arrays:

```
inputs = []
outputs = []
```

The model that acts as an input for the type receives a one-dimensional input and parses it through an embedding layer. The outputs of the embedding layer are then reshaped into flat arrays, as we can see in this code:

```
num_types = len(df['type'].unique())
type_embedding_dim = 3

type_in = Input(shape=(1,))
type_embedding = Embedding(num_types,type_embedding_dim,input_
length=1)(type_in)
```

```
type_out = Reshape(target_shape=
(type_embedding_dim,))(type_embedding)

type_model = Model(type_in,type_out)

inputs.append(type_in)
outputs.append(type_out)
```

The `type` embeddings have three layers here. This is an arbitrary choice, and experimentation with different numbers of dimensions could improve the results.

For all the other inputs, we create another input that has as many dimensions as there are non-categorical variables and consists of a single dense layer with no activation function. The dense layer is optional; the inputs could also be directly passed into the head model. More layers could also be added, including these:

```
num_rest = len(other_cols)

rest_in = Input(shape = (num_rest,))
rest_out = Dense(16)(rest_in)

rest_model = Model(rest_in,rest_out)

inputs.append(rest_in)
outputs.append(rest_out)
```

Now that we have created the two input models, we can concatenate them. On top of the two concatenated inputs, we will also build our head model. To begin this process, we must first run the following:

```
concatenated = Concatenate()(outputs)
```

Then, by running the following code, we can build and compile the overall model:

```
x = Dense(16)(concatenated)
x = Activation('sigmoid')(x)
x = Dense(1)(concatenated)
model_out = Activation('sigmoid')(x)

merged_model = Model(inputs, model_out)
merged_model.compile(loss='binary_crossentropy',
                     optimizer='adam',
                     metrics=['accuracy'])
```

Training the model

In this section we're going to train a model with multiple inputs. To do this, we need to provide a list of *X* values for each input. So, firstly we must split up our data frame. We can do this by running the following code:

```
types = df['type']
rest = df[other_cols]
target = df['isFraud']
```

Then, we can train the model by providing a list of the two inputs and the target, as we can see in the following code:

```
history = merged_model.fit([types.values,rest.values],target.values,
                epochs = 1,
                batch_size = 128)
```

```
out:
```

```
Epoch 1/1
```

```
6362620/6362620 [==============================] - 78s 12us/step - loss:
0.0208 - acc: 0.9987
```

Creating predictive models with Keras

Our data now contains the following columns:

```
amount,
oldBalanceOrig,
newBalanceOrig,
oldBalanceDest,
newBalanceDest,
isFraud,
isFlaggedFraud,
type_CASH_OUT,
type_TRANSFER, isNight
```

Now that we've got the columns, our data is prepared, and we can use it to create a model.

Extracting the target

To train the model, a neural network needs a target. In our case, `isFraud` is the target, so we have to separate it from the rest of the data. We can do this by running:

```
y_df = df['isFraud']
x_df = df.drop('isFraud',axis=1)
```

The first step only returns the `isFraud` column and assigns it to `y_df`.

The second step returns all columns except `isFraud` and assigns them to `x_df`.

We also need to convert our data from a pandas `DataFrame` to NumPy arrays. The pandas `DataFrame` is built on top of NumPy arrays but comes with lots of extra bells and whistles that make all the preprocessing we did earlier possible. To train a neural network, however, we just need the underlying data, which we can get by simply running the following:

```
y = y_df.values
X = x_df.values
```

Creating a test set

When we train our model, we run the risk of **overfitting**. Overfitting means that our model memorizes the x and y mapping in our training dataset but does not find the function that describes the true relationship between x and y. This is problematic because once we run our model **out of sample** – that is, on data not in our training set, it might do very poorly. To prevent this, we're going to create a so-called **test set**.

A test set is a holdout dataset, which we only use to evaluate our model once we think it is doing fairly well in order to see how well it performs on data it has not seen yet. A test set is usually randomly sampled from the complete data. Scikit-learn offers a convenient function to do this, as we can see in the following code:

```
from sklearn.model_selection import train_test_split
X_train, X_test, y_train, y_test = train_test_split(X, y,
test_size=0.33, random_state=42)
```

The element, `train_test_split` will randomly assign rows to either the train or test set. You can specify `test_size`, the share of data that goes into the test set (which in our case is 33%), as well as a random state. Assigning `random_state` makes sure that although the process is pseudo-random, it will always return the same split, which makes our work more reproducible. Note that the actual choice of number (for example, `42`) does not really matter. What matters is that the same number is used in all experiments.

Creating a validation set

Now you might be tempted to just try out a lot of different models until you get a really high performance on the test set. However, ask yourself this: how would you know that you have not selected a model that by chance works well on the test set but does not work in real life?

The answer is that every time you evaluate on the test set, you incur a bit of "information leakage," that is, information from the test set leaks into your model by influencing your choice of model. Gradually, the test set becomes less valuable. The validation set is a sort of a "dirty test set" that you can use to frequently test your models out of sample performance without worrying. Though it's key to note that we don't want to use the test set too often, but it is still used to measure out-of-sample performance frequently.

To this end, we'll create a "validation set," also known as a development set.

We can do this the same way we created the test set, by just splitting the training data again, as we can see in the following code:

```
X_train, X_test, y_train, y_test = train_test_split(X_train,
y_train, test_size=0.1, random_state=42)
```

Oversampling the training data

Remember that in our dataset, only a tiny fraction of transactions were fraudulent, and that a model that is always classifying transactions as genuine would have a very high level of accuracy. To make sure we train our model on true relationships, we can **oversample** the training data.

This means that we would add data that would be fraudulent to our dataset until we have the same amount of fraudulent transactions as genuine transactions.

Note: A useful library for this kind of task is `imblearn`, which includes a SMOTE function. See, `http://contrib.scikitlearn.org/imbalanced-learn/`.

Synthetic Minority Over-sampling Technique (SMOTE) is a clever way of oversampling. This method tries to create new samples while maintaining the same decision boundaries for the classes. We can oversample with SMOTE by simply running:

```
From imblearn.over_sampling import SMOTE
sm = SMOTE(random_state=42)
X_train_res, y_train_res = sm.fit_sample(X_train, y_train)
```

Building the model

We've successfully addressed several key learning points, and so it's now finally time to build a neural network! As in *Chapter 1, Neural Networks and Gradient-Based Optimization*, we need to import the required Keras modules using the following code:

```
from keras.models import Sequential
from keras.layers import Dense, Activation
```

In practice, many structured data problems require very low learning rates. To set the learning rate for the gradient descent optimizer, we also need to import the optimizer. We can do this by running:

```
from keras.optimizers import SGD
```

Creating a simple baseline

Before we dive into more advanced models, it is wise to start with a simple logistic regression baseline. This is to make sure that our model can actually train successfully.

To create a simple baseline, we need to run the following code:

```
model = Sequential()
model.add(Dense(1, input_dim=9))
model.add(Activation('sigmoid'))
```

You can see here a logistic regressor, which is the same as a one-layer neural network:

```
model.compile(loss='binary_crossentropy',
              optimizer=SGD(lr=1e-5),
              metrics=['acc'])
```

Here, we will compile the model. Instead of just passing SGD to specify the optimizer for Stochastic Gradient Descent, we'll create a custom instance of SGD in which we set the learning rate to 0.00001. In this example, tracking accuracy is not needed since we evaluate our models using the F1 score. Still, it still reveals some interesting behavior, as you can see in the following code:

```
model.fit(X_train_res,y_train_res,
          epochs=5,
          batch_size=256,
          validation_data=(X_val,y_val))
```

Notice how we have passed the validation data into Keras by creating a tuple in which we store data and labels. We will train this model for 5 epochs:

```
Train on 3331258 samples, validate on 185618 samples Epoch 1/5
3331258/3331258 [==============================] - 20s 6us/step - loss:
3.3568 - acc: 0.7900 - val_loss: 3.4959 - val_acc: 0.7807 Epoch 2/5
3331258/3331258 [==============================] - 20s 6us/step - loss:
3.0356 - acc: 0.8103 - val_loss: 2.9473 - val_acc: 0.8151 Epoch 3/5
3331258/3331258 [==============================] - 20s 6us/step - loss:
2.4450 - acc: 0.8475 - val_loss: 0.9431 - val_acc: 0.9408 Epoch 4/5
3331258/3331258 [==============================] - 20s 6us/step - loss:
2.3416 - acc: 0.8541 - val_loss: 1.0552 - val_acc: 0.9338 Epoch 5/5
3331258/3331258 [==============================] - 20s 6us/step - loss:
2.3336 - acc: 0.8546 - val_loss: 0.8829 - val_acc: 0.9446
```

Notice a few things here: first, we have trained on about 3.3 million samples, which is more data than we initially had. The sudden increase comes from the oversampling that we did earlier on in this chapter. Secondly, the training set's accuracy is significantly lower than the validation set's accuracy. This is because the training set is balanced, while the validation set is not.

We oversampled the data by adding more fraud cases to the training set than there are in real life, which as we discussed, helped our model detect fraud better. If we did not oversample, our model would be inclined to classify all transactions as genuine since the vast majority of samples in the training set are genuine.

By adding fraud cases, we are forcing the model to learn what distinguishes a fraud case. Yet, we want to validate our model on realistic data. Therefore, our validation set does not artificially contain many fraud cases.

A model classifying everything as genuine would have over 99% accuracy on the validation set, but just 50% accuracy on the training set. Accuracy is a flawed metric for such imbalanced datasets. It is a half-decent proxy and more interpretable than just a loss, which is why we keep track of it in Keras.

To evaluate our model, we should use the F1 score that we discussed at the beginning of this chapter. However, Keras is unable to directly track the F1 score in training since the calculation of an F1 score is somewhat slow and would end up slowing down the training of our model.

Note: Remember that accuracy on an imbalanced dataset can be very high, even if the model is performing poorly.

If the model exhibits a higher degree of accuracy on an imbalanced validation set than compared to that seen with a balanced training set, then it says little about the model performing well.

Compare the training set's performance against the previous training set's performance, and likewise the validation set's performance against the previous validation set's performance. However, be careful when comparing the training set's performance to that of the validation set's performance on highly imbalanced data. However, if your data is equally balanced, then comparing the validation set and the training set is a good way to gauge overfitting.

We are now in a position where we can make predictions on our test set in order to evaluate the baseline. We start by using `model.predict` to make predictions on the test set:

```
y_pred = model.predict(X_test)
```

Before evaluating our baseline, we need to turn the probabilities given by our model into absolute predictions. In our example, we'll classify everything that has a fraud probability above 50% as fraud. To do this, we need to run the following code:

```
y_pred[y_pred > 0.5] = 1
y_pred[y_pred < 0.5] = 0
```

Our F1 score is already significantly better than it was for the heuristic model, which if you go back, you'll see that it only achieved a rate of 0.013131315551742895:

```
f1_score(y_pred=y_pred,y_true=y_test)
```

out: 0.054384286716408395

By plotting the confusion matrix, we're able to see that our feature-based model has indeed improved on the heuristic model:

```
cm = confusion_matrix(y_pred=y_pred,y_true=y_test)
plot_confusion_matrix(cm, ['Genuine','Fraud'], normalize=False)
```

This code should produce the following confusion matrix:

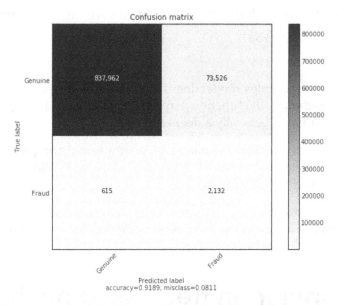

A confusion matrix for a simple Keras model

But what if we wanted to build more complex models that can express more subtle relationships, than the one that we've just built? Let's now do that!

Building more complex models

After we have created a simple baseline, we can go on to more complex models. The following code is an example of a two-layer network:

```
model = Sequential()
model.add(Dense(16,input_dim=9))
model.add(Activation('tanh'))
model.add(Dense(1))
model.add(Activation('sigmoid'))

model.compile(loss='binary_crossentropy',
              optimizer=SGD(lr=1e-5),
              metrics=['acc'])

model.fit(X_train_res,y_train_res,
          epochs=5, batch_size=256,
          validation_data=(X_val,y_val))

y_pred = model.predict(X_test)
y_pred[y_pred > 0.5] = 1
y_pred[y_pred < 0.5] = 0
```

After running that code, we'll then again benchmark with the F1 score:

```
f1_score(y_pred=y_pred,y_true=y_test)
```

out: 0.087220701988752675

In this case, the more complex model does better than the simple baseline created earlier. It seems as though the function mapping transaction data to fraud is complex and can be approximated better by a deeper network.

In this section we have built and evaluated both simple and complex neural network models for fraud detection. We have been careful to use the validation set to gauge the initial out-of-sample performance.

With all of that, we can build much more complex neural networks (and we will). But first we will have a look at the workhorse of modern enterprise-ready machine learning: tree-based methods.

A brief primer on tree-based methods

No chapter on structured data would be complete without mentioning tree-based methods, such as random forests or XGBoost.

It is worth knowing about them because, in the realm of predictive modeling for structured data, tree-based methods are very successful. However, they do not perform as well on more advanced tasks, such as image recognition or sequence-to-sequence modeling. This is the reason why the rest of the book does not deal with tree-based methods.

Note: For a deeper dive into XGBoost, check out the tutorials on the XGBoost documentation page: http://xgboost.readthedocs. io. There is a nice explanation of how tree-based methods and gradient boosting work in theory and practice under the **Tutorials** section of the website.

A simple decision tree

The basic idea behind tree-based methods is the decision tree. A decision tree splits up data to create the maximum difference in outcomes.

Let's assume for a second that our `isNight` feature is the greatest predictor of fraud. A decision tree would split our dataset according to whether the transactions happened at night or not. It would look at all the night-time transactions, looking for the next best predictor of fraud, and it would do the same for all day-time transactions.

Scikit-learn has a handy decision tree module. We can create one for our data by simply running the following code:

```
from sklearn.tree import DecisionTreeClassifier
dtree=DecisionTreeClassifier()
dtree.fit(X_train,y_train)
```

The resulting tree will look like this:

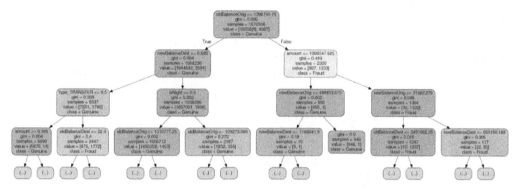

A decision tree for fraud detection

Simple decision trees, like the one we've produced, can give a lot of insight into data. For example, in our decision tree, the most important feature seems to be the old balance of the origin account, given that it is the first node in the tree.

A random forest

A more advanced version of a simple decision tree is a random forest, which is a collection of decision trees. A forest is trained by taking subsets of the training data and training decision trees on those subsets.

Often, those subsets do not include every feature of the training data. By doing it this way, the different decision trees can fit different aspects of the data and capture more information on aggregate. After a number of trees have been created, their predictions are averaged to create the final prediction.

The idea is that the errors presented by the trees are not correlated, and so by using multiple trees you cancel out the error. You can create and train a random forest classifier like this:

```
from sklearn.ensemble import RandomForestClassifier
rf = RandomForestClassifier(n_estimators=10,n_jobs=-1)
rf.fit(X_train_res,y_train_res)
```

You'll notice that with the code we've just generated, random forests have far fewer knobs to tune than neural networks. In this case, we just specify the number of estimators, that is, the number of trees we would like our forest to have.

The `n_jobs` argument tells the random forest how many trees we would like to train in parallel. Note that `-1` stands for "as many as there are CPU cores":

```
y_pred = rf.predict(X_test)
f1_score(y_pred=y_pred,y_true=y_test)
```

out: 0.8749502190362406

The random forest does an order of magnitude better than the neural network as its F1 score is close to 1, which is the maximum score. Its confusion plot, seen as follows, shows that the random forest significantly reduced the number of false positives:

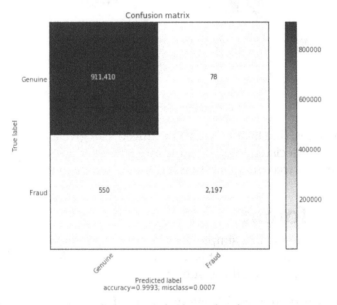

A confusion matrix for the random forest

A shallow learning approach, such as a random forest, often does better than deep learning on relatively simple problems. The reason for this is that simple relationships with low-dimensional data can be hard to learn for a deep learning model, which has to fit multiple parameters exactly in order to match the simple function.

As we will see in later chapters of this book, as soon as relationships do get more complex, deep learning gets to shine.

XGBoost

XGBoost stands for **eXtreme Gradient Boosting**. The idea behind gradient boosting is to train a decision tree, and then to train a second decision tree on the errors that the first decision tree made.

Through this method, multiple layers of decision trees can be added, which slowly reduces the total number of model errors. XGBoost is a popular library that implements gradient boosting very efficiently.

Note: XGBoost is installed on Kaggle kernels by default. If you are running these examples locally, see the XGBoost manual for installation instructions and more information: `http://xgboost.readthedocs.io/`.

Gradient boosting classifiers can be created and trained just like random forests from `sklearn`, as can be seen in the following code:

```
import xgboost as xgb
booster = xgb.XGBClassifier(n_jobs=-1)
booster = booster.fit(X_train,y_train)
y_pred = booster.predict(X_test)
f1_score(y_pred=y_pred,y_true=y_test)
```

out: 0.85572959604286891

The gradient booster performs at almost the same level as a random forest on this task. A common approach that is used is to take both a random forest and a gradient booster and to average the predictions in order to get an even better model.

The bulk of machine learning jobs in business today are done on relatively simple structured data. The methods we have learned today, random forests and gradient boosting, are therefore the standard tools that most practitioners use in the real world.

In most enterprise machine learning applications, value creation does not come from carefully tweaking a model or coming up with cool architectures, but from massaging data and creating good features. However, as tasks get more complex and more semantic understanding of unstructured data is needed, these tools begin to fail.

E2E modeling

Our current approach relies on engineered features. As we discussed at the start of this chapter, an alternative method is E2E modeling. In E2E modeling, both raw and unstructured data about a transaction is used. This could include the description text of a transfer, video feeds from cameras monitoring a cash machine, or other sources of data. E2E is often more successful than feature engineering, provided that you have enough data available.

To get valid results, and to successfully train the data with an E2E model it can take millions of examples. Yet, often this is the only way to gain an acceptable result, especially when it is hard to codify the rules for something. Humans can recognize things in images well, but it is hard to come up with exact rules that distinguish things, which is where E2E shines.

In the dataset used for this chapter, we do not have access to more data, but the rest of the chapters of this book demonstrate various E2E models.

Exercises

If you visit `https://kaggle.com`, search for a competition that has structured data. One example is the Titanic competition. Here you can create a new kernel, do some feature engineering, and try to build a predictive model.

How much can you improve it by investing time in feature engineering versus model tweaking? Is there an E2E approach to the problem?

Summary

In this chapter, we have taken a structured data problem from raw data to strong and reliable predictive models. We have learned about heuristic, feature engineering, and E2E modeling. We have also seen the value of clear evaluation metrics and baselines.

In the next chapter, we will look into a field where deep learning truly shines, computer vision. Here, we will discover the computer vision pipeline, from working with simple models to very deep networks augmented with powerful preprocessing software. The ability to "see" empowers computers to enter completely new domains.

3
Utilizing Computer Vision

When Snapchat first introduced a filter featuring a breakdancing hotdog, the stock price of the company surged. However, investors were less interested in the hotdog's handstand; what actually fascinated them was that Snapchat had successfully built a powerful form of computer vision technology.

The Snapchat app was now not only able to take pictures, but it was also able to find the surfaces within those pictures that a hotdog could breakdance on. Their app would then stick the hotdog there, something that could still be done when the user moved their phone, allowing the hotdog to keep dancing in the same spot.

While the dancing hotdog may be one of the sillier applications of computer vision, it successfully showed the world the potential of the technology. In a world full of cameras, from the billions of smartphones, security cameras, and satellites in use every day, to **Internet of Things (IoT)** devices, being able to interpret images yields great benefits for both consumers and producers.

Computer vision allows us to both perceive and interpret the real world at scale. You can think of it like this: no analyst could ever look at millions of satellite images to mark mining sites and track their activity over time; it's just not possible. Yet for computers, it's not just a possibility; it's something that's a reality here and now.

In fact, something that's being used in the real world now, by several firms, is retailers counting the number of cars in their parking lot in order to estimate what the sales of goods will be in a given period.

Another important application of computer vision can be seen in finance, specifically in the area of insurance. For instance, insurers might use drones to fly over roofs in order to spot issues before they become an expensive problem. This could extend to them using computer vision to inspect factories and equipment they insure.

Looking at another case in the finance sector, banks needing to comply with **Know-Your-Customer** (**KYC**) rules are automating back-office processes and identity verification. In financial trading, computer vision can be applied to candlestick charts in order to find new patterns for technical analysis. We could dedicate a whole book to the practical applications of computer vision.

In this chapter, we will be covering the building blocks of computer vision models. This will include a focus on the following topics:

- Convolutional layers.
- Padding.
- Pooling.
- Regularization to prevent overfitting.
- Momentum-based optimization.
- Batch normalization.
- Advanced architectures for computer vision beyond classification.
- A note on libraries.

Before we start, let's have a look at all the different libraries we will be using in this chapter:

- **Keras**: A high-level neural network library and an interface to TensorFlow.
- **TensorFlow**: A dataflow programming and machine learning library that we use for GPU-accelerated computation.
- **Scikit-learn**: A popular machine learning library with implementation of many classic algorithms as well as evaluation tools.
- **OpenCV**: An image processing library that can be used for rule-based augmentation
- **NumPy**: A library for handling matrices in Python.
- **Seaborn**: A plotting library.
- **tqdm**: A tool to monitor the progress of Python programs.

It's worth taking a minute to note that all of these libraries, except for OpenCV, can be installed via `pip`; for example, `pip install keras`.

OpenCV, however, will require a slightly more complex installation procedure. This is beyond the scope of this book, but the information is well documented online via OpenCV documentation, which you can view at the following URL: `https://docs.opencv.org/trunk/df/d65/tutorial_table_of_content_introduction.html`.

Alternately, it's worth noting that both Kaggle and Google Colab come with OpenCV preinstalled. To run the examples in this chapter, make sure you have OpenCV installed and can import with `import cv2`.

Convolutional Neural Networks

Convolutional Neural Networks, **ConvNets**, or **CNNs** for short, are the driving engine behind computer vision. ConvNets allow us to work with larger images while still keeping the network at a reasonable size.

The name Convolutional Neural Network comes from the mathematical operation that differentiates them from regular neural networks. Convolution is the mathematically correct term for sliding one matrix over another matrix. We'll explore in the next section, *Filters on MNIST*, why this is important for ConvNets, but also why this is not the best name in the world for them, and why ConvNets should, in reality, be called **filter nets**.

You may be asking, "but why filter nets?" The answer is simply because what makes them work is the fact that they use filters.

In the next section, we will be working with the MNIST dataset, which is a collection of handwritten digits that has become a standard "Hello, World!" application for computer vision.

Filters on MNIST

What does a computer actually see when it sees an image? Well, the values of the pixels are stored as numbers in the computer. So, when the computer *sees* a black-and-white image of a seven, it actually sees something similar to the following:

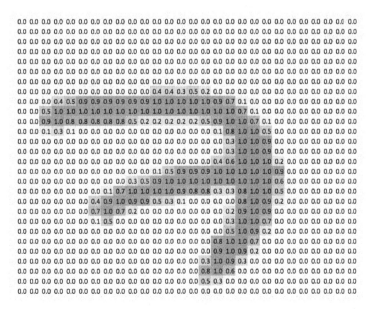

The number 7 from the MNIST dataset

The preceding is an example from the MNIST dataset. The handwritten number in the image has been highlighted to make the figure seven visible for humans, but for the computer, the image is really just a collection of numbers. This means we can perform all kinds of mathematical operations on the image.

When detecting numbers, there are a few lower-level features that make a number. For example, in this handwritten figure 7, there's a combination of one vertical straight line, one horizontal line on the top, and one horizontal line through the middle. In contrast, a 9 is made up of four rounded lines that form a circle at the top and a straight, vertical line.

We're now able to present the central idea behind ConvNets. We can use small filters that can detect a certain kind of low-level feature, such as a vertical line, and then slide it over the entire image to detect all the vertical lines in the image.

The following screenshot shows a vertical line filter. To detect vertical lines in our image, we need to slide this 3x3 matrix filter over the image.

1	0	-1
1	0	-1
1	0	-1

A vertical line filter

Using the MNIST dataset on the following page, we start in the top-left corner and slice out the top-left 3x3 grid of pixels, which in this case is all zeros.

We then perform an element-wise multiplication of all the elements in the filter with all elements in the slice of the image. The nine products then get summed up, and bias is added. This value then forms the output of the filter and gets passed on as a new pixel to the next layer:

$$Z_1 = \sum A_0 * F_1 + b_1$$

As a result, the output of our vertical line filter will look like this:

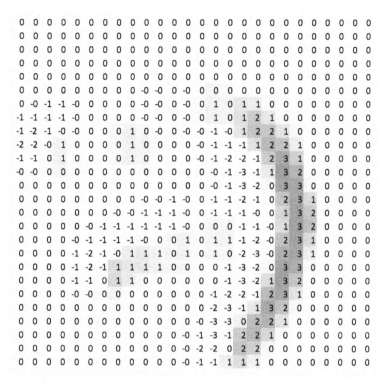

The output of a vertical line filter

Take a minute to notice that the vertical lines are visible while the horizontal lines are gone. Only a few artifacts remain. Also, notice how the filter captures the vertical line from one side.

Since it responds to high pixel values on the left and low pixel values on the right, only the right side of the output shows strong positive values. Meanwhile, the left side of the line actually shows negative values. This is not a big problem in practice as there are usually different filters for different kinds of lines and directions.

Adding a second filter

Our vertical filter is working, but we've already noticed that we also need to filter our image for horizontal lines in order to detect a seven.

Our horizontal line filter might look like this:

-1	-1	-1
0	0	0
1	1	1

A horizontal line filter

Using that example, we can now slide this filter over our image in the exact same way we did with the vertical filter, resulting in the following output:

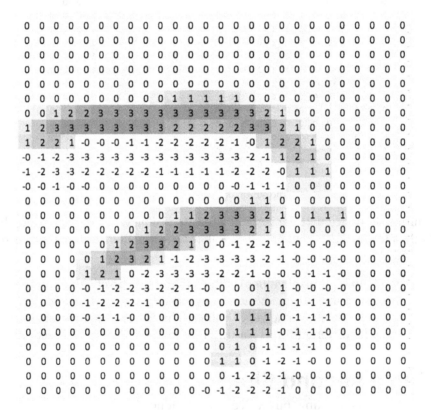

The output of the vertical line filter

See how this filter removes the vertical lines and pretty much only leaves the horizontal lines? The question now is what do we now pass onto the next layer? Well, we stack the outputs of both filters on top of each other, creating a three-dimensional cube:

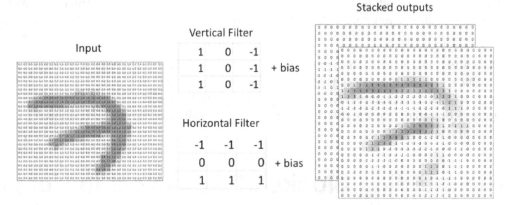

The MNIST convolution

By adding multiple convolutional layers, our ConvNet is able to extract ever more complex and semantic features.

Filters on color images

Of course, our filter technique is not only limited to black-and-white images. In this section we're going to have a look at color images.

The majority of color images consist of three layers or channels, and this is commonly referred to as RGB, the initialism for the three layers. They are made up of one red channel, one blue channel, and one green channel. When these three channels are laid on top of each other, they add up to create the traditional color image that we know.

Taking that concept, an image is therefore not flat, but actually a cube, a three-dimensional matrix. Combining this idea with our objective, we want to apply a filter to the image, and apply it to all three channels at once. We will, therefore, perform an element-wise multiplication between two three-dimensional cubes.

Our 3x3 filter now has a depth of three and thus nine parameters, plus the bias:

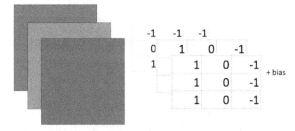

An example of a filter cube or convolutional kernel

This cube, which is referred to as a convolutional kernel, gets slid over the image just like the two-dimensional matrix did before. The element-wise products then again get summed up, the bias is added, and the outcome represents a pixel in the next layer.

Filters always capture the whole depth of the previous layer. The filters are moved over the width and height of the image. Likewise, filters are not moved across the depth, that is, the different channels, of an image. In technical terms, weights, the numbers that make up the filters, are shared over width and height, but not over different channels.

The building blocks of ConvNets in Keras

In this section, we will be building a simple ConvNet that can be used for classifying the MNIST characters, while at the same time, learning about the different pieces that make up modern ConvNets.

We can directly import the MNIST dataset from Keras by running the following code:

```
from keras.datasets import mnist
(x_train, y_train), (x_test, y_test) = mnist.load_data()
```

Our dataset contains 60,000 28x28-pixel images. MNIST characters are black and white, so the data shape usually does not include channels:

```
x_train.shape
```

out: (60000, 28, 28)

We will take a closer look at color channels later, but for now, let's expand our data dimensions to show that we only have a one-color channel. We can achieve this by running the following:

```
import numpy as np
x_train = np.expand_dims(x_train,-1)
x_test = np.expand_dims(x_test,-1)
x_train.shape
```

out: (60000, 28, 28, 1)

With the code being run, you can see that we now have a single color channel added.

Conv2D

Now we come to the meat and potatoes of ConvNets: using a convolutional layer in Keras. Conv2D is the actual convolutional layer, with one Conv2D layer housing several filters, as can be seen in the following code:

```
from keras.layers import Conv2D
from keras.models import Sequential

model = Sequential()

img_shape = (28,28,1)

model.add(Conv2D(filters=6,
                 kernel_size=3,
                 strides=1,
                 padding='valid',
                 input_shape=img_shape))
```

When creating a new Conv2D layer, we must specify the number of filters we want to use, and the size of each filter.

Kernel size

The size of the filter is also called `kernel_size`, as the individual filters are sometimes called kernels. If we only specify a single number as the kernel size, Keras will assume that our filters are squares. In this case, for example, our filter would be 3x3 pixels.

It is possible, however, to specify non-square kernel sizes by passing a tuple to the `kernel_size` parameter. For example, we could choose to have a 3x4-pixel filter through `kernel_size = (3,4)`. However, this is very rare, and in the majority of cases, filters have a size of either 3x3 or 5x5. Empirically, researchers have found that this is a size that yields good results.

Stride size

The `strides` parameter specifies the step size, also called the stride size, with which the convolutional filter slides over the image, usually referred to as the feature map. In the vast majority of cases, filters move pixel by pixel, so their stride size is set to 1. However, there are researchers that make more extensive use of larger stride sizes in order to reduce the spatial size of the feature map.

Like with `kernel_size`, Keras assumes that we use the same stride size horizontally and vertically if we specify only one value, and in the vast majority of cases that is correct. However, if we want to use a stride size of one horizontally, but two vertically, we can pass a tuple to the parameter as follows: `strides=(1,2)`. As in the case of the filter size, this is rarely done.

Padding

Finally, we have to add `padding` to our convolutional layer. Padding adds zeros around our image. This can be done if we want to prevent our feature map from shrinking.

Let's consider a 5x5-pixel feature map and a 3x3 filter. The filter only fits on the feature map nine times, so we'll end up with a 3x3 output. This both reduces the amount of information that we can capture in the next feature map, and how much the outer pixels of the input feature map can contribute to the task. The filter never centers on them; it only goes over them once.

There are three options for padding: not using padding, known as "No" padding, "Same" padding and "Valid" padding.

Let's have a look at each of the three paddings. First, No Padding:

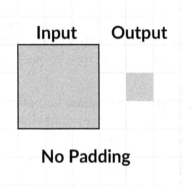

Option 1: No padding

Then we have Same Padding:

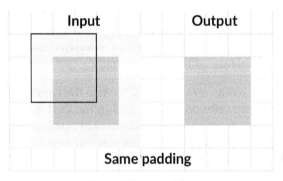

Option 2: Same padding

To ensure the output has the same size as the input, we can use `same` padding. Keras will then add enough zeros around the input feature map so that we can preserve the size. The default padding setting, however, is `valid`. This padding does not preserve the feature map size, but only makes sure that the filter and stride size actually fit on the input feature map:

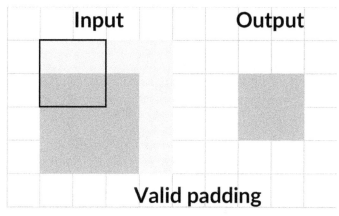

Option 3: Valid padding

Input shape

Keras requires us to specify the input shape. However, this is only required for the first layer. For all the following layers, Keras will infer the input shape from the previous layer's output shape.

Simplified Conv2D notation

The preceding layer takes a 28x28x1 input and slides six filters with a 2x2 filter size over it, going pixel by pixel. A more common way to specify the same layer would be by using the following code:

```
model.add(Conv2D(6,3,input_shape=img_shape))
```

The number of filters (here `6`) and the filter size (here `3`) are set as positional arguments, while `strides` and `padding` default to `1` and `valid` respectively. If this was a layer deeper in the network, we wouldn't even have to specify the input shape.

ReLU activation

Convolutional layers only perform a linear step. The numbers that make up the image get multiplied with the filter, which is a linear operation.

So, in order to approximate complex functions, we need to introduce non-linearity with an activation function. The most common activation function for computer vision is the Rectified Linear Units, or ReLU function, which we can see here:

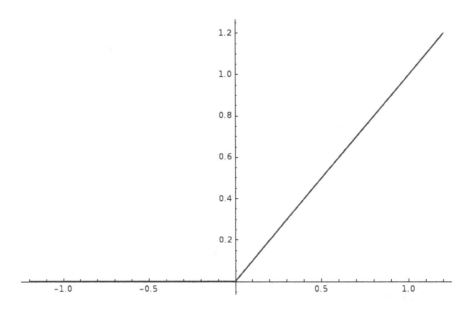

The ReLU activation function

The ReLU formula, which was used to produce the above chart, can be seen below:

$$ReLU(x) = max(x, 0)$$

In other words, the ReLU function returns the input if the input is positive. If it's not, then it returns zero. This very simple function has been shown to be quite useful, making gradient descent converge faster.

It is often argued that ReLU is faster because the derivative for all values above zero is just one, and it does not become very small as the derivative for some extreme values does, for example, with sigmoid or tanh.

ReLU is also less computationally expensive than both sigmoid and tanh. It does not require any computationally expensive calculations, input values below zero are just set to zero, and the rest is outputted. Unfortunately, though, ReLU activations are a bit fragile and can "die."

When the gradient is very large and moves multiple weights towards a negative direction, then the derivative of ReLU will also always be zero, so the weights never get updated again. This might mean that a neuron never fires again. However, this can be mitigated through a smaller learning rate.

Because ReLU is fast and computationally cheap, it has become the default activation function for many practitioners. To use the ReLU function in Keras, we can just name it as the desired activation function in the activation layer, by running this code:

```
from keras.layers import Activation
model.add(Activation('relu'))
```

MaxPooling2D

It's common practice to use a pooling layer after a number of convolutional layers. Pooling decreases the spatial size of the feature map, which in turn reduces the number of parameters needed in a neural network and thus reduces overfitting.

Below, we can see an example of Max Pooling:

Input				Output	
1	2	5	6		
3	4	2	1	4	6
2	1	6	5	2	6
1	1	5	5		

Max Pooling

Max pooling

Max pooling returns the maximum element out of a pool. This is in contrast to the example average of `AveragePooling2D`, which returns the average of a pool. Max pooling often delivers superior results to average pooling, so it is the standard most practitioners use.

Max pooling can be achieved by running the following:

```
from keras.layers import MaxPool2D

model.add(MaxPool2D(pool_size=2,
                    strides=None,
                    padding='valid'))
```

When using a max pooling layer in Keras, we have to specify the desired pool size. The most common value is a 2x2 pool. Just as with the `Conv2D` layer, we can also specify a stride size.

For pooling layers, the default stride size is `None`, in which case Keras sets the stride size to be the same as the pool size. In other words, pools are next to each other and don't overlap.

We can also specify padding, with `valid` being the default choice. However, specifying `same` padding for pooling layers is extremely rare since the point of a pooling layer is to reduce the spatial size of the feature map.

Our `MaxPooling2D` layer here takes 2x2-pixel pools next to each other with no overlap and returns the maximum element. A more common way of specifying the same layer is through the execution of the following:

```
model.add(MaxPool2D(2))
```

In this case, both `strides` and `padding` are set to their defaults, `None` and `valid` respectively. There is usually no activation after a pooling layer since the pooling layer does not perform a linear step.

Flatten

You might have noticed that our feature maps are three dimensional while our desired output is a one-dimensional vector, containing the probability of each of the 10 classes. So, how do we get from 3D to 1D? Well, we `Flatten` our feature maps.

The `Flatten` operation works similar to NumPy's `flatten` operation. It takes in a batch of feature maps with dimensions (`batch_size, height, width, channels`) and returns a set of vectors with dimensions (`batch_size, height * width * channels`).

It performs no computation and only reshapes the matrix. There are no hyperparameters to be set for this operation, as you can see in the following code:

```
from keras.layers import Flatten

model.add(Flatten())
```

Dense

ConvNets usually consist of a feature extraction part, the convolutional layers, as well as a classification part. The classification part is made up out of the simple fully connected layers that we've already explored in *Chapter 1, Neural Networks and Gradient-Based Optimization*, and *Chapter 2, Applying Machine Learning to Structured Data*.

To distinguish the plain layers from all other types of layers, we refer to them as `Dense` layers. In a dense layer, each input neuron is connected to an output neuron. We only have to specify the number of output neurons we would like, in this case, 10.

This can be done by running the following code:

```
from keras.layers import Dense
model.add(Dense(10))
```

After the linear step of the dense layer, we can add a `softmax` activation for multi-class regression, just as we did in the first two chapters, by running the following code:

```
model.add(Activation('softmax'))
```

Training MNIST

Let's now put all of these elements together so we can train a ConvNet on the MNIST dataset.

The model

First, we must specify the model, which we can do with the following code:

```
from keras.layers import Conv2D, Activation, MaxPool2D, Flatten, Dense
from keras.models import Sequential

img_shape = (28,28,1)

model = Sequential()

model.add(Conv2D(6,3,input_shape=img_shape))

model.add(Activation('relu'))

model.add(MaxPool2D(2))

model.add(Conv2D(12,3))

model.add(Activation('relu'))

model.add(MaxPool2D(2))

model.add(Flatten())

model.add(Dense(10))

model.add(Activation('softmax'))
```

In the following code, you can see the general structure of a typical ConvNet:

```
Conv2D
Pool

Conv2D
Pool

Flatten

Dense
```

The convolution and pooling layers are often used together in these blocks; you can find neural networks that repeat the `Conv2D`, `MaxPool2D` combination tens of times.

We can get an overview of our model with the following command:

```
model.summary()
```

Which will give us the following output:

Layer (type)	Output Shape	Param #
conv2d_2 (Conv2D)	(None, 26, 26, 6)	60
activation_3 (Activation)	(None, 26, 26, 6)	0
max_pooling2d_2 (MaxPooling2	(None, 13, 13, 6)	0
conv2d_3 (Conv2D)	(None, 11, 11, 12)	660
activation_4 (Activation)	(None, 11, 11, 12)	0
max_pooling2d_3 (MaxPooling2	(None, 5, 5, 12)	0
flatten_2 (Flatten)	(None, 300)	0
dense_2 (Dense)	(None, 10)	3010
activation_5 (Activation)	(None, 10)	0

```
Total params: 3,730
Trainable params: 3,730
Non-trainable params: 0
```

In this summary, you can clearly see how the pooling layers reduce the size of the feature map. It's a little bit less obvious from the summary alone, but you can see how the output of the first `Conv2D` layer is 26x26 pixels, while the input images are 28x28 pixels.

By using `valid` padding, `Conv2D` also reduces the size of the feature map, although only by a small amount. The same happens for the second `Conv2D` layer, which shrinks the feature map from 13x13 pixels to 11x11 pixels.

You can also see how the first convolutional layer only has 60 parameters, while the `Dense` layer has 3,010, over 50 times as many parameters. Convolutional layers usually achieve surprising feats with very few parameters, which is why they are so popular. The total number of parameters in a network can often be significantly reduced by convolutional and pooling layers.

Loading the data

The MNIST dataset we are using comes preinstalled with Keras. When loading the data, make sure you have an internet connection if you want to use the dataset directly via Keras, as Keras has to download it first.

You can import the dataset with the following code:

```
from keras.datasets import mnist
(x_train, y_train), (x_test, y_test) = mnist.load_data()
```

As explained at the beginning of the chapter, we want to reshape the dataset so that it can have a channel dimension as well. The dataset as it comes does not have a channel dimension yet, but this is something we can do:

```
x_train.shape
```

out:

`(60000, 28, 28)`

So, we add a channel dimension with NumPy, with the following code:

```
import numpy as np

x_train = np.expand_dims(x_train,-1)

x_test = np.expand_dims(x_test,-1)
```

Now there is a channel dimension, as we can see here:

```
x_train.shape
```

out:

`(60000, 28, 28,1)`

Compiling and training

In the previous chapters, we have used one-hot encoded targets for multiclass regression. While we have reshaped the data, the targets are still in their original form. They are a flat vector containing the numerical data representation for each handwritten figure. Remember that we have 60,000 of these in the MNIST dataset:

```
y_train.shape
```

out:

```
(60000,)
```

Transforming targets through one-hot encoding is a frequent and annoying task, so Keras allows us to just specify a loss function that converts targets to one-hot on the fly. This loss function is called sparse_categorical_crossentropy.

It's the same as the categorical cross-entropy loss used in earlier chapters, the only difference is that this uses sparse, that is, not one-hot encoded, targets.

Just as before, you still need to make sure that your network output has as many dimensions as there are classes.

We're now at a point where we can compile the model, which we can do with the following code:

```
model.compile(loss='sparse_categorical_crossentropy',
              optimizer='adam',
              metrics=['acc'])
```

As you can see, we are using an Adam optimizer. The exact workings of Adam are explained in the next section, *More bells and whistles for our neural network*, but for now, you can just think of it as a more sophisticated version of stochastic gradient descent.

When training, we can directly specify a validation set in Keras by running the following code:

```
history = model.fit(x_train,
                    y_train,
                    batch_size=32,
                    epochs=5,
                    validation_data=(x_test,y_test))
```

Once we have successfully run that code, we'll get the following output:

```
Train on 60000 samples, validate on 10000 samples
Epoch 1/10
60000/60000 [==============================] - 19s 309us/step - loss:
5.3931 - acc: 0.6464 - val_loss: 1.9519 - val_acc: 0.8542
```

```
Epoch 2/10
60000/60000 [==============================] - 18s 297us/step - loss:
0.8855 - acc: 0.9136 - val_loss: 0.1279 - val_acc: 0.9635

. . . .

Epoch 10/10
60000/60000 [==============================] - 18s 296us/step - loss:
0.0473 - acc: 0.9854 - val_loss: 0.0663 - val_acc: 0.9814
```

To better see what is going on, we can plot the progress of training with the following code:

```
import matplotlib.pyplot as plt

fig, ax = plt.subplots(figsize=(10,6))
gen = ax.plot(history.history['val_acc'], label='Validation
Accuracy')
fr = ax.plot(history.history['acc'],dashes=[5, 2], label='Training
Accuracy')

legend = ax.legend(loc='lower center', shadow=True)

plt.show()
```

This will give us the following chart:

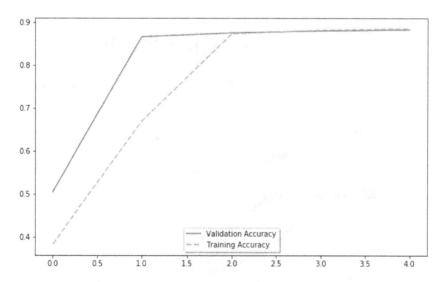

The visualized output of validation and training accuracy

As you can see in the preceding chart, the model achieves about 98% validation accuracy, which is pretty nice!

More bells and whistles for our neural network

Let's take a minute to look at some of the other elements of our neural network.

Momentum

In previous chapters we've explained gradient descent in terms of someone trying to find the way down a mountain by just following the slope of the floor. Momentum can be explained with an analogy to physics, where a ball is rolling down the same hill. A small bump in the hill would not make the ball roll in a completely different direction. The ball already has some momentum, meaning that its movement gets influenced by its previous movement.

Instead of directly updating the model parameters with their gradient, we update them with the exponentially weighted moving average. We update our parameter with an outlier gradient, then we take the moving average, which will smoothen out outliers and capture the general direction of the gradient, as we can see in the following diagram:

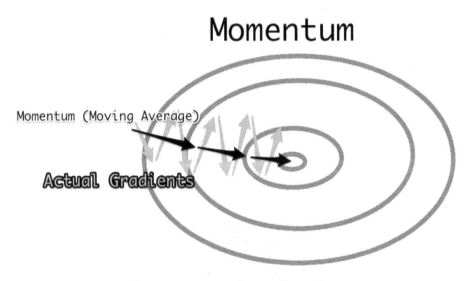

How momentum smoothens gradient updates

The exponentially weighted moving average is a clever mathematical trick used to compute a moving average without having to memorize a set of previous values. The exponentially weighted average, V, of some value, θ, would be as follows:

$$V_t = \beta * V_{t-1} + (1 - \beta) * \theta_t$$

A beta value of 0.9 would mean that 90% of the mean would come from the previous moving average, V_{t-1}, and 10% would come from the new value, θ_t.

Using momentum makes learning more robust against gradient descent pitfalls such as outlier gradients, local minima, and saddle points.

We can augment the standard stochastic gradient descent optimizer in Keras with momentum by setting a value for beta, which we do in the following code:

```
from keras.optimizers import SGD
momentum_optimizer = SGD(lr=0.01, momentum=0.9)
```

This little code snippet creates a stochastic gradient descent optimizer with a learning rate of 0.01 and a beta value of 0.9. We can use it when we compile our model, as we'll now do with this:

```
model.compile(optimizer=momentum_optimizer,
              loss='sparse_categorical_crossentropy',
              metrics=['acc'])
```

The Adam optimizer

Back in 2015, Diederik P. Kingma and Jimmy Ba created the **Adam (Adaptive Momentum Estimation)** optimizer. This is another way to make gradient descent work more efficiently. Over the past few years, this method has shown very good results and has, therefore, become a standard choice for many practitioners. For example, we've used it with the MNIST dataset.

First, the Adam optimizer computes the exponentially weighted average of the gradients, just like a momentum optimizer does. It achieves this with the following formula:

$$V_{dW} = \beta_1 * V_{dW} + (1 - \beta_1) * dW$$

It then also computes the exponentially weighted average of the squared gradients:

$$S_{dW} = \beta_2 * S_{dW} + (1 - \beta_2) * dW^2$$

It then updates the model parameters like this:

$$W = W - \alpha * \frac{V_{dW}}{\sqrt{S_{dW}} + \varepsilon}$$

Here ε is a very small number to avoid division by zero.

This division by the root of squared gradients reduces the update speed when gradients are very large. It also stabilizes learning as the learning algorithm does not get thrown off track by outliers as much.

Using Adam, we have a new hyperparameter. Instead of having just one momentum factor, β, we now have two, β_1 and β_2. The recommended values for β_1 and β_2 are 0.9 and 0.999 respectively.

We can use Adam in Keras like this:

```
from keras.optimizers import adam

adam_optimizer=adam(lr=0.1,
                beta_1=0.9,
                beta_2=0.999,
                epsilon=1e-08)

model.compile(optimizer=adam_optimizer,
            loss='sparse_categorical_crossentropy',
            metrics=['acc'])
```

As you have seen earlier in this chapter, we can also compile the model just by passing the adam string as an optimizer. In this case, Keras will create an Adam optimizer for us and choose the recommended values.

Regularization

Regularization is a technique used to avoid overfitting. Overfitting is when the model fits the training data too well, and as a result, it does not generalize well to either development or test data. You may see that overfitting is sometimes also referred to as "high variance," while underfitting, obtaining poor results on training, development, and test data, is referred to as "high bias."

In classical statistical learning, there is a lot of focus on the bias-variance tradeoff. The argument that is made is that a model that fits very well to the training set is likely to be overfitting and that some amount of underfitting (bias) has to be accepted in order to obtain good outcomes. In classical statistical learning, the hyperparameters that prevent overfitting also often prevent the training set fitting well.

Regularization in neural networks, as it is presented here, is largely borrowed from classical learning algorithms. Yet, modern machine learning research is starting to embrace the concept of "orthogonality," the idea that different hyperparameters influence bias and variance.

By separating those hyperparameters, the bias-variance tradeoff can be broken, and we can find models that generalize well and deliver accurate predictions. However, so far these efforts have only yielded small rewards, as low-bias and low-variance models require large amounts of training data.

L2 regularization

One popular technique to counter overfitting is L2 regularization. L2 regularization adds the sum of squared weights to the loss function. We can see an example of this in the formula below:

$$L_{Regularized}(W) = L(W) + \frac{\lambda}{2N}\sum W^2$$

Here N is the number of training examples and λ is the regularization hyperparameter, which determines how much we want to regularize, with a common value being around 0.01.

Adding this regularization to the loss function means that high weights increase losses and the algorithm is incentivized to reduce the weights. Small weights, those around zero, mean that the neural network will rely less on them.

Therefore, a regularized algorithm will rely less on every single feature and every single node activation, and instead will have a more holistic view, taking into account many features and activations. This will prevent the algorithm from overfitting.

L1 regularization

L1 regularization is very similar to L2 regularization, but instead of adding the sum of squares, it adds the sum of absolute values, as we can see in this formula:

$$L_{Regularized}(W) = L(W)\frac{\lambda}{2N}\sum \|W\|$$

In practice, it is often a bit uncertain as to which of the two will work best, but the difference between the two is not very large.

Regularization in Keras

In Keras, regularizers that are applied to the weights are called **kernel_regularizer**, and regularizers that are applied to the bias are called **bias_regularizer**. You can also apply regularization directly to the activation of the nodes to prevent them from being activated very strongly with **activity_regularizer**.

For now, let's add some L2 regularization to our network. To do this, we need to run the following code:

```
from keras.regularizers import l2

model = Sequential()


model.add(Conv2D(6,3,input_shape=img_shape, kernel_
regularizer=l2(0.01)))

model.add(Activation('relu'))

model.add(MaxPool2D(2))

model.add(Conv2D(12,3,activity_regularizer=l2(0.01)))

model.add(Activation('relu'))

model.add(MaxPool2D(2))

model.add(Flatten())

model.add(Dense(10,bias_regularizer=l2(0.01)))

model.add(Activation('softmax'))
```

Setting `kernel_regularizer` as done in the first convolutional layer in Keras means regularizing weights. Setting `bias_regularizer` regularizes the bias, and setting `activity_regularizer` regularizes the output activations of a layer.

In this following example, the regularizers are set to be shown off, but here they actually harm the performance to our network. As you can see from the preceding training results, our network is not actually overfitting, so setting regularizers harms performance here, and as a result, the model underfits.

As we can see in the following output, in this case, the model reaches about 87% validation accuracy:

```
model.compile(loss='sparse_categorical_crossentropy',
              optimizer = 'adam',
              metrics=['acc'])

history = model.fit(x_train,
                    y_train,
                    batch_size=32,
                    epochs=10,
                    validation_data=(x_test,y_test))
```

Train on 60000 samples, validate on 10000 samples

Epoch 1/10

60000/60000 [==============================] - 22s 374us/step - loss: 7707.2773 - acc: 0.6556 - val_loss: 55.7280 - val_acc: 0.7322

Epoch 2/10

60000/60000 [==============================] - 21s 344us/step - loss: 20.5613 - acc: 0.7088 - val_loss: 6.1601 - val_acc: 0.6771

. . . .

Epoch 10/10

60000/60000 [==============================] - 20s 329us/step - loss: 0.9231 - acc: 0.8650 - val_loss: 0.8309 - val_acc: 0.8749

You'll notice that the model achieves a higher accuracy on the validation than on the training set; this is a clear sign of underfitting.

Dropout

As the title of the 2014 paper by Srivastava et al gives away, *Dropout is A Simple Way to Prevent Neural Networks from Overfitting*. It achieves this by randomly removing nodes from the neural network:

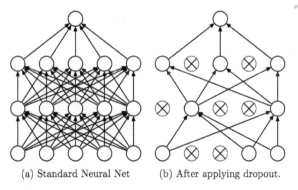

(a) Standard Neural Net   (b) After applying dropout.

Schematic of the dropout method. From Srivastava et al, "Dropout: A Simple Way to Prevent Neural Networks from Overfitting," 2014

With dropout, each node has a small probability of having its activation set to zero. This means that the learning algorithm can no longer rely heavily on single nodes, much like in L2 and L1 regularization. Dropout therefore also has a regularizing effect.

In Keras, dropout is a new type of layer. It's put after the activations you want to apply dropout to. It passes on activations, but sometimes it sets them to zero, achieving the same effect as a dropout in the cells directly. We can see this in the following code:

```
from keras.layers import Dropout
model = Sequential()

model.add(Conv2D(6,3,input_shape=img_shape))
model.add(Activation('relu'))
model.add(MaxPool2D(2))

model.add(Dropout(0.2))

model.add(Conv2D(12,3))
model.add(Activation('relu'))
model.add(MaxPool2D(2))

model.add(Dropout(0.2))

model.add(Flatten())

model.add(Dense(10,bias_regularizer=l2(0.01)))

model.add(Activation('softmax'))
```

A dropout value of 0.5 is considered a good choice if overfitting is a serious problem, while values that are over 0.5 are not very helpful, as the network would have too few values to work with. In this case, we chose a dropout value of 0.2, meaning that each cell has a 20% chance of being set to zero.

Note that dropout is used after pooling:

```
model.compile(loss='sparse_categorical_crossentropy',
              optimizer = 'adam',
              metrics=['acc'])

history = model.fit(x_train,
                    y_train,
                    batch_size=32,
                    epochs=10,
```

```
                   validation_data=(x_test,y_test))
```

```
Train on 60000 samples, validate on 10000 samples

Epoch 1/10

60000/60000 [==============================] - 22s 371us/step - loss:
5.6472 - acc: 0.6039 - val_loss: 0.2495 - val_acc: 0.9265

Epoch 2/10

60000/60000 [==============================] - 21s 356us/step - loss:
0.2920 - acc: 0.9104 - val_loss: 0.1253 - val_acc: 0.9627

....

Epoch 10/10

60000/60000 [==============================] - 21s 344us/step - loss:
0.1064 - acc: 0.9662 - val_loss: 0.0545 - val_acc: 0.9835
```

The low dropout value creates nice results for us, but again, the network does better on the validation set rather than the training set, a clear sign of underfitting taking place. Note that dropout is only applied at training time. When the model is used for predictions, dropout doesn't do anything.

Batchnorm

Batchnorm, short for **batch normalization**, is a technique for "normalizing" input data to a layer batch-wise. Each batchnorm computes the mean and standard deviation of the data and applies a transformation so that the mean is zero and the standard deviation is one.

This makes training easier because the loss surface becomes more "round." Different means and standard deviations along different input dimensions would mean that the network would have to learn a more complicated function.

In Keras, batchnorm is a new layer as well, as you can see in the following code:

```
from keras.layers import BatchNormalization

model = Sequential()

model.add(Conv2D(6,3,input_shape=img_shape))
model.add(Activation('relu'))
model.add(MaxPool2D(2))

model.add(BatchNormalization())
```

```
model.add(Conv2D(12,3))
model.add(Activation('relu'))
model.add(MaxPool2D(2))

model.add(BatchNormalization())

model.add(Flatten())

model.add(Dense(10,bias_regularizer=l2(0.01)))

model.add(Activation('softmax'))
model.compile(loss='sparse_categorical_crossentropy',
              optimizer = 'adam',
              metrics=['acc'])

history = model.fit(x_train,
      y_train,
      batch_size=32,
      epochs=10,
      validation_data=(x_test,y_test))
```

```
Train on 60000 samples, validate on 10000 samples
Epoch 1/10
60000/60000 [==============================] - 25s 420us/step - loss:
0.2229 - acc: 0.9328 - val_loss: 0.0775 - val_acc: 0.9768
Epoch 2/10
60000/60000 [==============================] - 26s 429us/step - loss:
0.0744 - acc: 0.9766 - val_loss: 0.0668 - val_acc: 0.9795
....
Epoch 10/10
60000/60000 [==============================] - 26s 432us/step - loss:
0.0314 - acc: 0.9897 - val_loss: 0.0518 - val_acc: 0.9843
```

Batchnorm often accelerates training by making it easier. You can see how the accuracy rate jumps up in the first epoch here:

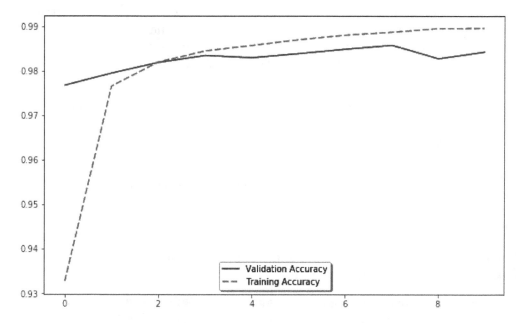

Training and validation accuracy of our MNIST classifier with batchnorm

Batchnorm also has a mildly regularizing effect. Extreme values are often overfitted to, and batchnorm reduces extreme values, similar to activity regularization. All this makes batchnorm an extremely popular tool in computer vision.

Working with big image datasets

Images tend to be big files. In fact, it's likely that you will not be able to fit your entire image dataset into your machine's RAM.

Therefore, we need to load the images from disk "just in time" rather than loading them all in advance. In this section, we will be setting up an image data generator that loads images on the fly.

We'll be using a dataset of plant seedlings in this case. This was provided by Thomas Giselsson and others, 2017, via their publication, *A Public Image Database for Benchmark of Plant Seedling Classification Algorithms*.

This dataset is available from the following link: `https://arxiv.org/abs/1711.05458`.

You may be wondering why we're looking at plants; after all, plant classifications are not a common problem that is faced in the finance sector. The simple answer is that this dataset lends itself to demonstrating many common computer vision techniques and is available under an open domain license; it's therefore a great training dataset for us to use.

Readers who wish to test their knowledge on a more relevant dataset should take a look at the *State Farm Distracted Driver* dataset as well as the *Planet: Understanding the Amazon from Space* dataset.

 The code and data for this section and the section on stacking pretrained models can be found and run here: https://www.kaggle.com/jannesklaas/stacking-vgg.

Keras comes with an image data generator that can load files from disk out of the box. To do this, you simply need to run:

```
from keras.preprocessing.image import ImageDataGenerator
```

To obtain a generator reading from the files, we first have to specify the generator. In Keras, `ImageDataGenerator` offers a range of image augmentation tools, but in our example, we will only be making use of the rescaling function.

Rescaling multiplies all values in an image with a constant. For most common image formats, the color values range from 0 to 255, so we want to rescale by 1/255. We can achieve this by running the following:

```
imgen = ImageDataGenerator(rescale=1/255)
```

This, however, is not yet the generator that loads the images for us. The `ImageDataGenerator` class offers a range of generators that can be created by calling functions on it.

To obtain a generator loading file, we have to call `flow_from_directory`.

We then have to specify the directory Keras should use, the batch size we would like, in this case 32, as well as the target size the images should be resized to, in this case 150x150 pixels. To do this, we can simply run the following code:

```
train_generator = imgen.flow_from_directory('train',
                                            batch_size=32,
                                            target_size=(150,150))

validation_generator = imgen.flow_from_directory('validation',
                                            batch_size=32,
                                            tar get_size=(150,150))
```

How did Keras find the images and how does it know which classes the images belong to? The Keras generator expects the following folder structure:

- Root:
  - Class 0
    - img
    - img
    - ...
  - Class 1
    - img
    - img
    - ...
  - Class 2
    - ...

Our dataset is already set up that way, and it's usually not hard to sort images to match the generator's expectations.

Working with pretrained models

Training large computer vision models is not only hard, but computationally expensive. Therefore, it's common to use models that were originally trained for another purpose and fine-tune them for a new purpose. This is an example of transfer learning.

Transfer learning aims to transfer the learning from one task to another task. As humans, we are very good at transferring what we have learned. When you see a dog that you have not seen before, you don't need to relearn everything about dogs for this particular dog; instead, you just transfer new learning to what you already knew about dogs. It's not economical to retrain a big network every time, as you'll often find that there are parts of the model that we can reuse.

In this section, we will fine-tune VGG-16, originally trained on the ImageNet dataset. The ImageNet competition is an annual computer vision competition, and the ImageNet dataset consists of millions of images of real-world objects, from dogs to planes.

In the ImageNet competition, researchers compete to build the most accurate models. In fact, ImageNet has driven much of the progress in computer vision over the recent years, and the models built for ImageNet competitions are a popular basis to fine-tune models from.

VGG-16 is a model architecture developed by the visual geometry group at Oxford University. The model consists of a convolutional part and a classification part. We will only be using the convolutional part. In addition, we will be adding our own classification part that can classify plants.

VGG-16 can be downloaded via Keras by using the following code:

```
from keras.applications.vgg16 import VGG16
vgg_model = VGG16(include_top=False, input_shape=(150,150,3))
```

out:

Downloading data from https://github.com/fchollet/deep-learning-models/ releases/download/v0.1/vgg16_weights_tf_dim_ordering_tf_kernels_notop.h5

58892288/58889256 [==============================] - 5s 0us/step

When downloading the data, we want to let Keras know that we don't want to include the top part (the classification part); we also want to let Keras know the desired input shape. If we do not specify the input shape, the model will accept any image size, and it will not be possible to add Dense layers on top:

```
vgg_model.summary()
```

out:

Layer (type)	Output Shape	Param #
input_1 (InputLayer)	(None, 150, 150, 3)	0
block1_conv1 (Conv2D)	(None, 150, 150, 64)	1792
block1_conv2 (Conv2D)	(None, 150, 150, 64)	36928
block1_pool (MaxPooling2D)	(None, 75, 75, 64)	0
block2_conv1 (Conv2D)	(None, 75, 75, 128)	73856
block2_conv2 (Conv2D)	(None, 75, 75, 128)	147584
block2_pool (MaxPooling2D)	(None, 37, 37, 128)	0
block3_conv1 (Conv2D)	(None, 37, 37, 256)	295168

block3_conv2 (Conv2D)	(None, 37, 37, 256)	590080
block3_conv3 (Conv2D)	(None, 37, 37, 256)	590080
block3_pool (MaxPooling2D)	(None, 18, 18, 256)	0
block4_conv1 (Conv2D)	(None, 18, 18, 512)	1180160
block4_conv2 (Conv2D)	(None, 18, 18, 512)	2359808
block4_conv3 (Conv2D)	(None, 18, 18, 512)	2359808
block4_pool (MaxPooling2D)	(None, 9, 9, 512)	0
block5_conv1 (Conv2D)	(None, 9, 9, 512)	2359808
block5_conv2 (Conv2D)	(None, 9, 9, 512)	2359808
block5_conv3 (Conv2D)	(None, 9, 9, 512)	2359808
block5_pool (MaxPooling2D)	(None, 4, 4, 512)	0

```
=================================================================
Total params: 14,714,688
Trainable params: 14,714,688
Non-trainable params: 0
```

As you can see, the VGG model is very large, with over 14.7 million trainable parameters. It also consists of both `Conv2D` and `MaxPooling2D` layers, both of which we've already learned about when working on the MNIST dataset.

From this point, there are two different ways we can proceed:

- Add layers and build a new model.
- Preprocess all the images through the pertained model and then train a new model.

Modifying VGG-16

In this section, we will be adding layers on top of the VGG-16 model, and then from there, we will train the new, big model.

We do not want to retrain all those convolutional layers that have been trained already, however. So, we must first "freeze" all the layers in VGG-16, which we can do by running the following:

```
for the layer in vgg_model.layers:
   layer.trainable = False
```

Keras downloads VGG as a functional API model. We will learn more about the functional API in *Chapter 6, Using Generative Models*, but for now, we just want to use the Sequential API, which allows us to stack layers through model.add(). We can convert a model with the functional API with the following code:

```
finetune = Sequential(layers = vgg_model.layers)
```

As a result of running the code, we have now created a new model called finetune that works just like a normal Sequential model. We need to remember that converting models with the Sequential API only works if the model can actually be expressed in the Sequential API. Some more complex models cannot be converted.

As a result of everything we've just done, adding layers to our model is now simple:

```
finetune.add(Flatten())
finetune.add(Dense(12))
finetune.add(Activation('softmax'))
```

The newly added layers are by default trainable, while the reused model socket is not. We can train this stacked model just as we would train any other model, on the data generator we defined in the previous section. This can be executed by running the following code:

```
finetune.compile(loss='categorical_crossentropy',
              optimizer='adam',
              metrics = ['acc'])

finetune.fit_generator(train_generator,
              epochs=8,
              steps_per_epoch= 4606 // 32,
              validation_data=validation_generator,
              validation_steps= 144//32)
```

After running this, the model manages to achieve a rate of about 75% validation accuracy.

Random image augmentation

A general problem in machine learning is that no matter how much data we have, having more data will always be better, as it would increase the quality of our output while also preventing overfitting and allowing our model to deal with a larger variety of inputs. It's therefore common to apply random augmentation to images, for example, a rotation or a random crop.

The idea is to get a large number of different images out of one image, therefore reducing the chance that the model will overfit. For most image augmentation purposes, we can just use Keras' ImageDataGenerator.

More advanced augmentations can be done with the OpenCV library. However, focusing on this is outside the scope of this chapter.

Augmentation with ImageDataGenerator

When using an augmenting data generator, we only usually use it for training. The validation generator should not use the augmentation features because when we validate our model, we want to estimate how well it is doing on unseen, actual data, and not augmented data.

This is different from rule-based augmentation, where we try to create images that are easier to classify. For this reason, we need to create two ImageDataGenerator instances, one for training and one for validation. This can be done by running the following code:

```
train_datagen = ImageDataGenerator(
   rescale = 1/255,
   rotation_range=90,
   width_shift_range=0.2,
   height_shift_range=0.2,
   shear_range=0.2,
   zoom_range=0.1,
   horizontal_flip=True,
   fill_mode='nearest')
```

This training data generator makes use of a few built-in augmentation techniques.

 Note: There are more commands available in Keras. For a full list, you should refer to the Keras documentation at https://keras.io/.

In the following list, we've highlighted several commonly used commands:

- `rescale` scales the values in the image. We used it before and will also use it for validation.
- `rotation_range` is a range (0 to 180 degrees) in which to randomly rotate the image.
- `width_shift_range` and `height_shift_range` are ranges (relative to the image size, so here 20%) in which to randomly stretch images horizontally or vertically.
- `shear_range` is a range (again, relative to the image) in which to randomly apply shear.
- `zoom_range` is the range in which to randomly zoom into a picture.
- `horizontal_flip` specifies whether to randomly flip the image.
- `fill_mode` specifies how to fill empty spaces created by, for example, rotation.

We can check out what the generator does by running one image through it multiple times.

First, we need to import the Keras image tools and specify an image path (this one was chosen at random). This can be done by running the following:

```
from keras.preprocessing import image
fname = 'train/Charlock/270209308.png'
```

We then need to load the image and convert it to a NumPy array, which is achieved with the following code:

```
img = image.load_img(fname, target_size=(150, 150))
img = image.img_to_array(img)
```

As before, we have to add a batch size dimension to the image:

```
img = np.expand_dims(img,axis=0)
```

We then use the `ImageDataGenerator` instance we just created, but instead of using `flow_from_directory`, we'll use `flow`, which allows us to pass the data directly into the generator. We then pass that one image we want to use, which we can do by running this:

```
gen = train_datagen.flow(img, batch_size=1)
```

In a loop, we then call `next` on our generator four times:

```
for i in range(4):
    plt.figure(i)
    batch = next(gen)
```

```
imgplot = plt.imshow(image.array_to_img(batch[0]))
```

```
plt.show()
```

This will produce the following output:

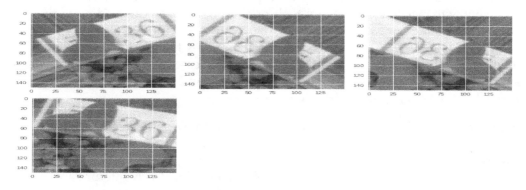

A few samples of the randomly modified image

The modularity tradeoff

This chapter has shown that it is possible, and often useful, to aid a machine learning model with some rule-based system. You might also have noticed that the images in the dataset were all cropped to show only one plant.

While we could have built a model to locate and classify the plants for us, in addition to classifying it, we could have also built a system that would output the treatment a plant should directly receive. This begs the question of how modular we should make our systems.

End-to-end deep learning was all the rage for several years. If given a huge amount of data, a deep learning model can learn what would otherwise have taken a system with many components much longer to learn. However, end-to-end deep learning does have several drawbacks:

- End-to-end deep learning needs huge amounts of data. Because models have so many parameters, a large amount of data is needed in order to avoid overfitting.

- End-to-end deep learning is hard to debug. If you replace your entire system with one black box model, you have little hope of finding out why certain things happened.

- Some things are hard to learn but easy to write down as a code, especially sanity-check rules.

Recently, researchers have begun to make their models more modular. A great example is Ha and Schmidthuber's *World Models*, which can be read here: https://worldmodels.github.io/. In this, they've encoded visual information, made predictions about the future, and chosen actions with three different models.

On the practical side, we can take a look at Airbnb, who combine structural modeling with machine learning for their pricing engine. You can read more about it here: https://medium.com/airbnb-engineering/learning-market-dynamics-for-optimal-pricing-97cffbcc53e3. Modelers knew that bookings roughly follow a Poisson Distribution and that there are also seasonal effects. So, Airbnb built a model to predict the parameters of the distribution and seasonality directly, rather than letting the model predict bookings directly.

If you have a small amount of data, then your algorithm's performance needs to come from human insight. If some subtasks can be easily expressed in code, then it's usually better to express them in code. If you need explainability and want to see why certain choices were made, a modular setup with clearly interpretable intermediate outputs is a good choice. However, if a task is hard and you don't know exactly what subtasks it entails, and you have lots of data, then it's often better to use an end-to-end approach.

It's very rare to use a *pure* end-to-end approach. Images, for example, are always preprocessed from the camera chip, you never really work with raw data.

Being smart about dividing a task can boost performance and reduce risk.

Computer vision beyond classification

As we have seen, there are many techniques that we can use to make our image classifier work better. These are techniques that you'll find used throughout this book, and not only for computer vision applications.

In this final section of the chapter, we will discuss some approaches that go beyond classifying images. These tasks often require more creative use of neural networks than what we've discussed throughout this chapter.

To get the most out of this section, you don't need to worry too much about the details of the techniques presented, but instead look at how researchers were creative about using neural networks. We're taking this approach because you will often find that the tasks you are looking to solve require similar creativity.

Facial recognition

Facial recognition has many applications for retail institutions. For instance, if you're in the front office, you might want to automatically recognize your customer at an ATM, or alternatively, you might want to offer face-based security features, such as the iPhone offers. In the back office, however, you need to comply with KYC regulations, which require you to identify which customer you are working with.

On the surface, facial recognition looks like a classification task. You give an image of a face to the machine, and it will predict which person it is. The trouble is that you might have millions of customers, but only one or two pictures per customer.

On top of that, you'll likely be continuously getting new customers. You can't change your model every time you get a new customer, and a simple classification approach will fail if it has to choose between millions of classes with only one example for each class.

The creative insight here is that instead of classifying the customer's face, you can see whether two images show the same face. You can see a visual representation of this idea in the following diagram:

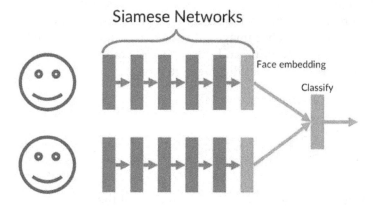

Schematic of a Siamese network

To this end, you'll have to run the two images through first. A Siamese network is a class of neural network architecture that contains two or more identical subnetworks, both of which are identical and contain the same weights. In Keras, you can achieve such a setup by defining the layers first and then using them in both networks. The two networks then feed into a single classification layer, which determines whether the two images show the same face.

To avoid running all of the customer images in our database through the entire Siamese network every time we want to recognize a face, it's common to save the final output of the Siamese network. The final output of the Siamese network for an image is called the face embedding. When we want to recognize a customer, we compare the embedding of the image of the customer's face with the embeddings stored in our database. We can do this with a single classification layer.

Storing facial embedding is very beneficial as it will save us a significant amount of computational cost, in addition to allowing for the clustering of faces. Faces will cluster together according to traits such as sex, age, and race. By only comparing an image to the images in the same cluster, we can save even more computational power and, as a result, get even faster recognition.

There are two ways to train Siamese networks. We can train them together with the classifier by creating pairs of matching and non-matching images and then using binary cross-entropy classification loss to train the entire model. However, another, and in many respects better, option is to train the model to generate face embeddings directly. This approach is described in Schroff, Kalenichenko, and Philbin's 2015 paper, *FaceNet: A Unified Embedding for Face Recognition and Clustering*, which you can read here: https://arxiv.org/abs/1503.03832.

The idea is to create triplets of images: one anchor image, one positive image showing the same face as the anchor image, and one negative image showing a different face than the anchor image. A triplet loss is used to make the distance between the anchor's embedding and the positive's embedding smaller, and the distance between the anchor and the negative larger.

The loss function looks like this:

$$L = \sum_{i}^{N} \left[\left\| f\left(x_i^a\right) - f\left(x_i^p\right) \right\|_2^2 - \left\| f\left(x_i^a\right) - f\left(x_i^n\right) \right\|_2^2 + \alpha \right]$$

Here x_i^a is an anchor image, and $f(x_i^a)$ is the output of the Siamese network, the anchor image's embedding. The triplet loss is the Euclidean distance between the anchor and the positive minus the Euclidean distance between the anchor and the negative. A small constant, α, is a margin enforced between positive and negative pairs. To reach zero loss, the difference between distances needs to be α.

You should be able to understand that you can use a neural network to predict whether two items are semantically the same in order to get around large classification problems. You can train the Siamese model through some binary classification tasks but also by treating the outputs as embeddings and using a triplet loss. This insight extends to more than faces. If you wanted to compare time series to classify events, then you could use the exact same approach.

Bounding box prediction

The likelihood is that at some point, you'll be interested in locating objects within images. For instance, say you are an insurance company that needs to inspect the roofs it insures. Getting people to climb on roofs to check them is expensive, so an alternative is to use satellite imagery. Having acquired the images, you now need to find the roofs in them, as we can see in the following screenshot. You can then crop out the roofs and send the roof images to your experts, who will check them:

California homes with bounding boxes around their roofs

What you need are bounding box predictions. A bounding box predictor outputs the coordinates of several bounding boxes together with predictions for what object is shown in the box.

There are two approaches to obtaining such bounding boxes.

A **Region-based Convolutional Neural Network (R-CNN)** reuses a classification model. It takes an image and slides the classification model over the image. The result is many classifications for different parts of the image. Using this feature map, a region proposal network performs a regression task to come up with bounding boxes and a classification network creates classifications for each bounding box.

The approach has been refined, culminating in Ren and others' 2016 paper, *Faster R-CNN: Towards Real-Time Object Detection with Region Proposal Networks*, which is available at https://arxiv.org/abs/1506.01497, but the basic concept of sliding a classifier over an image has remained the same.

You Only Look Once (YOLO), on the other hand, uses a single model consisting of only convolutional layers. It divides an image into a grid and predicts an object class for each grid cell. It then predicts several possible bounding boxes containing objects for each grid cell.

For each bounding box, it regresses coordinates and both width and height values, as well as a confidence score that this bounding box actually contains an object. It then eliminates all bounding boxes with a too low confidence score or with a too large overlap with another, a more confident bounding box.

For a more detailed description, read Redmon and Farhadi's 2016 paper, *YOLO9000: Better, Faster, Stronger*, available at https://arxiv.org/abs/1612.08242. Further reading includes the 2018 paper, *YOLOv3: An Incremental Improvement*. This is available at https://arxiv.org/abs/1804.027.

Both are well-written, tongue-in-cheek papers, that explain the YOLO concept in more detail.

The main advantage of YOLO over an R-CNN is that it's much faster. Not having to slide a large classification model is much more efficient. However, an R-CNN's main advantage is that it is somewhat more accurate than a YOLO model. If your task requires real-time analysis, you should use YOLO; however, if you do not need real-time speed but just want the best accuracy, then using an R-CNN is the way to go.

Bounding box detection is often used as one of many processing steps. In the insurance case, the bounding box detector would crop out all roofs. The roof images can then be judged by a human expert, or by a separate deep learning model that classifies damaged roofs. Of course, you could train an object locator to distinguish between damaged and intact roofs directly, but in practice, this is usually not a good idea.

If you're interested in reading more about this, *Chapter 4, Understanding Time Series*, has a great discussion on modularity.

Exercises

Fashion MNIST is a drop-in replacement for MNIST, but instead of handwritten digits, it is about classifying clothes. Try out the techniques we have used in this chapter on Fashion MNIST. How do they work together? What gives good results? You can find the dataset on Kaggle at https://www.kaggle.com/zalando-research/fashionmnist.

Take on the whale recognition challenge and read the top kernels and discussion posts. The link can be found here: https://www.kaggle.com/c/whale-categorization-playground. The task of recognizing whales by their fluke is similar to recognizing humans by their face. There are good kernels showing off bounding boxes as well as Siamese networks. We have not covered all the technical tools needed to solve the task yet, so do not worry about the code in detail but instead focus on the concepts shown.

Summary

In this chapter, you have seen the building blocks of computer vision models. We've learned about convolutional layers, and both the ReLU activation and regularization methods. You have also seen a number of ways to use neural networks creatively, such as with Siamese networks and bounding box predictors.

You have also successfully implemented and tested all these approaches on a simple benchmark task, the MNIST dataset. We scaled up our training and used a pretrained VGG model to classify thousands of plant images, before then using a Keras generator to load images from disk on the fly and customizing the VGG model to fit our new task.

We also learned about the importance of image augmentation and the modularity tradeoff in building computer vision models. Many of these building blocks, such as convolutions, batchnorm, and dropout, are used in other areas beyond computer vision. They are fundamental tools that you will see outside of computer vision applications as well. By learning about them here, you have set yourself up to discover a wide range of possibilities in, for example, time series or generative models.

Computer vision has many applications in the financial industry, especially in back-office functions as well as alternative alpha generation. It is one application of modern machine learning that can translate into real value for many corporations today. An increasing number of firms incorporate image-based data sources in their decision making; you are now prepared to tackle such problems head-on.

Over the course of this chapter, we've seen that an entire pipeline is involved in a successful computer vision project, and working on the pipeline often has a similar or greater benefit as compared to working on the model.

In the next chapter, we will look at the most iconic and common form of financial data: time series. We will tackle the task of forecasting web traffic using more traditional statistical methods, such as **ARIMA** (short for **AutoRegressive Integrated Moving Average**), as well as modern neural network-based approaches. You will also learn about feature engineering with autocorrelation and Fourier transformations. Finally, you will learn how to compare and contrast different forecasting methods and build a high-quality forecasting system.

4

Understanding Time Series

A time series is a form of data that has a temporal dimension and is easily the most iconic form of financial data out there. While a single stock quote is not a time series, take the quotes you get every day and line them up, and you get a much more interesting time series. Virtually all media materials related to finance sooner or later show a stock price gap; not a list of prices at a given moment, but a development of prices over time.

You'll often hear financial commenters discussing the movement of prices: "Apple Inc. is up 5%." But what does that mean? You'll hear absolute values a lot less, such as, "A share of Apple Inc. is $137.74." Again, what does that mean? This occurs because market participants are interested in how things will develop in the future and they try to extrapolate these forecasts from how things developed in the past:

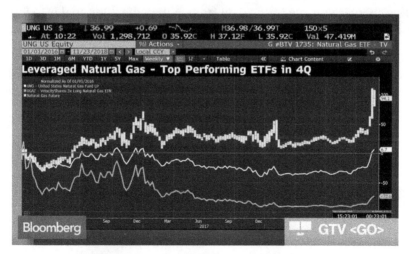

Multiple time series graphs as seen on Bloomberg TV

Most forecasting that is done involves looking at past developments over a period of time. The concept of a time series set of data is an important element related to forecasting; for example, farmers will look at a time series dataset when forecasting crop yields. Because of this, a vast body of knowledge and tools for working with time series has developed within the fields of statistics, econometrics, and engineering.

In this chapter, we will be looking at a few classic tools that are still very much relevant today. We will then learn how neural networks can deal with time series, and how deep learning models can express uncertainty.

Before we jump into looking at time series, I need to set your expectations for this chapter. Many of you might have come to this chapter to read about stock market forecasting, but I need to warn you that this chapter is not about stock market forecasting, neither is any other chapter in this book.

Economic theory shows that markets are somewhat efficient. The efficient market hypothesis states that all publicly available information is included in stock prices. This extends to information on how to process information, such as forecasting algorithms.

If this book were to present an algorithm that could predict prices on the stock market and deliver superior returns, many investors would simply implement this algorithm. Since those algorithms would all buy or sell in anticipation of price changes, they would change the prices in the present, thus destroying the advantage that you would gain by using the algorithm. Therefore, the algorithm presented would not work for future readers.

Instead, this chapter will use traffic data from Wikipedia. Our goal is to forecast traffic for a specific Wikipedia page. We can obtain the Wikipedia traffic data via the `wikipediatrend` CRAN package.

The dataset that we are going to use here is the traffic data of around 145,000 Wikipedia pages that has been provided by Google. The data can be obtained from Kaggle.

 The data can be found at the following links: `https://www.kaggle.com/c/web-traffic-time-series-forecasting`

`https://www.kaggle.com/muonneutrino/wikipedia-traffic-data-exploration`

Visualization and preparation in pandas

As we saw in *Chapter 2, Applying Machine Learning to Structured Data*, it's usually a good idea to get an overview of the data before we start training. You can achieve this for the data we obtained from Kaggle by running the following:

```
train = pd.read_csv('../input/train_1.csv').fillna(0)
train.head()
```

Running this code will give us the following table:

	Page	2015-07-01	2015-07-02	...	2016-12-31
0	2NE1_zh.wikipedia.org_all-access_spider	18.0	11.0	...	20.0
1	2PM_zh.wikipedia.org_all-access_spider	11.0	14.0	...	20.0

The data in the **Page** column contains the name of the page, the language of the Wikipedia page, the type of accessing device, and the accessing agent. The other columns contain the traffic for that page on that date.

So, in the preceding table, the first row contains the page of 2NE1, a Korean pop band, on the Chinese version of Wikipedia, by all methods of access, but only for agents classified as spider traffic; that is, traffic not coming from humans. While most time series work is focused on local, time-dependent features, we can enrich all of our models by providing access to **global features**.

Therefore, we want to split up the page string into smaller, more useful features. We can achieve this by running the following code:

```
def parse_page(page):
    x = page.split('_')
    return ' '.join(x[:-3]), x[-3], x[-2], x[-1]
```

We split the string by underscores. The name of a page could also include an underscore, so we separate off the last three fields and then join the rest to get the subject of the article.

As we can see in the following code, the third-from-last element is the sub URL, for example, en.wikipedia.org. The second-from-last element is the access, and the last element the agent:

```
parse_page(train.Page[0])
```

Out:

```
('2NE1', 'zh.wikipedia.org', 'all-access', 'spider')
```

When we apply this function to every page entry in the training set, we obtain a list of tuples that we can then join together into a new DataFrame, as we can see in the following code:

```
l = list(train.Page.apply(parse_page))
df = pd.DataFrame(l)
df.columns = ['Subject','Sub_Page','Access','Agent']
```

Finally, we must add this new DataFrame back to our original DataFrame before removing the original page column, which we can do by running the following:

```
train = pd.concat([train,df],axis=1)
del train['Page']
```

As a result of running this code, we have successfully finished loading the dataset. This means we can now move on to exploring it.

Aggregate global feature statistics

After all of this hard work, we can now create some aggregate statistics on global features.

The pandas value_counts() function allows us to plot the distribution of global features easily. By running the following code, we will get a bar chart output of our Wikipedia dataset:

```
train.Sub_Page.value_counts().plot(kind='bar')
```

As a result of running the previous code, we will output a bar chat that ranks the distributions of records within our dataset:

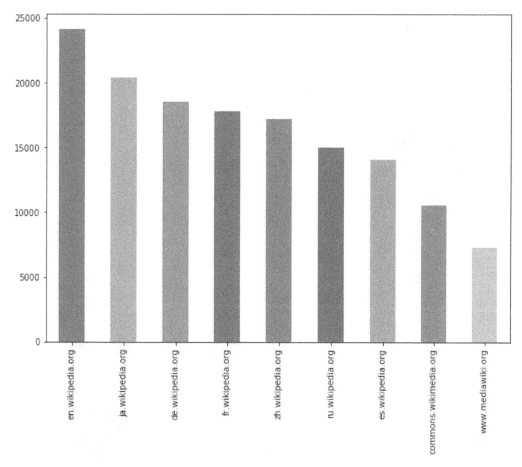

Distribution of records by Wikipedia country page

The preceding plot shows the number of time series available for each subpage. Wikipedia has subpages for different languages, and we can see that our dataset contains pages from the English (en), Japanese (ja), German (de), French (fr), Chinese (zh), Russian (ru), and Spanish (es) Wikipedia sites.

In the bar chart we produced you may have also noted two non-country based Wikipedia sites. Both `commons.wikimedia.org` and `www.mediawiki.org` are used to host media files such as images.

Let's run that command again, this time focusing on the type of access:

```
train.Access.value_counts().plot(kind='bar')
```

After running this code, we'll then see the following bar chart as the output:

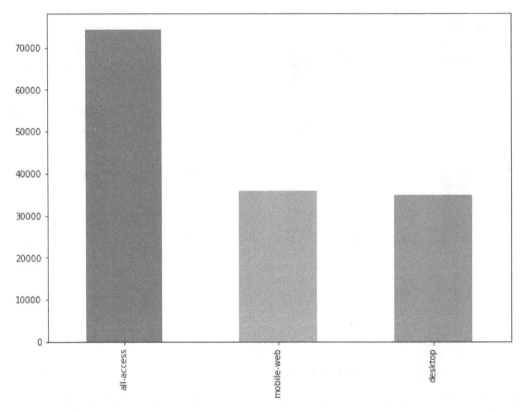

Distribution of records by access type

There are two possible access methods: **mobile** and **desktop**. There's also a third option **all-access**, which combines the statistics for mobile and desktop access.

We can then plot the distribution of records by agent by running the following code:

```
train.Agent.value_counts().plot(kind='bar')
```

After running that code, we'll output the following chart:

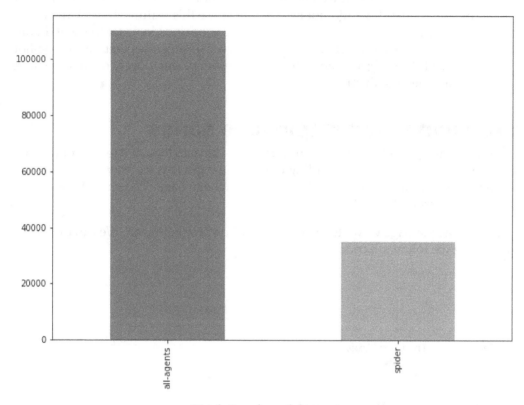

Distribution of records by agent

There are time series available not only for spider agents, but also for all other types of access. In classic statistical modeling, the next step would be to analyze the effect of each of these global features and build models around them. However, this is not necessary if there's enough data and computing power available.

If that's the case then a neural network is able to discover the effects of the global features itself and create new features based on their interactions. There are only two real considerations that need to be addressed for global features:

- **Is the distribution of features very skewed?** If this is the case then there might only be a few instances that possess a global feature, and our model might overfit on this global feature. Imagine that there were only a small number of articles from the Chinese Wikipedia in the dataset. The algorithm might distinguish too much based on the feature then overfit the few Chinese entries. Our distribution is relatively even, so we do not have to worry about this.

- **Can features be easily encoded?** Some global features cannot be one-hot encoded. Imagine that we were given the full text of a Wikipedia article with the time series. It would not be possible to use this feature straight away, as some heavy preprocessing would have to be done in order to use it. In our case, there are a few relatively straightforward categories that can be one-hot encoded. The subject names, however, cannot be one-hot encoded since there are too many of them.

Examining the sample time series

To examine the global features, of our dataset, we have to look at a few sample time series in order to get an understanding of the challenges that we may face. In this section, we will plot the views for the English language page of *Twenty One Pilots*, a musical duo from the USA.

To plot the actual page views together with a 10-day rolling mean. We can do this by running the following code:

```
idx = 39457

window = 10


data = train.iloc[idx,0:-4]
name = train.iloc[idx,-4]
days = [r for r in range(data.shape[0] )]

fig, ax = plt.subplots(figsize=(10, 7))

plt.ylabel('Views per Page')
plt.xlabel('Day')
plt.title(name)

ax.plot(days,data.values,color='grey')
ax.plot(np.convolve(data,
                    np.ones((window,))/window,
                    mode='valid'),color='black')


ax.set_yscale('log')
```

There is a lot going on in this code snippet, and it is worth going through it step by step. Firstly, we define which row we want to plot. The Twenty One Pilots article is row 39,457 in the training dataset. From there, we then define the window size for the rolling mean.

We separate the page view data and the name from the overall dataset by using the pandas `iloc` tool. This allows us to index the data by row and column coordinates. Counting the days rather than displaying all the dates of the measurements makes the plot easier to read, therefore we are going to create a day counter for the X-axis.

Next, we set up the plot and make sure it has the desired size by setting `figsize`. We also define the axis labels and the title. Next, we plot the actual page views. Our X coordinates are the days, and the Y coordinates are the page views.

To compute the mean, we are going to use a **convolve** operation, which you might be familiar with as we explored convolutions in *Chapter 3, Utilizing Computer Vision*. This convolve operation creates a vector of ones divided by the window size, in this case 10. The convolve operation slides the vector over the page view, multiplies 10-page views with 1/10, and then sums the resulting vector up. This creates a rolling mean with a window size 10. We plot this mean in black. Finally, we specify that we want to use a log scale for the Y axis:

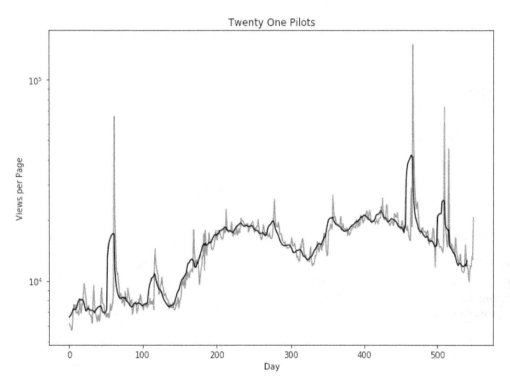

Access statistics for the Twenty One Pilots Wikipedia page with a rolling mean

You can see there are some pretty large spikes in the Twenty One Pilots graph we just generated, even though we used a logarithmic axis. On some days, views skyrocket to 10 times what they were just days before. Because of that, it quickly becomes clear that a good model will have to be able to deal with such extreme spikes.

Before we move on, it's worth pointing out that it's also clearly visible that there are global trends, as the page views generally increase over time.

For good measure, let's plot the interest in Twenty One Pilots for all languages. We can do this by running the following code:

```
fig, ax = plt.subplots(figsize=(10, 7))
plt.ylabel('Views per Page')
plt.xlabel('Day')
plt.title('Twenty One Pilots Popularity')
ax.set_yscale('log')


for country in ['de','en','es','fr','ru']:
    idx= np.where((train['Subject'] == 'Twenty One Pilots')
                   & (train['Sub_Page'] ==
'{}.wikipedia.org'.format(country)) &
(train['Access'] == 'all-access') &
(train['Agent'] == 'all-agents'))

    idx=idx[0][0]

    data = train.iloc[idx,0:-4]
    handle = ax.plot(days,data.values,label=country)


ax.legend()
```

In this snippet, we first set up the graph, as before. We then loop over the language codes and find the index of Twenty One Pilots. The index is an array wrapped in a tuple, so we have to extract the integer specifying the actual index. We then extract the page view data from the training dataset and plot the page views.

In the following chart, we can view the output of the code that we've just produced:

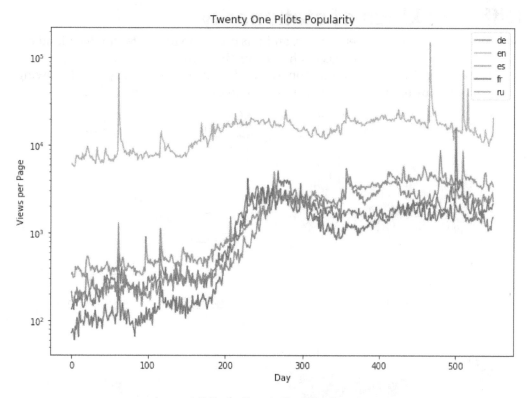

Access statistics for Twenty One Pilots by country

There is clearly some correlation between the time series. The English language version of Wikipedia (the top line) is, not surprisingly, by far the most popular. We can also see that the time series in our datasets are clearly not stationary; they change means and standard deviations over time.

A stationary process is one whose unconditional joint probability distribution stays constant over time. In other words, things such as the series mean or standard deviation should stay constant.

However, as you can see, between days 200-250 in the preceding graph, the mean views on the page changes dramatically. This result undermines some of the assumptions many classic modeling approaches make. Yet, financial time series are hardly ever stationary, so it is worthwhile dealing with these problems. By addressing these problems, we become familiar with several useful tools that can help us handle nonstationarity.

Different kinds of stationarity

Stationarity can mean different things, and it is crucial to understand which kind of stationarity is required for the task at hand. For simplicity, we will just look at two kinds of stationarity here: mean stationarity and variance stationarity. The following image shows four time series with different degrees of (non-)stationarity:

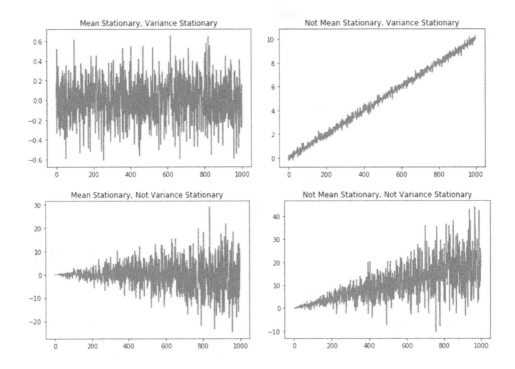

Mean stationarity refers to the level of a series being constant. Here, individual data points can deviate, of course, but the long-run mean should be stable. Variance stationarity refers to the variance from the mean being constant. Again, there may be outliers and short sequences whose variance seems higher, but the overall variance should be at the same level. A third kind of stationarity, which is difficult to visualize and is not shown here, is covariance stationarity. This refers to the covariance between different lags being constant. When people refer to covariance stationarity, they usually mean the special condition in which mean, variance, and covariances are stationary. Many econometric models, especially in risk management, operate under this covariance stationarity assumption.

Why stationarity matters

Many classic econometric methods assume some form of stationarity. A key reason for this is that inference and hypothesis testing work better when time series are stationary. However, even from a pure forecasting point of view, stationarity helps because it takes some work away from our model. Take a look at the **Not Mean Stationary** series in the preceding charts. You can see that a major part of forecasting the series is to recognize the fact that the series moves upward. If we can capture this fact outside of the model, the model has to learn less and can use its capacity for other purposes. Another reason is that it keeps the values we feed into the model in the same range. Remember that we need to standardize data before using a neural network. If a stock price grows from $1 to $1,000, we end up with non-standardized data, which will in turn make training difficult.

Making a time series stationary

The standard method to achieve mean stationarity in financial data (especially prices) is called differencing. It refers to computing the returns from prices. In the following image, you can see the raw and differenced versions of S&P 500. The raw version is not mean stationary as the value grows, but the differenced version is roughly stationary.

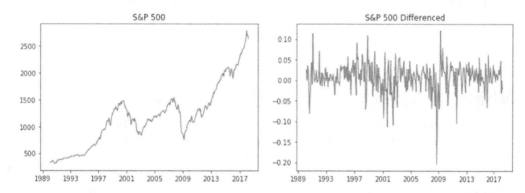

Another approach to mean stationarity is based on linear regression. Here, we fit a linear model to the data. A popular library for this kind of classical modeling is statsmodels, which has an inbuilt linear regression model. The following example shows how to use statsmodels to remove a linear trend from data:

```
time = np.linspace(0,10,1000)
series = time
series = series + np.random.randn(1000) *0.2
```

```
mdl = sm.OLS(time, series).fit()
trend = mdl.predict(time)
```

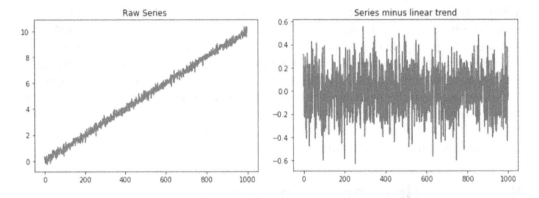

It is worth emphasizing that **stationarity is part of modeling and should be fit on the training set only**. This is not a big issue with differencing, but can lead to problems with linear detrending.

Removing variance non-stationarity is harder. A typical approach is to compute some rolling variance and divide new values by that variance. On the training set, you can also **studentize** the data. To do this, you need to compute the daily variance, and then divide all values by the root of it. Again, you may do this only on the training set, as the variance computation requires that you already know the values.

When to ignore stationarity issues

There are times when you should not worry about stationarity. When forecasting a sudden change, a so-called structural break, for instance. In the Wikipedia example, we are interested in knowing when the sites begin to be visited much more frequently than they were before. In this case, removing differences in level would stop our model from learning to predict such changes. Equally, we might be able to easily incorporate the non-stationarity into our model, or it can be ensured at a later stage in the pipeline. We usually only train a neural network on a small subsequence of the entire dataset. If we standardize each subsequence, the shift of mean within the subsequence might be negligible and we would not have to worry about it. Forecasting is a much more forgiving task than inference and hypothesis testing, so we might get away with a few non-stationarities if our model can pick up on them.

Fast Fourier transformations

Another interesting statistic we often want to compute about time series is the Fourier transformation (FT). Without going into the math, a Fourier transformation will show us the amount of oscillation within a particular frequency in a function.

You can imagine this like the tuner on an old FM radio. As you turn the tuner, you search through different frequencies. Every once in a while, you find a frequency that gives you a clear signal of a particular radio station. A Fourier transformation basically scans through the entire frequency spectrum and records at what frequencies there is a strong signal. In terms of a time series, this is useful when trying to find periodic patterns in the data.

Imagine that we found out that a frequency of one per week gave us a strong pattern. This would mean that knowledge about what the traffic was ton the same day one week ago would help our model.

When both the function and the Fourier transform are discrete, which is the case in a series of daily measurements, it is called the **discrete Fourier transform** (**DFT**). A very fast algorithm that is used for computing the DFT is known as the **Fast Fourier Transform** (**FFT**), which today has become an important algorithm in scientific computing. This theory was known to the mathematician Carl Gauss in 1805 but was brought to light more recently by American mathematicians James W. Cooley and John Tukey in 1965.

It's beyond the scope of this chapter to go into how and why the Fourier transformations work, so in this section we will only be giving a brief introduction. Imagine our function as a piece of wire. We take this wire and wrap it around a point, and if you wrap the wire so that the number of revolutions around the point matches the frequency of a signal, all of the signal peaks will be on one side of the pole. This means that the center of mass of the wire will move away from the point we wrapped the wire around.

In math, wrapping a function around a point can be achieved by multiplying the function $g(n)$ with $e^{-2\pi i f n}$, where f is the frequency of wrapping, n is the number of the item from the series, and i is the imaginary square root of -1. Readers that are not familiar with imaginary numbers can think of them as coordinates in which each number has a two-dimensional coordinate consisting of both a real and an imaginary number.

To compute the center of mass, we average the coordinates of the points in our discrete function. The DFT formula is, therefore, as follows:

$$y[f] = \sum_{n=0}^{N-1} e^{-2\pi i \frac{fn}{N}} x[n]$$

Here $y[f]$ is the fth element in the transformed series, and $x[n]$ is the nth element of the input series, x. N is the total number of points in the input series. Note that $y[f]$ will be a number with a real and a discrete element.

To detect frequencies, we are only really interested in the overall magnitude of $y[f]$. To get this magnitude we need to so we compute the root of the sum of the squares of the imaginary and real parts. In Python, we do not have to worry about all the math as we can use `scikit-learn's` `fftpack`, which has an FFT function built in.

The next step is to run the following code:

```
data = train.iloc[:,0:-4]
fft_complex = fft(data)
fft_mag = [np.sqrt(np.real(x)*np.real(x)+
               np.imag(x)*np.imag(x)) for x in fft_complex]
```

Here, we first extract the time series measurements without the global features from our training set. Then we run the FFT algorithm, before finally computing the magnitudes of the transformation.

After running that code, we now have the Fourier transformations for all the time series datasets. In order to allow us to get a better insight into the general behavior of the Fourier transformations we can average them by simply running:

```
arr = np.array(fft_mag)
fft_mean = np.mean(arr,axis=0)
```

This first turns the magnitudes into a NumPy array before then computing the mean. We want to compute the mean per frequency, not just the mean value of all the magnitudes, therefore we need to specify the `axis` along which to take the mean value.

In this case, the series are stacked in rows, so taking the mean column-wise (axis zero) will result in frequency-wise means. To better plot the transformation, we need to create a list of frequencies tested. The frequencies are in the form: day/ all days in the dataset for each day, so 1/550, 2/550, 3/550, and so on. To create the list we need to run:

```
fft_xvals = [day / fft_mean.shape[0] for day in
range(fft_mean.shape[0])]
```

In this visualization, we only care about the range of frequencies in a weekly range, so we will remove the second half of the transformation, which we can do by running:

```
npts = len(fft_xvals) // 2 + 1
fft_mean = fft_mean[:npts]
fft_xvals = fft_xvals[:npts]
```

Finally, we can plot our transformation:

```
fig, ax = plt.subplots(figsize=(10, 7))
ax.plot(fft_xvals[1:],fft_mean[1:])
plt.axvline(x=1./7,color='red',alpha=0.3)
plt.axvline(x=2./7,color='red',alpha=0.3)
plt.axvline(x=3./7,color='red',alpha=0.3)
```

Upon plotting the transformation, we will have successfully produced a chart similar to the one you see here:

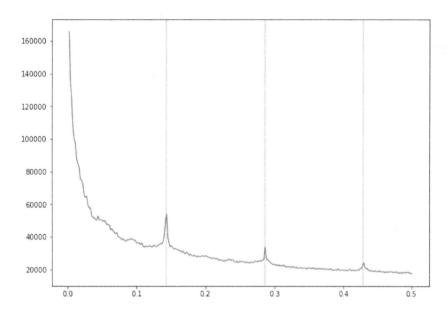

Fourier transformation of Wikipedia access statistics. Spikes marked by vertical lines

As you can see in the chart we produced, there are spikes at roughly 1/7 (0.14), 2/7 (0.28), and 3/7 (0.42). As a week has seven days, that is a frequency of one time per week, two times per week, and three times per week. In other words, page statistics repeat themselves (approximately) every week, so that, for example, access on one Saturday correlates with access on the previous Saturday.

Autocorrelation

Autocorrelation is the correlation between two elements of a series separated by a given interval. Intuitively, we would, for example, assume that knowledge about the last time step helps us in forecasting the next step. But how about knowledge from 2 time steps ago or from 100 time steps ago?

Running `autocorrelation_plot` will plot the correlation between elements with different lag times and can help us answer these questions. As a matter of fact, pandas comes with a handy autocorrelation plotting tool. To use it, we have to pass a series of data. In our case, we pass the page views of a page, selected at random.

We can do this by running the following code:

```
from pandas.plotting import autocorrelation_plot

autocorrelation_plot(data.iloc[110])
plt.title(' '.join(train.loc[110,['Subject', 'Sub_Page']]))
```

This will present us with the following diagram:

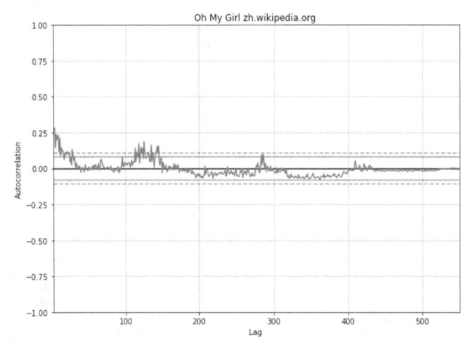

Autocorrelation of the Oh My Girl Chinese Wikipedia page

The plot in the preceding chart shows the correlation of page views for the Wikipedia page of *Oh My Girl*, a South Korean girl group, within the Chinese Wikipedia.

You can see that shorter time intervals between 1 and 20 days show a higher autocorrelation than longer intervals. Likewise there are also curious spikes, such as around 120 days and 280 days. It's possible that annual, quarterly, or monthly events could lead to an increase in the frequency of visits to the *Oh My Girl* Wikipedia page.

We can examine the general pattern of these frequencies by drawing 1,000 of these autocorrelation plots. To do this we run the following code:

```
a = np.random.choice(data.shape[0],1000)

for i in a:
    autocorrelation_plot(data.iloc[i])

plt.title('1K Autocorrelations')
```

This code snippet first samples 1,000 random numbers between 0 and the number of series in our dataset, which in our case is around 145,000. We use these as indices to randomly sample rows from our dataset for which we then draw the autocorrelation plot, which we can see in the following graphic:

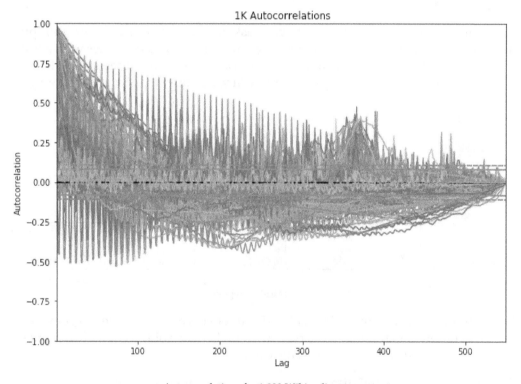

Autocorrelations for 1,000 Wikipedia pages

As you can see, autocorrelations can be quite different for different series and there is a lot of noise within the chart. There also seems to be a general trend toward higher correlations at around the 350-day mark.

Therefore, it makes sense to incorporate annual lagged page views as a time-dependent feature as well as the autocorrelation for one-year time intervals as a global feature. The same is true for quarterly and half-year lag as these seem to have high autocorrelations, or sometimes quite negative autocorrelations, which makes them valuable as well.

Time series analysis, such as in the examples shown previously, can help us engineer features for our model. Complex neural networks could, in theory, discover all of these features by themselves. However, it is often much easier to help them a bit, especially with information about long periods of time.

Establishing a training and testing regime

Even with lots of data available, we have to ask ourselves; How do we want to split data between *training*, *validation*, and *testing*. This dataset already comes with a test set of future data, therefore we don't have to worry about the test set, but for the validation set, there are two ways of splitting: a walk-forward split, and a side-by-side split:

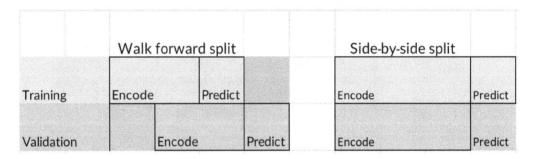

Possible testing regimes

In a walk-forward split, we train on all 145,000 series. To validate, we are going to use more recent data from all the series. In a side-by-side split, we sample a number of series for training and use the rest for validation.

Both have advantages and disadvantages. The disadvantage of walk-forward splitting is that we cannot use all of the observations of the series for our predictions. The disadvantage of side-by-side splitting is that we cannot use all series for training.

If we have few series, but multiple data observations per series, a walk-forward split is preferable. However, if we have a lot of series, but few observations per series, then a side-by-side split is preferable.

Establishing a training and testing regime also aligns more nicely with the forecasting problem at hand. In side-by-side splitting, the model might overfit to global events in the prediction period. Imagine that Wikipedia was down for a week in the prediction period used in side-by-side splitting. This event would reduce the number of views for all the pages, and as a result the model would overfit to this global event.

We would not catch the overfitting in our validation set because the prediction period would also be affected by the global event. However, in our case, we have multiple time series, but only about 550 observations per series. Therefore there seems to be no global events that would have significantly impacted all the Wikipedia pages in that time period.

However, there are some global events that impacted views for some pages, such as the Winter Olympics. Yet, this is a reasonable risk in this case, as the number of pages affected by such global events is still small. Since we have an abundance of series and only a few observations per series, a side-by-side split is more feasible in our case.

In this chapter, we're focusing on forecasting traffic for 50 days. So, we must first split the last 50 days of each series from the rest, as seen in the following code, before splitting the training and validation set:

```
from sklearn.model_selection import train_test_split

X = data.iloc[:,:500]
y = data.iloc[:,500:]

X_train, X_val, y_train, y_val = train_test_split(X.values,
                                                  y.values,
                                                  test_size=0.1,
                                                  random_state=42)
```

When splitting, we use `X.values` to only get the data, not a DataFrame containing the data. After splitting we are left with 130,556 series for training and 14,507 for validation.

In this example, we are going to use the **mean absolute percentage error (MAPE)** as a loss and evaluation metric. MAPE can cause division-by-zero errors if the true value of y is zero. Thus, to prevent division by zero occurring, we'll use a small-value epsilon:

```
def mape(y_true,y_pred):
    eps = 1
    err = np.mean(np.abs((y_true - y_pred) / (y_true + eps))) *
100
    return err
```

A note on backtesting

The peculiarities of choosing training and testing sets are especially important in both systematic investing and algorithmic trading. The main way to test trading algorithms is a process called **backtesting**.

Backtesting means we train the algorithm on data from a certain time period and then test its performance on *older* data. For example, we could train on data from a date range of 2015 to 2018 and then test on data from 1990 to 2015. By doing this, not only is the model's accuracy tested, but the backtested algorithm executes virtual trades so its profitability can be evaluated. Backtesting is done because there is plenty of past data available.

With all that being said, backtesting does suffer from several biases. Let's take a look at four of the most important biases that we need to be aware of:

- **Look-ahead bias**: This is introduced if future data is accidentally included at a point in the simulation where that data would not have been available yet. This can be caused by a technical bug in the simulator, but it can also stem from a parameter calculation. If a strategy makes use of the correlation between two securities, for example, and the correlation is calculated once for all time, a look-ahead bias is introduced. The same goes for the calculation of maxima or minima.

- **Survivorship bias**: This is introduced if only stocks that still exist at the time of testing are included in the simulation. Consider, for example, the 2008 financial crisis in which many firms went bankrupt. Leaving the stocks of these firms out when building a simulator in 2018 would introduce survivorship bias. After all, the algorithm could have invested in those stocks in 2008.

- **Psychological tolerance bias**: What looks good in a backtest might not be good in real life. Consider an algorithm that loses money for four months in a row before making it all back in a backtest. We might feel satisfied with this algorithm. However, if the algorithm loses money for four months in a row in real life and we don't know whether it will make that amount back, then will we sit tight or pull the plug? In the backtest, we know the final result, but in real life, we do not.

- **Overfitting**: This is a problem for all machine learning algorithms, but in backtesting, overfitting is a persistent and insidious problem. Not only does the algorithm potentially overfit, but the designer of the algorithm might also use knowledge about the past and build an algorithm that overfits to it. It is easy to pick stocks in hindsight, and knowledge can be incorporated into models that then look great in backtests. While it might be subtle, such as relying on certain correlations that held up well in the past, but it is easy to build bias into models that are evaluated in backtesting.

Building good testing regimes is a core activity of any quantitative investment firm or anyone working intensively with forecasting. One popular strategy for testing algorithms, other than backtesting, testing models on data that is statistically similar to stock data but differs because it's generated. We might build a generator for data that looks like real stock data but is not real, thus avoiding knowledge about real market events creeping into our models.

Another option is to deploy models silently and test them in the future. The algorithm runs but executes only virtual trades so that if things go wrong, no money will be lost. This approach makes use of future data instead of past data. However, the downside to this method is that we have to wait for quite a while before the algorithm can be used.

In practice, a combination regime is used. Statisticians carefully design regimes to see how an algorithm responds to different simulations. In our web traffic forecasting model, we will simply validate on different pages and then test on future data in the end.

Median forecasting

A good sanity check and an often underrated forecasting tool is medians. A median is a value separating the higher half of a distribution from the lower half; it sits exactly in the middle of the distribution. Medians have the advantage of removing noise, coupled with the fact that they are less susceptible to outliers than means, and the way they capture the midpoint of distribution means that they are also easy to compute.

To make a forecast, we compute the median over a look-back window in our training data. In this case, we use a window size of 50, but you could experiment with other values. The next step is to select the last 50 values from our X values and compute the median.

Take a minute to note that in the NumPy median function, we have to set `keepdims=True`. This ensures that we keep a two-dimensional matrix rather than a flat array, which is important when computing the error. So, to make a forecast, we need to run the following code:

```
lookback = 50

lb_data = X_train[:,-lookback:]

med = np.median(lb_data,axis=1,keepdims=True)

err = mape(y_train,med)
```

The output returned shows we obtain an error of about 68.1%; not bad given the simplicity of our method. To see how the medians work, let's plot the X values, the true y values, and predictions for a random page:

```
idx = 15000

fig, ax = plt.subplots(figsize=(10, 7))

ax.plot(np.arange(500),X_train[idx], label='X')
ax.plot(np.arange(500,550),y_train[idx],label='True')

ax.plot(np.arange(500,550),np.repeat(med[idx],50),
        label='Forecast')

plt.title(' '.join(train.loc[idx, ['Subject', 'Sub_Page']]))
ax.legend()
ax.set_yscale('log')
```

As you can see, our plotting consists of drawing three plots. For each plot, we must specify the X and Y values for the plot. For x_train, the X values range from 0 to 500, and for y_train and the forecast they range from 500 to 550. We then select the series we want to plot from our training data. Since we have only one median value, we repeat the median forecast of the desired series 50 times in order to draw our forecast.

The output can be seen here:

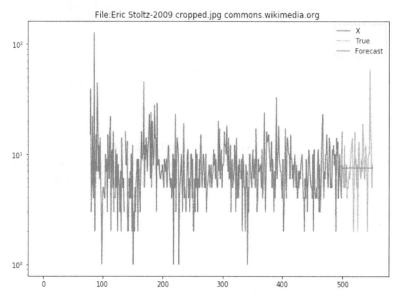

Median forecast and actual values for access of an image file. The True values are to the right-hand side of the plot, and the median forecast is the horizontal line in the center of them.

As you can see in the preceding output median forecast, the data for this page, in this case, an image of American actor Eric Stoltz, is very noisy, and the median cuts through all the noise. The median is especially useful here for pages that are visited infrequently and where there is no clear trend or pattern.

This is not all you can do with medians. Beyond what we've just covered, you could, for example, use different medians for weekends or use a median of medians from multiple look-back periods. A simple tool, such as median forecasting, is able to deliver good results with smart feature engineering. Therefore, it makes sense to spend a bit of time on implementing median forecasting as a baseline and performing a sanity check before using more advanced methods.

ARIMA

Earlier, in the section on exploratory data analysis, we talked about how seasonality and stationarity are important elements when it comes to forecasting time series. In fact, median forecasting has trouble with both. If the mean of a time series continuously shifts, then median forecasting will not continue the trend, and if a time series shows cyclical behavior, then the median will not continue with the cycle.

ARIMA which stands for **Autoregressive Integrated Moving Average**, is made up of three core components:

- **Autoregression**: The model uses the relationship between a value and a number of lagged observations.
- **Integrated**: The model uses the difference between raw observations to make the time series stationary. A time series going continuously upward will have a flat integral as the differences between points are always the same.
- **Moving Average**: The model uses residual errors from a moving average.

We have to manually specify how many lagged observations we want to include, p, how often we want to differentiate the series, d, and how large the moving average window should be, q. ARIMA then performs a linear regression against all the included lagged observations and moving average residuals on the differentiated series.

We can use ARIMA in Python with `statsmodels`, a library with many helpful statistical tools. To do this, we simply run this:

```
from statsmodels.tsa.arima_model import ARIMA
```

Then, to create a new ARIMA model, we pass the data we want to fit, in this case from our earlier example of views for 2NE1 from the Chinese Wikipedia, as well as the desired values for p, d, and q, in that order. In this case, we want to include five lagged observations, differentiate once, and take a moving average window of five. In code, this works out as follows:

```
model = ARIMA(X_train[0], order=(5,1,5))
```

We can then fit the model using `model.fit()`:

```
model = model.fit()
```

Running `model.summary()` at this point would output all the coefficients as well as significance values for statistical analysis. We, however, are more interested in how well our model does in forecasting. So, to complete this, and see the output, we simply run:

```
residuals = pd.DataFrame(model.resid)
ax.plot(residuals)

plt.title('ARIMA residuals for 2NE1 pageviews')
```

After running the previous code, we'll be able to output the results for 2NE1 page views, as we can see in this graph:

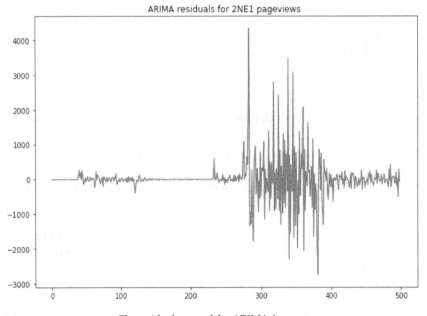

The residual error of the ARIMA forecast

In the preceding chart, we can see that the model does very well in the beginning but really begins to struggle at around the 300-day mark. This could be because page views are harder to predict or because there is more volatility in this period.

In order for us to ensure that our model is not skewed, we need to examine the distribution of the residuals. We can do this by plotting a *kernel density estimator*, which is a mathematical method designed to estimate distributions without needing to model them.

We can do this by running the following code:

```
residuals.plot(kind='kde',
               figsize=(10,7),
               title='ARIMA residual distribution 2NE1 ARIMA',
               legend = False)
```

This code will then output the following graph:

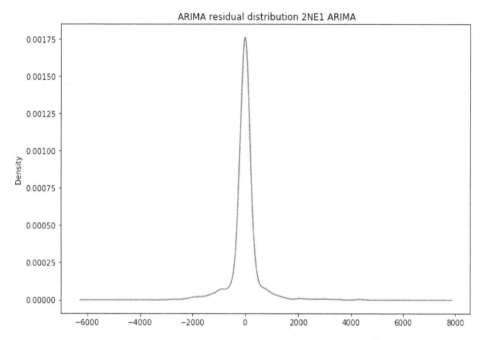

Approximately normally distributed residuals from ARIMA forecast

As you can see, our model roughly represents a Gaussian distribution with a mean of zero. So, it's all good on that front, but then the question arises, "how do we make forecasts?"

To use this model for forecasting, all we have to do is to specify the number of days we want to forecast, which we can do with the following code:

```
predictions, stderr, conf_int = model.forecast(50)
```

This forecast not only gives us predictions but also the standard error and confidence interval, which is 95% by default.

Let's plot the projected views against the real views to see how we are doing. This graph shows the last 20 days for our prediction basis as well as the forecast to keep things readable. To produce this, we must execute the following code:

```
fig, ax = plt.subplots(figsize=(10, 7))

ax.plot(np.arange(480,500),basis[480:], label='X')
ax.plot(np.arange(500,550),y_train[0], label='True')
ax.plot(np.arange(500,550),predictions, label='Forecast')

plt.title('2NE1 ARIMA forecasts')
ax.legend()
ax.set_yscale('log')
```

This code will output the following graph:

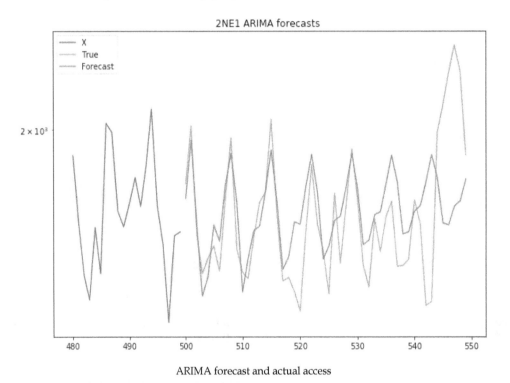

ARIMA forecast and actual access

You can see that ARIMA captures the periodicity of the series very well. Its forecast does steer off a bit toward the end, but in the beginning, it does a remarkable job.

Kalman filters

Kalman filters are a method of extracting a signal from either noisy or incomplete measurements. They were invented by Hungarian-born, American engineer, Rudolf Emil Kalman, for the purpose of electrical engineering, and were first used in the Apollo Space program in the 1960s.

The basic idea behind the Kalman filter is that there is some hidden state of a system that we cannot observe directly but for which we can obtain noisy measurements. Imagine you want to measure the temperature inside a rocket engine. You cannot put a measurement device directly into the engine, because it's too hot, but you can have a device on the outside of the engine.

Naturally, this measurement is not going to be perfect, as there are a lot of external factors occurring outside of the engine that make the measurement noisy. Therefore, to estimate the temperature inside the rocket, you need a method that can deal with the noise. We can think of the internal state in the page forecasting as the actual interest in a certain page, of which the page views represent only a noisy measurement.

The idea here is that the internal state, x_k, at time k is a state transition matrix, A, multiplied with the previous internal state, x_{k-1}, plus some process noise, q_{k-1}. How interest in the Wikipedia page of 2NE1 develops is to some degree random. The randomness is assumed to follow a Gaussian normal distribution with mean zero and variance Q:

$$x_k = Ax_{k-1} + q_{k-1}, \qquad q_{k-1} \sim N(0, Q)$$

The obtained measurement at time k, y_k, is an observation model, H, describing how states translate to measurements times the state, x_k, plus some observation noise, r_k. The observation noise is assumed to follow a Gaussian normal distribution with mean zero and variance R:

$$y_k = Hx_k + r_k, \qquad r_k \sim N(0, R)$$

Roughly speaking, Kalman filters fit a function by estimating A, H, Q, and R. The process of going over a time series and updating the parameters is called smoothing. The exact mathematics of the estimation process is complicated and not very relevant if all we want to do is forecasting. Yet, what is relevant is that we need to provide priors to these values.

We should note that our state does not have to be only one number. In this case, our state is an eight-dimensional vector, with one hidden level as well as seven levels to capture weekly seasonality, as we can see in this code:

```
n_seasons = 7

state_transition = np.zeros((n_seasons+1, n_seasons+1))

state_transition[0,0] = 1

state_transition[1,1:-1] = [-1.0] * (n_seasons-1)
state_transition[2:,1:-1] = np.eye(n_seasons-1)
```

The transition matrix, *A,* looks like the following table, describing one hidden level, which we might interpret as the real interest as well as a seasonality model:

```
array([[ 1.,   0.,   0.,   0.,   0.,   0.,   0.,   0.],
       [ 0.,  -1.,  -1.,  -1.,  -1.,  -1.,  -1.,   0.],
       [ 0.,   1.,   0.,   0.,   0.,   0.,   0.,   0.],
       [ 0.,   0.,   1.,   0.,   0.,   0.,   0.,   0.],
       [ 0.,   0.,   0.,   1.,   0.,   0.,   0.,   0.],
       [ 0.,   0.,   0.,   0.,   1.,   0.,   0.,   0.],
       [ 0.,   0.,   0.,   0.,   0.,   1.,   0.,   0.],
       [ 0.,   0.,   0.,   0.,   0.,   0.,   1.,   0.]])
```

The observation model, *H,* maps the general interest plus seasonality to a single measurement:

```
observation_model = [[1,1] + [0]*(n_seasons-1)]
```

The observation model looks like this:

```
[[1, 1, 0, 0, 0, 0, 0, 0]]
```

The noise priors are just estimates scaled by a "smoothing factor," which allows us to control the update process:

```
smoothing_factor = 5.0

level_noise = 0.2 / smoothing_factor
observation_noise = 0.2
season_noise = 1e-3

process_noise_cov = np.diag([level_noise, season_noise] +
[0]*(n_seasons-1))**2
observation_noise_cov = observation_noise**2
```

`process_noise_cov` is an eight-dimensional vector, matching the eight-dimensional state vector. Meanwhile, `observation_noise_cov` is a single number, as we have only a single measurement. The only real requirement for these priors is that their shapes must allow the matrix multiplications described in the two preceding formulas. Other than that, we are free to specify transition models as we see them.

Otto Seiskari, a mathematician and 8th place winner in the original Wikipedia traffic forecasting competition, wrote a very fast Kalman filtering library, which we will be using here. His library allows for the vectorized processing of multiple independent time series, which is very handy if you have 145,000 time series to process.

Note: The library's repository can be found here: `https://github.com/oseiskar/simdkalman`.

You can install his library using the following command:

`pip install simdkalman`

To import it, run the following code:

```
import simdkalman
```

Although `simdkalman` is very sophisticated, it is quite simple to use. Firstly, we are going to specify a Kalman filter using the priors we just defined:

```
kf = simdkalman.KalmanFilter(state_transition = state_transition,
                             process_noise = process_noise_cov,
                             observation_model =
observation_model,
                             observation_noise =
observation_noise_cov)
```

From there we can then estimate the parameters and compute a forecast in one step:

```
result = kf.compute(X_train[0], 50)
```

Once again, we make forecasts for 2NE1's Chinese page and create a forecast for 50 days. Take a minute to note that we could also pass multiple series, for example, the first 10 with `X_train[:10]`, and compute separate filters for all of them at once.

The result of the compute function contains the state and observation estimates from the smoothing process as well as predicted internal states and observations. States and observations are Gaussian distributions, so to get a plottable value, we need to access their mean.

Our states are eight-dimensional, but we only care about the non-seasonal state value, so we need to index the mean, which we can achieve by running the following:

```
fig, ax = plt.subplots(figsize=(10, 7))
ax.plot(np.arange(480,500),X_train[0,480:], label='X')
ax.plot(np.arange(500,550),y_train[0],label='True')

ax.plot(np.arange(500,550),
        result.predicted.observations.mean,
        label='Predicted observations')

ax.plot(np.arange(500,550),
        result.predicted.states.mean[:,0],
```

```
                 label='predicted states')

ax.plot(np.arange(480,500),
        result.smoothed.observations.mean[480:],
        label='Expected Observations')

ax.plot(np.arange(480,500),
        result.smoothed.states.mean[480:,0],
        label='States')




ax.legend()
ax.set_yscale('log')
```

The preceding code will then output the following chart:

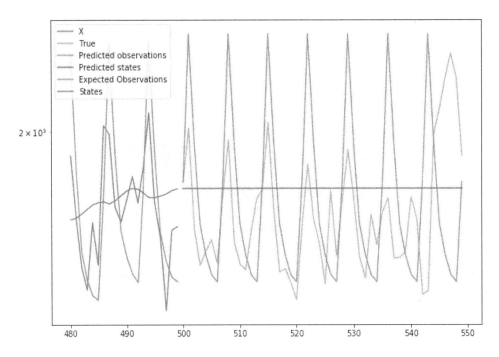

Predictions and inner states from the Kalman filter

We can clearly see in the preceding graph the effects of our prior modeling on the predictions. We can see the model predicts strong weekly oscillation, stronger than actually observed. Likewise, we can also see that the model does not anticipate any trends since we did not see model trends in our prior model.

Kalman filters are a useful tool and are used in many applications, from electrical engineering to finance. In fact, until relatively recently, they were the go-to tool for time series modeling. Smart modelers were able to create smart systems that described the time series very well. However, one weakness of Kalman filters is that they cannot discover patterns by themselves and need carefully engineered priors in order to work.

In the second half of this chapter, we will be looking at neural network-based approaches that can automatically model time series, and often with higher accuracy.

Forecasting with neural networks

The second half of the chapter is all about neural networks. In the first part, we will be building a simple neural network that only forecasts the next time step. Since the spikes in the series are very large, we will be working with log-transformed page views in input and output. We can use the short-term forecast neural network to make longer-term forecasts, too, by feeding its predictions back into the network.

Before we can dive in and start building forecast models, we need to do some preprocessing and feature engineering. The advantage of neural networks is that they can take in both a high number of features in addition to very high-dimensional data. The disadvantage is that we have to be careful about what features we input. Remember how we discussed look-ahead bias earlier in the chapter, including future data that would not have been available at the time of forecasting, which is a problem in backtesting.

Data preparation

For each series, we will assemble the following features:

- log_view: The natural logarithm of page views. Since the logarithm of zero is undefined, we will use log1p, which is the natural logarithm of page views plus one.
- days: One-hot encoded weekdays.
- year_lag: The value of log_view from 365 days ago. -1 if there is no value available.
- halfyear_lag: The value of log_view from 182 days ago. -1 if there is no value available.
- quarter_lag: The value of log_view from 91 days ago. -1 if there is no value available.
- page_enc: The one-hot encoded subpage.
- agent_enc: The one-hot encoded agent.

- acc_enc: The one-hot encoded access method.
- year_autocorr: The autocorrelation of the series of 365 days.
- halfyr_autocorr: The autocorrelation of the series of 182 days.
- quarter_autocorr: The autocorrelation of the series of 91 days.
- medians: The median of page views over the lookback period.

These features are assembled for each time series, giving our input data the shape (batch size, look back window size, 29).

Weekdays

The day of the week matters. Sundays may show different access behavior, when people are browsing from their couch, compared to Mondays, when people may be looking up things for work. So, we need to encode the weekday. A simple one-hot encoding will do the job:

```
import datetime
from sklearn.preprocessing import LabelEncoder
from sklearn.preprocessing import OneHotEncoder

weekdays = [datetime.datetime.strptime(date, '%Y-%m
-%d').strftime('%a')
                for date in train.columns.values[:-4]]
```

Firstly, we turn the date strings (such as 2017-03-02) into their weekday (Thursday). This is very simple to do, and can be done with the following code:

```
day_one_hot = LabelEncoder().fit_transform(weekdays)
day_one_hot = day_one_hot.reshape(-1, 1)
```

We then encode the weekdays into integers, so that "Monday" becomes 1, "Tuesday" becomes 2, and so on. We reshape the resulting array into a rank-2 tensor with shape (array length, 1) so that the one-hot encoder knows that we have many observations, but only one feature, and not the other way around:

```
day_one_hot =
OneHotEncoder(sparse=False).fit_transform(day_one_hot)
day_one_hot = np.expand_dims(day_one_hot,0)
```

Finally, we one-hot encode the days. We then add a new dimension to the tensor showing that we only have one "row" of dates. We will later repeat the array along this axis:

```
agent_int = LabelEncoder().fit(train['Agent'])
agent_enc = agent_int.transform(train['Agent'])
agent_enc = agent_enc.reshape(-1, 1)
agent_one_hot = OneHotEncoder(sparse=False).fit(agent_enc)

del agent_enc
```

We will need the encoders for the agents later when we encode the agent of each series.

Here, we first create a `LabelEncoder` instance that can transform the agent name strings into integers. We then transform all of the agents into such an integer string in order to set up a `OneHotEncoder` instance that can one-hot encode the agents. To save memory, we will then delete the already-encoded agents.

We do the same for subpages and access methods by running the following:

```
page_int = LabelEncoder().fit(train['Sub_Page'])
page_enc = page_int.transform(train['Sub_Page'])
page_enc = page_enc.reshape(-1, 1)
page_one_hot = OneHotEncoder(sparse=False).fit(page_enc)

del page_enc

acc_int = LabelEncoder().fit(train['Access'])
acc_enc = acc_int.transform(train['Access'])
acc_enc = acc_enc.reshape(-1, 1)
acc_one_hot = OneHotEncoder(sparse=False).fit(acc_enc)

del acc_enc
```

Now we come to the lagged features. Technically, neural networks could discover what past events are relevant for forecasting themselves. However, this is pretty difficult because of the vanishing gradient problem, something that is covered in more detail later, in the *LSTM* section of this chapter. For now, let's just set up a little function that creates an array lagged by a number of days:

```
def lag_arr(arr, lag, fill):
    filler = np.full((arr.shape[0],lag,1),-1)
    comb = np.concatenate((filler,arr),axis=1)
    result = comb[:,:arr.shape[1]]
    return result
```

This function first creates a new array that will fill up the "empty space" from the shift. The new array has as many rows as the original array but its series length, or width, is the number of days we want to lag. We then attach this array to the front of our original array. Finally, we remove elements from the back of the array in order to get back to the original array series length or width. We want to inform our model about the amount of autocorrelation for different time intervals. To compute the autocorrelation for a single series, we shift the series by the amount of lag we want to measure the autocorrelation for. We then compute the autocorrelation:

$$R(\tau) = \frac{\sum((X_t - \mu_t) * (X_{t+\tau} - \mu_{t+\tau}))}{\sigma_t * \sigma_{t+\tau}}$$

In this formula τ is the lag indicator. We do not just use a NumPy function since there is a real possibility that the divider is zero. In this case, our function will just return 0:

```
def single_autocorr(series, lag):
    s1 = series[lag:]
    s2 = series[:-lag]
    ms1 = np.mean(s1)
    ms2 = np.mean(s2)
    ds1 = s1 - ms1
    ds2 = s2 - ms2
    divider = np.sqrt(np.sum(ds1 * ds1)) * np.sqrt(np.sum
(ds2 * ds2))
    return np.sum(ds1 * ds2) / divider if divider != 0 else 0
```

We can use this function, which we wrote for a single series, to create a batch of autocorrelation features, as seen here:

```
def batc_autocorr(data, lag, series_length):
    corrs = []
    for i in range(data.shape[0]):
        c = single_autocorr(data, lag)
        corrs.append(c)
    corr = np.array(corrs)
    corr = np.expand_dims(corr, -1)
    corr = np.expand_dims(corr, -1)
    corr = np.repeat(corr, series_length, axis=1)
    return corr
```

Firstly, we calculate the autocorrelations for each series in the batch. Then we fuse the correlations together into one NumPy array. Since autocorrelations are a global feature, we need to create a new dimension for the length of the series and another new dimension to show that this is only one feature. We then repeat the autocorrelations over the entire length of the series.

The get_batch function utilizes all of these tools in order to provide us with one batch of data, as can be seen with the following code:

```
def get_batch(train, start=0, lookback = 100):          #1
    assert((start + lookback) <= (train.shape[1] - 5))  #2
    data = train.iloc[:, start:start + lookback].values #3
    target = train.iloc[:, start + lookback].values
    target = np.log1p(target)                           #4
```

```
    log_view = np.log1p(data)
    log_view = np.expand_dims(log_view,axis=-1)                     #5
    days = day_one_hot[:,start:start + lookback]
    days = np.repeat(days,repeats=train.shape[0],axis=0)            #6
    year_lag = lag_arr(log_view,365,-1)
    halfyear_lag = lag_arr(log_view,182,-1)
    quarter_lag = lag_arr(log_view,91,-1)                           #7
    agent_enc = agent_int.transform(train['Agent'])
    agent_enc = agent_enc.reshape(-1, 1)
    agent_enc = agent_one_hot.transform(agent_enc)
    agent_enc = np.expand_dims(agent_enc,1)
    agent_enc = np.repeat(agent_enc,lookback,axis=1)                #8
    page_enc = page_int.transform(train['Sub_Page'])
    page_enc = page_enc.reshape(-1, 1)
    page_enc = page_one_hot.transform(page_enc)
    page_enc = np.expand_dims(page_enc, 1)
    page_enc = np.repeat(page_enc,lookback,axis=1)                  #9
    acc_enc = acc_int.transform(train['Access'])
    acc_enc = acc_enc.reshape(-1, 1)
    acc_enc = acc_one_hot.transform(acc_enc)
    acc_enc = np.expand_dims(acc_enc,1)
    acc_enc = np.repeat(acc_enc,lookback,axis=1)                    #10
    year_autocorr = batc_autocorr(data,lag=365,
series_length=lookback)
    halfyr_autocorr = batc_autocorr(data,lag=182,
series_length=lookback)
    quarter_autocorr = batc_autocorr(data,lag=91,
series_length=lookback)                                            #11
    medians = np.median(data,axis=1)
    medians = np.expand_dims(medians,-1)
    medians = np.expand_dims(medians,-1)
    medians = np.repeat(medians,lookback,axis=1)                   #12
    batch = np.concatenate((log_view,
                            days,
                            year_lag,
                            halfyear_lag,
                            quarter_lag,
                            page_enc,
                            agent_enc,
                            acc_enc,
                            year_autocorr,
                            halfyr_autocorr,
                            quarter_autocorr,
                            medians),axis=2)

    return batch, target
```

That was a lot of code, so let's take a minute to walk through the preceding code step by step in order to fully understand it:

1. Ensures there is enough data to create a lookback window and a target from the given starting point.
2. Separates the lookback window from the training data.
3. Separates the target and then takes the one plus logarithm of it.
4. Takes the one plus logarithm of the lookback window and adds a feature dimension.
5. Gets the days from the precomputed one-hot encoding of days and repeats it for each time series in the batch.
6. Computes the lag features for year lag, half-year lag, and quarterly lag.
7. This step will encode the global features using the preceding defined encoders. The next two steps, 8 and 9, will echo the same role.
8. This step repeats step 7.
9. This step repeats step 7 and 8.
10. Calculates the year, half-year, and quarterly autocorrelation.
11. Calculates the median for the lookback data.
12. Fuses all these features into one batch.

Finally, we can use our get_batch function to write a generator, just like we did in *Chapter 3, Utilizing Computer Vision*. This generator loops over the original training set and passes a subset into the get_batch function. It then yields the batch obtained.

Note that we choose random starting points to make the most out of our data:

```
def generate_batches(train,batch_size = 32, lookback = 100):
    num_samples = train.shape[0]
    num_steps = train.shape[1] - 5
    while True:
        for i in range(num_samples // batch_size):
            batch_start = i * batch_size
            batch_end = batch_start + batch_size

            seq_start = np.random.randint(num_steps - lookback)
            X,y = get_batch(train.iloc[batch_start:batch_end],
start=seq_start)
            yield X,y
```

This function is what we will train and validate on.

Conv1D

You might remember Convolution Neural Networks (ConvNets, or CNNs) from *Chapter 3, Utilizing Computer Vision*, where we looked briefly at roofs and insurance. In computer vision, convolutional filters slide over the image two-dimensionally. There is also a version of convolutional filters that can slide over a sequence one-dimensionally. The output is another sequence, much like the output of a two-dimensional convolution was another image. Everything else about one-dimensional convolutions is exactly the same as two-dimensional convolutions.

In this section, we're going to start by building a ConvNet that expects a fixed input length:

```
n_features = 29
max_len = 100

model = Sequential()

model.add(Conv1D(16,5, input_shape=(100,29)))
model.add(Activation('relu'))
model.add(MaxPool1D(5))

model.add(Conv1D(16,5))
model.add(Activation('relu'))
model.add(MaxPool1D(5))
model.add(Flatten())
model.add(Dense(1))
```

Notice that next to `Conv1D` and `Activation`, there are two more layers in this network. `MaxPool1D` works exactly like `MaxPooling2D`, which we used earlier in the book. It takes a piece of the sequence with a specified length and returns the maximum element in the sequence. This is similar to how it returned the maximum element of a small window in two-dimensional convolutional networks.

Take note that max pooling always returns the maximum element for each channel. `Flatten` transforms the two-dimensional sequence tensor into a one-dimensional flat tensor. To use `Flatten` in combination with `Dense`, we need to specify the sequence length in the input shape. Here, we set it with the `max_len` variable. We do this because `Dense` expects a fixed input shape and `Flatten` will return a tensor based on the size of its input.

An alternative to using `Flatten` is `GlobalMaxPool1D`, which returns the maximum element of the entire sequence. Since the sequence is fixed in size, you can use a `Dense` layer afterward without fixing the input length.

Our model compiles just as you would expect:

```
model.compile(optimizer='adam',
loss='mean_absolute_percentage_error')
```

We then train it on the generator that we wrote earlier. To obtain separate train and validation sets, we must first split the overall dataset and then create two generators based on the two datasets. To do this, run the following code:

```
from sklearn.model_selection import train_test_split

batch_size = 128
train_df, val_df = train_test_split(train, test_size=0.1)
train_gen = generate_batches(train_df,batch_size=batch_size)
val_gen = generate_batches(val_df, batch_size=batch_size)

n_train_samples = train_df.shape[0]
n_val_samples = val_df.shape[0]
```

Finally, we can train our model on a generator, just like we did in computer vision:

```
model.fit_generator(train_gen,
                    epochs=20,
                    steps_per_epoch=n_train_samples // batch_size,
                    validation_data= val_gen,
                    validation_steps=n_val_samples // batch_size)
```

Your validation loss will still be quite high, around 12,798,928. The absolute loss value is never a good guide for how well your model is doing. You'll find that it's better to use other metrics in order to see whether your forecasts are useful. However, please note that we will reduce the loss significantly later in this chapter.

Dilated and causal convolution

As discussed in the section on backtesting, we have to make sure that our model does not suffer from look-ahead bias:

Standard Convolution

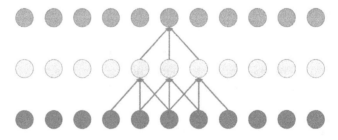

Standard convolution does not take the direction of convolution into account

As the convolutional filter slides over the data, it looks into the future as well as the past. Causal convolution ensures that the output at time t derives only from inputs from time $t - 1$:

Causal Convolution

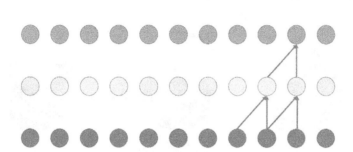

Causal convolution shifts the filter in the right direction

In Keras, all we have to do is set the `padding` parameter to `causal`. We can do this by executing the following code:

```
model.add(Conv1D(16,5, padding='causal'))
```

Another useful trick is dilated convolutional networks. Dilation means that the filter only accesses every nth element, as we can see in the image below.

Causal Dilated Convolution

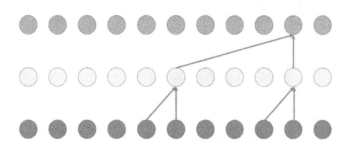

Dilated convolution skips over inputs while convolving

In the preceding diagram, the upper convolutional layer has a dilation rate of 4 and the lower layer a dilation rate of 1. We can set the dilation rate in Keras by running the following:

```
model.add(Conv1D(16,5, padding='causal', dilation_rate=4))
```

Simple RNN

Another method to make order matter within neural networks is to give the network some kind of memory. So far, all of our networks have done a forward pass without any memory of what happened before or after the pass. It's time to change that with a **recurrent neural network (RNN)**:

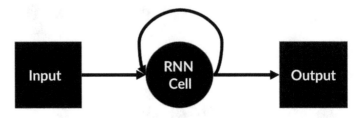

The scheme of an RNN

RNNs contain recurrent layers. Recurrent layers can remember their last activation and use it as their own input:

$$A_t = activation\left(W * in + U * A_{t-1} + b\right)$$

A recurrent layer takes a sequence as an input. For each element, it then computes a matrix multiplication ($W * in$), just like a Dense layer, and runs the result through an activation function, such as relu. It then retains its own activation. When the next item of the sequence arrives, it performs the matrix multiplication as before, but this time it also multiplies its previous activation with a second matrix ($U * A_{t-1}$). The recurrent layer adds the result of both operations together and passes it through the activation function again.

In Keras, we can use a simple RNN as follows:

```
from keras.layers import SimpleRNN

model = Sequential()
model.add(SimpleRNN(16,input_shape=(max_len,n_features)))
model.add(Dense(1))

model.compile(optimizer='adam',
loss='mean_absolute_percentage_error')
```

The only parameter we need to specify is the size of the recurrent layer. This is basically the same as setting the size of a Dense layer, as SimpleRNN layers are very similar to Dense layers except that they feed their output back in as input. RNNs, by default, only return the last output of the sequence.

To stack multiple RNNs, we need to set `return_sequences` to `True`, which we can do by running the following code:

```python
from keras.layers import SimpleRNN

model = Sequential()
model.add(SimpleRNN(16,return_sequences=True,
input_shape=(max_len,n_features)))
model.add(SimpleRNN(32, return_sequences = True))
model.add(SimpleRNN(64))
model.add(Dense(1))

model.compile(optimizer='adam',
loss='mean_absolute_percentage_error')
```

```
You can then fit the model on the generator as before:
```

```python
model.fit_generator(train_gen,
                    epochs=20,
                    steps_per_epoch=n_train_samples // batch_size,
                    validation_data= val_gen,
                    validation_steps=n_val_samples // batch_size)
```

As a result of this code, we'll be able to see that a simple RNN does much better than the convolutional model, with a loss of around 1,548,653. You'll remember that previously our loss was at 12,793,928. However, we can do much better using a more sophisticated version of the RNN.

LSTM

In the last section, we learned about basic RNNs. In theory, simple RNNs should be able to retain even long-term memories. However, in practice, this approach often falls short because of the vanishing gradients problem.

Over the course of many timesteps, the network has a hard time keeping up meaningful gradients. While this is not the focus of this chapter, a more detailed exploration of why this happens can be read in the 1994 paper, *Learning long-term dependencies with gradient descent is difficult,* available at -https://ieeexplore.ieee. org/document/279181 - by Yoshua Bengio, Patrice Simard, and Paolo Frasconi.

In direct response to the vanishing gradients problem of simple RNNs, the **Long Short-Term Memory (LSTM)** layer was invented. This layer performs much better at longer time series. Yet, if relevant observations are a few hundred steps behind in the series, then even LSTM will struggle. This is why we manually included some lagged observations.

Before we dive into details, let's look at a simple RNN that has been unrolled over time:

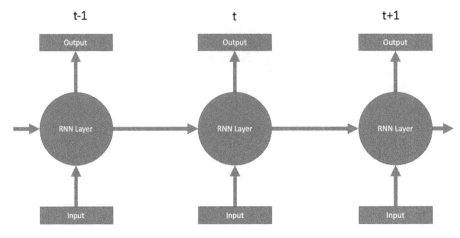

A rolled out RNN

As you can see, this is the same as the RNN that we saw in *Chapter 2, Applying Machine Learning to Structured Data*, except that this has been unrolled over time.

The carry

The central addition of an LSTM over an RNN is the *carry*. The carry is like a conveyor belt that runs along the RNN layer. At each time step, the carry is fed into the RNN layer. The new carry gets computed from the input, RNN output, and old carry, in a separate operation from the RNN layer itself::

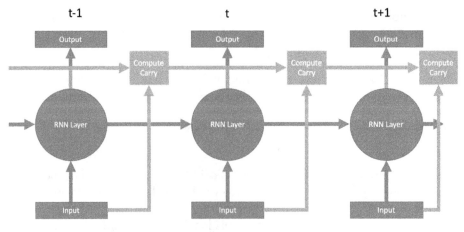

The LSTM schematic

To understand what the Compute Carry is, we should determine what should be added from the input and state:

$$i_t = a\left(s_t \cdot Ui + in_t \cdot Wi + bi\right)$$

$$k_t = a\left(s_t \cdot Uk + in_t \cdot Wk + bk\right)$$

In these formulas s_t is the state at time t (output of the simple RNN layer), in_t is the input at time t, and Ui, Wi, Uk, and Wk are the model parameters (matrices) that will be learned. $a()$ is an activation function.

To determine what should be forgotten from the state and input, we need to use the following formula:

$$f_t = a\left(s_t \cdot Uf\right) + in_t \cdot Wf + bf$$

The new carry is then computed as follows:

$$c_{t+1} = c_t * f_t + i_t * k_t$$

While the standard theory claims that the LSTM layer learns what to add and what to forget, in practice, nobody knows what really happens inside an LSTM. However, LSTM models have been shown to be quite effective at learning long-term memory.

Take this time to note that LSTM layers do not need an extra activation function as they already come with a `tanh` activation function out of the box.

LSTMs can be used in the same way as `SimpleRNN`:

```
from keras.layers import LSTM

model = Sequential()
model.add(LSTM(16, input_shape=(max_len, n_features)))
model.add(Dense(1))
```

To stack layers, you also need to set `return_sequences` to `True`. Note that you can easily combine `LSTM` and `SimpleRNN` using the following code:

```
model = Sequential()
model.add(LSTM(32, return_sequences=True,
input_shape=(max_len, n_features)))
model.add(SimpleRNN(16, return_sequences = True))
model.add(LSTM(16))
model.add(Dense(1))
```

Note: If you are using a GPU and TensorFlow backend with Keras, use `CuDNNLSTM` instead of `LSTM`. It's significantly faster while working in exactly the same way.

We'll now compile and run the model just as we did before:

```
model.compile(optimizer='adam',
loss='mean_absolute_percentage_error')

model.fit_generator(train_gen,
                    epochs=20,
                    steps_per_epoch=n_train_samples // batch_size,
                    validation_data= val_gen,
                    validation_steps=n_val_samples // batch_size)
```

This time, the loss went as low as 88,735, which is several orders of magnitude better than our initial model.

Recurrent dropout

Having read this far into the book, you've already encountered the concept of *dropout*. Dropout removes some elements of one layer of input at random. A common and important tool in RNNs is a *recurrent dropout*, which does not remove any inputs between layers but inputs between time steps:

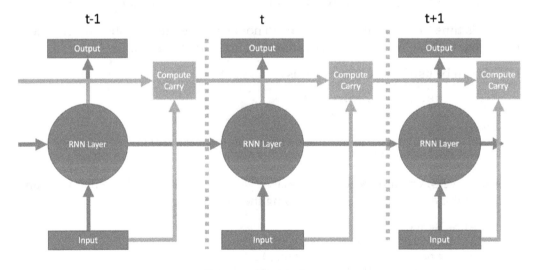

Recurrent dropout scheme

Just as with regular dropout, recurrent dropout has a regularizing effect and can prevent overfitting. It's used in Keras by simply passing an argument to the LSTM or RNN layer.

As we can see in the following code, recurrent dropout, unlike regular dropout, does not have its own layer:

```
model = Sequential()
model.add(LSTM(16,
               recurrent_dropout=0.1,
               return_sequences=True,
               input_shape=(max_len,n_features)))

model.add(LSTM(16,recurrent_dropout=0.1))

model.add(Dense(1))
```

Bayesian deep learning

We now have a whole set of models that can make forecasts on time series. But are the point estimates that these models give sensible estimates or just random guesses? How certain is the model? Most classic probabilistic modeling techniques, such as Kalman filters, can give confidence intervals for predictions, whereas regular deep learning cannot do this. The field of Bayesian deep learning combines Bayesian approaches with deep learning to enable models to express uncertainty.

The key idea in Bayesian deep learning is that there is inherent uncertainty in the model. Sometimes this is done by learning a mean and standard deviation for weights instead of just a single weight value. However, this approach increases the number of parameters required, so it did not catch on. A simpler hack that allows us to turn regular deep networks into Bayesian deep networks is to activate dropout during prediction time and then make multiple predictions.

In this section, we will be using a simpler dataset than before. Our x values are 20 random values between -5 and 5, and our y values are just the sine function applied to these values.

We start by running the following code:

```
X = np.random.rand(20,1) * 10-5
y = np.sin(X)
```

Our neural network is relatively straightforward, too. Note that Keras does not allow us to make a dropout layer the first layer, therefore we need to add a Dense layer that just passes through the input value. We can achieve this with the following code:

```
from keras.models import Sequential
from keras.layers import Dense, Dropout, Activation

model = Sequential()

model.add(Dense(1,input_dim = 1))
model.add(Dropout(0.05))

model.add(Dense(20))
model.add(Activation('relu'))
model.add(Dropout(0.05))

model.add(Dense(20))
model.add(Activation('relu'))
model.add(Dropout(0.05))

model.add(Dense(20))
model.add(Activation('sigmoid'))

model.add(Dense(1))
```

To fit this function, we need a relatively low learning rate, so we import the Keras vanilla stochastic gradient descent optimizer in order to set the learning rate there. We then train the model for 10,000 epochs. Since we are not interested in the training logs, we set verbose to 0, which makes the model train "quietly."

We do this by running the following:

```
from keras.optimizers import SGD
model.compile(loss='mse',optimizer=SGD(lr=0.01))
model.fit(X,y,epochs=10000,batch_size=10,verbose=0)
```

We want to test our model over a larger range of values, so we create a test dataset with 200 values ranging from -10 to 10 in 0.1 intervals. We can imitate the test by running the following code:

```
X_test = np.arange(-10,10,0.1)
X_test = np.expand_dims(X_test,-1)
```

And now comes the magic trick! Using keras.backend, we can pass settings to TensorFlow, which runs the operations in the background. We use the backend to set the learning phase parameter to 1. This makes TensorFlow believe that we are training, and so it will apply dropout. We then make 100 predictions for our test data. The result of these 100 predictions is a probability distribution for the y value at every instance of X.

Note: For this example to work, you have to load the backend, clear the session, and set the learning phase before defining and training the model, as the training process will leave the setting in the TensorFlow graph. You can also save the trained model, clear the session, and reload the model. See the code for this section for a working implementation.

To start this process, we first run:

```
import keras.backend as K
K.clear_session()
K.set_learning_phase(1)
```

And now we can obtain our distributions with the following code:

```
probs = []
for i in range(100):
    out = model.predict(X_test)
    probs.append(out)
```

Next we can calculate the mean and standard deviation for our distributions:

```
p = np.array(probs)

mean = p.mean(axis=0)
std = p.std(axis=0)
```

Finally, we plot the model's predictions with one, two, and four standard deviations (corresponding to different shades of blue):

```
plt.figure(figsize=(10,7))
plt.plot(X_test,mean,c='blue')

lower_bound = mean - std * 0.5
upper_bound =   mean + std * 0.5
plt.fill_between(X_test.flatten(),upper_bound.flatten(),
lower_bound.flatten(),alpha=0.25, facecolor='blue')

lower_bound = mean - std
upper_bound =   mean + std
plt.fill_between(X_test.flatten(),upper_bound.flatten(),
lower_bound.flatten(),alpha=0.25, facecolor='blue')

lower_bound = mean - std * 2
upper_bound =   mean + std * 2
plt.fill_between(X_test.flatten(),upper_bound.flatten(),
lower_bound.flatten(),alpha=0.25, facecolor='blue')

plt.scatter(X,y,c='black')
```

As a result of running this code, we will see the following graph:

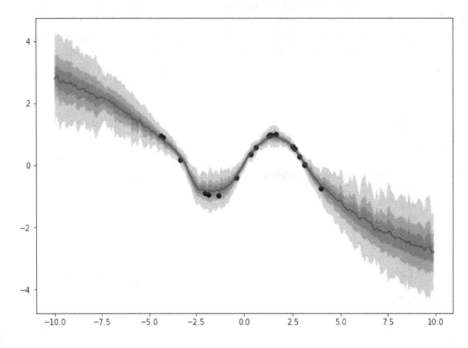

Predictions with uncertainty bands

As you can see, the model is relatively confident around areas where it had data and becomes less and less confident the further away it gets from the data points.

Getting uncertainty estimates from our model increases the value we can get from it. It also helps in improving the model if we can detect where the model is over or under confident. Right now, Bayesian deep learning is only in its infancy, and we will certainly see many advances in the next few years.

Exercises

Now we're at the end of the chapter, why not try some of the following exercises? You'll find guides on how to complete them all throughout this chapter:

- A good trick is to use LSTMs on top of one-dimensional convolution, as one-dimensional convolution can go over large sequences while using fewer parameters. Try to implement an architecture that first uses a few convolutional and pooling layers and then a few LSTM layers. Try it out on the web traffic dataset. Then try adding (recurrent) dropout. Can you beat the LSTM model?

- Add uncertainty to your web traffic forecasts. To do this, remember to run your model with dropout turned on at inference time. You will obtain multiple forecasts for one time step. Think about what this would mean in the context of trading and stock prices.

- Visit the Kaggle datasets page and search for time series data. Make a forecasting model. This involves feature engineering with autocorrelation and Fourier transformation, picking the right model from the ones introduced (for example, ARIMA versus neural networks), and then training your model. A hard task, but you will learn a lot! Any dataset will do, but I suggest that you may want to try the stock market dataset here: `https://www.kaggle.com/szrlee/stock-time-series-20050101-to-20171231`, or the electric power consumption dataset here: `https://www.kaggle.com/uciml/electric-power-consumption-data-set`.

Summary

In this chapter, you learned about a wide range of conventional tools for dealing with time series data. You also learned about one-dimensional convolution and recurrent architectures, and finally, you learned a simple way to get your models to express uncertainty.

Time series are the most iconic form of financial data. This chapter has given you a rich toolbox for dealing with time series. Let's recap all of the things that we've covered on the example of forecasting web traffic for Wikipedia:

- Basic data exploration to understand what we are dealing with

- Fourier transformation and autocorrelation as tools for feature engineering and understanding data

- Using a simple median forecast as a baseline and sanity check

- Understanding and using ARIMA and Kalman filters as classic prediction models

- Designing features, including building a data loading mechanism for all our time series

- Using one-dimensional convolutions and variants such as causal convolutions and dilated convolutions

- Understanding the purpose and use of RNNs and their more powerful variant, LSTMs

- Getting to grips with understanding how to add uncertainty to our forecasts with the dropout trick, taking our first step into Bayesian learning

This rich toolbox of time series techniques comes in especially handy in the next chapter, where we will cover natural language processing. Language is basically a sequence, or time series, of words. This means we can reuse many tools from time series modeling for natural language processing.

In the next chapter, you will learn how to find company names in text, how to group text by topic, and even how to translate text using neural networks.

5
Parsing Textual Data with Natural Language Processing

It's no accident that Peter Brown, Co-CEO of Renaissance Technologies, one of the most successful quantitative hedge funds of all time, had previously worked at IBM, where he applied machine learning to natural language problems.

As we've explored in earlier chapters, in today's world, information drives finance, and the most important source of information is written and spoken language. Ask any finance professional what they are actually spending time on, and you will find that a significant part of their time is spent on reading. This can cover everything from reading headlines on tickers, to reading a Form 10K, the financial press, or various analyst reports; the list goes on and on. Automatically processing this information can increase the speed of trades occurring and widen the breadth of information considered for trades while at the same time reducing overall costs.

Natural language processing (NLP) is making inroads into the finance sector. As an example, insurance companies are increasingly looking to process claims automatically, while retail banks try to streamline their customer service and offer better products to their clients. The understanding of text is increasingly becoming the go-to application of machine learning within the finance sector.

Historically, NLP has relied on hand-crafted rules that were created by linguists. Today, the linguists are being replaced by neural networks that are able to learn the complex, and often hard to codify, rules of language.

In this chapter, you will learn how to build powerful natural language models with Keras, as well as how to use the spaCy NLP library.

The focus of this chapter will be on the following:

- Fine-tuning spaCy's models for your own custom applications
- Finding parts of speech and mapping the grammatical structure of sentences
- Using techniques such as Bag-of-Words and TF-IDF for classification
- Understanding how to build advanced models with the Keras functional API
- Training models to focus with attention, as well as to translate sentences with a sequence to sequence (seq2seq) model

So, let's get started!

An introductory guide to spaCy

spaCy is a library for advanced NLP. The library, which is pretty fast to run, also comes with a range of useful tools and pretrained models that make NLP easier and more reliable. If you've installed Kaggle, you won't need to download spaCy, as it comes preinstalled with all the models.

To use spaCy locally, you will need to install the library and download its pretrained models separately.

To install the library, we simply need to run the following command:

```
$ pip install -U spacy
$ python -m spacy download en
```

Note: This chapter makes use of the English language models, but more are available. Most features are available in English, German, Spanish, Portuguese, French, Italian, and Dutch. Entity recognition is available for many more languages through the multi-language model.

The core of spaCy is made up of the Doc and Vocab classes. A Doc instance contains one document, including its text, tokenized version, and recognized entities. The Vocab class, meanwhile, keeps track of all the common information found across documents.

spaCy is useful for its pipeline features, which contain many of the parts needed for NLP. If this all seems a bit abstract right now, don't worry, as this section will show you how to use spaCy for a wide range of practical tasks.

 You can find the data and code for this section on Kaggle at `https://www.kaggle.com/jannesklaas/analyzing-the-news`.

The data that we'll use for this first section is from a collection of 143,000 articles taken from 15 American publications. The data is spread out over three files. We are going to load them separately, merge them into one large DataFrame, and then delete the individual DataFrames in order to save memory.

To achieve this, we must run:

```
a1 = pd.read_csv('../input/articles1.csv',index_col=0)
a2 = pd.read_csv('../input/articles2.csv',index_col=0)
a3 = pd.read_csv('../input/articles3.csv',index_col=0)

df = pd.concat([a1,a2,a3])

del a1, a2, a3
```

As a result of running the preceding code, the data will end up looking like this:

id	title	publication	author	date	year	month	url	content
17283	House Republicans Fret...	New York Times	Carl Hulse	2016-12-31	2016.0	12.0	NaN	WASHINGTON — Congressional Republicans...

After getting our data to this state, we can then plot the distribution of publishers to get an idea of what kind of news we are dealing with.

To achieve this, we must run the following code:

```
import matplotlib.pyplot as plt
plt.figure(figsize=(10,7))
df.publication.value_counts().plot(kind='bar')
```

After successfully running this code, we'll see this chart showing the distribution of news sources from our dataset:

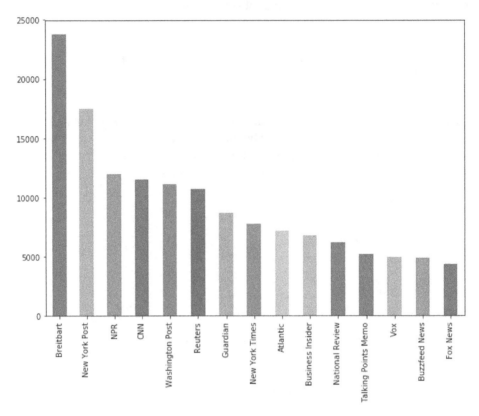

News page distribution

As you can see in the preceding graph the dataset that we extracted contains no articles from classical financial news media, instead it mostly contains articles from mainstream and politically oriented publications.

Named entity recognition

A common task in NLP is **named entity recognition (NER)**. NER is all about finding things that the text explicitly refers to. Before discussing more about what is going on, let's jump right in and do some hands-on NER on the first article in our dataset.

The first thing we need to do is load spaCy, in addition to the model for English language processing:

```
import spacy
nlp = spacy.load('en')
```

Next, we must select the text of the article from our data:

```
text = df.loc[0,'content']
```

Finally, we'll run this piece of text through the English language model pipeline. This will create a `Doc` instance, something we explained earlier on in this chapter. The file will hold a lot of information, including the named entities:

```
doc = nlp(text)
```

One of the best features of spaCy is that it comes with a handy visualizer called `displacy`, which we can use to show the named entities in text. To get the visualizer to generate the display, based on the text from our article, we must run this code:

```
from spacy import displacy
displacy.render(doc,                    #1
                style='ent',            #2
                jupyter=True)           #3
```

With that command now executed, we've done three important things, which are:

1. We've passed the document
2. We have specified that we would like to render entities
3. We let `displacy` know that we are running this in a Jupyter notebook so that rendering works correctly

The output of the previous NER using spaCy tags

And voilà! As you can see, there are a few mishaps, such as blank spaces being classified as organizations, and "Obama" being classified as a place.

So, why has this happened? It's because the tagging has been done by a neural network and neural networks are strongly dependent on the data that they were trained on. So, because of these imperfections, we might find that we need to fine-tune the tagging model for our own purposes, and in a minute, we will see how that works.

You can also see in our output that NER offers a wide range of tags, some of which come with strange abbreviations. For now, don't worry as we will examine a full list of tags later on in this chapter.

Right now, let's answer a different question: what organizations does the news in our dataset write about? To make this exercise run faster, we will create a new pipeline in which we will disable everything but NER.

To find out the answer to this question, we must first run the following code:

```
nlp = spacy.load('en',
                 disable=['parser',
                          'tagger',
                          'textcat'])
```

In the next step, we'll loop over the first 1,000 articles from our dataset, which can be done with the following code:

```
from tqdm import tqdm_notebook

frames = []
for i in tqdm_notebook(range(1000)):
    doc = df.loc[i,'content']                              #1
    text_id = df.loc[i,'id']                               #2
    doc = nlp(doc)                                          #3
    ents = [(e.text, e.start_char, e.end_char, e.label_)   #4
               for e in doc.ents
               if len(e.text.strip(' -—')) > 0]
    frame = pd.DataFrame(ents)                              #5
    frame['id'] = text_id                                  #6
    frames.append(frame)                                   #7

npf = pd.concat(frames)                                    #8

npf.columns = ['Text','Start','Stop','Type','id']          #9
```

The code we've just created has nine key points. Let's take a minute to break it down, so we are confident in understanding what we've just written. Note that in the preceding code, the hashtag, #, refers to the number it relates to in this following list:

1. We get the content of the article at row i.

2. We get the id of the article.
3. We run the article through the pipeline.
4. For all the entities found, we save the text, index of the first and last character, as well as the label. This only happens if the tag consists of more than white spaces and dashes. This removes some of the mishaps we encountered earlier when the classification tagged empty segments or delimiters.
5. We create a pandas DataFrame out of the array of tuples created.
6. We add the id of the article to all records of our named entities.
7. We add the DataFrame containing all the tagged entities of one document to a list. This way, we can build a collection of tagged entities over a larger number of articles.
8. We concatenate all DataFrames in the list, meaning that we create one big table with all tags.
9. For easier use, we give the columns meaningful names

Now that we've done that, the next step is to plot the distribution of the types of entities that we found. This code will produce a chart which can be created with the following code:

```
npf.Type.value_counts().plot(kind='bar')
```

The output of the code being this graph:

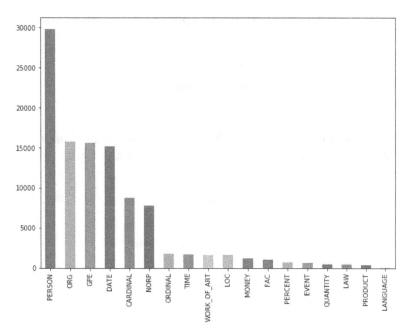

spaCy tag distribution

After seeing the preceding graph, it is a fair question to ask which categories spaCy can identify and where they come from. The English language NER that comes with spaCy is a neural network trained on the *OntoNotes 5.0 corpus*, meaning it can recognize the following categories:

- **PERSON**: People, including fictional characters
- **ORG**: Companies, agencies, institutions
- **GPE**: Places including countries, cities, and states
- **DATE**: Absolute (for example, January 2017) or relative dates (for example, two weeks)
- **CARDINAL**: Numerals that are not covered by other types
- **NORP**: Nationalities or religious or political groups
- **ORDINAL**: "first," "second," and so on
- **TIME**: Times shorter than a day (for example, two hours)
- **WORK_OF_ART**: Titles of books, songs, and so on
- **LOC**: Locations that are not GPEs, for example, mountain ranges or streams
- **MONEY**: Monetary values
- **FAC**: Facilities such as airports, highways or bridges
- **PERCENT**: Percentages
- **EVENT**: Named hurricanes, battles, sporting events, and so on
- **QUANTITY**: Measurements such as weights or distance
- **LAW**: Named documents that are laws
- **PRODUCT**: Objects, vehicles, food, and so on
- **LANGUAGE**: Any named language

Using this list, we will now look at the 15 most frequently named organizations, categorized as ORG. As part of this, we will produce a similar graph showing us that information.

To get the graph, we must run the following:

```
orgs = npf[npf.Type == 'ORG']
orgs.Text.value_counts()[:15].plot(kind='bar')
```

The resulting code will give us the following graph:

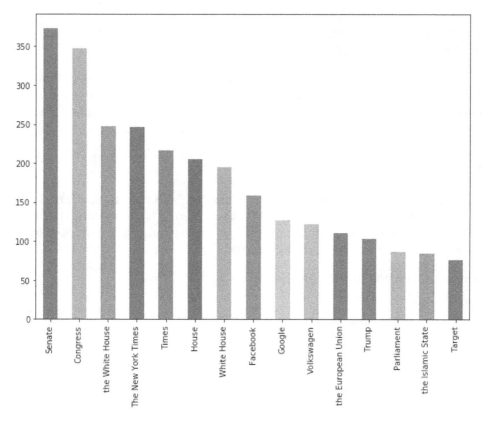

spaCy organization distance

As you can see, political institutions such as the *senate* are most frequently named in our news dataset. Likewise, some companies, such as *Volkswagen*, that were in the center of media attention can also be found in the chart. Take a minute to also notice how **the White House** and **White House** are listed as two separate organizations, despite us knowing they are the same entity.

Depending on your needs, you might want to do some post-processing, such as removing "the" from organization names. Python comes with a built-in string replacement method that you can use with pandas. This would allow you to achieve post-processing. However, this is not something we will cover in depth here.

Should you want to look at it in more detail, you can get the documentation and example from the following link: `https://pandas.pydata.org/pandas-docs/stable/generated/pandas.Series.str.replace.html`

Also, note how **Trump** is shown here as an organization. However, if you look at the tagged text, you will also see that "Trump" is tagged several times as an NORP, a political organization. This has happened because the NER infers the type of tag from the context. Since Trump is the U.S. president, his name often gets used in the same context as (political) organizations.

This pretrained NER gives you a powerful tool that can solve many common NLP tasks. So, in reality, from here you could conduct all kinds of other investigations. For example, we could fork the notebook to see whether The New York Times is mentioned as different entities more often than the Washington Post or Breitbart.

Fine-tuning the NER

A common issue you may find is that the pretrained NER does not perform well enough on the specific types of text that you want it to work with. To solve this problem, you will need to fine-tune the NER model by training it with custom data. Achieving this will be the focus of this section.

The training data you're using should be in a form like this:

```
TRAIN_DATA = [
    ('Who is Shaka Khan?', {
        'entities': [(7, 17, 'PERSON')]
    }),
    ('I like London and Berlin.', {
        'entities': [(7, 13, 'LOC'), (18, 24, 'LOC')]
    })
]
```

As you can see, you provide a list of tuples of the string, together with the start and end points, as well as the types of entities you want to tag. Data such as this is usually collected through manual tagging, often on platforms such as Amazon's **Mechanical Turk (MTurk)**.

The company behind spaCy, Explosion AI, also make a (paid) data tagging system called *Prodigy*, which enables efficient data collection. Once you have collected enough data, you can either fine-tune a pretrained model or initialize a completely new model.

To load and fine-tune a model, we need to use the `load()` function:

```
nlp = spacy.load('en')
```

Alternatively, to create a new and empty model from scratch that is ready for the English language, use the `blank` function:

```
nlp = spacy.blank('en')
```

Either way, we need to get access to the NER component. If you have created a blank model, you'll need to create an NER pipeline component and add it to the model.

If you have loaded an existing model, you can just access its existing NER by running the following code:

```
if 'ner' not in nlp.pipe_names:
    ner = nlp.create_pipe('ner')
    nlp.add_pipe(ner, last=True)
else:
    ner = nlp.get_pipe('ner')
```

The next step is to ensure that our NER can recognize the labels we have. Imagine our data contained a new type of named entity such as ANIMAL. With the add_label function, we can add a label type to an NER.

The code to achieve this can be seen below, but don't worry if it doesn't make sense right now, we'll break it down on the next page:

```
for _, annotations in TRAIN_DATA:
    for ent in annotations.get('entities'):
        ner.add_label(ent[2])
import random


                                                            #1
other_pipes = [pipe for pipe in nlp.pipe_names if pipe != 'ner']

with nlp.disable_pipes(*other_pipes):
    optimizer = nlp._optimizer                              #2
    if not nlp._optimizer:
        optimizer = nlp.begin_training()
    for itn in range(5):                                    #3
        random.shuffle(TRAIN_DATA)                          #4
        losses = {} #5
        for text, annotations in TRAIN_DATA:                #6
            nlp.update(                                     #7
                [text],
                [annotations],
                drop=0.5,                                   #8
                sgd=optimizer,                              #9
                losses=losses)                              #10
        print(losses)
```

What we've just written is made up of 10 key elements:

1. We disable all pipeline components that are not the NER by first getting a list of all the components that are not the NER and then disabling them for training.
2. Pretrained models come with an optimizer. If you have a blank model, you will need to create a new optimizer. Note that this also resets the model weights.
3. We now train for a number of epochs, in this case, 5.
4. At the beginning of each epoch, we shuffle the training data using Python's built-in `random` module.
5. We create an empty dictionary to keep track of the losses.
6. We then loop over the text and annotations in the training data.
7. `nlp.update` performs one forward and backward pass, and updates the neural network weights. We need to supply text and annotations, so that the function can figure out how to train a network from it.
8. We can manually specify the dropout rate we want to use while training.
9. We pass a stochastic gradient descent optimizer that performs the model updates. Note that you cannot just pass a Keras or TensorFlow optimizer here, as spaCy has its own optimizers.
10. We can also pass a dictionary to write losses that we can later print to monitor progress.

Once you've run the code, the output should look something like this:

```
{'ner': 5.0091189558407585}
{'ner': 3.9693684224622108}
{'ner': 3.984836024903589}
{'ner': 3.457960373417813}
{'ner': 2.570318400714134}
```

What you are seeing is the loss value of a part of the spaCy pipeline, in this case, the **named entity recognition** (**NER**) engine. Similar to the cross-entropy loss we discussed in previous chapters, the actual value is hard to interpret and does not tell you very much. What matters here is that the loss is decreasing over time and that it reaches a value much lower than the initial loss.

Part-of-speech (POS) tagging

On Tuesday, October 10, 2017, between 9:34 AM and 9:36 AM, the US Dow Jones newswire encountered a technical error that resulted in it posting some strange headlines. One of them was, "Google to buy Apple." These four words managed to send Apple stock up over two percent.

The algorithmic trading systems obviously failed here to understand that such an acquisition would be impossible as Apple had a market capitalization of $800 billion at the time, coupled with the fact that the move would likely not find regulatory approval.

So, the question arises, why did the trading algorithms choose to buy stock based on these four words? The answer is through **part-of-speech** (**POS**) tagging. POS tagging allows an understanding of which words take which function in a sentence and how the words relate to each other.

spaCy comes with a handy, pretrained POS tagger. In this section we're going to apply this to the Google/Apple news story. To start the POS tagger, we need to run the following code:

```
import spacy
from spacy import displacy
nlp = spacy.load('en')

doc = 'Google to buy Apple'
doc = nlp(doc)
displacy.render(doc,style='dep',jupyter=True,
options={'distance':120})
```

Again, we will load the pretrained English model and run our sentence through it. Then we'll use `displacy` just as we did for NER.

To make the graphics fit better in this book, we will set the `distance` option to something shorter than the default, in this case, 1,120, so that words get displayed closer together, as we can see in the following diagram:

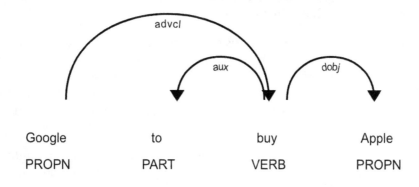

spaCy POS tagger

As you can see, the POS tagger identified **buy** as a verb and **Google** and **Apple** as the nouns in the sentence. It also identified that **Apple** is the object the action is applied to and that **Google** is applying the action.

We can access this information for nouns through this code:

```
nlp = spacy.load('en')
doc = 'Google to buy Apple'
doc = nlp(doc)

for chunk in doc.noun_chunks:
    print(chunk.text, chunk.root.text, chunk.root.dep_,
chunk.root.head.text)
```

After running the preceding code, we get the following table featured as the result:

Text	Root Text	Root dep	Root Head Text
Google	Google	ROOT	Google
Apple	Apple	dobj	buy

In our example, Google is the root of the sentence, while Apple is the object of the sentence. The verb applied to Apple is "buy."

From there, it is only a hard-coded model of price developments under an acquisition (demand for the target stock goes up and with it the price) and a stock lookup table to a simple event-driven trading algorithm. Making these algorithms understand the context and plausibility is another story, however.

Rule-based matching

Before deep learning and statistical modeling took over, NLP was all about rules. That's not to say that rule-based systems are dead! They are often easy to set up and perform very well when it comes to doing simple tasks.

Imagine you wanted to find all mentions of Google in a text. Would you really train a neural network-based named entity recognizer? If you did, you would have to run all of the text through the neural network and then look for Google in the entity texts. Alternatively, would you rather just search for text that exactly matches Google with a classic search algorithm? Well, we're in luck, as spaCy comes with an easy-to-use, rule-based matcher that allows us to do just that.

Before we start this section, we first must make sure that we reload the English language model and import the matcher. This is a very simple task that can be done by running the following code:

```
import spacy
from spacy.matcher import Matcher

nlp = spacy.load('en')
```

The matcher searches for patterns, which we encode as a list of dictionaries. It operates token by token, that is, word for word, except for punctuation and numbers, where a single symbol can be a token.

As a starting example, let's search for the phrase "hello, world." To do this, we would define a pattern as follows:

```
pattern = [{'LOWER': 'hello'}, {'IS_PUNCT': True},
{'LOWER': 'world'}]
```

This pattern is fulfilled if the lower case first token is `hello`. The `LOWER` attribute checks if both words would match if they were both converted to lowercase. That means if the actual token text is "Hello" or "HELLO," then it would also fulfill the requirement. The second token has to be punctuation to pick up the comma, so the phrases "hello. world" or "hello! world" would both work, but not "hello world."

The lower case of the third token has to be "world," so "WoRlD" would also be fine.

The possible attributes for a token can be the following:

- `ORTH`: The token text has to match exactly
- `LOWER`: The lower case of the token has to match
- `LENGTH`: The length of the token text has to match
- `IS_ALPHA`, `IS_ASCII`, `IS_DIGIT`: The token text has to consist of alphanumeric characters, ASCII symbols, or digits
- `IS_LOWER`, `IS_UPPER`, `IS_TITLE`: The token text has to be lower case, upper case, or title case
- `IS_PUNCT`, `IS_SPACE`, `IS_STOP`: The token text has to be punctuation, white space, or a stop word
- `LIKE_NUM`, `LIKE_URL`, `LIKE_EMAIL`: The token has to resemble a number, URL, or email
- `POS`, `TAG`, `DEP`, `LEMMA`, `SHAPE`: The token's position, tag, dependency, lemma, or shape has to match
- `ENT_TYPE`: The token's entity type from NER has to match

spaCy's lemmatization is extremely useful. A lemma is the base version of a word. For example, "was" is a version of "be," so "be" is the lemma for "was" but also for "is." spaCy can lemmatize words in context, meaning it uses the surrounding words to determine what the actual base version of a word is.

To create a matcher, we have to pass on the vocabulary the matcher works on. In this case, we can just pass the vocabulary of our English language model by running the following:

```
matcher = Matcher(nlp.vocab)
```

In order to add the required attributes to our matcher, we must call the following:

```
matcher.add('HelloWorld', None, pattern)
```

The `add` function expects three arguments. The first is a name of the pattern, in this case, `HelloWorld`, so that we can keep track of the patterns we added. The second is a function that can process matches once found. Here we pass `None`, meaning no function will be applied, though we will use this tool later. Finally, we need to pass the list of token attributes we want to search for.

To use our matcher, we can simply call `matcher(doc)`. This will give us back all the matches that the matcher found. We can call this by running the following:

```
doc = nlp(u'Hello, world! Hello world!')
matches = matcher(doc)
```

If we print out the matches, we can see the structure:

```
matches
```

```
[(15578876784678163569, 0, 3)]
```

The first thing in a match is the hash of the string found. This is just to identify what was found internally; we won't use it here. The next two numbers indicate the range in which the matcher found something, here tokens 0 to 3.

We can get the text back by indexing the original document:

```
doc[0:3]
```

```
Hello, world
```

In the next section we will look at how we can add custom functions to matchers.

Adding custom functions to matchers

Let's move on to a more complex case. We know that the iPhone is a product. However, the neural network-based matcher often classifies it as an organization. This happens because the word "iPhone" gets used a lot in a similar context as organizations, as in "The iPhone offers..." or "The iPhone sold...."

Let's build a rule-based matcher that always classifies the word "iPhone" as a product entity.

First, we have to get the hash of the word PRODUCT. Words in spaCy can be uniquely identified by their hash. Entity types also get identified by their hash. To set an entity of the product type, we have to be able to provide the hash for the entity name.

We can get the name from the language model's vocabulary by running the following:

```
PRODUCT = nlp.vocab.strings['PRODUCT']
```

Next, we need to define an on_match rule. This function will be called every time the matcher finds a match. on_match rules have four arguments:

- matcher: The matcher that made the match.
- doc: The document the match was made in.
- i: The index of a match. The first match in a document would have index zero, the second would have index one, and so on.
- matches: A list of all matches made.

There are two things happening in our on_match rule:

```
def add_product_ent(matcher, doc, i, matches):
    match_id, start, end = matches[i]          #1
    doc.ents += ((PRODUCT, start, end),)       #2
```

Let's break down what they are:

1. We index all matches to find our match at index i. One match is a tuple of a match_id, the start of the match, and the end of the match.

2. We add a new entity to the document's named entities. An entity is a tuple of the hash of the type of entity (the hash of the word PRODUCT here), the start of the entity, and the end of the entity. To append an entity, we have to nest it in another tuple. Tuples that only contain one value need to include a comma at the end. It is important not to overwrite doc.ents, as we otherwise would remove all the entities that we have already found.

Now that we have an on_match rule, we can define our matcher.

We should note that matchers allow us to add multiple patterns, so we can add a matcher for just the word "iPhone" and another pattern for the word "iPhone" together with a version number, as in "iPhone 5":

```
pattern1 = [{'LOWER': 'iPhone'}]                        #1
pattern2 = [{'ORTH': 'iPhone'}, {'IS_DIGIT': True}]     #2

matcher = Matcher(nlp.vocab)                            #3
matcher.add('iPhone', add_product_ent,pattern1, pattern2) #4
```

So, what makes these commands work?

1. We define the first pattern.
2. We define the second pattern.

3. We create a new empty matcher.

4. We add the patterns to the matcher. Both will fall under the rule called iPhone, and both will call our on_match rule called add_product_ent.

We will now pass one of the news articles through the matcher:

```
doc = nlp(df.content.iloc[14])          #1
matches = matcher(doc)                   #2
```

This code is relatively simple, with only two steps:

1. We run the text through the pipeline to create an annotated document.

2. We run the document through the matcher. This modifies the document created in the step before. We do not care as much about the matches but more about how the on_match method adds the matches as entities to our documents.

Now that the matcher is set up, we need to add it to the pipeline so that spaCy can use it automatically. This will be the focus in the next section.

Adding the matcher to the pipeline

Calling the matcher separately is somewhat cumbersome. To add it to the pipeline, we have to wrap it into a function, which we can achieve by running the following:

```
def matcher_component(doc):
    matches = matcher(doc)
    return doc
```

The spaCy pipeline calls the components of the pipeline as functions and always expects the annotated document to be returned. Returning anything else could break the pipeline.

We can then add the matcher to the main pipeline, as can be seen in the following code:

```
nlp.add_pipe(matcher_component, last=True)
```

The matcher is now the last piece of the pipeline. From this point onward iPhones will now get tagged based on the matcher's rules.

And boom! All mentions of the word "iPhone" (case independent) are now tagged as named entities of the product type. You can validate this by displaying the entities with displacy as we have done in the following code:

```
displacy.render(doc, style='ent', jupyter=True)
```

The results of that code can be seen in the following screenshot:

services, as well as uncommon surfaces on which to enlarge photos for display, be it burlap, wood boards, acrylic or fabric. Why not try some fresh sites and methods? I recently sent some `ORG`
quality `iPhone` `PRODUCT` vacation photos to a handful of companies that I'd never used before and had them enlarged to various sizes and printed on different surfaces. I've also offered some
guidance about bulk digitizing those boxes of old travel photos sitting in your closet or basement so that you can begin `the New Year` `EVENT` if not with a vacation, then with a `ORG` home. Of
all the ways to turn photos into wall art, I was most interested in trying engineer prints, named for the large, lightweight prints used by architects. For less than the cost of a couple of movie tickets,
you can make huge enlargements. Mind you, it's a particular aesthetic, one that's most likely to appeal to people who are after an industrial, shabby chic or bohemian look. The paper is thin and the

spaCy now finds the iPhone as a product

Combining rule-based and learning-based systems

One especially interesting aspect of spaCy's pipeline system is that it is relatively easy to combine different aspects of it. We can, for example, combine neural network-based named entity recognition with a rule-based matcher in order to find something such as executive compensation information.

Executive compensation is often reported in the press but hard to find in aggregate. One possible rule-based matching pattern for executive compensation could look like this:

```
pattern = [{'ENT_TYPE':'PERSON'},
           {'LEMMA':'receive'},
           {'ENT_TYPE':'MONEY'}]
```

A matcher looking for this pattern would pick up any combination of a person's name, for example, John Appleseed, or Daniel; any version of the word receive, for example, received, receives, and so on; followed by an expression of money, for example, $4 million.

This matcher could be run over a large text corpus with the on_match rule handily saving the found snippets into a database. The machine learning approach for naming entities and the rule-based approach go hand in hand seamlessly.

Since there is much more training data available with annotations for names and money, rather than statements about executive education, it is much easier to combine the NER with a rule-based method rather than training a new NER.

Regular expressions

Regular expressions, or regexes, are a powerful form of rule-based matching. Invented back in the 1950s, they were, for a very long time, the most useful way to find things in text and proponents argue that they still are.

No chapter on NLP would be complete without mentioning regexes. With that being said, this section is by no means a complete regex tutorial. It's intended to introduce the general idea and show how regexes can be used in Python, pandas, and spaCy.

A very simple regex pattern could be "a." This would only find instances of the lower-case letter a followed by a dot. However, regexes also allow you to add ranges of patterns; for example, "[a-z]." would find any lower-case letter followed by a dot, and "xy." would find only the letters "x" or "y" followed by a dot.

Regex patterns are case sensitive, so "A-Z" would only capture upper-case letters. This is useful if we are searching for expressions in which the spelling is frequently different; for example, the pattern "seriali[sz]e" would catch the British as well as the American English version of the word.

The same goes for numbers. "0-9" captures all numbers from 0 to 9. To find repetitions, you can use "*," which captures zero or more occurrences, or "+," which captures one or more occurrences. For example, "[0-9]+" would capture any series of numbers, which might be useful when looking for years. While "[A-Z][a-z] + [0-9] +," for example, would find all words starting with a capital letter followed by one or more digit, such as "March 2018" but also "Jaws 2."

Curly brackets can be used to define the number of repetitions. For instance, "[0-9] {4}" would find number sequences with exactly four digits. As you can see, a regex does not make any attempt to understand what is in the text, but rather offers a clever method of finding text that matches patterns.

A practical use case in the financial industry is finding the VAT number of companies in invoices. These follow a pretty strict pattern in most countries that can easily be encoded. VAT numbers in the Netherlands, for example, follow this regex pattern: "NL[0-9]{9}B[0-9]{2}".

Using Python's regex module

Python has a built-in tool for regexes called `re`. While it does not need to be installed because it is part of Python itself, we can import it with the following code:

```
import re
```

Imagine we are working on an automatic invoice processor, and we want to find the VAT number of the company that sent us the invoice. For simplicity's sake, we're going to only deal with Dutch VAT numbers (the Dutch for "VAT" is "BTW"). As mentioned before, we know the pattern for a Dutch VAT number is as follows:

```
pattern = 'NL[0-9]{9}B[0-9]{2}'
```

A string for finding a BTW number might look like this:

```
my_string = 'ING Bank N.V. BTW:NL003028112B01'
```

So, to find all the occurrences of a BTW number in the string, we can call `re.findall`, which will return a list of all strings matching the pattern found. To call this, we simply run:

```
re.findall(pattern,my_string)
```

```
['NL003028112B01']
```

`re` also allows the passing of flags to make the development of regex patterns a bit easier. For example, to ignore the case of letters when matching a regular expression, we can add a `re.IGNORECASE` flag, like we've done here:

```
re.findall(pattern,my_string, flags=re.IGNORECASE)
```

Often, we are interested in a bit more information about our matches. To this end, there is a `match` object. `re.search` yields a `match` object for the first match found:

```
match = re.search(pattern,my_string)
```

We can get more information out of this object, such as the location of our match, simply by running:

```
match.span()
```

```
(18, 32)
```

The span, the start and the end of our match, is the characters 18 to 32.

Regex in pandas

The data for NLP problems often comes in pandas DataFrames. Luckily for us, pandas natively supports regex. If, for example, we want to find out whether any of the articles in our news dataset contain a Dutch BTW number, then we can pass the following code:

```
df[df.content.str.contains(pattern)]
```

This would yield all the articles that include a Dutch BTW number, but unsurprisingly no articles in our dataset do.

When to use regexes and when not to

A regex is a powerful tool, and this very short introduction does not do it justice. In fact, there are several books longer than this one written purely on the topic of regexes. However, for the purpose of this book, we're only going to briefly introduce you to the topic.

A regex, as a tool, works well on simple and clear-to-define patterns. VAT/BTW numbers are a perfect example, as are email addresses and phone numbers, both of which are very popular use cases for regexes. However, a regex fails when the pattern is hard to define or if it can only be inferred from context. It is not possible to create a rule-based named entity recognizer that can spot that a word refers to the name of a person, because names follow no clear distinguishing pattern.

So, the next time you are looking to find something that is easy to spot for a human but hard to describe in rules, use a machine learning-based solution. Likewise, the next time you are looking for something clearly encoded, such as a VAT number, use regexes.

A text classification task

A common NLP task is to classify text. The most common text classification is done in sentiment analysis, where texts are classified as positive or negative. In this section, we will consider a slightly harder problem, classifying whether a tweet is about an actual disaster happening or not.

Today, investors have developed a number of ways to gain information from tweets. Twitter users are often faster than news outlets to report disasters, such as a fire or a flood. In the case of finance, this speed advantage can be used and translated to event-driven trading strategies.

However, not all tweets that contain words associated with disasters are actually about disasters. A tweet such as, "California forests on fire near San Francisco" is a tweet that should be taken into consideration, whereas "California this weekend was on fire, good times in San Francisco" can safely be ignored.

The goal of the task here is to build a classifier that separates the tweets that relate to real disasters from irrelevant tweets. The dataset that we are using consists of hand-labeled tweets that were obtained by searching Twitter for words common to disaster tweets such as "ablaze" or "fire."

 Note: In preparation for this section, the code and data can be found on Kaggle at https://www.kaggle.com/jannesklaas/nlp-disasters.

Preparing the data

Preparing the text is a task in its own right. This is because in the real world, text is often messy and cannot be fixed with a few simple scaling operations. For instance, people can often make typos after adding unnecessary characters as they are adding text encodings that we cannot read. NLP involves its own set of data cleaning challenges and techniques.

Sanitizing characters

To store text, computers need to encode the characters into bits. There are several different ways to do this, and not all of them can deal with all the characters out there.

It is good practice to keep all the text files in one encoding scheme, usually UTF-8, but of course, that does not always happen. Files might also be corrupted, meaning that a few bits are off, therefore rendering some characters unreadable. Therefore, before we do anything else, we need to sanitize our inputs.

Python offers a helpful `codecs` library, which allows us to deal with different encodings. Our data is UTF-8 encoded, but there are a few special characters in there that cannot be read easily. Therefore, we have to sanitize our text of these special characters, which we can do by running the following:

```
import codecs
input_file = codecs.open('../input/socialmedia-disaster-tweets-
DFE.csv',
                         'r',',
                         encoding='utf-8',
                         errors='replace')
```

In the preceding code, `codecs.open` acts as a stand-in replacement for Python's standard file opening function. It returns a file object, which we can later read line by line. We specify the input path that we want to read the file (with `r`), the expected encoding, and what to do with errors. In this case, we are going to replace the errors with a special unreadable character marker.

To write to the output file, we can just use Python's standard `open()` function. This function will create a file at the specified file path we can write to:

```
output_file = open('clean_socialmedia-disaster.csv', 'w')
```

Now that's done, all we have to do is loop over the lines in our input file that we read with our `codecs` reader and save it as a regular CSV file again. We can achieve this by running the following:

```
for line in input_file:
    out = line
    output_file.write(line)
```

Likewise, it's good practice to close the file objects afterward, which we can do by running:

```
input_file.close()
output_file.close()
```

Now we can read the sanitized CSV file with pandas:

```
df = pd.read_csv('clean_socialmedia-disaster.csv')
```

Lemmatization

Lemmas have already made several appearances throughout this chapter. A lemma in the field of linguistics, also called a headword, is the word under which the set of related words or forms appears in a dictionary. For example, "was" and "is" appear under "be," "mice" appears under "mouse," and so on. Quite often, the specific form of a word does not matter very much, so it can be a good idea to convert all your text into its lemma form.

spaCy offers a handy way to lemmatize text, so once again, we're going to load a spaCy pipeline. Only that in this case, we don't need any pipeline module aside from the tokenizer. The tokenizer splits the text into separate words, usually by spaces. These individual words, or tokens, can then be used to look up their lemma. In our case, it looks like this:

```
import spacy
nlp = spacy.load('en',disable=['tagger','parser','ner'])
```

Lemmatization can be slow, especially for big files, so it makes sense to track our progress. `tqdm` allows us to show progress bars on the pandas `apply` function. All we have to do is import `tqdm` as well as the notebook component for pretty rendering in our work environment. We then have to tell `tqdm` that we would like to use it with pandas. We can do this by running the following:

```
from tqdm import tqdm, tqdm_notebook
tqdm.pandas(tqdm_notebook)
```

We can now run `progress_apply` on a DataFrame just as we would use the standard `apply` method, but here it has a progress bar.

For each row, we loop over the words in the `text` column and save the lemma of the word in a new `lemmas` column:

```
df['lemmas'] = df["text"].progress_apply(lambda row:
[w.lemma_ for w in nlp(row)])
```

Our `lemmas` column is now full of lists, so to turn the lists back into text, we will join all of the elements of the lists with a space as a separator, as we can see in the following code:

```
df['joint_lemmas'] = df['lemmas'].progress_apply
(lambda row: ' '.join(row))
```

Preparing the target

There are several possible prediction targets in this dataset. In our case, humans were asked to rate a tweet, and, they were given three options, `Relevant`, `Not Relevant`, and `Can't Decide`, as the lemmatized text shows:

```
df.choose_one.unique()
array(['Relevant', 'Not Relevant', "Can't Decide"], dtype=object)
```

The tweets where humans cannot decide whether it is about a real disaster are not interesting to us. Therefore, we will just remove the category, *Can't Decide*, which we can do in the following code:

```
df = df[df.choose_one != "Can't Decide"]
```

We are also only interested in mapping text to relevance, therefore we can drop all the other metadata and just keep these two columns, which we do here:

```
df = df[['text','choose_one']]
```

Finally, we're going to convert the target into numbers. This is a binary classification task, as there are only two categories. So, we map `Relevant` to 1 and `Not Relevant` to 0:

```
f['relevant'] = df.choose_one.map({'Relevant':1,'Not Relevant':0})
```

Preparing the training and test sets

Before we start building models, we're going to split our data into two sets, the training dataset and the test dataset. To do this we simply need to run the following code:

```
from sklearn.model_selection import train_test_split
X_train, X_test, y_train, y_test = train_test_split(df['joint_
lemmas'],
                                                    df['relevant'],
                                                    test_size=0.2,
                                                    random_state=42)
```

Bag-of-words

A simple yet effective way of classifying text is to see the text as a bag-of-words. This means that we do not care for the order in which words appear in the text, instead we only care about which words appear in the text.

One of the ways of doing a bag-of-words classification is by simply counting the occurrences of different words from within a text. This is done with a so-called **count vector**. Each word has an index, and for each text, the value of the count vector at that index is the number of occurrences of the word that belong to the index.

Picture this as an example: the count vector for the text "I see cats and dogs and elephants" could look like this:

i	see	cats	and	dogs	elephants
1	1	1	2	1	1

In reality, count vectors are pretty sparse. There are about 23,000 different words in our text corpus, so it makes sense to limit the number of words we want to include in our count vectors. This could mean excluding words that are often just gibberish or typos with no meaning. As a side note, if we kept all the rare words, this could be a source of overfitting.

We are using `sklearn`'s built-in count vectorizer. By setting `max_features`, we can control how many words we want to consider in our count vector. In this case, we will only consider the 10,000 most frequent words:

```
from sklearn.feature_extraction.text import CountVectorizer
count_vectorizer = CountVectorizer(max_features=10000)
```

Our count vectorizer can now transform texts into count vectors. Each count vector will have 10,000 dimensions:

```
X_train_counts = count_vectorizer.fit_transform(X_train)
X_test_counts = count_vectorizer.transform(X_test)
```

Once we have obtained our count vectors, we can then perform a simple logistic regression on them. While we could use Keras for logistic regression, as we did in the first chapter of this book, it is often easier to just use the logistic regression class from scikit-learn:

```
from sklearn.linear_model import LogisticRegression
clf = LogisticRegression()

clf.fit(X_train_counts, y_train)

y_predicted = clf.predict(X_test_counts)
```

Now that we have predictions from our logistic regressor, we can measure the accuracy of it with `sklearn`:

```
from sklearn.metrics import accuracy_score
accuracy_score(y_test, y_predicted)
```

```
0.8011049723756906
```

As you can see, we've got 80% accuracy, which is pretty decent for such a simple method. A simple count vector-based classification is useful as a baseline for more advanced methods, which we will be discussing later.

TF-IDF

TF-IDF stands for **Term Frequency, Inverse Document Frequency**. It aims to address a problem of simple word counting, that being words that frequently appear in a text are important, while words that appear in *all* texts are not important.

The TF component is just like a count vector, except that TF divides the counts by the total number of words in a text. Meanwhile, the IDF component is the logarithm of the total number of texts in the entire corpus divided by the number of texts that include a specific word.

TF-IDF is the product of these two measurements. TF-IDF vectors are like count vectors, except they contain the TF-IDF scores instead of the counts. Rare words will gain a high score in the TF-IDF vector.

We create TF-IDF vectors just as we created count vectors with `sklearn`:

```
from sklearn.feature_extraction.text import TfidfVectorizer
tfidf_vectorizer = TfidfVectorizer()

X_train_tfidf = tfidf_vectorizer.fit_transform(X_train)
X_test_tfidf = tfidf_vectorizer.transform(X_test)
```

Once we have the TF-IDF vectors, we can train a logistic regressor on them just like we did for count vectors:

```
clf_tfidf = LogisticRegression()
clf_tfidf.fit(X_train_tfidf, y_train)

y_predicted = clf_tfidf.predict(X_test_tfidf)
```

In this case, TF-IDF does slightly worse than count vectors. However, because the performance difference is very small, this poorer performance might be attributable to chance in this case:

```
accuracy_score(y_pred=y_predicted, y_true=y_test)
```

```
0.7978821362799263
```

Topic modeling

A final, very useful application of word counting is topic modeling. Given a set of texts, are we able to find clusters of topics? The method to do this is called **Latent Dirichlet Allocation (LDA)**.

> **Note**: The code and data for this section can be found on Kaggle at `https://www.kaggle.com/jannesklaas/topic-modeling-with-lda`.

While the name is quite a mouth full, the algorithm is a very useful one, so we will look at it step by step. LDA makes the following assumption about how texts are written:

1. First, a topic distribution is chosen, say 70% machine learning and 30% finance.

2. Second, the distribution of words for each topic is chosen. For example, the topic "machine learning" might be made up of 20% the word "tensor," 10% the word "gradient," and so on. This means that our topic distribution is a *distribution of distributions*, also called a Dirichlet distribution.

3. Once the text gets written, two probabilistic decisions are made for each word: first, a topic is chosen from the distribution of topics in the document. Then, a word is chosen for the distribution of words in that document.

Note that not all documents in a corpus have the same distribution of topics. We need to specify a fixed number of topics. In the learning process, we start out by assigning each word in the corpus randomly to one topic. For each document, we then calculate the following:

$$p(t \mid d)$$

The preceding formula is the probability of each topic, *t*, to be included in document *d*. For each word, we then calculate:

$$p(w \mid t)$$

That is the probability of a word, *w*, to belong to a topic, *t*. We then assign the word to a new topic, *t*, with the following probability:

$$p(t \mid d) * p(w \mid t)$$

In other words, we assume that all of the words are already correctly assigned to a topic except for the word currently under consideration. We then try to assign words to topics to make documents more homogenous in their topic distribution. This way, words that actually belong to a topic cluster together.

Scikit-learn offers an easy-to-use LDA tool that will help us achieve this. To use this, we must first create a new LDA analyzer and specify the number of topics, called components that we expect.

This can be done by simply running the following:

```
from sklearn.decomposition import LatentDirichletAllocation
lda = LatentDirichletAllocation(n_components=2)
```

We then create count vectors, just as we did for the bag-of-words analysis. For LDA, it is important to remove frequent words that don't mean anything, such as "an" or "the," so-called stop words. CountVectorizer comes with a built-in stopword dictionary that removes these words automatically. To use this, we'll need to run the following code:

```
from sklearn.feature_extraction.text import TfidfVectorizer,
CountVectorizer
vectorizer = CountVectorizer(stop_words='english')
tf = vectorizer.fit_transform(df['joint_lemmas'])
```

Next, we fit the LDA to the count vectors:

```
lda.fit(tf)
```

To inspect our results, we can print out the most frequent words for each topic. To this end, we first need to specify the number of words per topic we want to print, in this case 5. We also need to extract the mapping word count vector indices to words:

```
n_top_words = 5
tf_feature_names = vectorizer.get_feature_names()
```

Now we can loop over the topics of the LDA, in order to print the most frequent words:

```
for topic_idx, topic in enumerate(lda.components_):
        message = "Topic #%d: " % topic_idx
        message += " ".join([tf_feature_names[i]
                            for i in topic.argsort()[:-
n_top_words - 1:-1]])
        print(message)
Topic #0: http news bomb kill disaster
Topic #1: pron http like just https
```

As you can see, the LDA seems to have discovered the grouping into serious tweets and non-serious ones by itself without being given the targets.

This method is very useful for classifying news articles, too. Back in the world of finance, investors might want to know if there is a news article mentioning a risk factor they are exposed to. The same goes for support requests for consumer-facing organizations, which can be clustered this way.

Word embeddings

The order of words in a text matters. Therefore, we can expect higher performance if we do not just look at texts in aggregate but see them as a sequence. This section makes use of a lot of the techniques discussed in the previous chapter; however, here we're going to add a critical ingredient, word vectors.

Words and word tokens are categorical features. As such, we cannot directly feed them into a neural network. Previously, we have dealt with categorical data by turning it into one-hot encoded vectors. Yet for words, this is impractical. Since our vocabulary is 10,000 words, each vector would contain 10,000 numbers that are all zeros except for one. This is highly inefficient, so instead, we will use an embedding.

In practice, embeddings work like a lookup table. For each token, they store a vector. When the token is given to the embedding layer, it returns the vector for that token and passes it through the neural network. As the network trains, the embeddings get optimized as well.

Remember that neural networks work by calculating the derivative of the loss function with respect to the parameters (weights) of the model. Through backpropagation, we can also calculate the derivative of the loss function with respect to the input of the model. Thus we can optimize the embeddings to deliver ideal inputs that help our model.

Preprocessing for training with word vectors

Before we start with training word embeddings, we need to do some preprocessing steps. Namely, we need to assign each word token a number and create a NumPy array full of sequences.

Assigning numbers to tokens makes the training process smoother and decouples the tokenization process from the word vectors. Keras has a `Tokenizer` class, which can create numeric tokens for words. By default, this tokenizer splits text by spaces. While this works mostly fine in English, it can be problematic and cause issues in other languages. A key learning point to take away is that it's better to tokenize the text with spaCy first, as we already did for our two previous methods, and then assign numeric tokens with Keras.

The `Tokenizer` class also allows us to specify how many words we want to consider, so once again we will only use the 10,000 most used words, which we can specify by running:

```
from keras.preprocessing.text import Tokenizer
import numpy as np

max_words = 10000
```

The tokenizer works a lot like `CountVectorizer` from `sklearn`. First, we create a new `tokenizer` object. Then we fit the tokenizer, and finally, we can transform the text into tokenized sequences:

```
tokenizer = Tokenizer(num_words=max_words)
tokenizer.fit_on_texts(df['joint_lemmas'])
sequences = tokenizer.texts_to_sequences(df['joint_lemmas'])
```

The `sequences` variable now holds all of our texts as numeric tokens. We can look up the mapping of words to numbers from the tokenizer's word index with the following code:

```
word_index = tokenizer.word_index
print('Token for "the"',word_index['the'])
print('Token for "Movie"',word_index['movie'])
```

Token for "the" 4

Token for "Movie" 333

As you can see, frequently used words such as "the" have lower token numbers than less frequent words such as "movie." You can also see that `word_index` is a dictionary. If you are using your model in production, you can save this dictionary to disk in order to convert words into tokens at a later time.

Finally, we need to turn our sequences into sequences of equal length. This is not always necessary, as some model types can deal with sequences of different lengths, but it usually makes sense and is often required. We will examine which models need equal length sequences in the next section on building custom NLP models.

Keras' `pad_sequences` function allows us to easily bring all of the sequences to the same length by either cutting off sequences or adding zeros at the end. We will bring all the tweets to a length of 140 characters, which for a long time was the maximum length tweets could have:

```
from keras.preprocessing.sequence import pad_sequences

maxlen = 140

data = pad_sequences(sequences, maxlen=maxlen)
```

Finally, we split our data into a training and validation set:

```
from sklearn.model_selection import train_test_split
X_train, X_test, y_train, y_test = train_test_split(data,
                                    df['relevant'],
                                    test_size = 0.2,
                                    shuffle=True,
                                    random_state = 42)
```

Now we are ready to train our own word vectors.

Embeddings are their own layer type in Keras. To use them, we have to specify how large we want the word vectors to be. The 50-dimensional vector that we have chosen to use is able to capture good embeddings even for quite large vocabularies. Additionally, we also have to specify how many words we want embeddings for and how long our sequences are. Our model is now a simple logistic regressor that trains its own embeddings:

```
from keras.models import Sequential
from keras.layers import Embedding, Flatten, Dense

embedding_dim = 50

model = Sequential()
model.add(Embedding(max_words, embedding_dim,
input_length=maxlen))
model.add(Flatten())
model.add(Dense(1, activation='sigmoid'))
```

Notice how we do not have to specify an input shape. Even specifying the input length is only necessary if the following layers require knowledge of the input length. Dense layers require knowledge about the input size, but since we are using dense layers directly, we need to specify the input length here.

Word embeddings have *many* parameters. This is something you can see if you are printing out the models summary:

```
model.summary()
```

Layer (type)	Output Shape	Param #
embedding_2 (Embedding)	(None, 140, 50)	500000
flatten_2 (Flatten)	(None, 7000)	0
dense_3 (Dense)	(None, 1)	7001

```
Total params: 507,001
Trainable params: 507,001
Non-trainable params: 0
```

As you can see, the embedding layer has 50 parameters for 10,000 words equaling 500,000 parameters in total. This makes training slower and can increase the chance of overfitting.

The next step is for us to compile and train our model as usual:

```
model.compile(optimizer='adam',
              loss='binary_crossentropy',
              metrics=['acc'])

history = model.fit(X_train, y_train,
                    epochs=10,
                    batch_size=32,
                    validation_data=(X_test, y_test))
```

This model achieves about 76% accuracy on the test set but over 90% accuracy on the training set. However, the large number of parameters in the custom embeddings has led us to overfitting. To avoid overfitting and reduce training time, it's often better to use pretrained word embeddings.

Loading pretrained word vectors

Like in computer vision, NLP models can benefit from using pretrained pieces of other models. In this case, we will use the pretrained GloVe vectors. **GloVe** stands for **Global Vectors** for Word 8 and is a project of the Stanford NLP group. GloVe provides different sets of vectors trained in different texts.

In this section, we will be using word embeddings trained on Wikipedia texts as well as the Gigaword dataset. In total, the vectors were trained on a text of 6 billion tokens.

With all that being said, there are alternatives to GloVe, such as Word2Vec. Both GloVe and Word2Vec are relatively similar, although the training method for them is different. They each have their strengths and weaknesses, and in practice it is often worth trying out both.

A nice feature of GloVe vectors is that they encode word meanings in vector space so that "word algebra" becomes possible. The vector for "king" minus the vector for "man" plus the vector for "woman," for example, results in a vector pretty close to "queen." This means the differences between the vectors for "man" and "woman" are the same as the differences for the vectors of "king" and "queen," as the differentiating features for both are nearly the same.

Equally, words describing similar things such as "frog" and "toad" are very close to each other in the GloVe vector space. Encoding semantic meanings in vectors offer a range of other exciting opportunities for document similarity and topic modeling, as we will see later in this chapter. Semantic vectors are also pretty useful for a wide range of NLP tasks, such as our text classification problem.

The actual GloVe vectors are in a text file. We will use the 50-dimensional embeddings trained on 6 billion tokens. To do this, we need to open the file:

```
import os
glove_dir = '../input/glove6b50d'
f = open(os.path.join(glove_dir, 'glove.6B.50d.txt'))
```

Then we create an empty dictionary that will later map words to embeddings:

```
embeddings_index = {}
```

In the dataset, each line represents a new word embedding. The line starts with the word, and the embedding values follow. We can read out the embeddings like this:

```
for line in f:                                              #1
    values = line.split()                                   #2
    word = values[0]                                        #3
    embedding = np.asarray(values[1:], dtype='float32')     #4
    embeddings_index[word] = embedding dictionary           #5
f.close()                                                   #6
```

But what does that mean? Let's take a minute to break down the meaning behind the code, which has six key elements:

1. We loop over all lines in the file. Each line contains a word and embedding.
2. We split the line by whitespace.
3. The first thing in the line is always the word.
4. Then come the embedding values. We immediately transform them into a NumPy array and make sure that they are all floating-point numbers, that is, decimals.
5. We then save the embedding vector in our embedding dictionary.
6. Once we are done with it, we close the file.

As a result of running this code, we now have a dictionary mapping words to their embeddings:

```
print('Found %s word vectors.' % len(embeddings_index))
```

Found 400000-word vectors.

This version of GloVe has vectors for 400,000 words, which should be enough to cover most of the words that we will encounter. However, there might be some words where we still do not have a vector. For these words, we will just create random vectors. To make sure these vectors are not too far off, it is a good idea to use the same mean and standard deviation for the random vectors as from the trained vectors.

To this end, we need to calculate the mean and standard deviation for the GloVe vectors:

```
all_embs = np.stack(embeddings_index.values())
emb_mean = all_embs.mean()
emb_std = all_embs.std()
```

Our embedding layer will be a matrix with a row for each word and a column for each element of the embedding. Therefore, we need to specify how many dimensions one embedding has. The version of GloVe we loaded earlier has 50-dimensional vectors:

```
embedding_dim = 50
```

Next, we need to find out how many words we actually have. Although we have set the maximum to 10,000, there might be fewer words in our corpus. At this point, we also retrieve the word index from the tokenizer, which we will use later:

```
word_index = tokenizer.word_index
nb_words = min(max_words, len(word_index))
```

To create our embedding matrix, we first create a random matrix with the same `mean` and `std` as the embeddings:

```
embedding_matrix = np.random.normal(emb_mean,
                                    emb_std,
                                    (nb_words, embedding_dim))
```

Embedding vectors need to be in the same position as their token number. A word with token 1 needs to be in row 1 (rows start with zero), and so on. We can now replace the random embeddings for the words for which we have trained embeddings:

```
for word, i in word_index.items():                      #1
    if i >= max_words:                                  #2
        continue
    embedding_vector = embeddings_index.get(word)       #3
    if embedding_vector is None:                        #4
        embedding_matrix[i] = embedding_vector
```

This command has four key elements that we should explore in more detail before we move on:

1. We loop over all the words in the word index.

2. If we are above the number of words we want to use, we do nothing.

3. We get the embedding vector for the word. This operation might return none if there is no embedding for this word.

4. If there is an embedding vector, we put it in the embedding matrix.

To use the pretrained embeddings, we just have to set the weights in the embedding layer to the embedding matrix that we just created. To make sure the carefully created weights are not destroyed, we are going to set the layer to be non-trainable, which we can achieve by running the following:

```
model = Sequential()
model.add(Embedding(max_words,
                    embedding_dim,
                    input_length=maxlen,
                    weights = [embedding_matrix],
                    trainable = False))

model.add(Flatten())
model.add(Dense(1, activation='sigmoid'))
```

This model can be compiled and trained just like any other Keras model. You will notice that it trains much faster than the model in which we trained our own embeddings and suffers less from overfitting. However, the overall performance on the test set is roughly the same.

Word embeddings are pretty cool in reducing training time and helping to build accurate models. However, semantic embeddings go further. They can, for example, be used to measure how similar two texts are on a semantical level, even if they include different words.

Time series models with word vectors

Text is a time series. Different words follow each other and the order in which they do matters. Therefore, every neural network-based technique from the previous chapter can also be used for NLP. In addition, there are some building blocks that were not introduced in *Chapter 4, Understanding Time Series* that are useful for NLP.

Let's start with an LSTM, otherwise known as long short-term memory. All you have to change from the implementation in the last chapter is that the first layer of the network should be an embedding layer. This example below uses a CuDNNLSTM layer, which trains much faster than a regular LSTM layer.

Other than this, the layer remains the same. If you do not have a GPU, replace
CuDNNLSTM with LSTM:

```
from keras.layers import CuDNNLSTM
model = Sequential()
model.add(Embedding(max_words,
                    embedding_dim,
                    input_length=maxlen,
                    weights = [embedding_matrix], trainable =
False))
model.add(CuDNNLSTM(32))
model.add(Dense(1, activation='sigmoid'))
```

One technique used frequently in NLP but less frequently in time series forecasting is
a bidirectional **recurrent neural network (RNN)**. A bidirectional RNN is effectively
just two RNNs where one gets fed the sequence forward, while the other one gets fed
the sequence backward:

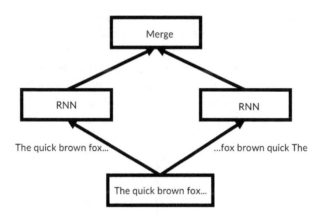

A bidirectional RNN

In Keras, there is a `Bidirectional` layer that we can wrap any RNN layer around,
such as an LSTM. We achieve this in the following code:

```
from keras.layers import Bidirectional
model = Sequential()
model.add(Embedding(max_words,
                    embedding_dim,
                    input_length=maxlen,
                    weights = [embedding_matrix], trainable =
False))
model.add(Bidirectional(CuDNNLSTM(32)))
model.add(Dense(1, activation='sigmoid'))
```

Word embeddings are great because they enrich neural networks. They are a space-efficient and powerful method that allows us to transform words into numbers that a neural network can work with. With that being said, there are more advantages to encoding semantics as vectors, such as how we can perform vector math on them! This is useful if we want to measure the similarity between two texts, for instance.

Document similarity with word embeddings

The practical use case of word vectors is to compare the semantic similarity between documents. If you are a retail bank, insurance company, or any other company that sells to end users, you will have to deal with support requests. You'll often find that many customers have similar requests, so by finding out how similar texts are semantically, previous answers to similar requests can be reused, and your organization's overall service can be improved.

spaCy has a built-in function to measure the similarity between two sentences. It also comes with pretrained vectors from the Word2Vec model, which is similar to GloVe. This method works by averaging the embedding vectors of all the words in a text and then measuring the cosine of the angle between the average vectors. Two vectors pointing in roughly the same direction will have a high similarity score, whereas vectors pointing in different directions will have a low similarity score. This is visualized in the following graph:

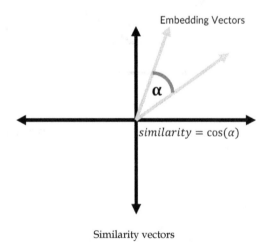

Similarity vectors

We can see the similarity between two phrases by running the following command:

```
sup1 = nlp('I would like to open a new checking account')
sup2 = nlp('How do I open a checking account?')
```

As you can see, these requests are pretty similar, achieving a rate of 70%:

```
sup1.similarity(sup2)
```

```
0.7079433112862716
```

As you can see, their similarity score is quite high. This simple averaging method works pretty decently. It is not, however, able to capture things such as negations or a single deviating vector, which might not influence the average too much.

For example, "I would like to close a checking account" has a semantically different meaning than, "I would like to open a checking account." However, the model sees them as being pretty similar. Yet, this approach is still useful and a good illustration of the advantages of representing semantics as vectors.

A quick tour of the Keras functional API

So far, we've used sequential models. In the sequential model, layers get stacked on top of each other when we call `model.add()`. The advantage of the functional API is that it is simple and prevents errors. The disadvantage is that it only allows us to stack layers linearly:

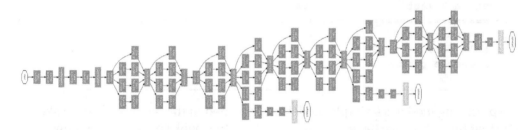

GoogLeNet Architecture from Szegedy and others' "Going Deeper with Convolutions"

Take a look at the preceding GoogLeNet architecture. While the graph is very detailed, what we need to take away is the fact that the model is not just a number of layers stacked on top of each other. Instead, there are multiple layers in parallel; in this case, the model has three outputs. However, the question remains, how did the authors build this complicated model? The sequential API wouldn't have allowed them to, but the functional API makes it easy to string up layers like a pearl string and create architectures such as the preceding one.

For many NLP applications, we need more complex models in which, for example, two separate layers run in parallel. In the Keras functional API, we have more control and can specify how layers should be connected. We can use this to create much more advanced and complex models.

We will use the functional API a lot more from now on. This section of the chapter aims to provide a brief overview of the Keras functional API, as we will be going into much more depth in later chapters. Firstly, let's look at a simple two-layer network in both the sequential and functional way:

```
from keras.models import Sequential
from keras.layers import Dense, Activation

model = Sequential()
model.add(Dense(64, input_dim=64))
model.add(Activation('relu'))
model.add(Dense(4))
model.add(Activation('softmax'))
model.summary()
```

Layer (type)	Output Shape	Param #
dense_1 (Dense)	(None, 64)	4160
activation_1 (Activation)	(None, 64)	0
dense_2 (Dense)	(None, 4)	260
activation_2 (Activation)	(None, 4)	0

```
Total params: 4,420
Trainable params: 4,420
Non-trainable params: 0
```

The preceding model is a simple model implemented in the sequential API. Take note that this is how we have done it throughout this book so far. We will now implement the same model in the functional API:

```
from keras.models import Model                          #1
from keras.layers import Dense, Activation, Input

model_input = Input(shape=(64,))                        #2
x = Dense(64)(model_input)                              #3
x = Activation('relu')(x)                               #4
x = Dense(4)(x)
model_output = Activation('softmax')(x)

model = Model(model_input, model_output)                #5
model.summary()
```

Notice the differences to the sequential API:

1. Instead of defining the model first with `model = Sequential()`, you now define the computational graph first and then turn it into a model using the `Model` class.

2. Inputs are now their own layer.

3. Instead of using `model.add()`, you define the layer and then pass on an input layer or the output tensor of the previous layer.

4. You create models by stringing layers on a chain. `Dense(64)(model_input)`, for instance, returns a tensor. You pass on this tensor to the next layer, like in `Activation('relu')(x)`. This function will return a new output tensor, which you can pass to the next layer, and so on. This way, you create a computational graph like a chain.

5. To create a model, you pass the model input layer as well as the final output tensor of your graph into the `Model` class.

Functional API models can be used just like sequential API models. In fact, from the output of this model's summary, you can see it is pretty much the same as the model we just created with the sequential API:

```
Layer (type)                 Output Shape              Param #
=================================================================
input_2 (InputLayer)         (None, 64)                0

dense_3 (Dense)              (None, 64)                4160

activation_3 (Activation)    (None, 64)                0

dense_4 (Dense)              (None, 4)                 260

activation_4 (Activation)    (None, 4)                 0
=================================================================
Total params: 4,420
Trainable params: 4,420
Non-trainable params: 0
```

You can see that the functional API can connect layers in more advanced ways than the sequential API. We can also separate the layer creation and connection step. This keeps the code clean and allows us to use the same layer for different purposes.

The following code segment will create the exact same model as the preceding segment, but with separate layer creation and connection steps:

```
model_input = Input(shape=(64,))

dense = Dense(64)

x = dense(model_input)

activation = Activation('relu')

x = activation(x)

dense_2 = Dense(4)

x = dense_2(x)

model_output = Activation('softmax')(x)

model = Model(model_input, model_output)
```

Layers can be reused. For example, we could train some layers in one computational graph and then use them for another, as we will do in the section on seq2seq models later in the chapter.

One more caveat before we move on to use the functional API to build advanced models. We should note that the activation function of any layer can also be specified directly in the layer. So far, we have used a separate activation layer, which increases clarity but is not strictly required. A Dense layer with a relu activation function can also be specified as:

```
Dense(24, activation='relu')
```

When using the functional API, this can be easier than adding an activation function.

Attention

Are you paying attention? If so, certainly not to everyone equally. In any text, some words matter more than others. An attention mechanism is a way for a neural network to *focus* on a certain element in a sequence. Focusing, for neural networks, means amplifying what is important:

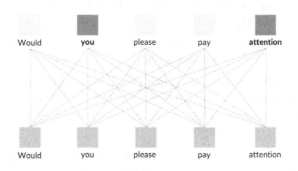

An example of an attention mechanism

Attention layers are fully connected layers that take in a sequence and output the weighting for a sequence. The sequence is then multiplied with the weightings:

```
def attention_3d_block(inputs,time_steps,
single_attention_vector = False):
    input_dim = int(inputs.shape[2])                          #1
    a = Permute((2, 1),name='Attent_Permute')(inputs)         #2
    a = Reshape((input_dim, time_steps),name='Reshape')(a)    #3
    a = Dense(time_steps, activation='softmax',
name='Attent_Dense')(a) # Create attention vector            #4
    if single_attention_vector:                               #5
        a = Lambda(lambda x: K.mean(x, axis=1),
            name='Dim_reduction')(a)                          #6
        a = RepeatVector(input_dim, name='Repeat')(a)         #7
        a_probs = Permute((2, 1), name='Attention_vec')(a)    #8
    output_attention_mul = Multiply(name='Attention_mul')
([inputs, a_probs])                                          #9
    return output_attention_mul
```

Let's break down the sequence we've just created. As you can see, it's made up of nine key elements:

1. Our input has the shape `(batch_size, time_steps, input_dim)`, where `time_steps` is the length of the sequence, and `input_dim` is the dimensionality of the input. If we applied this directly to a text series with the embeddings used, `input_dim` would be 50, the same as the embedding dimensionality.

2. We then swap (permute) the axis for `time_steps` and `input_dim` so that the tensor has a shape of `(batch_size, input_dim, time_steps)`.

3. If everything went fine, our tensor is already in the shape that we want it to be in. Here we are adding a reshaping operation just to be sure.

4. Now comes the trick. We run our input through a `dense` layer with a `softmax` activation. This will generate a weighting for each element in the series, just as shown previously. This `dense` layer is what is trained inside the `attention` block.

5. By default, the `dense` layer computes attention for each input dimension individually. That is, for our word vectors, it would compute 50 different weightings. That can be useful if we are working with time series models where the input dimensions actually represent different things. In this case, we want to weight words as a whole.

6. To create one attention value per word, we average the attention layer across the input dimensions. Our new tensor has the shape `(batch_size, 1, time_steps)`.

7. In order to multiply the attention vector with the input, we need to repeat the weightings across the input dimension. After repetition, the tensor has the shape `(batch_size, input_dim, time_steps)` again, but with the same weights across the `input_dim` dimension.

8. To match the shape of the input, we permute the axis for `time_steps` and `input_dim` back, so that the attention vector once again has a shape of `(batch_size, time_steps, input_dim)`.

9. Finally, we apply the attention to the input by element-wise multiplying the attention vector with the input. We return the resulting tensor.

The following flowchart gives an overview of the process:

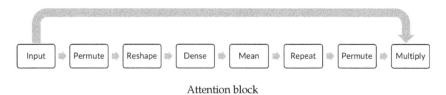

Attention block

Notice how the preceding function defines takes a tensor as an input, defines a graph, and returns a tensor. We can now call this function as part of our model building process:

```
input_tokens = Input(shape=(maxlen,),name='input')

embedding = Embedding(max_words,
                      embedding_dim,
                      input_length=maxlen,
                      weights = [embedding_matrix],
                      trainable = False,
name='embedding')(input_tokens)

attention_mul = attention_3d_block(inputs = embedding,
                                   time_steps = maxlen,
                                   single_attention_vector = True)

lstm_out = CuDNNLSTM(32, return_sequences=True, name='lstm')
(attention_mul)



attention_mul = Flatten(name='flatten')(attention_mul)
output = Dense(1, activation='sigmoid',name='output')
(attention_mul)
model = Model(input_tokens, output)
```

In this case, we are using the attention block right after the embeddings. This means that we can amplify or suppress certain word embeddings. Equally, we could use the attention block after the LSTM. In many cases, you will find attention blocks to be powerful tools in your arsenal when it comes to building models that deal with any kind of sequence, especially in NLP.

To become more comfortable with how the functional API strings up layers and how the attention block reshapes tensors, take a look at this model summary:

```
model.summary()
```

Layer (type)	Output Shape	Param #	Connected to
input (InputLayer)	(None, 140)	0	
embedding (Embedding)	(None, 140, 50)	500000	input[0]

```
[0]
```

Attent_Permute (Permute) embedding[0][0]	(None, 50, 140)	0	
Reshape (Reshape) Permute[0][0]	(None, 50, 140)	0	Attent_
Attent_Dense (Dense) Reshape[0][0]	(None, 50, 140)	19740	
Dim_reduction (Lambda) Dense[0][0]	(None, 140)	0	Attent_
Repeat (RepeatVector) reduction[0][0]	(None, 50, 140)	0	Dim_
Attention_vec (Permute) Repeat[0][0]	(None, 140, 50)	0	
Attention_mul (Multiply) embedding[0][0] Attention_vec[0][0]	(None, 140, 50)	0	
flatten (Flatten) Attention_mul[0][0]	(None, 7000)	0	
output (Dense) flatten[0][0]	(None, 1)	7001	

```
================================================================================
================================
Total params: 526,741
Trainable params: 26,741
Non-trainable params: 500,000
```

This model can be trained, just as any Keras model can be, and achieves around 80% accuracy on the validation set.

Seq2seq models

In 2016, Google announced that it had replaced the entire Google Translate algorithm with a single neural network. The special thing about the Google Neural Machine Translation system is that it translates mutliple languages "end-to-end" using only a single model. It works by encoding the semantics of a sentence and then decoding the semantics into the desired output language.

The fact that such a system is possible at all baffled many linguists and other researchers, as it shows that machine learning can create systems that accurately capture high-level meanings and semantics without being given any explicit rules.

These semantic meanings are represented as an encoding vector, and while we don't quite yet know how to interpret these vectors, there are a lot of useful applications for them. Translating from one language to another is one such popular method, but we could use a similar approach to "translate" a report into a summary. Text summarization has made great strides, but the downside is that it requires a lot of computing power to deliver meaningful results, so we will be focusing on language translation.

Seq2seq architecture overview

If all phrases had the exact same length, we could simply use an LSTM (or multiple LSTMs). Remember that an LSTM can also return a full sequence of the same length as the input sequence. However, in many cases, sequences will not have the same length.

To deal with different lengths of phrases, we'll need to create an encoder that aims to capture the sentence's semantic meaning. We then create a decoder that has two inputs: the *encoded semantics* and the *sequence* that was already produced. The decoder then predicts the next item in the sequence. For our character-level translator, it looks like this:

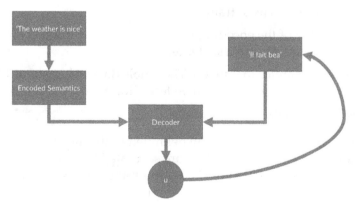

Seq2seq architecture overview

Note how the output of the decoder is used as the input of the decoder again. This process is only stopped once the decoder produces a <STOP> tag, which indicates that the sequence is over.

> **Note**: The data and code for this section can be found on Kaggle at `https://www.kaggle.com/jannesklaas/a-simple-seq2seq-translator.`

The data

We use a dataset of English phrases and their translation. This dataset was obtained from the **Tabotea** project, a translation database, and you can find the file attached to the code on Kaggle. We implement this model on a character level, which means that unlike previous models, we won't tokenize words, but characters. This makes the task harder for our network because it now has to also learn how to spell words! However, on the other hand, there are a lot fewer characters than words, therefore we can just one-hot encode characters instead of having to work with embeddings. This makes our model a bit simpler.

To get started, we have to set a few parameters:

```
batch_size = 64                     #1
epochs = 100                        #2
latent_dim = 256                    #3
num_samples = 10000                 #4
data_path = 'fra-eng/fra.txt'   #5
```

But what are the parameters that we've set up?

1. Batch size for training.

2. The number of epochs to train for.

3. Dimensionality of the encoding vectors. How many numbers we use to encode the meaning of a sentence.

4. A number of samples to train on. The whole dataset has about 140,000 samples. However, we will train on fewer for memory and time reasons.

5. The path to the data `.txt` file on disk.

Input (English) and target (French) is tab delimited in the data file. Each row represents a new phrase. The translations are separated by a tab (escaped character: \t). So, we loop over the lines and read out inputs and targets by splitting the lines at the tab symbol.

To build up our tokenizer, we also need to know which characters are present in our dataset. So, for all of the characters, we need to check whether they are already in our set of seen characters, and if not, add them to it.

To do this, we must first set up the holding variables for texts and characters:

```
input_texts = []
target_texts = []
input_characters = set()
target_characters = set()
```

Then we loop over as many lines as we want samples and extract the texts and characters:

```
lines = open(data_path).read().split('\n')
for line in lines[: min(num_samples, len(lines) - 1)]:

    input_text, target_text = line.split('\t')          #1

    target_text = '\t' + target_text + '\n'             #2
    input_texts.append(input_text)
    target_texts.append(target_text)

    for char in input_text:                             #3
        if char not in input_characters:
            input_characters.add(char)

    for char in target_text:                            #4
        if char not in target_characters:
            target_characters.add(char)
```

Let's break this code down so that we can understand it in more detail:

1. Input and target are split by tabs, English TAB French, so we split the lines by tabs to obtain input and target texts.

2. We use \t as the "start sequence" character for the targets, and \n as "end sequence" character. This way, we know when to stop decoding.

3. We loop over the characters in the input text, adding all characters that we have not seen yet to our set of input characters.

4. We loop over the characters in the output text, adding all characters that we have not seen yet to our set of output characters.

Encoding characters

We now need to create lists of alphabetically sorted input and output characters, which we can do by running:

```
input_characters = sorted(list(input_characters))
target_characters = sorted(list(target_characters))
```

We're also going to count how many input and output characters we have. This is important since we need to know how many dimensions our one-hot encodings should have. We can find this by writing the following:

```
num_encoder_tokens = len(input_characters)
num_decoder_tokens = len(target_characters)
```

Instead of using the Keras tokenizer, we will build our own dictionary mapping characters to token numbers. We can do this by running the following:

```
input_token_index = {char: i for i,
char in enumerate(input_characters)}
target_token_index = {char: i for i,
char in enumerate(target_characters)}
```

We can see how this works by printing the token numbers for all characters in a short sentence:

```
for c in 'the cat sits on the mat':
    print(input_token_index[c], end = ' ')
```

63 51 48 0 46 44 63 0 62 52 63 62 0 58 57 0 63 51 48 0 56 44 63

Next, we build up our model training data. Remember that our model has two inputs but only one output. While our model can handle sequences of any length, it is handy to prepare the data in NumPy and thus to know how long our longest sequence is:

```
max_encoder_seq_length = max([len(txt) for txt in input_texts])
max_decoder_seq_length = max([len(txt) for txt in target_texts])

print('Max sequence length for inputs:', max_encoder_seq_length)
print('Max sequence length for outputs:', max_decoder_seq_length)
```

Max sequence length for inputs: 16
Max sequence length for outputs: 59

Now we prepare input and output data for our model. `encoder_input_data` is a 3D array of shape (`num_pairs, max_english_sentence_length, num_english_ characters`) containing a one-hot vectorization of the English sentences:

```
encoder_input_data = np.zeros((len(input_texts),
max_encoder_seq_length, num_encoder_tokens),dtype='float32')
```

`decoder_input_data` is a 3D array of shape (`num_pairs`, `max_french_sentence_`
`length`, `num_french_characters`) containing a one-hot vectorization of the French
sentences:

```
decoder_input_data = np.zeros((len(input_texts),
max_decoder_seq_length, num_decoder_tokens),dtype='float32')
```

`decoder_target_data` is the same as `decoder_input_data` but offset by one
timestep. `decoder_target_data[:, t, :]` will be the same as `decoder_input_`
`data[:, t + 1, :]`.

```
decoder_target_data = np.zeros((len(input_texts),
max_decoder_seq_length, num_decoder_tokens),dtype='float32')
```

You can see that the input and output of the decoder are the same except that the
output is one timestep ahead. This makes sense when you consider that we feed an
unfinished sequence into the decoder and want it to predict the next character. We
will use the functional API to create a model with two inputs.

You can see that the decoder also has two inputs: the *decoder inputs* and the *encoded
semantics*. The encoded semantics, however, are not directly the outputs of the
encoder LSTM but its *states*. In an LSTM, states are the hidden memory of the cells.
What happens is that the first "memory" of our decoder is the encoded semantics.
To give the decoder this first memory, we can initialize its states with the states of
the decoder LSTM.

To return states, we have to set the `return_state` argument, configuring an
RNN layer to return a list where the first entry is the outputs and the next entries
are the internal RNN states. Once again, we are using CuDNNLSTM. If you do
not have a GPU, replace it with LSTM, but note that training this model without
a GPU can take a very long time to complete:

```
encoder_inputs = Input(shape=(None, num_encoder_tokens),
                    name = 'encoder_inputs')                  #1
encoder = CuDNNLSTM(latent_dim,
                    return_state=True,
                    name = 'encoder')                         #2
encoder_outputs, state_h, state_c = encoder(encoder_inputs)   #3

encoder_states = [state_h, state_c]                           #4
```

Let's look at the four key elements of the code:

1. We create an input layer for our encoder
2. We create the LSTM encoder
3. We link the LSTM encoder to the input layer and get back the outputs and states
4. We discard `encoder_outputs` and only keep the states

Now we define the decoder. The decoder uses the states of the encoder as initial states for its decoding LSTM.

You can think of it like this: imagine you were a translator translating English to French. When tasked with translating, you would first listen to the English speaker and form ideas about what the speaker wants to say in your head. You would then use these ideas to form a French sentence expressing the same idea.

It is important to understand that we are not just passing a variable, but a piece of the computational graph. This means that we can later backpropagate from the decoder to the encoder. In the case of our previous analogy, you might think that your French translation suffered from a poor understanding of the English sentence, so you might start changing your English comprehension based on the outcomes of your French translation, for example:

```
decoder_inputs = Input(shape=(None, num_decoder_tokens),
                       name = 'decoder_inputs')                          #1
decoder_lstm = CuDNNLSTM(latent_dim,
                         return_sequences=True,
                         return_state=True,
                         name = 'decoder_lstm')                          #2

decoder_outputs, _, _ = decoder_lstm(decoder_inputs,
                                     initial_state=encoder_states) #3

decoder_dense = Dense(num_decoder_tokens,
                      activation='softmax',
                      name = 'decoder_dense')

decoder_outputs = decoder_dense(decoder_outputs)                         #4
```

The preceding code is made up of four key elements:

1. Set up the decoder inputs.

2. We set up our decoder to return full output sequences, and to return internal states as well. We don't use the return states in the training model, but we will use them for inference.

3. Connect the decoder to the decoder inputs and specify the internal state. As mentioned previously, we don't use the internal states of the decoder for training, so we discard them here.

4. Finally, we need to decide which character we want to use as the next character. This is a classification task, so we will use a simple Dense layer with a softmax activation function.

We now have the pieces we need to define our model with two inputs and one output:

```
model = Model([encoder_inputs, decoder_inputs], decoder_outputs)
```

If you have the graphviz library installed, you can visualize the model very nicely using the following code lines. Unfortunately, however, this code snippet won't work on Kaggle:

```
from IPython.display import SVG
from keras.utils.vis_utils import model_to_dot

SVG(model_to_dot(model).create(prog='dot', format='svg'))
```

As you can see, this visualization is represented in the following diagram:

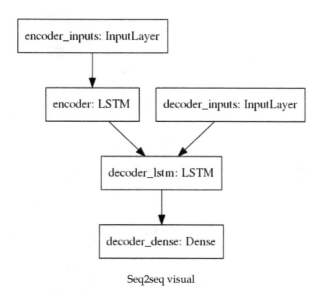

Seq2seq visual

You can now compile and train the model. Since we have to choose between a number of possible characters to output next, this is basically a multi-class classification task. Therefore, we'll use a categorical cross-entropy loss:

```
model.compile(optimizer='rmsprop',
loss='categorical_crossentropy')
history = model.fit([encoder_input_data, decoder_input_data],
                    decoder_target_data,
                    batch_size=batch_size,
                    epochs=epochs,
                    validation_split=0.2)
```

The training process takes about 7 minutes on a GPU. However, if we were to plot the model's progress, you can see that it's overfitting:

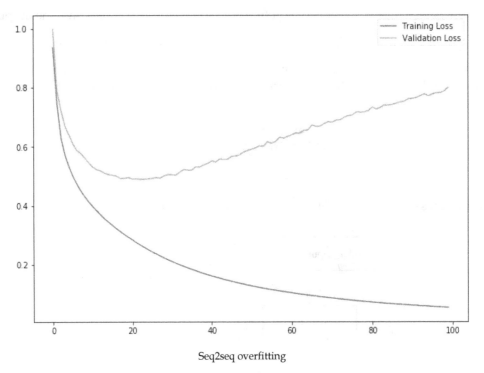

Seq2seq overfitting

The reason it's overfitting is largely because we used only 10,000 sentence pairs of only relatively short sentences. To get a bigger model, a real translation or summarization system would have to be trained on many more examples. To allow you to follow the examples without owning a massive datacenter, we are just using a smaller model to give an example of what a seq2seq architecture can do.

Creating inference models

Overfitting or not, we would like to use our model now. Using a seq2seq model for inference, in this case for doing translations, requires us to build a separate inference model that uses the weights trained in the training model, but does the routing a bit differently. More specifically, we will separate the encoder and decoder. This way, we can first create the encoding once and then use it for decoding instead of creating it again and again.

The encoder model maps from the encoder inputs to the encoder states:

```
encoder_model = Model(encoder_inputs, encoder_states)
```

The decoder model then takes in the encoder memory plus its own memory from the last character as an input. It then spits out a prediction plus its own memory to be used for the next character:

```
#Inputs from the encoder
decoder_state_input_h = Input(shape=(latent_dim,))       #1
decoder_state_input_c = Input(shape=(latent_dim,))

#Create a combined memory to input into the decoder
decoder_states_inputs = [decoder_state_input_h,
decoder_state_input_c]                                    #2

#Decoder
decoder_outputs, state_h, state_c = decoder_lstm(decoder_inputs,
initial_state=decoder_states_inputs)                      #3

decoder_states = [state_h, state_c]                       #4

#Predict next char
decoder_outputs = decoder_dense(decoder_outputs)          #5

decoder_model = Model(
    [decoder_inputs] + decoder_states_inputs,
    [decoder_outputs] + decoder_states)                   #6
```

Let's look at the six elements of this code:

1. The encoder memory consists of two states. We need to create two inputs for both of them.
2. We then combine the two states into one memory representation.
3. We then connect the decoder LSTM we trained earlier to the decoder inputs and the encoder memory.
4. We combine the two states of the decoder LSTM into one memory representation.
5. We reuse the dense layer of the decoder to predict the next character.
6. Finally, we set up the decoder model to take in the character input as well as the state input and map it to the character output as well as the state output.

Making translations

We can now start to use our model. To do this, we must first create an index that maps tokens to characters again:

```
reverse_input_char_index = {i: char for char,
i in input_token_index.items()}
reverse_target_char_index = {i: char for char,
i in target_token_index.items()}
```

When we translate a phrase, we must first encode the input. We'll then loop, feeding the decoder states back into the decoder until we receive a STOP; in our case, we use the tab character to signal STOP.

`target_seq` is a NumPy array representing the last character predicted by the decoder:

```
def decode_sequence(input_seq):

    states_value = encoder_model.predict(input_seq)        #1

    target_seq = np.zeros((1, 1, num_decoder_tokens))      #2

    target_seq[0, 0, target_token_index['\t']] = 1.        #3

    stop_condition = False                                 #4
    decoded_sentence = ''

    while not stop_condition:                              #5
```

```
        output_tokens, h, c = decoder_model.predict(
            [target_seq] + states_value)                          #6

        sampled_token_index = np.argmax(output_tokens[0, -1, :])   #7

        sampled_char = reverse_target_char_index[
sampled_token_index]                                               #8

        decoded_sentence += sampled_char                           #9


        if (sampled_char == '\n' or                                #10
            len(decoded_sentence) > max_decoder_seq_length):
            stop_condition = True

        target_seq = np.zeros((1, 1, num_decoder_tokens))          #11
        target_seq[0, 0, sampled_token_index] = 1.

        states_value = [h, c]                                      #12

    return decoded_sentence
```

For the final time in this chapter, let's break down the code:

1. Encode the input as state vectors
2. Generate an empty target sequence of length one
3. Populate the first character of the target sequence with the start character
4. There was no stop sign, and the decoded sequence is empty so far
5. Loop until we receive a stop sign
6. Get output and internal states of the decoder
7. Get the predicted token (the token with the highest probability)
8. Get the character belonging to the token number
9. Append a character to the output
10. Exit condition: either hit max length or find stop character
11. Update the target sequence (of length one)
12. Update states

Now we can translate English into French! At least for some phrases, it works quite well. Given that we did not supply our model with any rules about French words or grammar, this is quite impressive. Translation systems such as Google Translate, of course, use much bigger datasets and models, but the underlying principles are the same.

To translate a text, we first create a placeholder array full of zeros:

```
my_text = 'Thanks!'
placeholder = np.zeros((1,len(my_text)+10,num_encoder_tokens))
```

We then one-hot encode all characters in the text by setting the element at the index of the characters' token numbers to 1:

```
for i, char in enumerate(my_text):
    print(i,char, input_token_index[char])
    placeholder[0,i,input_token_index[char]] = 1
```

This will print out the characters' token numbers alongside the character and its position in the text:

```
0 T 38
1 h 51
2 a 44
3 n 57
4 k 54
5 s 62
6 ! 1
```

Now we can feed this placeholder into our decoder:

```
decode_sequence(placeholder)
```

And we get the translation back:

```
'Merci !\n'
```

Seq2seq models are useful not only for translating between languages. They can be trained on just about anything that takes a sequence as an input and also outputs a sequence.

Remember our forecasting task from the last chapter? The winning solution to the forecasting problem was a seq2seq model. Text summarization is another useful application. Seq2seq models can also be trained to output a series of actions, such as a sequence of trades that would minimize the impact of a large order.

Exercises

Now that we're at the end of the chapter, let's see what we've learned. To finish this chapter, I've included three exercises that will challenge you based on what we've covered in this chapter:

1. Add an extra layer to the encoder of the translation model. The translation model might work better if it had a bit more capacity to learn the structure of French sentences. Adding one more LSTM layer will be a good exercise to learn about the functional API.

2. Add attention to the encoder of the translation model. Attention will allow the model to focus on the (English) words that really matter for translation. It is best to use attention as the last layer. This task is a bit harder than the previous one, but you will understand the inner workings of attention much better.

3. Visit *Daily News for Stock Market Prediction* at `https://www.kaggle.com/ aaron7sun/stocknews`. The task is to use the daily news as an input to predict stock prices. There are a number of kernels already that can help you with this. Use what you have learned in this chapter to predict some stock prices!

Summary

In this chapter, you have learned the most important NLP techniques. There was a lot that we've learned, and here's a big list of things we covered in this chapter and everything you should now feel confident about understanding:

*   Finding named entities
*   Fine-tuning spaCy's models for your own custom applications
*   Finding parts of speech and mapping the grammatical structure of sentences
*   Using regular expressions
*   Preparing text data for classification tasks
*   Using techniques such as bag-of-words and TF-IDF for classification
*   Modeling the topics present in a text with LDA
*   Using pretrained word embeddings
*   Building advanced models with the Keras functional API
*   Training your model to focus on attention
*   Translating sentences with the seq2seq model

You now have a big set of tools in your toolbox that will allow you to tackle NLP problems. Throughout the rest of this book, you will see some of these techniques again, being used in different contexts to solve hard problems. These techniques are useful across the industry, from retail banking to hedge fund investing. While the problem your institution is trying to solve might require a bit of tweaking, the general approaches are quite transferable.

In the next chapter, we will look at a technique that has gained a lot of attention since DeepMind beat a human Go champion: reinforcement learning. This technique is especially useful when working in financial markets and is in many ways a natural extension of what many quantitative investment firms are already doing. So, stay tuned, and I'll see you on the other side.

6
Using Generative Models

Generative models generate new data. In a way, they are the exact opposite of the models that we've dealt with in prior chapters. While an image classifier takes in a high-dimensional input, the image, and outputs a low-dimensional output such as the content of the image, a generative model goes about things in exactly the opposite way around. It might, for example, draw images from the description of what's in them.

Generative models are still in the experimental phase of their development, and are currently used mostly in image applications. However, they are an important model as shown by the fact that there have already been several applications that have used generative models that have caused an uproar within the industry.

In 2017, so-called *DeepFakes* began to appear on the internet. **Generative Adversarial Networks (GANs)**, which we will cover later in this chapter, were used to generate pornographic videos featuring famous celebrities. The year before, in 2016, researchers showcased a system in which they could generate videos of politicians saying anything the researcher wanted them to say, complete with realistic mouth movements and facial expressions. An example of this can be seen in a fake speech made by former US president Barack Obama that news site BuzzFeed produced in 2018: https://youtu.be/cQ54GDmleL0.

This technology is not completely negative, there are positive applications as well, especially if the generative model's data is sparse. If this is the case, generative models can generate realistic data that other models can then train on. Generative models are able to "translate" images, a prime example being taking satellite images and turning them into street maps. Another example is that generative models can generate code from website screenshots. They can even be used to combat unfairness and discrimination in machine learning models, as we will see in *Chapter 9*, *Fighting Bias*.

In the field of finance, data is frequently sparse. Think back to the fraud case from *Chapter 2*, *Applying Machine Learning to Structured Data*, in which we were classifying fraudulent transactions from transaction metadata. We found that there was not much fraud taking place in the dataset that we used, so the model had a hard time detecting when fraud was taking place. Usually, when this occurs, engineers make assumptions and create synthetic data. Machine learning models, however, can do this themselves, and in the process, they might even discover some useful features that can help with fraud detection.

In algorithmic trading, data is frequently generated in simulators. Want to know how your algorithm would do in a global selloff? Luckily, there are not that many global selloffs, so engineers at quantitative analysis firms spend a lot of their time creating simulations of selloffs. These simulators are often biased by the engineer's experience and their feelings about what a selloff should look like. However, what if the models could learn what a selloff fundamentally looks like, and then create data describing an infinite number of selloffs?

In this chapter, we'll be focusing on two families of generative models: autoencoders and GANs. Firstly there is the family of **autoencoders**, which aim to compress data into a lower dimensional representation and then reconstruct the data faithfully. The second family is that of the **GANs**, which aim to train a generator so that a separate discriminator cannot tell fake images from true images.

Understanding autoencoders

Technically, autoencoders are not generative models since they cannot create completely new kinds of data. Yet, variational autoencoders, a minor tweak to vanilla autoencoders, can. So, it makes sense to first understand autoencoders by themselves, before adding the generative element.

Autoencoders by themselves have some interesting properties that can be exploited for applications such as detecting credit card fraud, which is useful in our focus on finance.

Given an input, x, an autoencoder learns how to output x. It aims to find a function, f, so that the following is true:

$$x = f(x)$$

This might sound trivial at first, but the trick here is that autoencoders have a bottleneck. The middle hidden layer's size is smaller than the size of the input, x. Therefore, the model has to learn a compressed representation that captures all of the important elements of x in a smaller vector.

This can best be shown in the following diagram, where we can see a compressed representation of the Autoencoder scheme:

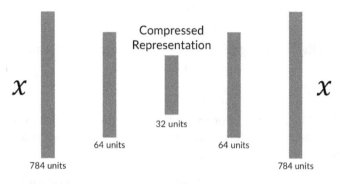

Autoencoder scheme

This compressed representation aims to capture the essence of the input, which turns out to be useful for us. We might, for example, want to capture what essentially distinguishes a fraudulent transaction from a genuine one. Vanilla autoencoders accomplish this with something similar to standard **principal component analysis (PCA)**. They allow us to reduce the dimensionality of our data and focus on what matters. But in contrast to PCA, autoencoders can be extended in order to generate more data of a certain type. For example, autoencoders can better deal with image or video data since they can make use of the spatiality of data using convolutional layers.

In this section, we will build two autoencoders. The first will be used for handwritten digits from the MNIST dataset. Generative models are easier to debug and understand for visual data due to the fact that humans are intuitively good at judging whether two pictures show something similar, but are less good at judging abstract data. The second autoencoder is for a fraud detection task, using similar methods as the MNIST dataset.

Autoencoder for MNIST

Let's start with a simple autoencoder for the MNIST dataset of handwritten digits. An MNIST image is 28x28 pixels and can be flattened into a vector of 784 elements, which equals 28x28. We will compress this data into a vector with only 32 elements by using an autoencoder.

Before diving into the code described here, make sure you have saved the MNIST dataset on the right path, successfully imported both the NumPy and Matplotlib libraries, and set a random seed to ensure that your experiments are reproducible.

Note: You can find the code for the MNIST autoencoder and variational autoencoder under the following URL https://www.kaggle.com/jannesklaas/mnist-autoencoder-vae.

We're going to set the encoding dimensionality hyperparameter now so that we can use it later:

```
encoding_dim = 32
```

Then, we construct the autoencoder using the Keras functional API. While a simple autoencoder could be constructed using the sequential API, this is a good refresher for us on how the functional API works.

First, we import the `Model` class, which allows us to create functional API models. We also need to import both the `Input` and `Dense` layers. You'll remember from previous chapters how the functional API needs a separate input layer, while the sequential API does not need one. To import both layers, we need to run the following:

```
from keras.models import Model
from keras.layers import Input, Dense
```

Now we are chaining up the autoencoder's layers: an `Input` layer followed by a `Dense` layer that encodes the image to a smaller representation.

This is followed by a `Dense` decoding layer that aims to reconstruct the original image:

```
input_img = Input(shape=(784,))

encoded = Dense(encoding_dim, activation='relu')(input_img)

decoded = Dense(784, activation='sigmoid')(encoded)
```

After we have created and chained up the layers, we are then able to create a model that maps from the input to the decoded image:

```
autoencoder = Model(input_img, decoded)
```

To get a better idea of what is going on, we can plot a visualization of the resulting autoencoder model with the following code:

```
from keras.utils import plot_model
plot_model(autoencoder, to_file='model.png', show_shapes=True) plt.
figure(figsize=(10,10))
plt.imshow(plt.imread('model.png'))
```

You can see our autoencoder as follows:

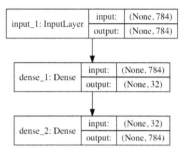

| input_1: InputLayer | input: | (None, 784) |
| | output: | (None, 784) |

| dense_1: Dense | input: | (None, 784) |
| | output: | (None, 32) |

| dense_2: Dense | input: | (None, 32) |
| | output: | (None, 784) |

Autoencoder model

Which we can compile with:

```
autoencoder.compile(optimizer='adadelta',
loss='binary_crossentropy')
```

To train this autoencoder, we use the *X* values as both the input and output:

```
autoencoder.fit(X_train_flat, X_train_flat,
                epochs=50,
                batch_size=256,
                shuffle=True,
                validation_data=(X_test_flat, X_test_flat))
```

After we train this autoencoder, which will take between one and two minutes, we can visually inspect how well it is doing. To do this, we first extract a single image from the test set, before adding a batch dimension to the image in order to run it through the model, which is what we use np.expand_dims for:

```
original = np.expand_dims(X_test_flat[0],0)
```

Now we're going to run the original image through the autoencoder. You'll remember that the original MNIST image showed us a number seven, so we're hoping that the output of our autoencoder shows a seven as well:

```
seven = autoencoder.predict(original)
```

Next, we're going to reshape both the autoencoder output as well as the original image back into 28x28-pixel images:

```
seven = seven.reshape(1,28,28)
original = original.reshape(1,28,28)
```

We then plot the original and reconstructed image next to each other. matplotlib does not allow the image to have a batch dimension, therefore we need to pass an array without it. By indexing the images with [0, :, :], we'll only pass the first item in the batch with all pixels.

This first item now doesn't have a batch dimension anymore:

```
fig = plt.figure(figsize=(7, 10))
a=fig.add_subplot(1,2,1)
a.set_title('Original')
imgplot = plt.imshow(original[0,:,:])

b=fig.add_subplot(1,2,2)
b.set_title('Autoencoder')
imgplot = plt.imshow(seven[0,:,:])
```

After running that code, you'll see that our hopes have been achieved! Compared to the original image (left), our autoencoder image (right) is also showing a seven!:

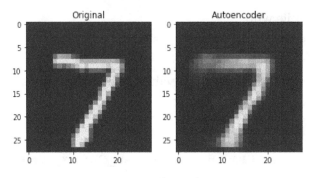

Autoencoder result

As you can see in the preceding screenshot, the reconstructed seven is still a seven, so the autoencoder was able to capture the general idea of what a seven is. It's not perfect though, as you can see it's a bit blurry around the edges, especially in the top left. It seems that while the autoencoder is unsure about the length of the lines, it does have a good idea that there are two lines in a seven and it is aware of the general direction they follow.

An autoencoder such as this one performs nonlinear PCA. It learns which components matter the most for a seven to be a seven. The usefulness of being able to learn this representation goes beyond images. Within credit card fraud detection, such principal components would make for good features that another classifier would be able to work with.

In the next section, we will apply an autoencoder to the credit card fraud problem.

Autoencoder for credit cards

Throughout this section, we will once again be dealing with the problem of credit card fraud. This time, we will be using a slightly different dataset from that in *Chapter 2, Applying Machine Learning to Structured Data*.

This new dataset contains records of actual credit card transactions with anonymized features; however, it does not lend itself much to feature engineering. Therefore, we will have to rely on end-to-end learning methods in order to build a good fraud detector.

 Note: You can find the dataset at: `https://www.kaggle.com/mlg-ulb/creditcardfraud` and the notebook with an implementation of an autoencoder and variational autoencoder at: `https://www.kaggle.com/jannesklaas/credit-vae`.

As usual, we first load the data. The `Time` feature shows the absolute time of the transaction, which makes the data a bit hard to deal with here. Therefore, we will just drop it, which we can do by running:

```
df = pd.read_csv('../input/creditcard.csv')
df = df.drop('Time',axis=1)
```

We then separate the `X` data on the transaction from the classification of the transaction and extract the NumPy array that underlies the pandas DataFrame:

```
X = df.drop('Class',axis=1).values
y = df['Class'].values
```

Now we need to scale the features. Feature scaling makes it easier for our model to learn a good representation of the data. This time around, we're going employ a slightly different method of feature scaling than what we did before. We'll scale all features to be between zero and one, as opposed to having a mean of zero and a standard deviation of one. By doing this, we ensure that there are neither any very high nor very low values in the dataset.

We must be aware that this method is susceptible to outliers influencing the result. For each column, we first subtract the minimum value, so that the new minimum value becomes zero. Next, we divide by the maximum value so that the new maximum value becomes one.

By specifying `axis=0`, we perform the scaling column-wise:

```
X -= X.min(axis=0)
X /= X.max(axis=0)
```

Then, finally, we split our data:

```
from sklearn.model_selection import train_test_split
X_train, X_test, y_train,y_test =
train_test_split(X,y,test_size=0.1)
```

We then create the exact same autoencoder as we did before; however, this time, we do it with different dimensions. Our input now has 29 dimensions, which we compress down to 12 dimensions before aiming to restore the original 29-dimensional output.

While 12 dimensions is a somewhat arbitrary choice here, it allows for enough capacity to capture all the relevant information while still significantly compressing the data:

```
from keras.models import Model
from keras.layers import Input, Dense
```

We are going to use the sigmoid activation function for the decoded data. This is only possible because we've scaled the data to have values between zero and one. We are also using a tanh activation within the encoded layer. This is just a style choice that worked well in experiments and ensures that encoded values are all between minus one and one. With that being said, you may use different activation functions depending on your individual needs.

If you are working with images or deeper networks, a ReLU activation is usually a good choice. However, if you are working with a shallower network, as we are doing here, then a tanh activation often works well:

```
data_in = Input(shape=(29,))
encoded = Dense(12,activation='tanh')(data_in)
decoded = Dense(29,activation='sigmoid')(encoded)
autoencoder = Model(data_in,decoded)
```

In this example, we've used a mean squared error loss. This seems a bit of an unusual choice at first, using a sigmoid activation with a mean squared error loss, yet it makes sense. Most people think that sigmoid activations have to be used with a cross-entropy loss, but cross-entropy loss encourages values to either be zero or one, which works well for classification tasks where this is the case.

In our credit card example, most values will be around 0.5. Mean squared error, which we can see being implemented in the code below, is better at dealing with values where the target is not binary, but on a spectrum. Binary cross entropy forces values to be close to zero and one, which is not what we always want:

```
autoencoder.compile(optimizer='adam',loss='mean_squared_error')
```

After training, which will take around two minutes, the autoencoder converges to a low loss:

```
autoencoder.fit(X_train,
                X_train,
                epochs = 20,
                batch_size=128,
                validation_data=(X_test,X_test))
```

The reconstruction loss is low, but how do we know whether our autoencoder is working well? Once again, a visual inspection will come to the rescue. As we've explained before, humans are very good at judging things visually, but not very good at judging abstract numbers.

To run a visual inspection, first we must make some predictions, in which we'll run a subset of our test set through the autoencoder:

```
pred = autoencoder.predict(X_test[0:10])
```

We must can then plot individual samples. The following code produces an overlaid bar chart comparing the original transaction data with the reconstructed transaction data:

```
import matplotlib.pyplot as plt
import numpy as np

width = 0.8

prediction   = pred[9]
true_value   = X_test[9]

indices = np.arange(len(prediction))

fig = plt.figure(figsize=(10,7))

plt.bar(indices, prediction, width=width,
        color='b', label='Predicted Value')

plt.bar([i+0.25*width for i in indices], true_value,
        width=0.5*width, color='r', alpha=0.5, label='True Value')

plt.xticks(indices+width/2.,
            ['V{}'.format(i) for i in range(len(prediction))] )

plt.legend()

plt.show()
```

This code will then give us the following chart:

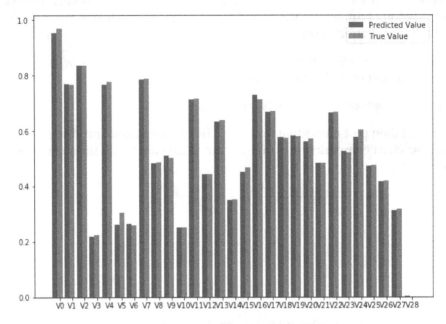

Autoencoder reconstruction versus original data

As you can see, our model does a fine job at reconstructing the original values. The reconstructed values often match the true values, and if they don't, then they only deviate by a small margin. As you can see, visual inspection gives more insight than looking at abstract numbers.

Visualizing latent spaces with t-SNE

We now have an autoencoder that takes in a credit card transaction and outputs a credit card transaction that looks more or less the same. However, this is not why we built the autoencoder. The main advantage of an autoencoder is that we can now encode the transaction into a lower dimensional representation that captures the main elements of the transaction.

To create the encoder model, all we have to do is to define a new Keras model that maps from the input to the encoded state:

```
encoder = Model(data_in,encoded)
```

Note that you don't need to train this model again. The layers keep the weights from the previously trained autoencoder.

To encode our data, we now use the encoder model:

```
enc = encoder.predict(X_test)
```

But how would we know whether these encodings contain any meaningful information about fraud? Once again, visual representation is key. While our encodings have fewer dimensions than the input data, they still have 12 dimensions. It's impossible for humans to think about a 12-dimensional space, so we need to draw our encodings in a lower dimensional space while still preserving the characteristics we care about.

In our case, the characteristic we care about is *proximity*. We want points that are close to each other in the 12-dimensional space to be close to each other in the 2-dimensional plot. More precisely, we care about the neighborhood. We want the points that are closest to each other in the high-dimensional space to also be closest to each other in the low-dimensional space.

Preserving the neighborhood is important because we want to find clusters of fraud. If we find that fraudulent transactions form a cluster in our high-dimensional encodings, then we can use a simple check if a new transaction falls into the fraud cluster to flag a transaction as fraudulent. A popular method to project high-dimensional data into low-dimensional plots while preserving neighborhoods is called **t-distributed stochastic neighbor embedding, or t-SNE**.

In a nutshell, t-SNE aims to faithfully represent the probability that two points are neighbors in a random sample of all points. That is, it tries to find a low-dimensional representation of data in which points in a random sample have the same probability of being the closest neighbors as in the high-dimensional data:

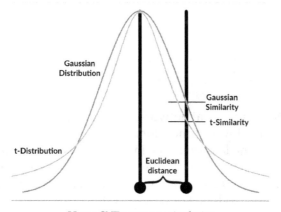

How t-SNE measures similarity

The t-SNE algorithm follows these steps:

1. Calculate the Gaussian similarity between all points. This is done by calculating the Euclidean (spatial) distance between points and then calculating the value of a Gaussian curve at that distance, as you can see in the preceding diagram. The Gaussian similarity for all points, j, from point i can be calculated as follows:

$$p_{i|j} = \frac{exp\left(-\|x_i - x_j\|^2 / 2\sigma_i^2\right)}{\sum_{k \neq i} exp\left(-\|x_i - x_k\|^2 / 2\sigma_i^2\right)}$$

In the preceding formula, σ_i^2 is the variance of the Gaussian distribution. We will look at how to determine this variance later on in this chapter. Note that since the similarity between points i and j is scaled by the sum of distances between i and all other points (expressed as k), the similarity between i and j, $p_{i|j}$, can be different from the similarity between j and i, $p_{j|i}$. Therefore, we average the two similarities to gain the final similarity that we'll work with going forward:

$$p_{ij} = \frac{p_{i|j} + p_{j,i}}{2n}$$

In the preceding formula, n is the number of data points.

2. Randomly position the data points in the lower dimensional space.

3. Calculate the *t-similarity* between all the points in the lower dimensional space:

$$q_{ij} = \frac{\left(1 + \|y_i - y_j\|^2\right)^{-1}}{\sum_{k \neq l}\left(1 + \|y_k - y_l\|^2\right)^{-1}}$$

4. Just like in training neural networks, we will optimize the positions of the data points in the lower dimensional space by following the gradient of a loss function. The loss function, in this case, is the **Kullback–Leibler (KL)** divergence between the similarities in the higher and lower dimensional space. We will give the KL divergence a closer look in the section on variational autoencoders. For now, just think of it as a way to measure the difference between two distributions. The derivative of the loss function with respect to the position y_i of data point i in the lower dimensional space is as follows:

$$\frac{dL}{dy_i} = 4\sum\left(p_{ij} - q_{ij}\right)\left(y_i - y_j\right)\left(1 + \|y_i - y_j\|^2\right)^{-1}$$

5. Adjust the data points in the lower dimensional space by using gradient descent, moving points that were close in the high-dimensional data closer together and moving points that were further away further from each other:

$$y^{(t)} = y^{(t-1)} + \frac{dL}{dy} + \alpha(t)\left(y^{(t-1)} - y^{(t-2)}\right)$$

6. You will recognize this as a form of gradient descent with momentum, as the previous gradient is incorporated into the updated position.

The t-distribution used always has one degree of freedom. This freedom leads to a simpler formula as well as some nice numerical properties that lead to faster computation and more useful charts.

The standard deviation of the Gaussian distribution can be influenced by the user with a *perplexity* hyperparameter. Perplexity can be interpreted as the number of neighbors we expect a point to have. A low perplexity value emphasizes local proximities, while a high perplexity value emphasizes global perplexity values. Mathematically, perplexity can be calculated as follows:

$$Perp\left(P_i\right) = 2^{H(P_i)}$$

Here P_i is a probability distribution over the position of all data points in the dataset and $H(P_i)$ is the Shanon entropy of this distribution, calculated as follows:

$$H\left(P_i\right) = -\sum p_{j|i} log_2 p_{j|i}$$

While the details of this formula are not very relevant to using t-SNE, it is important to know that t-SNE performs a search over values of the standard deviation, σ, so that it finds a global distribution, P_i, for which the entropy over our data is of our desired perplexity. In other words, you need to specify the perplexity by hand, but what that perplexity means for your dataset also depends on the dataset itself.

Laurens Van Maarten and Geoffrey Hinton, the inventors of t-SNE, report that the algorithm is relatively robust for choices of perplexity between 5 and 50. The default value in most libraries is 30, which is a fine value for most datasets. However, if you find that your visualizations are not satisfactory, then tuning the perplexity value is probably the first thing you would want to do.

For all the math involved, using t-SNE is surprisingly simple. Scikit-learn has a handy t-SNE implementation that we can use just like any algorithm in scikit-learn.

We first import the TSNE class, and then we can create a new TSNE instance. We define that we want to train for 5000 epochs, and use the default perplexity of 30 and the default learning rate of 200. We also specify that we would like output during the training process. We then call `fit_transform`, which transforms our 12 encodings into 2-dimensional projections:

```
from sklearn.manifold import TSNE
tsne = TSNE(verbose=1,n_iter=5000)
res = tsne.fit_transform(enc)
```

As a word of warning, t-SNE is quite slow as it needs to compute the distances between all the points. By default, scikit-learn uses a faster version of t-SNE called the Barnes Hut approximation. While it's not as precise, it's significantly faster.

There's also a faster Python implementation of t-SNE that can be used as a drop-in replacement of the scikit-learn implementation. However, this is not as well documented and contains fewer features, therefore we will not be covering it in this book.

> **Note**: You can find the faster implementation with installation instructions under the following URL https://github.com/DmitryUlyanov/Multicore-TSNE.

We can then plot our t-SNE results as a scatterplot. For illustration, we will distinguish frauds from non-frauds by color, with frauds being plotted in red and non-frauds being plotted in blue. Since the actual values of t-SNE do not matter as much, we will hide the axes:

```
fig = plt.figure(figsize=(10,7))
scatter =plt.scatter(res[:,0],res[:,1],c=y_test,
cmap='coolwarm', s=0.6)
scatter.axes.get_xaxis().set_visible(False)
scatter.axes.get_yaxis().set_visible(False)
```

Let's now see, what the output chart will look like:

t-SNE results in the form of a scatter graph

For easier spotting, and for those reading the print version, the cluster containing the most frauds, those that are marked red, has been marked with a circle. You can see that the frauds are nicely separate from the rest of the genuine transactions, those in blue. Clearly, our autoencoder has found a way to distinguish frauds from the genuine transaction without being given labels. This is a form of unsupervised learning.

In fact, plain autoencoders perform an approximation of PCA, which is useful for unsupervised learning. In the output chart, you can see that there are a few more clusters that are clearly separate from the other transactions, yet these are not frauds. Using autoencoders and unsupervised learning, it is possible to separate and group our data in ways that we did not even think of before. For example, we might be able to cluster transactions by purchase type.

Using our autoencoder, we could now use the encoded information as features for a classifier. However, what's even better is that with only a slight modification of the autoencoder, we can generate more data that has the underlying properties of a fraud case while having different features. This is done with a variational autoencoder, which will be the focus of the next section.

Variational autoencoders

Autoencoders are basically an approximation for PCA. However, they can be extended to become generative models. Given an input, **variational autoencoders (VAEs)** can create encoding *distributions*. This means that for a fraud case, the encoder would produce a distribution of possible encodings that all represent the most important characteristics of the transaction. The decoder would then turn all of the encodings back into the original transaction.

This is useful since it allows us to generate data about transactions. One problem of fraud detection that we discovered earlier is that there are not all that many fraudulent transactions. Therefore, by using a VAE, we can sample any amount of transaction encodings and train our classifier with more fraudulent transaction data.

So, how do VAEs do it? Instead of having just one compressed representation vector, a VAE has two: one for the mean encoding, μ, and one for the standard deviation of this encoding, σ:

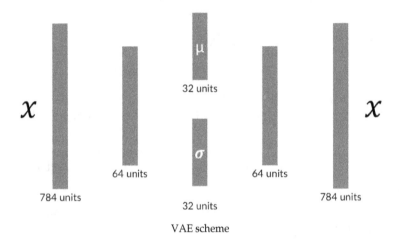

VAE scheme

Both the mean and standard deviation are vectors, just as with the encoding vector we used for the vanilla autoencoder. However, to create the actual encoding, we simply need to add random noise with the standard deviation, σ, to our encoding vector.

To achieve a broad distribution of values, our network trains with a combination of two losses: the reconstruction loss, which you know from the vanilla autoencoder; and the KL divergence loss between the encoding distribution and a standard Gaussian distribution with a standard deviation of one.

MNIST example

Now on to our first VAE. This VAE will work with the MNIST dataset and give you a better idea about how VAEs work. In the next section, we will build the same VAE for credit card fraud detection.

Firstly, we need to import several elements, which we can do simply by running:

```
from keras.models import Model
from keras.layers import Input, Dense, Lambda
from keras import backend as K
from keras import metrics
```

Notice the two new imports, the `Lambda` layer and the `metrics` module. The `metrics` module provides metrics, such as the cross-entropy loss, which we will use to build our custom loss function. Meanwhile the `Lambda` layer allows us to use Python functions as layers, which we will use to sample from the encoding distribution. We will see just how the `Lambda` layer works in a bit, but first, we need to set up the rest of the neural network.

The first thing we need to do is to define a few hyperparameters. Our data has an original dimensionality of 784, which we compress into a latent vector with 32 dimensions. Our network has an intermediate layer between the input and the latent vector, which has 256 dimensions. We will train for 50 epochs with a batch size of 100:

```
batch_size = 100
original_dim = 784
latent_dim = 32
intermediate_dim = 256
epochs = 50
```

For computational reasons, it is easier to learn the log of the standard deviation rather than the standard deviation itself. To do this we create the first half of our network, in which the input, x, maps to the intermediate layer, h. From this layer, our network splits into z_mean, which expresses μ and z_log_var, which expresses $log\,\sigma$:

```
x = Input(shape=(original_dim,))
h = Dense(intermediate_dim, activation='relu')(x)
z_mean = Dense(latent_dim)(h)
z_log_var = Dense(latent_dim)(h)
```

Using the Lambda layer

The Lambda layer wraps an arbitrary expression, that is, a Python function, as a Keras layer. Yet there are a few requirements in order to make this work. For backpropagation to work, the function needs to be differentiable. After all, we want to update the network weights by the gradient of the loss. Luckily, Keras comes with a number of functions in its backend module that are all differentiable, and simple Python math, such as $y = x + 4$, is fine as well.

Additionally, a Lambda function can only take one input argument. In the layer we want to create, the input is just the previous layer's output tensor. In this case, we want to create a layer with two inputs, μ and σ. Therefore, we will wrap both inputs into a tuple that we can then take apart.

You can see the function for sampling below:

```
def sampling(args):
    z_mean, z_log_var = args                                      #1
    epsilon = K.random_normal(shape=(K.shape(z_mean)[0],
latent_dim),
                              mean=0.,
                              stddev=1.0)                         #2
    return z_mean + K.exp(z_log_var / 2) * epsilon               #3
```

Let's take a minute to break down the function:

1. We take apart the input tuple and have our two input tensors.

2. We create a tensor containing random, normally distributed noise with a mean of zero and a standard deviation of one. The tensor has the shape as our input tensors (batch_size, latent_dim).

3. Finally, we multiply the random noise with our standard deviation to give it the learned standard deviation and add the learned mean. Since we are learning the log standard deviation, we have to apply the exponent function to our learned tensor.

All these operations are differentiable since we are using the Keras backend functions. Now we can turn this function into a layer and connect it to the previous two layers with one line:

```
z = Lambda(sampling)([z_mean, z_log_var])
```

And voilà! We've now got a custom layer that samples from a normal distribution described by two tensors. Keras can automatically backpropagate through this layer and train the weights of the layers before it.

Now that we have encoded our data, we also need to decode it as well. We are able to do this with two `Dense` layers:

```
decoder_h = Dense(intermediate_dim, activation='relu')(z)
x_decoded = Dense(original_dim, activation='sigmoid')
decoder_mean(h_decoded)
```

Our network is now complete. This network will encode any MNIST image into a mean and a standard deviation tensor from which the decoding part then reconstructs the image. The only thing missing is the custom loss incentivizing the network to both reconstruct images and produce a normal Gaussian distribution in its encodings. Let's address that now.

Kullback–Leibler divergence

To create the custom loss for our VAE, we need a custom loss function. This loss function will be based on the **Kullback-Leibler** (**KL**) divergence.

KL divergence, is one of the metrics, just like cross-entropy, that machine learning inherited from information theory. While it is used frequently, there are many struggles you can encounter when trying to understand it.

At its core, KL divergence measures how much information is lost when distribution p is approximated with distribution q.

Imagine you are working on a financial model and have collected data on the returns of a security investment. Your financial modeling tools all assume a normal distribution of returns. The following chart shows the actual distribution of returns versus an approximation using a normal distribution model. For the sake of this example, let's assume there are only discrete returns. Before we go ahead, be assured that we'll cover continuous distributions later:

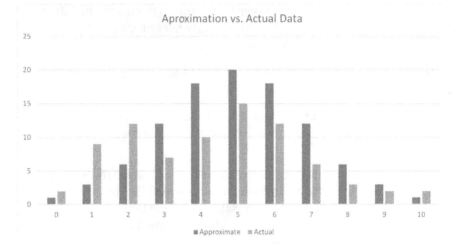

Approximation versus actual

Of course, the returns in your data are not exactly normally distributed. So, just how much information about returns would you lose if you did lose the approximation? This is exactly what the KL divergence is measuring:

$$D_{KL}\left(p\|q\right) = \sum_{i=1}^{N} p\left(x_i\right)\cdot\left(\log p\left(x_i\right) - \log q\left(x_i\right)\right)$$

Here $p(x_i)$ and $q(x_i)$ are the probabilities that x, in this case, the return, has some value i, say 5%. The preceding formula effectively expresses the expected difference in the logarithm of probabilities of the distributions p and q:

$$D_{KL} = E\left[\log p\left(x\right) - \log q\left(x\right)\right]$$

This expected difference of log probabilities is the same as the average information lost if you approximate distribution p with distribution q. See the following:

$$\log a - \log b = \log \frac{a}{b}$$

Given that the KL divergence is usually written out as follows:

$$D_{KL}\left(p\|q\right) = \sum_{i=1}^{N} p\left(x_i\right)\cdot\log \frac{p\left(x_i\right)}{q\left(x_i\right)}$$

It can also be written in its continuous form as:

$$D_{KL}\left(p\|q\right)=\int_{-\infty}^{\infty}p\left(x_i\right)\cdot log\frac{p\left(x_i\right)}{q\left(x_i\right)}$$

For VAEs, we want the distribution of encodings to be a normal Gaussian distribution with a mean of zero and a standard deviation of one.

When p is substituted with the normal Gaussian distribution, $N(0,1)$, and the approximation q is a normal distribution with a mean of μ and a standard deviation of σ, $N(\mu,\sigma)$, the KL divergence, simplifies to the following:

$$D_{KL}=-0.5*\left(1+log\left(\sigma\right)-\mu^2-\sigma\right)$$

The partial derivatives to our mean and standard deviation vectors are, therefore as follows:

$$\frac{dD_{KL}}{d\mu}=\mu$$

With the other being:

$$\frac{dD_{KL}}{d\sigma}=-0.5*\frac{\left(\sigma-1\right)}{\sigma}$$

You can see that the derivative with respect to μ is zero if μ is zero, and the derivative with respect to σ is zero if σ is one. This loss term is added to the reconstruction loss.

Creating a custom loss

The VAE loss is a combination of two losses: a reconstruction loss incentivizing the model to reconstruct its input well, and a KL divergence loss which is incentivizing the model to approximate a normal Gaussian distribution with its encodings. To create this combined loss, we have to first calculate the two loss components separately before combining them.

The reconstruction loss is the same loss that we applied for the vanilla autoencoder. Binary cross-entropy is an appropriate loss for MNIST reconstruction. Since Keras' implementation of a binary cross-entropy loss already takes the mean across the batch, an operation we only want to do later, we have to scale the loss back up, so that we can divide it by the output dimensionality:

```
reconstruction_loss = original_dim *
metrics.binary_crossentropy(x, x_decoded)
```

The KL divergence loss is the simplified version of KL divergence, which we discussed earlier on in the section on KL divergence:

$$D_{KL} = -0.5 * \left(1 + log\left(\sigma\right) - \mu^2 - \sigma\right)$$

Expressed in Python, the KL divergence loss appears like the following code:

```
kl_loss = - 0.5 * K.sum(1 + z_log_var - K.square(z_mean)
                              - K.exp(z_log_var), axis=-1)
```

Our final loss is then the mean of the sum of the reconstruction loss and KL divergence loss:

```
vae_loss = K.mean(reconstruction_loss + kl_loss)
```

Since we have used the Keras backend for all of the calculations, the resulting loss is a tensor that can be automatically differentiated. Now we can create our model as usual:

```
vae = Model(x, x_decoded)
```

Since we are using a custom loss, we have the loss separately, and we can't just add it in the `compile` statement:

```
vae.add_loss(vae_loss)
```

Now we will compile the model. Since our model already has a loss, we only have to specify the optimizer:

```
vae.compile(optimizer='rmsprop')
```

Another side effect of the custom loss is that it compares the *output* of the VAE with the *input* of the VAE, which makes sense as we want to reconstruct the input. Therefore, we do not have to specify the *y* values, as only specifying an input is enough:

```
vae.fit(X_train_flat,
        shuffle=True,
        epochs=epochs,
        batch_size=batch_size,
        validation_data=(X_test_flat, None))
```

In the next section we will learn how we can use a VAE to generate data.

Using a VAE to generate data

So, we've got our autoencoder, but how do we generate more data? Well, we take an input, say, a picture of a seven, and run it through the autoencoder multiple times. Since the autoencoder is randomly sampling from a distribution, the output will be slightly different at each run.

To showcase this, from our test data, we're going to take a seven:

```
one_seven = X_test_flat[0]
```

We then add a batch dimension and repeat the seven across the batch four times. After which we now have a batch of four, identical sevens:

```
one_seven = np.expand_dims(one_seven,0)
one_seven = one_seven.repeat(4,axis=0)
```

We can then make a prediction on that batch, in which case, we get back the reconstructed sevens:

```
s = vae.predict(one_seven)
```

The next step is broken in two parts. Firstly, we're going to reshape all the sevens back into image form:

```
s= s.reshape(4,28,28)
```

Then we are going to plot them:

```
fig=plt.figure(figsize=(8, 8))
columns = 2
rows = 2
for i in range(1, columns*rows +1):
    img = s[i-1]
    fig.add_subplot(rows, columns, i)
    plt.imshow(img)
plt.show()
```

As a result of running the code that we've just walked through, we'll then see the following screenshot showing our four sevens as our output:

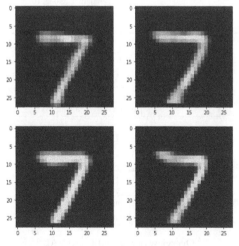

A collection of sevens

As you can see, all of the images show a seven. While they look quite similar, if you look closely, you can see that there are several distinct differences. The seven on the top left has a less pronounced stroke than the seven on the bottom left. Meanwhile, the seven on the bottom right has a sight bow at the end.

What we've just witnessed is the VAE successfully creating new data. While using this data for more training is not as good as compared to using using completely new real-world data, it is still very useful. While generative models such as this one are nice on the eye we will now discuss how this technique can be used for credit card fraud detection.

VAEs for an end-to-end fraud detection system

To transfer the VAE from an MNIST example to a real fraud detection problem, all we have to do is change three hyperparameters: the input, the intermediate, and the latent dimensionality of the credit card VAE, which are all smaller than for the MNIST VAE. Everything else will remain the same:

```
original_dim = 29
latent_dim = 6
intermediate_dim = 16
```

The following visualization shows the resulting VAE including both the input and output shapes:

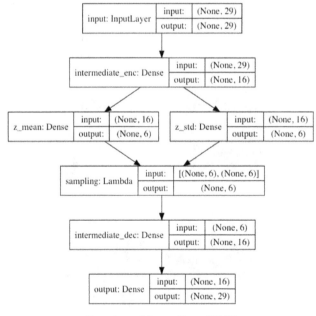

Overview of the credit card VAE

Armed with a VAE that can encode and generate credit card data, we can now tackle the task of an end-to-end fraud detection system. This can reduce bias in predictions as we can learn complicated rules directly from data.

We are using the encoding part of the autoencoder as a feature extractor as well as a method to give us more data where we need it. How exactly that works will be covered in the section on active learning, but for now, let's take a little detour and look at how VAEs work for time series.

VAEs for time series

This section covers the how and why of time series VAEs and gives a couple of examples where they have been used. Time series are such a big topic in finance that *Chapter 4, Understanding Time Series,* is heavily focused to it.

Autoencoders have found applications in connection to time series as they are able to encode a long time series into a single, descriptive vector. This vector can then, for example, be used to efficiently compare one time series to another time series, based on specific and complex patterns that cannot be captured with a simple correlation, for instance.

Consider the 2010 "Flash Crash." On May 6, 2010, starting at 02:32, US markets saw a major loss of value. The Dow Jones Industrial Average lost about 9%, which equates to about a trillion dollars' worth of value being wiped out in a couple of minutes. 36 minutes later, the crash was over, most of the lost value was regained, and people started wondering what on earth had just happened.

Five years later, a man named Navinder Singh Sarao was arrested for having in part caused the flash crash and having made $40 million in the process. Sarao engaged in a practice called "spoofing" in which he used an automated bot to place large sell orders that could not be filled in the market but would drive prices down.

The bot would leave the orders in the order books of the stock exchange for only a short period of time before canceling them. In the mean time, Sarao would buy the stock at the new lower prices and then profit when the stocks started rebounding after the canceled sales orders. While Sarao was certainly not the only one responsible for the flash crash, practices such as spoofing are now illegal, and exchanges, such as the NASDAQ (US), Tokyo (Japan), and Bombay (India) Stock Exchanges, now have to monitor and flag such cases.

If you dig back into old blog posts about high-frequency trading, such as Bloomberg's *Spoofers Keep Markets Honest*, which you can view at `https://www.bloomberg.com/opinion/articles/2015-01-23/high-frequency-trading-spoofers-and-front-running`, then you will find that some traders working at large firms openly recommend spoofing or front-running large orders, but that is a story for another time.

How would we detect when someone engages in spoofing? One way is to use an autoencoder. By using a large amount of order book information, we can train an autoencoder to reconstruct "normal" trading behavior. For traders whose trading patterns deviate a lot from normal trading, the reconstruction loss of the trained autoencoder for the transaction will be quite high.

Another option is to train the autoencoder on different kinds of patterns, whether these are illegal or not, and then cluster the patterns in the latent space, just as we did for the fraudulent credit card transactions.

Recurrent neural networks (RNNs), by default, take in a time series and output a single vector. They can also output sequences if Keras' `return_sequences` argument is set to `True`. Using recurrent neural networks such as LSTMs, building an autoencoder for time series can be done using the following code:

```
from keras.models import Sequential
from keras.layers import LSTM, RepeatVector

model = Sequential()                                              #1
model.add(LSTM(latent_dim, input_shape=(maxlen, nb_features)))    #2
model.add(RepeatVector(maxlen))                                   #3
model.add(LSTM(nb_features, return_sequences=True))              #4
```

Let's pause for a second and break down what we've just coded. As you can see, there are four key elements to this code:

1. A simple autoencoder is built using the sequential API.

2. We first feed our sequence length, `maxlen`, along with the number of features equal to `nb_features` into an LSTM. The LSTM will only return its last output, a single vector of dimension `latent_dim`. This vector is the encoding of our sequence.

3. To decode the vector, we need to repeat it over the length of the time series. This is done by the `RepeatVector` layer.

4. Now we feed the sequence of repeated encodings into a decoding LSTM, which this time returns the full sequence.

VAEs can also find their way into trading. They can be used to augment backtesting by generating new, unseen data for testing. Likewise, we can use VAEs to generate data about contracts where data is missing.

It is reasonable to assume that just because two market days look a bit different, the same forces might be at work. Mathematically, we can assume that market data $\{x_i\}$ is sampled from a probability distribution, $p(x)$, with a small number of latent variables, h. Using an autoencoder, we can then approximate $p(h \mid x)$, the distribution of h given x. This will allow us to analyze the driving forces, h, in a market.

This solves the problem that a standard maximum likelihood model for this kind of problem is computationally intractable. Two other methods performing the same feat are the *Markov Chain Monte Carlo* and *Hamilton Monte Carlo* methods. While neither will be covered in depth here, though they will be featured in later chapters, it's worth understanding that VAEs address long-standing problems in mathematical finance in a computationally tractable way.

Generative models can also be used to solve problems beyond the scope of traditional methods. Financial markets are fundamentally adversarial environments in which investors are trying to achieve something that is impossible in aggregate: above-average returns. Knowing that a company is doing well is not enough: if everyone knows the company is doing well, then the stock price will be high and returns will be low. The key is knowing that a company is doing well while everyone else believes it is doing poorly. Markets are a zero-sum game-theoretic environment. GANs make use of these dynamics to generate realistic data.

GANs

GANs work a lot like an art forger and a museum curator. Every day, the art forger tries to sell some fake art to the museum, and every day the curator tries to distinguish whether a certain piece is real or fake. The forger learns from their failures. By trying to fool the curator and observing what leads to success and failure, they become a better forger. But the curator learns too. By trying to stay ahead of the forger, they become a better curator. As time passes, the forgeries become better and so does the distinguishing process. After years of battle, the art forger is an expert that can draw just as well as Picasso and the curator is an expert that can distinguish a real painting by tiny details.

Technically, a GAN consists of two neural networks: a *generator,* which produces data from a random latent vector, and a *discriminator,* which classifies data as "real," that is, stemming from the training set, or "fake," that is, stemming from the generator.

We can visualize a GAN scheme, as we can see in the following diagram:

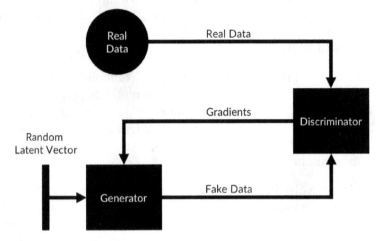

GAN scheme

Once again, generative models are easier to understand when images are generated, so in this section, we will look at image data, although all kinds of data can be used.

The training process for a GAN works as follows:

1. A latent vector containing random numbers is created.

2. The latent vector is fed into the generator, which produces an image.

3. A set of fake images from the generator is mixed with a set of real images from the training set. The discriminator is trained in the binary classification of real and fake data.

4. After the discriminator has been trained for a while we feed in the fake images again. This time, we set the label of the fake images to "real." We backpropagate through the discriminator and obtain the loss gradient with respect to the *input* of the discriminator. We do *not* update the weights of the discriminator based on this information.

5. We now have gradients describing how we would have to change our fake image so that the discriminator would classify it as a real image. We use these gradients to backpropagate and train the generator.

6. With our new and improved generator, we once again create fake images, which get mixed with real images in order to train the discriminator, whose gradients are used to train the generator again.

Note: GAN training has a lot of similarities to the visualization of the network layers that we discussed in *Chapter 3, Utilizing Computer Vision,* only this time we don't just create one image that maximizes an activation function, instead we create a generative network that specializes in maximizing the activation function of another network.

Mathematically, generator G and discriminator D play a mini-max two-player game with the value function $V(G,D)$:

$$\min_{G} \max_{D} V(G,D) = \mathbb{E}_{x \sim p_{data}(x)} \Big[\log D(x)\Big] + \mathbb{E}_{z \sim p_z(z)} \Big[\log\big(1 - D\big(G(z)\big)\big)\Big]$$

In this formula x is an item drawn from the distribution of real data, p_{data}, and z is a latent vector drawn from the latent vector space, p_z.

The output distribution of the generator is noted as p_g. It can be shown that the global optimum of this game is $p_g = p_{data}$, that is, if the distribution of the generated data is equal to the distribution of actual data.

GANs get optimized following a game-theoretic value function. Solving this type of optimization problem with deep learning is an active area of research, and an area we will visit again in *Chapter 8, Privacy, Debugging, and Launching Your Products,* where we will discuss reinforcement learning. The fact that deep learning can be used to solve Minimax games is exciting news for the field of finance and economics, which features many such problems.

A MNIST GAN

Let's now implement a GAN in order to generate MNIST characters. Before we start, we need to do some imports. GANs are large models, and in this section you will see how to combine sequential and functional API models for easy model building:

```
from keras.models import Model, Sequential
```

In this example we will be using a few new layer types:

```
from keras.layers import Input, Dense, Dropout, Flatten
from keras.layers import LeakyReLU, Reshape
from keras.layers import Conv2D, UpSampling2D
```

Let's look at some of the key elements:

- LeakyReLU is just like ReLU, except that the activation allows for small negative values. This prevents the gradient from ever becoming zero. This activation function works well for GANs, something we will discuss in the next section:

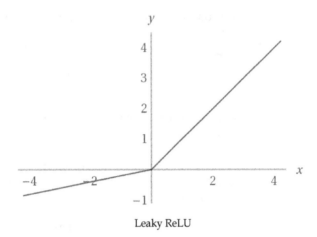

Leaky ReLU

- Reshape does the same as np.reshape: it brings a tensor into a new form.
- UpSampling2D scales a 2D feature map up, for example, by a factor of two, by repeating all numbers in the feature map.

We will be using the Adam optimizer as we often do:

```
from keras.optimizers import Adam
```

Neural network layers get initialized randomly. Usually, the random numbers are drawn from a distribution that supports learning well. For GANs, it turns out that a normal Gaussian distribution is a better alternative:

```
from keras.initializers import RandomNormal
```

Now we're going to build the generator model:

```
generator = Sequential()                                          #1

generator.add(Dense(128*7*7, input_dim=latent_dim,
              kernel_initializer=RandomNormal(stddev=0.02)))      #2

generator.add(LeakyReLU(0.2))                                     #3
generator.add(Reshape((128, 7, 7)))                               #4
generator.add(UpSampling2D(size=(2, 2)))                          #5

generator.add(Conv2D(64,kernel_size=(5, 5),padding='same'))       #6
```

```
generator.add(LeakyReLU(0.2))                              #7
generator.add(UpSampling2D(size=(2, 2)))                   #8

generator.add(Conv2D(1, kernel_size=(5, 5),
                        padding='same',
                        activation='tanh'))                #9

adam = Adam(lr=0.0002, beta_1=0.5)
generator.compile(loss='binary_crossentropy', optimizer=adam) #10
```

Again, let's take a look at the generator model code, which consists of 10 key steps:

1. We construct the generator as a sequential model.
2. The first layer takes in the random latent vector and maps it to a vector with dimensions $128 * 7 * 7 = 6,272$. It already significantly expands the dimensionality of our generated data. For this fully connected layer, it is important to initialize weights from a normal Gaussian distribution with a relatively small standard deviation. A Gaussian distribution, as opposed to a uniform distribution, will have fewer extreme values, which will make training easier.
3. The activation function for the first layer is LeakyReLU. We need to specify how steep the slope for negative inputs is; in this case, negative inputs are multiplied with 0.2.
4. Now we reshape our flat vector into a 3D tensor. This is the opposite of using a Flatten layer, which we did in *Chapter 3, Utilizing Computer Vision*. We now have a tensor with 128 channels in a 7x7-pixel image or feature map.
5. Using UpSampling2D, we enlarge this image to 14x14 pixels. The size argument specifies the multiplier factor for width and height.
6. Now we can apply a standard Conv2D layer. As opposed to the case with most image classifiers, we use a relatively large kernel size of 5x5 pixels.
7. The activation following the Conv2D layer is another LeakyReLU.
8. We upsample again, bringing the image to 28x28 pixels, the same dimensions as an MNIST image.
9. The final convolutional layer of our generator outputs only a single channel image, as MNIST images are only black and white. Notice how the activation of this final layer is a tanh activation. Tanh squishes all values to between negative one and one. This might be unexpected as image data usually does not feature any values below zero. Empirically, it turned out, however, that tanh activations work much better for GANs than sigmoid activations.
10. Finally, we compile the generator to train with the Adam optimizer with a very small learning rate and smaller-than-usual momentum.

The discriminator is a relatively standard image classifier that classifies images as real or fake. There are only a few GAN-specific modifications:

```
#Discriminator
discriminator = Sequential()
discriminator.add(Conv2D(64, kernel_size=(5, 5),
                        strides=(2, 2),
                        padding='same',
                        input_shape=(1, 28, 28),
                        kernel_initializer=RandomNormal(stdd
ev=0.02)))                                              #1

discriminator.add(LeakyReLU(0.2))
discriminator.add(Dropout(0.3))
discriminator.add(Conv2D(128, kernel_size=(5, 5),
                        strides=(2, 2),
                        padding='same'))
discriminator.add(LeakyReLU(0.2))
discriminator.add(Dropout(0.3))                         #2
discriminator.add(Flatten())
discriminator.add(Dense(1, activation='sigmoid'))
discriminator.compile(loss='binary_crossentropy', optimizer=adam)
```

There are two key elements here:

1. As with the generator, the first layer of the discriminator should be initialized randomly from a Gaussian distribution.

2. Dropout is commonly used in image classifiers. For GANs, it should also be used just before the last layer.

Now we have both a generator and a discriminator. To train the generator, we have to get the gradients from the discriminator to backpropagate through and train the generator. This is where the power of Keras' modular design comes into play.

[**Note:** Keras models can be treated just like Keras layers.]

The following code creates a GAN model that can be used to train the generator from the discriminator gradients:

```
discriminator.trainable = False                          #1
ganInput = Input(shape=(latent_dim,))                    #2
x = generator(ganInput)                                  #3
ganOutput = discriminator(x)                             #4
gan = Model(inputs=ganInput, outputs=ganOutput)          #5
gan.compile(loss='binary_crossentropy', optimizer=adam)  #6
```

Within that code, there are six key stages:

1. When training the generator, we do not want to train `discriminator`. When setting `discriminator` to non-trainable, the weights are frozen only for the model that is compiled with the non-trainable weights. That is, we can still train the `discriminator` model on its own, but as soon as it becomes part of the GAN model that is compiled again, its weights are frozen.

2. We create a new input for our GAN, which takes in the random latent vector.

3. We connect the generator model to the `ganInput` layer. The model can be used just like a layer under the functional API.

4. We now connect the discriminator with frozen weights to the generator. Again, we call the model in the same way we would use a layer in the functional API.

5. We create a model that maps an input to the output of the discriminator.

6. We compile our GAN model. Since we call `compile` here, the weights of the discriminator model are frozen for as long as they are part of the GAN model. Keras will throw a warning on training time that the weights are not frozen for the actual discriminator model.

Training our GAN requires some customization of the training process and a couple of GAN-specific tricks as well. More specifically, we have to write our own training loop, something that we'll achieve with the following code:

```
epochs=50
batchSize=128
batchCount = X_train.shape[0] // batchSize                      #1

for e in range(1, epochs+1):                                    #2
    print('-'*15, 'Epoch %d' % e, '-'*15)
    for _ in tqdm(range(batchCount)):                           #3

        noise = np.random.normal(0, 1,
                          size=[batchSize, latent_dim])  #4
        imageBatch = X_train[np.random.randint(0,
                                  X_train.shape[0],
                                  size=batchSize)]  #5


        generatedImages = generator.predict(noise)             #6
        X = np.concatenate([imageBatch, generatedImages])      #7

        yDis = np.zeros(2*batchSize)                            #8
        yDis[:batchSize] = 0.9
```

```
labelNoise = np.random.random(yDis.shape)                #9
yDis += 0.05 * labelNoise + 0.05


discriminator.trainable = True                           #10
dloss = discriminator.train_on_batch(X, yDis)            #11


noise = np.random.normal(0, 1,
                         size=[batchSize, latent_dim])   #12
yGen = np.ones(batchSize)                                #13
discriminator.trainable = False                          #14
gloss = gan.train_on_batch(noise, yGen)                  #15

dLosses.append(dloss)                                    #16
gLosses.append(gloss)
```

That was a lot of code we just introduced. So, let's take a minute to pause and think about the 16 key steps:

1. We have to write a custom loop to loop over the batches. To know how many batches there are, we need to make an integer division of our dataset size by our batch size.

2. In the outer loop, we iterate over the number of epochs we want to train.

3. In the inner loop, we iterate over the number of batches we want to train on in each epoch. The tqdm tool helps us keep track of progress within the batch.

4. We create a batch of random latent vectors.

5. We randomly sample a batch of real MNIST images.

6. We use the generator to generate a batch of fake MNIST images.

7. We stack the real and fake MNIST images together.

8. We create the target for our discriminator. Fake images are encoded with 0, and real images with 0.9. This technique is called soft labels. Instead of hard labels (zero and one), we use something softer in order to not train the GAN too aggressively. This technique has been shown to make GAN training more stable.

9. On top of using soft labels, we add some noise to the labels. This, once again, will make the training more stable.

10. We make sure that the discriminator is trainable.

11. We train the discriminator on a batch of real and fake data.

12. We create some more random latent vectors for training the generator.

13. The target for generator training is always one. We want the discriminator to give us the gradients that would have made a fake image look like a real one.

14. Just to be sure, we set the discriminator to be non-trainable, so that we can not break anything by accident.

15. We train the GAN model. We feed in a batch of random latent vectors and train the generator part of the GAN so that the discriminator part will classify the generated images as real.

16. We save the losses from training.

In the following figure, you can see some of the generated MNIST characters:

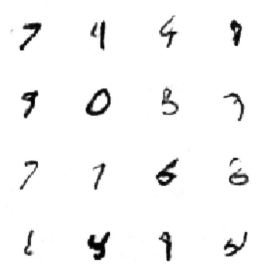

GAN-generated MNIST characters

Most of these characters look like identifiable numbers, although some, such as those in the bottom left and right, seem a bit off.

The code that we wrote and explored is now outputted in the following chart, showing us the Discriminitive and Generative loss of an increasing number of Epochs.

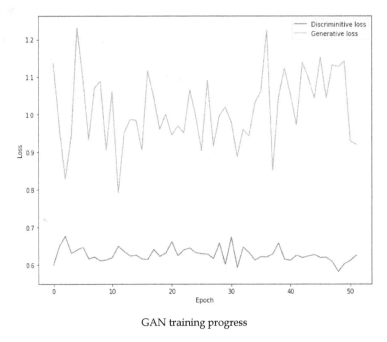

GAN training progress

Note that the loss in GAN training is not interpretable as it is for supervised learning. The loss of a GAN will not decrease even as the GAN makes progress.

The loss of a generator and discriminator is dependent on how well the other model does. If the generator gets better at fooling the discriminator, then the discriminator loss will stay high. If one of the losses goes to zero, it means that the other model lost the race and cannot fool or properly discriminate the other model anymore.

This is one of the things that makes GAN training so hard: **GANs don't converge to a low loss solution**; they converge to an *equilibrium* in which the generator fools the discriminator not all the time, but many times. That equilibrium is not always stable. Part of the reason so much noise is added to labels and the networks themselves is that it increases the stability of the equilibrium.

As GANs are unstable and difficult, yet useful, a number of tricks has been developed over time that makes GAN training more stable. Knowing these tricks can help you with your GAN building process and save you countless hours, even though there is often no theoretical reason for why these tricks work.

Understanding GAN latent vectors

For autoencoders, the latent space was a relatively straightforward approximation of PCA. VAEs create a latent space of distributions, which is useful but still easy to see as a form of PCA. So, what is the latent space of a GAN if we just sample randomly from it during training? As it turns out, GANs self-structure the latent space. Using the latent space of a GAN, you would still be able to cluster MNIST images by the characters they display.

Research has shown that the latent space of GANs often has some surprising features, such as "smile vectors," which arrange face images according to the width of the person's smile. Researchers have also shown that GANs can be used for latent space algebra, where adding the latent representation of different objects creates realistic, new objects. Yet, research on the latent space of GANs is still in its infancy and drawing conclusions about the world from its latent space representations is an active field of research.

GAN training tricks

GANs are tricky to train. They might collapse, diverge, or fail in a number of different ways. Researchers and practitioners have come up with a number of tricks that make GANs work better. While it may seem odd, it's not known why these work, but all that matters to us is that they help in practice:

- **Normalize the inputs**: GANs don't work well with extreme values, so make sure you always have normalized inputs between -1 and 1. This is also the reason why you should use the tanh function as your generator output.

- **Don't use the theoretical correct loss function**: If you read papers on GANs, you will find that they give the generator optimization goal as the following formula:

$$min \, log \, (1-D)$$

In this formula, D is the discriminator output. In practice, it works better if the objective of the generator is this:

$$max \, log \, D$$

In other words, instead of minimizing the negative discriminator output, it is better to maximize the discriminator output. The reason is that the first objective often has vanishing gradients at the beginning of the GAN training process.

- **Sample from a normal Gaussian distribution**: There are two reasons to sample from normal distributions instead of uniform distributions. First, GANs don't work well with extreme values, and normal distributions have fewer extreme values than uniform distributions. Additionally, it has turned out that if the latent vectors are sampled from a normal distribution, then the latent space becomes a sphere. The relationships between latent vectors in this sphere are easier to describe than latent vectors in a cube space.

- **Use batch normalization**: We've already seen that GANs don't work well with extreme values since they are so fragile. Another way to reduce extreme values is to use batch normalization, as we discussed in *Chapter 3, Utilizing Computer Vision*.

- **Use separate batches for real and fake data**: In the beginning of this process, real and fake data might have very different distributions. As batch norm applies normalization over a batch, using the batches' mean and standard deviation, it is more advisable to keep the real and fake data separate. While this does lead to slightly less accurate gradient estimates, the gain from fewer extreme values is great.

- **Use soft and noisy labels**: GANs are fragile; the use of soft labels reduces the gradients and keeps the gradients from tipping over. Adding some random noise to labels also helps to stabilize the system.

- **Use basic GANs**: There is now a wide range of GAN models. Many of them claim wild performance improvements, whereas in reality they do not work much better, and are often worse, than a simple **deep convolutional generative adversarial network,** or **DCGAN**. That does not mean they have no justification for existing, but for the bulk of tasks, more basic GANs will perform better. Another GAN that works well is the adversarial autoencoder, which combines a VAE with a GAN by training the autoencoder on the gradients of a discriminator.

- **Avoid ReLU and MaxPool**: ReLU activations and MaxPool layers are frequently used in deep learning, but they have the disadvantage of producing "sparse gradients." A ReLU activation will not have any gradient for negative inputs, and a MaxPool layer will not have any gradients for all inputs that were not the maximum input. Since gradients are what the generator is being trained on, sparse gradients will hurt generator training.

- **Use the Adam optimizer**: This optimizer has been shown to work very well with GANs, while many other optimizers do not work well with them.

- **Track failures early**: Sometimes, GANs can fail for random reasons. Just choosing the "wrong" random seed could set your training run up for failure. Usually, it is possible to see whether a GAN goes completely off track by observing outputs. They should slowly become more like real data.

If the generator goes completely off track and produces only zeros, for instance, you will be able to see it before spending days of GPU time on training that will go nowhere.

- **Don't balance loss via statistics**: Keeping the balance between the generator and discriminator is a delicate task. Many practitioners, therefore, try to help the balance by training either the generator or discriminator a bit more depending on statistics. Usually, that does not work. GANs are very counterintuitive and trying to help them with an intuitive approach usually makes matters worse. That is not to say there are no ways to help out GAN equilibriums, but the help should stem from a principled approach, such as "train the generator while the generator loss is above X."

- **If you have labels, use them**: A slightly more sophisticated version of a GAN discriminator can not only classify data as real or fake but also classify the class of the data. In the MNIST case, the discriminator would have 11 outputs: an output for the 10 real numbers as well as an output for a fake. This allows us to create a GAN that can show more specific images. This is useful in the domain of semi-supervised learning, which we will cover in the next section.

- **Add noise to inputs, reduce it over time**: Noise adds stability to GAN training so it comes as no surprise that noisy inputs can help, especially in the early, unstable phases of training a GAN. Later, however, it can obfuscate too much and keep the GAN from generating realistic images. So, we should reduce the noise applied to inputs over time.

- **Use dropouts in G in both the train and test phases**: Some researchers find that using dropout on inference time leads to better results for the generated data. Why that is the case is still an open question.

- **Historical averaging**: GANs tend to "oscillate," with their weights moving rapidly around a mean during training. Historical averaging penalizes weights that are too far away from their historical average and reduces oscillation. It, therefore, increases the stability of GAN training.

- **Replay buffers**: Replay buffers keep a number of older generated images so they can be reused for training the discriminator. This has a similar effect as historical averaging, reducing oscillation and increasing stability. It also reduces the correlation and the test data.

- **Target networks**: Another "anti-oscillation" trick is to use target networks. That is, to create copies of both the generator and discriminator, and then train the generator with a frozen copy of the discriminator and train the discriminator with a frozen copy of the generator.

- **Entropy regularization**: Entropy regularization means rewarding the network for outputting more different values. This can prevent the generator network from settling on a few things to produce, say, only the number seven. It is a regularization method as it prevents overfitting.

- **Use dropout or noise layers**: Noise is good for GANs. Keras not only features dropout layers, but it also features a number of noise layers that add different kinds of noise to activations in a network. You can read the documentation of these layers to see whether they are helpful for your specific GAN application: `https://keras.io/layers/noise/`.

Using less data – active learning

Part of the motivation for generative models, be they GANs or VAEs, was always that they would allow us to generate data and therefore require less data. As data is inherently sparse, especially in finance, and we never have enough of it, generative models seem as though they are the free lunch that economists warn us about. Yet even the best GAN works with *no* data. In this section, we will have a look at the different methods used to bootstrap models with as little data as possible. This method is also called active learning or semi-supervised learning.

Unsupervised learning uses unlabeled data to cluster data in different ways. An example is autoencoders, where images can be transformed into learned and latent vectors, which can then be clustered without the need for labels that describe the image.

Supervised learning uses data with labels. An example is the image classifier we built in *Chapter 3, Utilizing Computer Vision,* or most of the other models that we've built in this book.

Semi-supervised learning aims to perform tasks usually done by supervised models, but with less data at hand and using either unsupervised or generative methods. There are three ways this can work: firstly, by making smarter use of humans; secondly, by making better use of unlabeled data, and thirdly, by using generative models.

Using labeling budgets efficiently

For all the talk about AI replacing humans, an awful lot of humans are required to train AI systems. Although the numbers are not clear, it's a safe bet that there are between 500,000 and 750,000 registered "Mechanical Turkers" on Amazon's MTurk service.

MTurk is an Amazon website that offers, according to its own site, "Human intelligence through an API." In practice, this means that companies and researchers post simple jobs such as filling out a survey or classifying an image and people all over the world perform these tasks for a few cents per task. For an AI to learn, humans need to provide labeled data. If the task is large scale, then many companies will hire MTurk users in order to let humans do the labeling. If it is a small task, you will often find the company's own staff labeling the data.

Surprisingly little thought goes into what these humans label. Not all labels are equally useful. The following diagram shows a linear classifier. As you can see, the frontier point, which is close to the frontier between the two classes, determines where the decision boundary is, while the points further in the back are not as relevant:

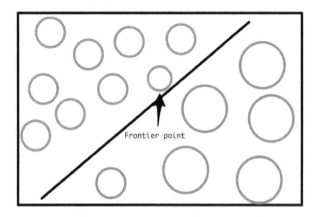

Frontier points are more valuable

As such, the frontier points are more valuable than points further away from the decision boundary. You can train on less data by doing the following:

1. Labeling only a few images
2. Training a weak model
3. Letting that weak model make predictions for some unlabeled images
4. Labeling the images that the model is least confident about and adding them to your training set
5. Repeating the process

This process of labeling data is much more efficient than just randomly labeling data and can accelerate your efforts quite drastically.

Leveraging machines for human labeling

In labeling, many companies rely on Microsoft Excel. They have human labelers look at something to label, such as an image or a text, and then that person will type the label into an Excel spreadsheet. While this is incredibly inefficient and error prone, it's a common practice. Some slightly more advanced labeling operations include building some simple web applications that let the user see the item to label and directly click on the label or press a hotkey. This can accelerate the labeling process quite substantially. However, it's still not optimal if there are a large number of label categories.

Another way is to once again label a few images and pretrain a weak model. At the point where the labeling takes place, the computer shows the labeler the data as well as a label. The labeler only has to decide whether this label is correct. This can be done easily with hotkeys and the time it takes to label a single item goes down dramatically. If the label was wrong, the label interface can either bring up a list of possible options, sorted by the probability the model assigned to them, or just put the item back on the stack and display the next most likely label the next time.

A great implementation of this technique is "Prodigy," a labeling tool by the company that makes spaCy, which we learned about in *Chapter 5, Parsing Textual Data with Natural Language Processing*, we can see an example of the Prodigy tool in the following screenshot:

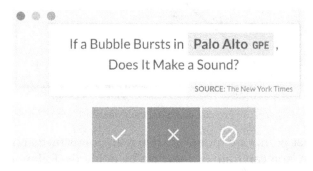

Screenshot of the Prodigy labeling tool

Prodigy is a labeling tool that leverages machines, you can find more out about it by reading its official documentation here: `https://prodi.gy/`.

 Note: A better user interface design and smart implementation of weak models can greatly accelerate the speed and quality of labeling.

Pseudo labeling for unlabeled data

Often there is plenty of unlabeled data available, but only a small amount of data that has been labeled. That unlabeled data can still be used. First, you train a model on the labeled data that you have. Then you let that model make predictions on your corpus of unlabeled data. You treat those predictions as if they were true labels and train your model on the full pseudo-labeled dataset. However, actual true labels should be used more often than pseudo labels.

The exact sampling rate for pseudo labels can vary for different circumstances. This works under the condition that errors are random. If they are biased, your model will be biased as well. This simple method is surprisingly effective and can greatly reduce labeling efforts.

Using generative models

As it turns out, GANs extend quite naturally to semi-supervised training. By giving the discriminator two outputs, we can train it to be a classifier as well.

The first output of the discriminator only classifies data as real or fake, just as it did for the GAN previously. The second output classifies the data by its class, for example, the digit an image represents, or an extra "is fake" class. In the MNIST example, the classifying output would have 11 classes, 10 digits plus the "is fake" class. The trick is that the generator is one model and only the output, that is, the last layer, is different. This forces the "real or not" classification to share weights with the "which digit" classifier.

The idea is that to determine whether an image is real or fake, the classifier would have to figure out whether it can classify this image into one class. If it can, the image is probably real. This approach, called **semi-supervised generative adversarial network (SGAN)**, has been shown to generate more realistic data and deliver better results on limited data than standard supervised learning. Of course, GANs can be applied to more than just images.

In the next section, we will apply them to our fraud detection task.

SGANs for fraud detection

As the final applied project of this chapter, let's consider the credit card problem again. In this section, we will create an SGAN as follows:

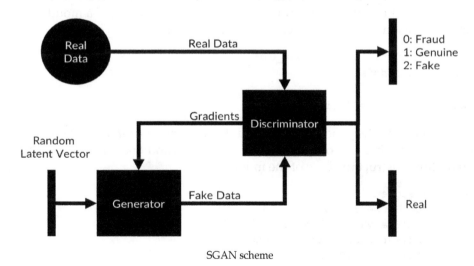

SGAN scheme

We will train this model on fewer than 1,000 transactions and still get a decent fraud detector.

 Note: You can find the code for the SGAN on Kaggle under this link: `https://www.kaggle.com/jannesklaas/semi-supervised-gan-for-fraud-detection/code`.

In this case, our data has 29 dimensions. We set our latent vectors to have 10 dimensions:

```
latent_dim=10
data_dim=29
```

The generator model is constructed as a fully connected network with `LeakyReLU` activations and batch normalization. The output activation is a `tanh` activation:

```
model = Sequential()
model.add(Dense(16, input_dim=latent_dim))
model.add(LeakyReLU(alpha=0.2))
model.add(BatchNormalization(momentum=0.8))
model.add(Dense(32, input_dim=latent_dim))
model.add(LeakyReLU(alpha=0.2))
model.add(BatchNormalization(momentum=0.8))
model.add(Dense(data_dim,activation='tanh'))
```

To use the generator model better, we wrap the model we created into a functional API model that maps the noise vector to a generated transaction record. Since most GAN literature is about images, and "transaction record" is a bit of a mouthful, therefore we just name our transaction records as "images":

```
noise = Input(shape=(latent_dim,))
img = model(noise)

generator = Model(noise, img)
```

Just as we did with the generator, we build the discriminator in the sequential API. The discriminator has two output: one for the classes, and one for fake or not fake. We first only construct the base of the model:

```
model = Sequential()
model.add(Dense(31,input_dim=data_dim))
model.add(LeakyReLU(alpha=0.2))
model.add(BatchNormalization(momentum=0.8))
model.add(Dropout(0.25))
model.add(Dense(16,input_dim=data_dim))
model.add(LeakyReLU(alpha=0.2))
```

Now we'll map the input of the discriminator to its two heads using the functional API:

```
img = Input(shape=(data_dim,))                              #1
features = model(img)                                       #2
valid = Dense(1, activation="sigmoid")(features)            #3
label = Dense(num_classes+1, activation="softmax")(features) #4

discriminator = Model(img, [valid, label])                  #5
```

Let's take a minute to look at the five key aspects of the preceding code:

1. We create an input placeholder for the noise vector
2. We get the feature tensor from the discriminator base model
3. We create a `Dense` layer for classifying a transaction as real or not and map it to the feature vector
4. We create a second `Dense` layer for classifying transactions as genuine or fake
5. We create a model mapping the input to the two heads

To compile the discriminator with two heads, we need to use a few advanced model-compiling tricks:

```
optimizer = Adam(0.0002, 0.5)                               #1
discriminator.compile(loss=['binary_crossentropy',
                      'categorical_crossentropy'],          #2
                      loss_weights=[0.5, 0.5],              #3
                      optimizer=optimizer,                  #4
                      metrics=['accuracy'])                 #5
```

Breaking that code down, we see five key elements:

1. We define an `Adam` optimizer with a learning rate of `0.0002` and a momentum of `0.5`.
2. Since we have two model heads, we can specify two losses. Our fake or not head is a binary classifier, so we use `binary_crossentropy` for it. Our classifying head is a multi-class classifier, so we use `categorical_crossentropy` for the second head.
3. We can specify how we want to weight the two different losses. In this case, we give all losses a 50% weight.
4. We optimize our predefined `Adam` optimizer.
5. As long as we are not using soft labels, we can track progress using the accuracy metric.

Finally, we create our combined GAN model:

```
noise = Input(shape=(latent_dim,))            #1
img = generator(noise)                        #2
discriminator.trainable = False               #3
valid,_ = discriminator(img)                  #4
combined = Model(noise , valid)               #5
combined.compile(loss=['binary_crossentropy'],
                    optimizer=optimizer)
```

Again, looking at the code, we can see the following key points:

1. We create a placeholder for the noise vector input.
2. We obtain a tensor representing the generated image by mapping the generator to the noise placeholder.
3. We make sure we do not destroy the discriminator by setting it to not trainable.
4. We only want the discriminator to believe the generated transactions are real, so we can discard the classification output tensor.
5. We map the noise input to the "fake or not fake" output of the discriminator.

For training, we define a `train` function, which handles all the training for us:

```
def train(X_train,y_train,
          X_test,y_test,
          generator,discriminator,
          combined,
          num_classes,
          epochs,
          batch_size=128):

    f1_progress = []                                        #1
    half_batch = int(batch_size / 2)                        #2

    cw1 = {0: 1, 1: 1}                                      #3
    cw2 = {i: num_classes / half_batch for i in
range(num_classes)}
    cw2[num_classes] = 1 / half_batch

    for epoch in range(epochs):

        idx = np.random.randint(0, X_train.shape[0], half_batch) #4
        imgs = X_train[idx]

        noise = np.random.normal(0, 1, (half_batch, 10))        #5
```

```
        gen_imgs = generator.predict(noise)

        valid = np.ones((half_batch, 1))                        #6
        fake = np.zeros((half_batch, 1))

        labels = to_categorical(y_train[idx],
num_classes=num_classes+1)                                      #7

        fake_labels = np.full((half_batch, 1),num_classes)      #8
        fake_labels = to_categorical(fake_labels,
num_classes=num_classes+1)
        d_loss_real = discriminator.train_on_batch(imgs,
                                [valid, labels],
                                class_weight=[cw1, cw2])    #9
        d_loss_fake = discriminator.train_on_batch(gen_imgs,
                                [fake, fake_labels],
                                class_weight=[cw1, cw2])    #10
        d_loss = 0.5 * np.add(d_loss_real, d_loss_fake)         #11

        noise = np.random.normal(0, 1, (batch_size, 10))        #12
        validity = np.ones((batch_size, 1))
        g_loss = combined.train_on_batch(noise,
                                validity,
                                class_weight=[cw1, cw2]) #13

        print ("%d [D loss: %f] [G loss: %f]" % (epoch, g_loss)) #14

        if epoch % 10 == 0:                                     #15
            _,y_pred = discriminator.predict(X_test,
                    batch_size=batch_size)
            y_pred = np.argmax(y_pred[:,:-1],axis=1)

            f1 = f1_score(y_test,y_pred)
            print('Epoch: {}, F1: {:.5f}'.format(epoch,f1))
            f1_progress.append(f1)

    return f1_progress
```

Take a minute to pause: that was a very long and complicated function to code. Before we summarize this chapter, let's look at the 15 key elements of that code:

1. We create an empty array to monitor the F1 score of the discriminator on the test set.

2. Since we use separate batch training steps for real and fake data, we effectively use a half batch for each of the training steps.

3. The classification head of the discriminator has a class label for "this is fake." Since half of the images are fake, we want to give this class a higher weight.

4. We now draw a random sample of real data.

5. We generate some random noise vectors and use the generator to create some fake data.

6. For the "fake or not" head, we create labels. All of the real images have the label 1 (real), while all the fake images have the label 0 (fake).

7. We one-hot encode the labels of our real data. By specifying that our data has one more class than it actually has, we leave space for the "is fake" class.

8. Our fake data is all labeled with the "is fake" label. We create a vector of those labels, and one-hot encode them, too.

9. First, we train the discriminator on the real data.

10. Then we train the discriminator on the fake data.

11. The total loss of the discriminator for this epoch is the mean of the loss from the real and fake data.

12. Now we train the generator. We generate a batch full of noise vectors as well as a batch full of labels saying, "this is real data."

13. With this data in hand, we train the generator.

14. To keep track of what is going on, we print out the progress. Remember that we do not want the losses to go down; we want them to stay roughly constant. If either the generator or discriminator starts performing much better than the other, then the equilibrium breaks.

15. Finally, we calculate and output the F1 score of using the discriminator as a fraud detection classifier for the data. This time, we only care about the classification data and discard the "real or fake" head. We classify the transactions by the highest value that is not the "is real" class of the classifier.

Now that we have everything set up, we are going to train our SGAN for 5,000 epochs. This will take about 5 minutes on a GPU but could take much longer if you do not have a GPU:

```
f1_p = train(X_res,y_res,
             X_test,y_test,
             generator,discriminator,
             combined,
             num_classes=2,
             epochs=5000,
             batch_size=128)
```

Finally, we plot the F1 score of our semi-supervised fraud classifier over time:

```
fig = plt.figure(figsize=(10,7))
plt.plot(f1_p)
plt.xlabel('10 Epochs')
plt.ylabel('F1 Score Validation')
```

This would output as the following graph:

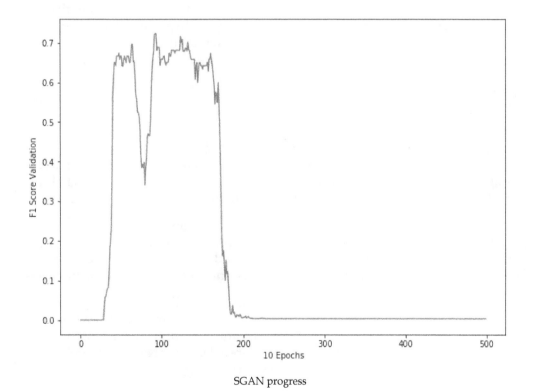

SGAN progress

As you can see, the model learns pretty quickly at first, but then collapses with its F1 score going to zero. This is a textbook example of a collapsing GAN. As mentioned previously, GANs are unstable. If the delicate balance between the generator and discriminator breaks, performance quickly deteriorates.

Making GANs more stable is an active area of research. So far, many practitioners will just attempt to try multiple runs with different hyperparameters and random seeds in a hope to get lucky. Another popular method is just to save the model every couple of epochs. The model seems to be a pretty decent fraud detector at around epoch 150 despite being trained on fewer than 1,000 transactions.

Exercises

To get more comfortable with generative models, try your hand at these exercises:

1. Create an SGAN in order to train an MNIST image classifier. How few images can you use to achieve over 90% classification accuracy?

2. Using LSTMs, you can build an autoencoder for stock price movements. Using a dataset such as the DJIA stock prices, build an autoencoder that encodes stock movements. Then visualize what happens to the outputs as you move through the latent space. You can find the dataset here: `https://www.kaggle.com/szrlee/stock-time-series-20050101-to-20171231`.

Summary

In this chapter, you have learned about the two most important types of generative models: autoencoders and GANs. We first developed an autoencoder for MNIST images. We then used a similar architecture to encode credit card data and detect fraud. Afterward, we expanded the autoencoder to a VAE. This allowed us to learn distributions of encodings and generate new data that we could use for training.

Afterward, we learned about GANs, again first in the context of MNIST images and then in the context of credit card fraud. We used an SGAN to reduce the amount of data we needed to train our fraud detector. We used model outputs to reduce the amount of labeling necessary through active learning and smarter labeling interfaces.

We've also discussed and learned about latent spaces and the use they have for financial analysis. We saw the t-SNE algorithm and how it can be used to visualize higher dimensional (latent) data. You also got a first impression of how machine learning can solve game-theoretic optimization problems. GANs solve a minimax problem, which is frequent in economics and finance.

In the next chapter, we will deep dive into exactly that type of optimization as we cover reinforcement learning.

7

Reinforcement Learning for Financial Markets

Humans don't learn from millions of labeled examples. Instead, we often learn from positive or negative experiences that we associate with our actions. Children that touch a hot stove once will never touch it again. Learning from experiences and the associated rewards or punishments is the core idea behind **reinforcement learning (RL)**. RL allows us to learn sophisticated decision-making rules while having no data at all. Through this approach, several high-profile breakthroughs occurred in AI, such as AlphaGo, which beat the world Go champion in 2016.

In finance, reinforcement learning, also known as RL, is making inroads as well. In its 2017 report, *Machine learning in investment management* (https://www.ahl.com/machine-learning), Man AHL outlined a reinforcement system for order routing in the FX and futures market. Order routing is a classic problem in quantitative finance. When placing an order, funds can usually choose from different brokers and place their orders at different times. The goal is to fill the order as cheaply as possible. This also means minimizing the market impact, as large orders can lift prices of stocks.

Traditional algorithms with colorful names such as *Sniper* or *Guerilla* rely on statistics from historical data and smart engineering. The RL-based routing system learned an optimal routing policy by itself. The advantage is that this system can adapt to changing markets and because of that it outperforms traditional methods in data-rich markets such as the FX market.

However, RL can do more. Researchers at OpenAI have used RL to predict when agents will collaborate or fight. Meanwhile at DeepMind, researchers there have used RL to yield new insights into the workings of the frontal cortex in the brain and the role of the dopamine hormone.

This chapter will start with an intuitive introduction to RL using a simple "catch the fruit" game. We will then dive into the underlying theory before covering more advanced RL applications. The examples in this chapter rely on visualizations that are not easily rendered in Kaggle kernels. In order to simplify them, the example algorithms are also not optimized for GPU usage. It is, therefore, best to run these examples on your local machine.

The algorithms in this chapter run relatively quickly, so you won't have to wait too long for them to run. The chapter code was written on a Mid-2012 MacBook Pro, and no example took longer than 20 minutes to run on that machine. Of course, you can also run the code on Kaggle, however the visualizations will not work there.

Catch – a quick guide to reinforcement learning

Catch is a straightforward arcade game that you might have played as a child. Fruits fall from the top of the screen, and the player has to catch them with a basket. For every fruit caught, the player scores a point. For every fruit lost, the player loses a point.

The goal here is to let the computer play Catch by itself. We will be using a simplified version in this example in order to make the task easier:

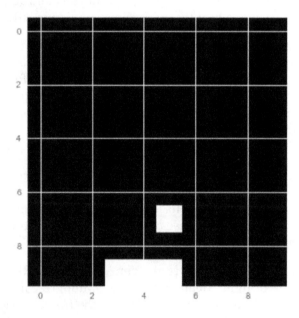

The "Catch" game that we will be creating

While playing Catch, the player decides between three possible actions. They can move the basket to the left, to the right, or make it stay put.

The basis for this decision is the current state of the game; in other words, the positions of the falling fruit and of the basket. Our goal is to create a model that, given the content of the game screen, chooses the action that leads to the highest score possible. This task can be seen as a simple classification problem. We could ask expert human players to play the game multiple times and record their actions. Then, we could train a model to choose the "correct" action that mirrors the expert players.

This is not how humans learn, however. Humans can learn a game such as Catch by themselves, without guidance. This is very useful, because imagine if you had to hire a bunch of experts to perform a task thousands of times every time you wanted to learn something as simple as Catch: it would be expensive and slow.

In reinforcement learning, the model trains from experience, rather than labeled data. Instead of providing the model with the correct actions, we provide it with rewards and punishments. The model receives information about the current state of the environment, for example, the computer game screen. It then outputs an action, such as a joystick movement. The environment reacts to this action and provides the next state, along with any rewards:

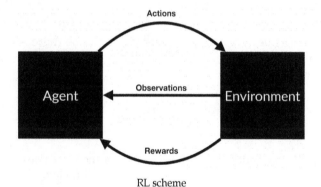

RL scheme

The model then learns to find actions that lead to maximum rewards. There are many ways this can work in practice. Right now, we are going to look at **Q-learning**. Q-learning made a splash when it was used to train a computer to play Atari video games. Today, it is still a relevant concept. Most modern RL algorithms are based on some adaptation of Q-learning.

An excellent way to understand Q-learning is to compare playing Catch with playing chess. In both games, you are given a state, s. With chess, this is the position of the figures on the board. In Catch, this is the location of the fruit and the basket. The player then has to take an action, a. In chess, this is moving a figure. In Catch, this is moving the basket left or right or remaining in the current position.

As a result, there will be some reward, *r*, and a new state, s'. The problem with both Catch and chess is that the rewards do not appear immediately after the action.

In Catch, you only earn rewards when the fruits hit the basket or fall on the floor, and in chess, you only earn a reward when you win or lose the game. This means that rewards are sparsely distributed. Most of the time, *r* will be zero. When there is a reward, it is not always a result of the action taken immediately before. Some action taken long before might have caused the victory. Figuring out which action is responsible for the reward is often referred to as the credit assignment problem. Because rewards are delayed, good chess players do not choose their plays only by the immediate reward. Instead, they choose the expected future reward.

For example, they do not only think about whether they can eliminate an opponent's figure in the next move, they also consider how taking a specific action now will help them in the long run. In Q-learning, we choose our action based on the highest expected future reward. We use a **Q-function** to calculate this. This is a mathematical function that takes two arguments: the current state of the game, and a given action. We can write this as *Q(state, action)*.

While in state *s*, we estimate the future reward for each possible action, *a*. We assume that after we have taken action *a* and moved to the next state, s', everything works out perfectly. The expected future reward, *q(s,a)*, for a given state and action is calculated as the immediate reward, plus the expected future reward thereafter, $Q(s',a')$. We assume the next action, a', is optimal. Because there is uncertainty about the future, we discount $Q(s',a')$ by the factor gamma, γ. We, therefore, arrive at an expected reward of this:

$$Q(s,a) = r + \gamma * \max Q(s',a')$$

 Note: We discount future rewards in RL for the same reason we discount future returns in finance. They are uncertain. Our choice here reflects how much we value future returns.

Good chess players are very good at estimating future rewards in their head. In other words, their Q-function, *Q(s,a)*, is very precise.

Most chess practice revolves around developing a better Q-function. Players peruse many old games to learn how specific moves played out in the past, and how likely a given action is to lead to victory. However, this raises the question, how can a machine estimate a good Q-function? This is where neural networks come into play.

Q-learning turns RL into supervised learning

When playing a game, we generate lots of "experiences." These experiences consist of the following:

- The initial state, s
- The action taken, a
- The reward earned, r
- The state that followed, s'

These experiences are our training data. We can frame the problem of estimating $Q(s,a)$ as a regression problem. To solve this, we can use a neural network. Given an input vector consisting of s and a, the neural network is supposed to predict the value of $Q(s,a)$ equal to the target: $r + \gamma * maxQ(s',a')$. If we are good at predicting $Q(s,a)$ for different states s and actions a, we will have a good approximation of the Q-function.

[**Note**: We estimate $Q(s',a')$ through the same neural network as $Q(s,a)$. This leads to some instability as our targets now change as the networks learn, just as with **generative adversarial networks** (GANs).]

Given a batch of experiences, $<s,a,r,s'>$, the training process then looks as follows:

1. For each possible action, a', (left, right, stay), predict the expected future reward, $Q(s',a')$, using the neural network.

2. Choose the highest value of the three predictions as the max, $Q(s',a')$.

3. Calculate $r + \gamma * maxQ(s',a')$. This is the target value for the neural network.

4. Train the neural network using a loss function. This is a function that calculates how near or far the predicted value is from the target value. Here, we will use $0.5 * \left(predicted_Q(s,a) - target \right)^2$ as the loss function. Effectively, we want to minimize the squared error between prediction and target. The factor of 0.5 is just there to make the gradient nicer.

During gameplay, all the experiences are stored in a replay memory. This acts like a simple buffer in which we store $<s,a,r,s'>$ pairs. The `ExperienceReplay` class also handles preparing the data for training.

Check out the following code:

```
class ExperienceReplay(object):                              #1
    def __init__(self, max_memory=100, discount=.9):
        self.max_memory = max_memory                         #2
        self.memory = []
```

```
        self.discount = discount

    def remember(self, states, game_over):                      #3
        self.memory.append([states, game_over])
        if len(self.memory) > self.max_memory:
            del self.memory[0]                                  #4

    def get_batch(self, model, batch_size=10):                  #5
        len_memory = len(self.memory)                           #6
        num_actions = model.output_shape[-1]
        env_dim = self.memory[0][0][0].shape[1]

        inputs = np.zeros((min(len_memory, batch_size), env_dim)) #7
        targets = np.zeros((inputs.shape[0], num_actions))

        for i, idx in enumerate(np.random.randint(0, len_memory,
                                size=inputs.shape[0])):         #8
            state_t, action_t, reward_t, state_tp1 =
                self.memory[idx][0]                             #9
            game_over = self.memory[idx][1]

            inputs[i:i+1] = state_t                             #10

            targets[i] = model.predict(state_t)[0]             #11

            Q_sa = np.max(model.predict(state_tp1)[0])         #12

            if game_over:                                       #13
                targets[i, action_t] = reward_t
            else:
                targets[i, action_t] = reward_t + self.discount * Q_sa
        return inputs, targets
```

Let's pause for a second and break down the code that we've just created:

1. Firstly, we implement the experience replay buffer as a Python class. A
    replay buffer object is responsible for storing experiences and generating
    training data. Therefore, it has to implement some of the most critical pieces
    of the Q-learning algorithm.

2. To initialize a replay object, we need to let it know how large its buffer should be and what the discount rate, γ, is. The replay memory itself is a list of lists following this scheme:

```
[...
[experience, game_over]
[experience, game_over]
...]
```

3. Within this, `experience` is a tuple holding the experience information and `game_over` is a binary Boolean value indicating whether the game was over after this step.

4. When we want to remember a new experience, we add it to our list of experiences. Since we cannot store infinite experiences, we delete the oldest experience if our buffer exceeds its maximum length.

5. With the `get_batch` function, we can obtain a single batch of training data. To calculate $Q(s',a')$, we need a neural network as well, so we need to pass a Keras model to use the function.

6. Before we start generating a batch, we need to know how many experiences we have stored in our replay buffer, how many possible actions there are, and how many dimensions a game state has.

7. Then we need to set up placeholder arrays for the inputs and targets we want to train the neural network on.

8. We loop over the experience replay in a random order until we have either sampled all stored experiences or filled the batch.

9. We load the experience data as well as the `game_over` indicator from the replay buffer.

10. We add state s to the input matrix. Later, the model will train to map from this state to the expected reward.

11. We then fill the expected reward for all actions with the expected reward calculated by the current model. This ensures that our model only trains on the action that was actually taken since the loss for all other actions is zero.

12. Next, we calculate $Q(s',a')$. We simply assume that for the next state, s', or `state_tp1` in code, the neural network will estimate the expected reward perfectly. As the network trains, this assumption slowly becomes true.

13. Finally, if the game ended after state S, the expected reward from the action, a, should be the received reward, r. If it did not end, then the expected reward should be the received reward as well as the discounted expected future reward.

Defining the Q-learning model

Now it is time to define the model that will learn a Q-function for Catch. It turns out that a relatively simple model can already learn the function well. We need to define the number of possible actions as well as the grid size. There are three possible actions, which are *move left*, *stay in position*, and *move right*. Additionally, the game is being played on a 10x10-pixel grid:

```
num_actions = 3
grid_size = 10
```

As this is a regression problem, the final layer has no activation function, and the loss is a mean squared error loss. We optimize the network using stochastic gradient descent without momentum or any other bells and whistles:

```
model = Sequential()
model.add(Dense(100, input_shape=(grid_size**2,),
activation='relu'))
model.add(Dense(100, activation='relu'))
model.add(Dense(num_actions))
model.compile(optimizer='sgd', loss='mse')
```

Training to play Catch

The final ingredient to Q-learning is exploration. Everyday life shows that sometimes you have to do something weird and/or random to find out whether there is something better than your daily trot.

The same goes for Q-learning. By always choosing the best option, you might miss out on some unexplored paths. To avoid this, the learner will sometimes choose a random option, and not necessarily the best one.

Now we can define the training method:

```
def train(model,epochs):
    win_cnt = 0                                              #1

    win_hist = []

    for e in range(epochs):                                 #2
        loss = 0.
        env.reset()
        game_over = False
        input_t = env.observe()

        while not game_over:                                #3
            input_tm1 = input_t                             #4
```

```
    if np.random.rand() <= epsilon:                        #5
        action = np.random.randint(0, num_actions, size=1)
    else:
        q = model.predict(input_tm1)                       #6
        action = np.argmax(q[0])

    input_t, reward, game_over = env.act(action)           #7
    if reward == 1:
        win_cnt += 1

    exp_replay.remember([input_tm1, action, reward,
                        input_t],game_over)                #8

    inputs, targets = exp_replay.get_batch(model,
                        batch_size=batch_size)             #9

    batch_loss = model.train_on_batch(inputs, targets)

    loss += batch_loss

win_hist.append(win_cnt)
return win_hist
```

Before we go further, again let's break down the code so we can see what we're doing:

1. We want to keep track of the progress of our Q-learner, so we count the wins of the model over time.

2. We now play for a number of games, specified by the epoch argument. At the beginning of a game, we first reset the game, set the game_over indicator to False, and observe the initial state of the game.

3. We will then be playing frame by frame until the game is over.

4. At the start of a frame cycle, we save the previously observed input as input_tm1, the input at time *t* minus one.

5. Now comes the exploration part. We draw a random number between zero and one. If the number is smaller than epsilon, we pick a random action. This technique is also called "epsilon greedy," as we pick a random action with a probability of epsilon and greedily choose the action promising the highest rewards otherwise.

6. If we choose a non-random action, we let the neural network predict the expected rewards for all actions. We then pick the action with the highest expected reward.

7. We now act with our chosen or random action and observe a new state, a reward, and information about whether the game is over. The game gives a reward of one if we win, so we eventually have to increase our win counter.

8. We store the new experience in our experience replay buffer.

9. We then sample a new training batch from the experience replay and train on that batch.

The following graph shows the rolling mean of successful games. After about 2,000 epochs of training, the neural network should be quite good at playing Catch:

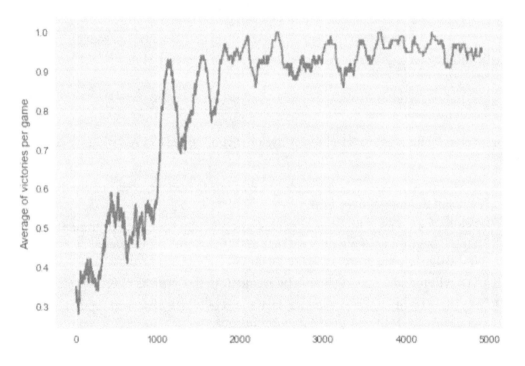

The progress of a Q-learning neural network playing Catch

Looking at the preceding graph, it's safe to say that you have now successfully created your first reinforcement learning system, as after 5000 epochs the average of victories per games is between 90% and 100%. In the next section, we will explore the theoretical foundations of reinforcement learning and discover how the same system that learns to play catch can learn to route orders in the futures market.

Markov processes and the bellman equation – A more formal introduction to RL

Following the long history of modern deep learning being a continuation of quantitative finance with more GPUs, the theoretical foundation of reinforcement learning lies in Markov models.

> **Note**: This section requires a bit of mathematical background knowledge. If you are struggling, there is a beautiful visual introduction by Victor Powell here: `http://setosa.io/ev/markov-chains/`.
>
> A more formal, but still simple, introduction is available on the website Analytics Vidhya: `https://www.analyticsvidhya.com/blog/2014/07/markov-chain-simplified/`.

A Markov model describes a stochastic process with different states in which the probability of ending up in a specific state is purely dependent on the state one is currently in. In the following diagram, you can see a simple Markov model describing recommendations given for a stock:

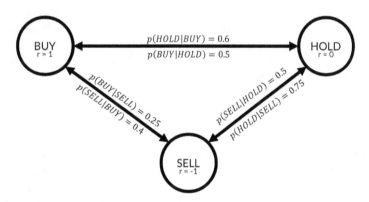

The Markov model

As you can see, there are three states in this model, **BUY, HOLD,** and **SELL**. For every two states, there is a transition probability. For example, the probability that a state gets a **BUY** recommendation if it had a **HOLD** recommendation in the previous round is described by $p(BUY|HOLD)$, which is equal to 0.5. There is a 50% chance that a stock that is currently in **HOLD** will move to **BUY** in the next round.

States are associated with rewards. If you own stock, and that stock has a **BUY** recommendation, the stock will go up, and you will earn a reward of **1**. If the stock has a sell recommendation, you will gain a negative reward, or punishment, of **-1**.

Note: In some textbooks, the rewards are associated with state transitions and not states themselves. It turns out to be mathematically equivalent, and for the ease of notation, we are associating the rewards with states here.

In a Markov model, an agent can follow a policy, usually denoted as $\pi(s,a)$. A policy describes the probability of taking action a when in state s. Say you are a trader: you own stock and that stock gets a **SELL** recommendation. In that case, you might choose to sell the stock in 50% of cases, hold the stock in 30% of cases, and buy more in 20% of cases. In other words, your policy for the state **SELL** can be described as follows:

$$\pi(SELL, sell) = 0.5$$

$$\pi(SELL, hold) = 0.3$$

$$\pi(SELL, buy) = 0.2$$

Some traders have a better policy and can make more money from a state than others. Therefore, the value of state s depends on the policy, π. The value function, V, describes the value of state s when policy π is followed. It is the expected return from state s when policy π is followed:

$$V^\pi(s) = \mathbb{E}_\pi[R_t \mid s_t = s]$$

The expected return is the reward gained immediately plus the discounted future rewards:

$$R_t = r_{t+1} + \gamma * r_{t+2} + \gamma^2 * r_{t+3} + \gamma^3 * r_{t+3} = \sum_{k=0}^{\infty} \gamma^k * r_{t+k+1}$$

The other value function frequently used in RL is the function $Q(s,a)$, which we have already seen in the previous section. Q describes the expected return of taking action a in state s if policy π is followed:

$$Q^\pi(s,a) = \mathbb{E}[R_t \mid s_t = s, a_t = a]$$

Note: We use the expected value since our environment and our actions are stochastic. We cannot say for certain that we will land in a specific state; we can only give a probability.

Q and V describe the same thing. If we find ourselves in a certain state, what should we do? V gives recommendations regarding which state we should seek, and Q gives advice on which action we should take. Of course, V implicitly assumes we have to take some action and Q assumes that the result of our actions is landing in some state. In fact, both Q and V are derived from the so-called Bellman equation, which brings us back to the Markov model from the beginning of this section.

If you assume that the environment you operate in can be described as a Markov model, you would really want to know two things. First, you would want to find out the *state transition probabilities*. If you are in state s, what is the chance $\mathcal{P}_{ss'}^a$ ends in state s' if you take action a? Mathematically, it is as follows:

$$\mathcal{P}_{ss'}^a = Pr\left(s_{t+1} = s' \mid s_t = s, a_t = a\right)$$

Equally, you would be interested in the expected reward $\mathcal{R}_{ss'}^a$ of being in state s, taking action a and ending up in state s':

$$\mathcal{R}_{ss'}^a = \mathbb{E}\left[r_{t+1} \mid s_t = s, s_{t+1} = s', a_t = a\right]$$

With this in mind, we can now derive the two Bellman equations for Q and V. First, we rewrite the equation describing V to contain the actual formula for R_t:

$$V^\pi = \mathbb{E}_\pi\left[\sum_{k=0}^{\infty} \gamma^k * r_{t+k+1} \mid s_t = s\right]$$

We can pull the first reward out of the sum:

$$V^\pi(s) = \mathbb{E}_\pi\left[r_{t+1} + \gamma * \sum_{k=0}^{\infty} \gamma^k * r_{t+k+2} \mid s_t = s\right]$$

The first part of our expectation is the expected reward we directly receive from being in state s and the following policy, π:

$$\mathbb{E}_\pi\left[r_{t+1} \mid s_t = s\right] = \sum_a \pi(s,a) \sum_{s'} \mathcal{P}_{ss'}^a \mathcal{R}_{ss'}^a$$

The preceding equation shows a nested sum. First, we sum over all actions, a, weighted by their probability of occurrence under policy π. For each action, we then sum over the distribution of rewards $\mathcal{R}$ from the transition from state s to the next state, s', after action a, weighted by the probability of this transition occurring following the transition probability $\mathcal{P}$.

The second part of our expectation can be rewritten as follows:

$$\mathbb{E}_\pi\left[\gamma\sum_{k=0}^{\infty}\gamma^k r_{t+k+2}|s_t = s\right] = \sum_a \pi(s,a)\sum_{s'}\mathcal{P}^a_{ss'}\gamma\mathbb{E}_\pi\left[\sum_{k=0}^{\infty}\gamma^k r_{t+k+2}|s_{t+1} = s'\right]$$

The expected discounted value of the future rewards after state s is the discounted expected future value of all states, s', weighted by their probability of occurrence, $\mathcal{P}$, and the probability of action a being taken following policy π.

This formula is quite a mouthful, but it gives us a glimpse into the recursive nature of the value function. If we now replace the expectation in our value function, it becomes clearer:

$$V^\pi(s) = \sum_a \pi(s,a)\sum_{s'}\mathcal{P}^a_{ss'}\left[\mathcal{R}^a_{ss'} + \gamma\mathbb{E}_\pi\left[\sum_{k=0}^{\infty}\gamma^k r_{t+k+2}|s_{t+1} = s'\right]\right]$$

The inner expectation represents the value function for the next step, s'! That means we can replace the expectation with the value function, $V(s')$:

$$V^\pi(s) = \sum_a \pi(s,a)\sum_{s'}\mathcal{P}^a_{ss'}\left[\mathcal{R}^a_{ss'} + \gamma V^\pi(s')\right]$$

Following the same logic, we can derive the Q function as follows:

$$Q(s,a) = \sum_{s'}\mathcal{P}^a_{ss'}\left[\mathcal{R}^a_{ss'} + \gamma Q^\pi(s',a')\right]$$

Congratulations, you have just derived the Bellman equation! For now, pause and take a second to ponder and make sure you really understand the mechanics behind these equations. The core idea is that the value of a state can be expressed as the value of other states. For a long time, the go-to approach to optimizing the Bellman equation was to build a model of the underlying Markov model and its state transition and reward probabilities.

However, the recursive structure calls for a technique called dynamic programming. The idea behind dynamic programming is to solve easier sub-problems. You've already seen this in action in the Catch example. There, we used a neural network to estimate $Q^\pi(s',a')$, except for states that ended the game. For these games, finding the reward associated with the state is easy: it is the final reward received at the end of the game. It was these states for which the neural network first developed an accurate estimate of the function Q. From there, it could then go backward and learn the values of states that were further away from the end of the game. There are more possible applications of this dynamic programming and model-free approach to reinforcement learning.

Before we jump into the different kinds of systems that can be built using this theoretical foundation, we will pay a brief visit to the applications of the Bellman equation in economics. Readers who are familiar with the work discussed here will find reference points that they can use to develop a deeper understanding of Bellman equations. Readers unfamiliar with these works will find inspiration for further reading and applications for techniques discussed throughout this chapter.

The Bellman equation in economics

While the first application of the Bellman equation to economics occurred in 1954, Robert C. Merton's 1973 article, *An Intertemporal Capital Asset Pricing Model* (http://www.people.hbs.edu/rmerton/Intertemporal%20Capital%20Asset%20 Pricing%20Model.pdf), is perhaps the most well-known application. Using the Bellman equation, Merton developed a capital asset pricing model that, unlike the classic CAPM model, works in continuous time and can account for changes in an investment opportunity.

The recursiveness of the Bellman equation inspired the subfield of recursive economics. Nancy Stokey, Robert Lucas, and Edward Prescott wrote an influential 1989 book titled *Recursive Methods in Economic Dynamics* (http://www.hup.harvard. edu/catalog.php?isbn=9780674750968) in which they apply the recursive approach to solve problems in economic theory. This book inspired others to use recursive economics to address a wide range of economic problems, from the principal-agent problem to optimal economic growth.

Avinash Dixit and Robert Pindyck developed and applied the approach successfully to capital budgeting in their 1994 book, *Investment Under Uncertainty* (https:// press.princeton.edu/titles/5474.html). Patrick Anderson applied it to the valuation of private businesses in his 2009 article, *The Value of Private Businesses in the United States* (https://www.andersoneconomicgroup.com/the-value-of- private-businesses-in-the-united-states/).

While recursive economics still has many problems, including the tremendous compute power required for it, it is a promising subfield of the science.

Advantage actor-critic models

Q-learning, as we saw in the previous sections, is quite useful but it does have its drawbacks. For example, as we have to estimate a Q value for each action, there has to be a discrete, limited set of actions. So, what if the action space is continuous or extremely large? Say you are using an RL algorithm to build a portfolio of stocks.

In this case, even if your universe of stocks consisted only of two stocks, say, AMZN and AAPL, there would be a huge amount of ways to balance them: 10% AMZN and 90% AAPL, 11% AMZM and 89% AAPL, and so on. If your universe gets bigger, the amount of ways you can combine stocks explodes.

A workaround to having to select from such an action space is to learn the policy, π, directly. Once you have learned a policy, you can just give it a state, and it will give back a distribution of actions. This means that your actions will also be stochastic. A stochastic policy has advantages, especially in a game theoretic setting.

Imagine you are playing rock, paper, scissors and you are following a deterministic policy. If your policy is to pick rock, you will always pick rock, and as soon as your opponent figures out that you are always picking rock, you will always lose. The Nash equilibrium, the solution of a non-cooperative game, for rock, paper, scissors is to pick actions at random. Only a stochastic policy can do that.

To learn a policy, we have to be able to compute a gradient with respect to policy. Contrary to most people's expectations, policies are differentiable. In this section, we will build up a policy gradient step by step and use it to create an **advantage actor-critic (A2C)** model for continuous control.

The first part in the process of differentiating policies is to look at the advantage we can have by picking a particular action, a, rather than just following the policy, π:

$$A(s,a) = Q_\pi(s,a) - V^P i(s)$$

The advantage of action a in state s is the value of executing a in s minus the value of s under the policy, π. We measure how good our policy, π, is with $J(\pi)$, a function expressing the expected value of the starting state, s_0:

$$J(\pi) = \mathbb{E}_p s_0 [V(s_0)]$$

Now, to compute the gradient of the policy, we have to do two steps, which are shown inside the expectation in the policy gradient formula:

$$\nabla_\theta J(\pi) = \mathbb{E}_{s \sim p^\pi, a \sim \pi(s)} [A(s,a).\nabla_\theta \pi(a|s)]$$

First, we have to calculate the advantage of a given action, a, with A(s,a). Then we have to calculate the derivative of the weights of the neural network, ∇_θ, with respect to increasing the probability, $\pi(a|s)$, that a is picked under policy π.

For actions with a positive advantage, A(s,a), we follow the gradient that would make a more likely. For actions with a negative advantage, we go in the exact opposite direction. The expectation says that we are doing this for all states and all actions. In practice, we manually multiply the advantage of actions with their increased likelihood gradients.

One thing left for us to look at is how we compute the advantage. The value of taking an action is the reward earned directly as a result of taking the action, as well as the value of the state we find ourselves in after taking that action:

$$Q(s,a) = r + \gamma V(s')$$

So, we can substitute Q(s,a) in the advantage calculation:

$$A(s,a) = Q(s,a) - V(s) = r + \gamma V(s') - V(s)$$

As calculating V turns out to be useful for calculating the policy gradient, researchers have come up with the A2C architecture. A single neural network with two heads that learns both V and π. As it turns out, sharing weights for learning the two functions is useful because it accelerates the training if both heads have to extract features from the environment:

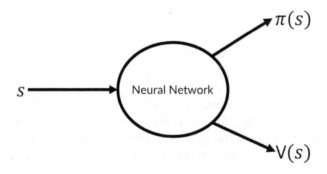

A2C scheme

If you are training an agent that operates on high-dimensional image data, for instance, the value function and the policy head then both need to learn how to interpret the image. Sharing weights would help master the common task. If you are training on lower dimensional data, it might make more sense to not share weights.

If the action space is continuous, π is represented by two outputs, those being the mean, μ, and standard deviation, σ. This allows us to sample from a learned distribution just as we did for the autoencoder.

A common variant of the A2C approach is the **asynchronous advantage actor-critic** or **A3C**. A3C works exactly like A2C, except that at training time, multiple agents are simulated in parallel. This means that more independent data can be gathered. Independent data is important as too-correlated examples can make a model overfit to specific situations and forget other situations.

Since both A3C and A2C work by the same principles, and the implementation of parallel gameplay introduces some complexity that obfuscates the actual algorithm, we will just stick with A2C in the following examples.

Learning to balance

In this section, we will train an A2C model to swing up and balance a pendulum:

Pendulum gym

The pendulum is controlled by a rotational force that can be applied in either direction. In the preceding diagram, you can see the arrow that shows the force being applied. Control is continuous; the agent can apply more or less force. At the same time, force can be applied in both directions as a positive and negative force.

This relatively simple control task is a useful example of a continuous control that can be easily extended to a stock trading task, which we will look at later. In addition, the task can be visualized so that we can get an intuitive grasp of how the algorithm learns, including any pitfalls.

Note: When implementing a new algorithm, try it out on a task you can visualize. Failures are often subtle and easier to spot visually than through data.

The pendulum environment is part of the OpenAI Gym, a suite of games made to train reinforcement learning algorithms. You can install it via the command line as follows:

```
pip install gym
```

 Note: See http://gym.openai.com/ for more information in regard to the suite of games.

Before we start, we have to make some imports:

```
import gym                                        #1

import numpy as np                                #2

from scipy.stats import norm                      #3
from keras.layers import Dense, Input, Lambda
from keras.models import Model
from keras.optimizers import Adam
from keras import backend as K

from collections import deque                     #4
import random
```

There are quite a few new imports, so let's walk through them one by one:

1. OpenAI's `gym` is a toolkit for developing reinforcement learning algorithms. It provides a number of game environments, from classic control tasks, such as a pendulum, to Atari games and robotics simulations.

2. `gym` is interfaced by `numpy` arrays. States, actions, and environments are all presented in a `numpy`-compatible format.

3. Our neural network will be relatively small and based around the functional API. Since we once again learn a distribution, we need to make use of SciPy's `norm` function, which helps us take the norm of a vector.

4. The `deque` Python data structure is a highly efficient data structure that conveniently manages a maximum length for us. No more manually removing experiences! We can randomly sample from `deque` using Python's `random` module.

Now it is time to build the agent. The following methods all form the A2CAgent class:

```
def __init__(self, state_size, action_size):

    self.state_size = state_size                        #1
    self.action_size = action_size
    self.value_size = 1

    self.exp_replay = deque(maxlen=2000)                #2


    self.actor_lr = 0.0001                              #3
    self.critic_lr = 0.001
    self.discount_factor = .9


    self.actor, self.critic = self.build_model()        #4

    self.optimize_actor = self.actor_optimizer()        #5
    self.optimize_critic = self.critic_optimizer()
```

Let's walk through the code step by step:

1. First, we need to define some game-related variables. The state space size and the action space size are given by the game. Pendulum states consist of three variables dependent on the angle of the pendulum. A state consists of the sine of theta, the cosine of theta, and the angular velocity. The value of a state is just a single scalar.

2. Next, we set up our experience replay buffer, which can save at maximum 2,000 states. Larger RL experiments have much larger replay buffers (often around 5 million experiences), but for this task 2,000 will do.

3. As we are training a neural network, we need to set some hyperparameters. Even if the actor and critic share weights, it turns out that the actor learning rate should usually be lower than the critic learning rate. This is because the policy gradient we train the actor on is more volatile. We also need to set the discount rate, γ. Remember that the discount rate in reinforcement learning is applied differently than it is usually in finance. In finance, we discount by dividing future values by one plus the discount factor. In reinforcement learning, we multiply with the discount rate. Therefore, a higher discount factor, γ, means that future values are less discounted.

4. To actually build the model, we define a separate method, which we will discuss next.

5. The optimizers for actor and critic are custom optimizers. To define these, we
    also create a separate function. The optimizers themselves are functions that
    can be called at training time:

```
def build_model(self):

    state = Input(batch_shape=(None, self.state_size))          #1

    actor_input = Dense(30,                                     #2
                    activation='relu',
                    kernel_initializer='he_uniform')(state)

    mu_0 = Dense(self.action_size,                              #3
                activation='tanh',
                kernel_initializer='he_uniform')(actor_input)

    mu = Lambda(lambda x: x * 2)(mu_0)                          #4

    sigma_0 = Dense(self.action_size,                           #5
                activation='softplus',
                kernel_initializer='he_uniform')(actor_input)


    sigma = Lambda(lambda x: x + 0.0001)(sigma_0)              #6

    critic_input = Dense(30,                                    #7
                    activation='relu',
                    kernel_initializer='he_uniform')(state)

    state_value = Dense(1, kernel_initializer='he_uniform')(critic_
input)                                                          #8


    actor = Model(inputs=state, outputs=(mu, sigma))            #9
    critic = Model(inputs=state, outputs=state_value)           #10


    actor._make_predict_function()                              #11
    critic._make_predict_function()

    actor.summary()                                             #12
    critic.summary()

    return actor, critic                                        #13
```

The preceding function sets up the Keras model. It is quite complicated, so let's go through it:

1. As we are using the functional API, we have to define an input layer that we can use to feed the state to the actor and critic.

2. The actor has a hidden first layer as an input to the actor value function. It has 30 hidden units and a `relu` activation function. It is initialized by an `he_uniform` initializer. This initializer is only slightly different from the default `glorot_uniform` initializer. The `he_uniform` initializer draws from a uniform distribution with the limits $\pm\sqrt{6/i}$, where i is the input dimension. The default glorot uniform samples from a uniform distribution with the limits $\pm\sqrt{6/(i+o)}$, with o being the output dimensionality. The difference between the two is rather small, but as it turns out, the `he_uniform` initializer works better for learning the value function and policy.

3. The action space of the pendulum ranges from -2 to 2. We use a regular `tanh` activation, which ranges from -1 to 1 first and corrects the scaling later.

4. To correct the scaling of the action space, we now multiply the outputs of the `tanh` function by two. Using the `Lambda` layer, we can define such a function manually in the computational graph.

5. The standard deviation should not be negative. The `softplus` activation works in principle just like `relu`, but with a soft edge:

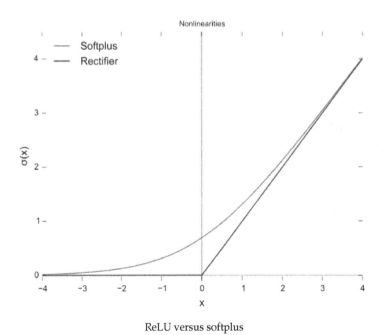

ReLU versus softplus

6. To make sure the standard deviation is not zero, we add a tiny constant to it. Again we use the `Lambda` layer for this task. This also ensures that the gradients get calculated correctly, as the model is aware of the constant added.

7. The critic also has a hidden layer to calculate its value function.

8. The value of a state is just a single scalar that can have any value. The value head thus only has one output and a linear, that is: the default, activation function.

9. We define the actor to map from a state to a policy as expressed by the mean, μ, and standard deviation, σ.

10. We define the critic to map from a state to a value of that state.

11. While it is not strictly required for A2C, if we want to use our agents for an asynchronous, A3C approach, then we need to make the predict function threading safe. Keras loads the model on a GPU the first time you call `predict()`. If that happens from multiple threads, things can break. `_make_predict_function()` makes sure the model is already loaded on a GPU or CPU and is ready to predict, even from multiple threads.

12. For debugging purposes, we print the summaries of our models.

13. Finally, we return the models.

Now we have to create the optimizer for the actor. The actor uses a custom optimizer that optimizes it along the policy gradient. Before we define the optimizer; however, we need to look at the last piece of the policy gradient. Remember how the policy gradient was dependent on the gradient of the weights, $\nabla_{\theta}\pi(a|s)$, that would make action a more likely? Keras can calculate this derivative for us, but we need to provide Keras with the value of policy π.

To this end, we need to define a probability density function. π is a normal distribution with mean μ and standard deviation σ, so the probability density function, f, is as follows:

$$f\left(x;\mu,\sigma^2\right) = \frac{1}{\sqrt{2\pi\sigma^2}} * e^{\frac{-(a-\mu)^2}{2\sigma}}$$

In this term, π stands for the constant, 3.14..., not for the policy. Later, we only need to take the logarithm of this probability density function. Why the logarithm? Because taking the logarithm results in a smoother gradient. Maximizing the log of a probability means maximizing the probability, so we can just use the "log trick," as it is called, to improve learning.

The value of policy π is the advantage of each action a, times the log probability of this action occurring as expressed by the probability density function, f.

The following function optimizes our actor model. Let's go through the optimization procedure:

```
def actor_optimizer(self):
    action = K.placeholder(shape=(None, 1))                            #1
    advantages = K.placeholder(shape=(None, 1))

    mu, sigma_sq = self.actor.output                                   #2

    pdf = 1. / K.sqrt(2. * np.pi * sigma_sq) * \
                K.exp(-K.square(action - mu) /
                (2. * sigma_sq))                                       #3

    log_pdf = K.log(pdf + K.epsilon())                                 #4

    exp_v = log_pdf * advantages                                       #5

    entropy = K.sum(0.5 * (K.log(2. * np.pi * sigma_sq) + 1.))  #6
    exp_v = K.sum(exp_v + 0.01 * entropy)                              #7
    actor_loss = -exp_v                                                #8

    optimizer = Adam(lr=self.actor_lr)                                 #9

    updates = optimizer.get_updates(self.actor.trainable_weights,
                                    [], actor_loss)                    #10

    train = K.function([self.actor.input, action, advantages], [],
                    updates=updates)                                   #11

    return train                                                       #12
```

1. First, we need to set up some placeholders for the action taken and the advantage of that action. We will fill in these placeholders when we call the optimizer.

2. We get the outputs of the actor model. These are tensors that we can plug into our optimizer. Optimization of these tensors will be backpropagated and optimizes the whole model.

3. Now we set up the probability density function. This step can look a bit intimidating, but if you look closely, it is the same probability density function we defined previously.

4. Now we apply the log trick. To ensure that we don't accidentally take the logarithm of zero, we add a tiny constant, `epsilon`.

5. The value of our policy is now the probability of action *a* times the probability of this action occurring.

6. To reward the model for a probabilistic policy, we add an entropy term. The entropy is calculated with the following term:

$$\sum 0.5\left(\log\left(2\pi\sigma^2\right)+1\right)$$

Here, again, π is a constant 3.14... and σ is the standard deviation. While the proof that this term expresses the entropy of a normal distribution is outside of the scope of this chapter, you can see that the entropy goes up if the standard deviation goes up.

7. We add the entropy term to the value of the policy. By using `K.sum()`, we sum the value over the batch.

8. We want to maximize the value of the policy, but by default, Keras performs gradient descent that minimizes losses. An easy trick is to turn the value negative and then minimize the negative value.

9. To perform gradient descent, we use the `Adam` optimizer.

10. We can retrieve an update tensor from the optimizer. `get_updates()` takes three arguments, `parameters`, `constraints`, and `loss`. We provide the parameters of the model, that is, its weights. Since we don't have any constraints, we just pass an empty list as a constraint. For a loss, we pass the actor loss.

11. Armed with the updated tensor, we can now create a function that takes as its input the actor model input, that is, the state, as well as the two placeholders, the action, and the advantages. It returns nothing but the empty list that applies the update tensor to the model involved. This function is callable, as we will see later.

12. We return the function. Since we call `actor_optimizer()` in the `init` function of our class, the optimizer function we just created becomes `self.optimize_actor`.

For the critic, we also need to create a custom optimizer. The loss for the critic is the mean squared error between the predicted value and the reward plus the predicted value of the next state:

```
def critic_optimizer(self):
    discounted_reward = K.placeholder(shape=(None, 1))          #1

    value = self.critic.output
```

```
loss = K.mean(K.square(discounted_reward - value))        #2

optimizer = Adam(lr=self.critic_lr)                        #3

updates = optimizer.get_updates(self.critic.trainable_weights,
                                [], loss)

train = K.function([self.critic.input, discounted_reward],
                   [],
                   updates=updates)                        #4

return train
```

The preceding function optimizes our critic model:

1. Again we set up a placeholder for the variable we need. discounted_reward contains the discounted future value of state s' as well as the reward immediately earned.

2. The critic loss is the mean squared error between the critic's output and the discounted reward. We first obtain the output tensor before calculating the mean squared error between the output and the discounted reward.

3. Again we use an Adam optimizer from which we obtain an update tensor, just as we did previously.

4. Again, and finally, as we did previously, we'll roll the update into a single function. This function will become self.optimize_critic.

For our agent to take actions, we need to define a method that produces actions from a state:

```
def get_action(self, state):
    state = np.reshape(state, [1, self.state_size])        #1
    mu, sigma_sq = self.actor.predict(state)               #2
    epsilon = np.random.randn(self.action_size)            #3
    action = mu + np.sqrt(sigma_sq) * epsilon              #4
    action = np.clip(action, -2, 2)                        #5
    return action
```

With this function, our actor can now act. Let's go through it:

1. First, we reshape the state to make sure it has the shape the model expects.

2. We predict the means and variance, σ^2, for this action from the model.

3. Then, as we did for the autoencoder, we first sample a random normal distribution with a mean of zero and a standard deviation of 1.

4. We add the mean and multiply by the standard deviation. Now we have our action, sampled from the policy.

5. To make sure we are within the bounds of the action space, we clip the action at -2, 2, so it won't be outside of those boundaries.

At last, we need to train the model. The `train_model` function will train the model after receiving one new experience:

```
def train_model(self, state, action, reward, next_state, done):
    self.exp_replay.append((state, action, reward,
                            next_state, done))                     #1

    (state, action, reward, next_state, done) =
            random.sample(self.exp_replay,1)[0]                    #2
    target = np.zeros((1, self.value_size))                        #3
    advantages = np.zeros((1, self.action_size))

    value = self.critic.predict(state)[0]                          #4
    next_value = self.critic.predict(next_state)[0]

    if done:                                                       #5
        advantages[0] = reward - value
        target[0][0] = reward
    else:
        advantages[0] = reward + self.discount_factor *
(next_value) - value
        target[0][0] = reward + self.discount_factor * next_value

    self.optimize_actor([state, action, advantages])              #6
    self.optimize_critic([state, target])
```

And this is how we optimize both actor and critic:

1. First, the new experience is added to the experience replay.

2. Then, we immediately sample an experience from the experience replay. This way, we break the correlation between samples the model trains on.

3. We set up placeholders for the advantages and targets. We will fill them at *step 5*.

4. We predict the values for state s and s'.

5. If the game ended after the current state, s, the advantage is the reward we earned minus the value we assigned to the state, and the target for the value function is just the reward we earned. If the game did not end after this state, the advantage is the reward earned plus the discounted value of the next state minus the value of this state. The target, in that case, is the reward earned plus the discounted value of the next state.

6. Knowing the advantage, the action taken, and the value target, we can optimize both the actor and critic with the optimizers we created earlier.

And that is it; our `A2CAgent` class is done. Now it is time to use it. We define a `run_experiment` function. This function plays the game for a number of episodes. It is useful to first train a new agent without rendering, because training takes around 600 to 700 games until the agent does well. With your trained agent, you can then watch the gameplay:

```
def run_experiment(render=False, agent=None, epochs = 3000):
    env = gym.make('Pendulum-v0')                                   #1

    state_size = env.observation_space.shape[0]                     #2
    action_size = env.action_space.shape[0]

    if agent = None:                                                #3
        agent = A2CAgent(state_size, action_size)

    scores = []                                                     #4

    for e in range(epochs):                                         #5
        done = False                                                #6
        score = 0
        state = env.reset()
        state = np.reshape(state, [1, state_size])

        while not done:                                             #7
            if render:                                              #8
                env.render()

            action = agent.get_action(state)                        #9
            next_state, reward, done, info = env.step(action)       #10
            reward /= 10                                            #11
            next_state = np.reshape(next_state,
```

```
                                  [1, state_size])                    #12
              agent.train_model(state, action, reward,
                            next_state, done)                          #13

              score += reward                                          #14
              state = next_state                                       #15

              if done:                                                 #16
                  scores.append(score)
                  print("episode:", e, "  score:", score)

              if np.mean(scores[-min(10, len(scores)):]) > -20:        #17
                  print('Solved Pendulum-v0 after {}
                          iterations'.format(len(scores)))
                  return agent, scores
```

Our experiment boils down to these functions:

1. First, we set up a new gym environment. This environment contains the pendulum game. We can pass actions to it and observe states and rewards.

2. We obtain the action and state space from the game.

3. If no agent was passed to the function, we would create a new one.

4. We set up an empty array to keep track of the scores over time.

5. Now we play the game for a number of rounds specified by epochs.

6. At the beginning of a game, we set the "game over indicator" to false, score to 0, and reset the game. By resetting the game, we obtain the initial starting state.

7. Now we play the game until it is over.

8. If you passed render = True to the function, the game would be rendered on screen. Note that this won't work on a remote notebook such as in Kaggle or Jupyter.

9. We get an action from the agent and act in the environment.

10. When acting in the environment, we observe a new state, a reward, and whether the game is over. gym also passes an info dictionary, which we can ignore.

11. The rewards from the game are all negative, with a higher reward closer to zero being better. The rewards can be quite large, though, so we reduce them. Too extreme rewards can lead to too large gradients while training. That would hinder training.

12. Before training with the model, we reshape the state, just to be sure.

13. Now we train the agent on a new experience. As you have seen, the agent will store the experience in its replay buffer and draw a random old experience to train from.

14. We increase the overall reward to track the rewards earned during one game.

15. We set the new state to be the current state to prepare for the next frame of the game.

16. If the game is over, we track and print out the game score.

17. The agent usually does pretty well after 700 epochs. We declare the game solved if the average reward over the last 20 games was better than -20. If that is the case, we will exit the function and return the trained agent together with its scores.

Learning to trade

Reinforcement learning algorithms are largely developed in games and simulations where a failing algorithm won't cause any damage. However, once developed, an algorithm can be adapted to other, more serious tasks. To demonstrate this ability, we are now going to create an A2C agent that learns how to balance a portfolio of stocks within a large universe of stocks.

Note: Please do not trade based on this algorithm. It is only a simplified and slightly naive implementation to demonstrate the concept and shouldn't be used in the real world.

To train a new reinforcement learning algorithm, we first need to create a training environment. In this environment, the agent trades in real-life stock data. The environment can be interfaced just like an OpenAI Gym environment. Following the Gym conventions for interfacing reduces the complexity of development. Given a 100-day look back of the percentile returns of stocks in the universe, the agent has to return an allocation in the form of a 100-dimensional vector.

The allocation vector describes the share of assets the agent wants to allocate on one stock. A negative allocation means the agent is short trading the stock. For simplicity's sake, transaction costs and slippage are not added to the environment. It would not be too difficult to add them, however.

Tip: The full implementation of the environment and agent can be found at https://www.kaggle.com/jannesklaas/a2c-stock-trading.

The environment looks like this:

```
class TradeEnv():
    def reset(self):
        self.data = self.gen_universe()             #1
        self.pos = 0                                #2
        self.game_length = self.data.shape[0]       #3
        self.returns = []                           #4

        return self.data[0,:-1,:]                   #5

    def step(self,allocation):                      #6
        ret = np.sum(allocation * self.data[self.pos,-1,:])   #7
        self.returns.append(ret)                    #8
        mean = 0                                    #9
        std = 1
        if len(self.returns) >= 20:                 #10
            mean = np.mean(self.returns[-20:])
            std = np.std(self.returns[-20:]) + 0.0001

        sharpe = mean / std                         #11

        if (self.pos +1) >= self.game_length:       #12
            return None, sharpe, True, {}
        else:                                       #13
            self.pos +=1
            return self.data[self.pos,:-1,:], sharpe, False, {}

    def gen_universe(self):                         #14
        stocks = os.listdir(DATA_PATH)
        stocks = np.random.permutation(stocks)
        frames = []
        idx = 0
        while len(frames) < 100:                    #15
            try:
                stock = stocks[idx]
                frame = pd.read_csv(os.path.join(DATA_PATH,stock),
                                index_col='Date')
                frame = frame.loc['2005-01-01':].Close
                frames.append(frame)
            except:
                e = sys.exc_info()[0]
            idx += 1

        df = pd.concat(frames,axis=1,ignore_index=False)    #16
```

```
df = df.pct_change()
df = df.fillna(0)
batch = df.values
episodes = []                                          #17
for i in range(batch.shape[0] - 101):
    eps = batch[i:i+101]
    episodes.append(eps)
data = np.stack(episodes)
assert len(data.shape) == 3
assert data.shape[-1] == 100
return data
```

Our trade environment is somewhat similar to the pendulum environment. Let's see how we set it up:

1. We load data for our universe.

2. Since we are stepping through the data where each day is a step, we need to keep track of our position in time.

3. We need to know when the game ends, so we need to know how much data we have.

4. To keep track of returns over time, we set up an empty array.

5. The initial state is the data for the first episode, until the last element, which is the return of the next day for all 100 stocks in the universe.

6. At each step, the agent needs to provide an allocation to the environment. The reward the agent receives is the sharpe ratio, the ratio between the mean and standard deviation of returns, over the last 20 days. You could modify the reward function to, for example, include transaction costs or slippage. If you do want to do this, then refer to the section on reward shaping later in this chapter.

7. The return on the next day is the last element of the episode data.

8. To calculate the Sharpe ratio, we need to keep track of past returns.

9. If we do not have 20 returns yet, the mean and standard deviation of returns will be zero and one respectively.

10. If we do have enough data, we calculate the mean and standard deviation of the last 20 elements in our return tracker. We add a tiny constant to the standard deviation to avoid division by zero.

11. We can now calculate the Sharpe ratio, which will provide the reward for the agent.

12. If the game is over, the environment will return no next state, the reward, and an indicator that the game is over, as well as an empty information dictionary in order to stick to the OpenAI Gym convention.

13. If the game is not over, the environment will return the next state, a reward, and an indicator that the game is not over, along with an empty information dictionary.

14. This function loads the daily returns of a universe of 100 random stocks.

15. The selector moves in random order over the files containing stock prices. Some of them are corrupted so that loading them will result in an error. The loader keeps trying until it has 100 pandas DataFrames containing stock prices assembled. Only closing prices starting in 2005 will be considered.

16. In the next step, all DataFrames are concatenated. The percentile change in stock price is calculated. All missing values are filled with zero, for no change. Finally, we extract the values from the data as a NumPy array.

17. The last thing to do is transform the data into a time series. The first 100 steps are the basis for the agent's decision. The 101st element is the next day's return, on which the agent will be evaluated.

We only have to make minor edits in the `A2CAgent` agent class. Namely, we only have to modify the model so that it can take in the time series of returns. To this end, we add two `LSTM` layers, which actor and critic share:

```
def build_model(self):
        state = Input(batch_shape=(None,                      #1
                                    self.state_seq_length,
                                    self.state_size))

        x = LSTM(120,return_sequences=True)(state)            #2
        x = LSTM(100)(x)

        actor_input = Dense(100, activation='relu',           #3
                        kernel_initializer='he_uniform')(x)

        mu = Dense(self.action_size, activation='tanh',       #4
                    kernel_initializer='he_uniform')(actor_input)

        sigma_0 = Dense(self.action_size, activation='softplus',
                        kernel_initializer='he_uniform')
                        (actor_input)

        sigma = Lambda(lambda x: x + 0.0001)(sigma_0)

        critic_input = Dense(30, activation='relu',
                            kernel_initializer='he_uniform')(x)

        state_value = Dense(1, activation='linear',
```

```
                        kernel_initializer='he_uniform')
                        (critic_input)

    actor = Model(inputs=state, outputs=(mu, sigma))
    critic = Model(inputs=state, outputs=state_value)

    actor._make_predict_function()
    critic._make_predict_function()

    actor.summary()
    critic.summary()

    return actor, critic
```

Again, we have built a Keras model in a function. It is only slightly different from the model before. Let's explore it:

1. The state now has a time dimension.

2. The two LSTM layers are shared across actor and critic.

3. Since the action space is larger; we also have to increase the size of the actor's hidden layer.

4. Outputs should lie between -1 and 1, and 100% short and 100% long, so that we can save ourselves the step of multiplying the mean by two.

And that is it! This algorithm can now learn to balance a portfolio just as it could learn to balance before.

Evolutionary strategies and genetic algorithms

Recently, a decades-old optimization algorithm for reinforcement learning algorithms has come back into fashion. **Evolutionary strategies (ES)** are much simpler than Q-learning or A2C.

Instead of training one model through backpropagation, in ES we create a population of models by adding random noise to the weights of the original model. We then let each model run in the environment and evaluate its performance. The new model is the performance-weighted average of all the models.

In the following diagram, you can see a visualization of how evolution strategies work:

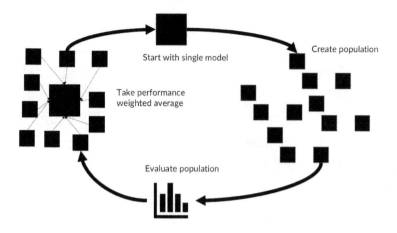

Evolutionary strategy

To get a better grip on how this works, consider the following example. We want to find a vector that minimizes the mean squared error to a solution vector. The learner is not given the solution, but only the total error as a reward signal:

```
solution = np.array([0.5, 0.1, -0.3])
def f(w):
  reward = -np.sum(np.square(solution - w))
  return reward
```

A key advantage of evolutionary strategies is that they have fewer hyperparameters. In this case, we need just three:

```
npop =    50 #1
sigma = 0.1 #2
alpha = 0.1 #3
```

1. **Population size**: We will create 50 versions of the model at each iteration
2. **Noise standard deviation**: The noise we add will have mean of zero and a standard deviation of 0.1
3. **Learning rate**: Weights don't just simply get set to the new average but are slowly moved in the direction to avoid overshooting

The optimization algorithm will look like the following code:

```
w = np.random.randn(3)                          #1
for i in range(300):                            #2
  N = np.random.randn(npop, 3) * sigma          #3
  R = np.zeros(npop)
```

```
for j in range(npop):                           #4
    w_try = w + N[j]
    R[j] = f(w_try)

A = (R - np.mean(R)) / np.std(R)                 #5
w = w + alpha * np.dot(N.T, A)/npop              #6
```

Genetic optimization is relatively short in code, so let's go through it:

1. We start off with a random solution.

2. Just like with the other RL algorithm, we train for a number of epochs, here 300.

3. We create a noise matrix of 50 noise vectors with a mean of zero and a standard deviation of `sigma`.

4. We now create and immediately evaluate our population by adding noise to the original weights and running the resulting vector through the evaluation function.

5. We standardize the rewards by subtracting the mean and dividing by the standard deviation. The result can be interpreted as an advantage, in this case, that a particular member of the population has over the rest.

6. Finally, we add the weighted average noise vector to the weight solution. We use a learning rate to slow down the process and avoid overshooting.

Similar to neural networks themselves, evolutionary strategies are loosely inspired by nature. In nature, species optimize themselves for survival using natural selection. Researchers have come up with many algorithms to imitate this process. The preceding neural evolution strategy algorithm works not only for single vectors but for large neural networks as well. Evolutionary strategies are still a field of active research, and at the time of writing, no best practice has been settled on.

Reinforcement learning and evolutionary strategies are the go-to techniques if no supervised learning is possible, but a reward signal is available. There are many applications in the financial industry where this is the case from simple "multi-armed bandit" problems, such as the DHL order routing system, to complex trading systems.

Practical tips for RL engineering

In this section, we will be introducing some practical tips for building RL systems. We will also highlight some current research frontiers that are highly relevant to financial practitioners.

Designing good reward functions

Reinforcement learning is the field of designing algorithms that maximize a reward function. However, creating good reward functions is surprisingly hard. As anyone who has ever managed people will know, both people and machines game the system.

The literature on RL is full of examples of researchers finding bugs in Atari games that had been hidden for years but were found and exploited by an RL agent. For example, in the game "Fishing Derby," OpenAI has reported a reinforcement learning agent achieving a higher score than is ever possible according to the game makers, and this is without catching a single fish!

While it is fun for games, such behavior can be dangerous when it occurs in financial markets. An agent trained on maximizing returns from trading, for example, could resort to illegal trading activities such as spoofing trades, without its owners knowing about it. There are three methods to create better reward functions, which we will look at in the next three subsections.

Careful, manual reward shaping

By manually creating rewards, practitioners can help the system to learn. This works especially well if the natural rewards of the environment are sparse. If, say, a reward is usually only given if a trade is successful, and this is a rare event, it helps to manually add a function that gives a reward if the trade was nearly successful.

Equally, if an agent is engaging in illegal trading, a hard-coded "robot policy" can be set up that gives a huge negative reward to the agent if it breaks the law. Reward shaping works if the rewards and the environment are relatively simple. In complex environments, it can defeat the purpose of using machine learning in the first place. Creating a complex reward function in a very complex environment can be just as big a task as writing a rule-based system acting in the environment.

Yet, especially in finance, and more so in trading, hand-crafted reward shaping is useful. Risk-averse trading is an example of creating a clever objective function. Instead of maximizing the expected reward, risk-averse reinforcement learning maximizes an evaluation function, u, which is an extension of the utility-based shortfall to a multistage setting:

$$\mathcal{U}_{s,a}(X) = \sup\left\{m \in \mathbb{R} \mid \mathbb{E}_{s\sim p^\pi, a\sim\pi(s)}\left[u(X - m) \geq 0\right]\right\}$$

Here u is a concave, continuous, and strictly increasing function that can be freely chosen according to how much risk the trader is willing to take. The RL algorithm now maximizes as follows:

$$J(\pi) = \mathcal{U}\left[V(s_0)\right]$$

Inverse reinforcement learning

In **inverse reinforcement learning (IRL)**, a model is trained to predict the reward function of a human expert. A human expert is performing a task, and the model observes states and actions. It then tries to find a value function that explains the human expert's behavior. More specifically, by observing the expert, a policy trace of states and actions is created. One example is the maximum likelihood inverse reinforcement learning, or IRL, algorithm which works as follows:

1. Guess a reward function, R

2. Compute the policy, π, that follows from R, by training an RL agent

3. Compute the probability that the actions observed, D, were a result of π, $p(D|\pi)$

4. Compute the gradient with respect to R and update it

5. Repeat this process until $p(D|\pi)$ is very high

Learning from human preferences

Similar to IRL, which produces a reward function from human examples, there are also algorithms that learn from human preferences. A reward predictor produces a reward function under which policy is trained.

The goal of the reward predictor is to produce a reward function that results in a policy that has a large human preference. Human preference is measured by showing the human the results of two policies and letting the human indicate which one is more preferable:

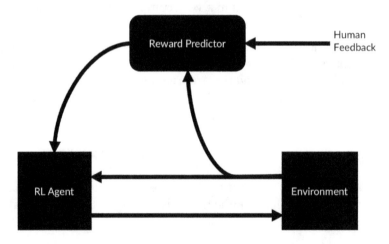

Learning from preferences

Robust RL

Much like for GANs, RL can be fragile and can be hard to train for good results. RL algorithms are quite sensitive to hyperparameter choices. But there are a few ways to make RL more robust:

- **Using a larger experience replay buffer**: The goal of using experience replay buffers is to collect uncorrelated experiences. This can be achieved by just creating a larger buffer or a whole buffer database that can store millions of examples, possibly from different agents.

- **Target networks**: RL is unstable in part because the neural network relies on its own output for training. By using a frozen target network for generating training data, we can mitigate problems. The frozen target network should only be updated slowly by, for example, moving the weights of the target network only a few percent every few epochs in the direction of the trained network.

- **Noisy inputs**: Adding noise to the state representation helps the model generalize to other situations and avoids overfitting. It has proven especially useful if the agent is trained in a simulation but needs to generalize to the real, more complex world.

- **Adversarial examples**: In a GAN-like setup, an adversarial network can be trained to fool the model by changing the state representations. The model can, in turn, learn to ignore the adversarial attacks. This makes learning more robust.

- **Separating policy learning from feature extraction**: The most well-known results in reinforcement learning have learned a game from raw inputs. However, this requires the neural network to interpret, for example, an image by learning how that image leads to rewards. It is easier to separate the steps by, for example, first training an autoencoder that compresses state representations, then training a dynamics model that can predict the next compressed state, and then training a relatively small policy network from the two inputs.

Similar to the GAN tips, there is little theoretical reason for why these tricks work, but they will make your RL work better in practice.

Frontiers of RL

You have now seen the theory behind and application of the most useful RL techniques. Yet, RL is a moving field. This book cannot cover all of the current trends that might be interesting to practitioners, but it can highlight some that are particularly useful for practitioners in the financial industry.

Multi-agent RL

Markets, by definition, include many agents. Lowe and others, 2017, *Multi-Agent Actor-Critic for Mixed Cooperative-Competitive Environments* (see `https://arxiv.org/abs/1706.02275`), shows that reinforcement learning can be used to train agents that cooperate, compete, and communicate depending on the situation.

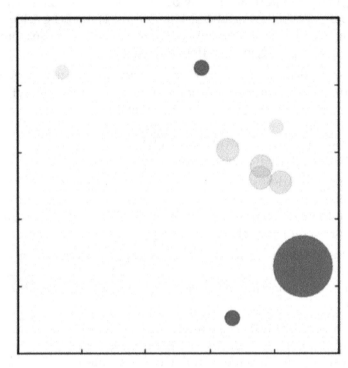

Multiple agents (in red) working together to chase the green dots. From the OpenAI blog.

In an experiment, Lowe and others let agents communicate by including a communication vector into the action space. The communication vector that one agent outputted was then made available to other agents. They showed that the agents learned to communicate to solve a task. Similar research showed that agents adopted collaborative or competitive strategies based on the environment.

In a task where the agent had to collect reward tokens, agents collaborated as long as plenty of tokens were available and showed competitive behavior as tokens got sparse. Zheng and others, 2017, *MAgent: A Many-Agent Reinforcement Learning Platform for Artificial Collective Intelligence* (see `https://arxiv.org/abs/1712.00600`), scaled the environment to include hundreds of agents. They showed that agents developed more complex strategies such as an encirclement attack on other agents through a combination of RL algorithms and clever reward shaping.

Foerster and others, 2017, *Learning with Opponent-Learning Awareness* (see `https://arxiv.org/abs/1709.04326`), developed a new kind of RL algorithm that allows the agent to learn how another agent will behave and develop actions to influence the other agent.

Learning how to learn

A shortcoming of deep learning is that skilled humans have to develop neural networks. Because of that, one longstanding dream of researchers and companies who are currently having to pay Ph.D. students is to automate the process of designing neural networks.

One example of this so-called AutoML is the **neural evolution of augmenting topologies**, known as the NEAT algorithm. NEAT uses an evolutionary strategy to design a neural network that is then trained by standard backpropagation:

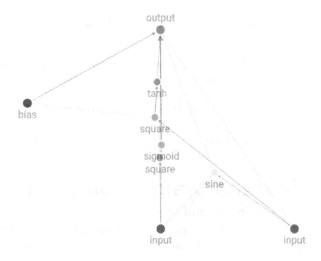

A network developed by the NEAT algorithm

As you can see in the preceding diagram, the networks developed by NEAT are often smaller than traditional, layer-based neural networks. They are hard to come up with. This is the strength of AutoML; it can find effective strategies that humans would not have discovered.

An alternative to using evolutionary algorithms for network design is to use reinforcement learning, which yields similar results. There are a couple "off-the-shelf" AutoML solutions:

- **tpot** (`https://github.com/EpistasisLab/tpot`): This is a data science assistant that optimizes machine learning pipelines using genetic algorithms. It is built on top of scikit-learn, so it does not create deep learning models but models useful for structured data, such as random forests.

- **auto-sklearn** (`https://github.com/automl/auto-sklearn`): This is also based on scikit-learn but focuses more on creating models rather than feature extraction.

- **AutoWEKA** (`https://github.com/automl/autoweka`): This is similar to `auto-sklearn`, except that it is built on the WEKA package, which runs on Java.

- **H2O AutoML** (`http://docs.h2o.ai/h2o/latest-stable/h2o-docs/automl.html`): This is an AutoML tool that is part of the H2O software package, which provides model selection and ensembling.

- **Google Cloud AutoML** (`https://cloud.google.com/automl/`): This is currently focused on pipelines for computer vision.

For the subfield of hyperparameter search, there are a few packages available as well:

- **Hyperopt** (`https://github.com/hyperopt/hyperopt`): This package allows for distributed, asynchronous hyperparameter search in Python.

- **Spearmint** (`https://github.com/HIPS/Spearmint`): This package is similar to Hyperopt, optimizing hyperparameters but using a more advanced Bayesian optimization process.

AutoML is still an active field of research, but it holds great promise. Many firms struggle to use machine learning due to a lack of skilled employees. If machine learning could optimize itself, more firms could start using machine learning.

Understanding the brain through RL

The other emerging field in finance and economics is behavioral economics. More recently, reinforcement learning has been used to understand how the human brain works. Wang and others, in 2018, published a paper titled, *Prefrontal cortex as a meta-reinforcement learning system* (see `http://dx.doi.org/10.1038/s41593-018-0147-8`), which provided new insights into the frontal cortex and the function of dopamine.

Similarly, Banino and others in 2018 published a report titled, *Vector-based navigation using grid-like representations in artificial agents* (see `https://doi.org/10.1038/s41586-018-0102-6`), where they replicated so-called "grid cells" that allow mammals to navigate using reinforcement learning.

The method is similar because both papers train RL algorithms on tasks related to the area of research, for example, navigation. They then examine the learned weights of the model for emergent properties. Such insight can be used to create more capable RL agents but also to further the field of neuroscience.

As the world of economics gets to grips with the idea that humans are not rational, but irrational in predictable ways, understanding the brain becomes more important when understanding economics. The results of neuroeconomics are particularly relevant to finance as they deal with how humans act under uncertainty and deal with risk, such as why humans are loss averse. Using RL is a promising avenue to yield further insight into human behavior.

Exercises

As we've now completed the task, let's try our hand at two appropriate exercises based on the content that we've covered.

1. **A simple RL task**: Go to `https://github.com/openai/gym`. Once there, install the Gym environment and train an agent to solve the "Cartpole" problem.

2. **A multi-agent RL task**: Go to `https://github.com/crazymuse/snakegame-numpy`. This is a Gym environment that lets you play multiple agents in a "Snake" game. Experiment with different strategies. Can you create an agent that fools the other agent? What is the emergent behavior of the snakes?

Summary

In this chapter, you learned about the main algorithms in RL, Q-learning, policy gradients, and evolutionary strategies. You saw how these algorithms could be applied to trading and learned about some of the pitfalls of applying RL. You also saw the direction of current research and how you can benefit from this research today. At this point in the book, you are now equipped with a number of advanced machine learning algorithms, which are hopefully useful to you when developing machine learning models.

In the next chapter, we will discuss the practicalities of developing, debugging, and deploying machine learning systems. We will break out of the data-science sandbox and get our models into the real world.

8

Privacy, Debugging, and Launching Your Products

Over the course of the last seven chapters we've developed a large toolbox of machine learning algorithms that we could use for machine learning problems in finance. To help round-off this toolbox, we're now going to look at what you can do if your algorithms don't work.

Machine learning models fail in the worst way: silently. In traditional software, a mistake usually leads to the program crashing, and while they're annoying for the user, they are helpful for the programmer. At least it's clear that the code failed, and often the developer will find an accompanying crash report that describes what went wrong. Yet as you go beyond this book and start developing your own models, you'll sometimes encounter machine learning code crashes too, which, for example, could be caused if the data that you fed into the algorithm had the wrong format or shape.

These issues can usually be debugged by carefully tracking which shape the data had at what point. More often, however, models that fail just output poor predictions. They'll give no signal that they have failed, to the point that you might not even be aware that they've even failed at all, but at other times, the model might not train well, it won't converge, or it won't achieve a low loss rate.

In this chapter, we'll be focusing on how you debug these silent failures so that they don't impact the machine learning algorithms that you've created. This will include looking at the following subject areas:

- Finding flaws in your data that lead to flaws in your learned model
- Using creative tricks to make your model learn more from less data
- Unit testing data in production or training to ensure standards are met

- Being mindful of privacy and regulation, such as GDPR
- Preparing data for training and avoiding common pitfalls
- Inspecting the model and peering into the "black box"
- Finding optimal hyperparameters
- Scheduling learning rates in order to reduce overfitting
- Monitoring training progress with TensorBoard
- Deploying machine learning products and iterating on them
- Speeding up training and inference

The first step you must take, before even attempting to debug your program, is to acknowledge that even good machine learning engineers fail frequently. There are many reasons why machine learning projects fail, and most have nothing to do with the skills of the engineers, so don't think that just because it's not working, you're at fault.

If these bugs are spotted early enough, then both time and money can be saved. Furthermore, in high-stakes environments, including finance-based situations, such as trading, engineers that are aware can pull the plug when they notice their model is failing. This should not be seen as a failure, but as a success to avoid problems.

Debugging data

You'll remember that back in the first chapter of this book, we discussed how machine learning models are a function of their training data, meaning that, for example, bad data will lead to bad models, or as we put it, garbage in, garbage out. If your project is failing, your data is the most likely culprit. Therefore, in this chapter we will start by looking at the data first, before moving on to look at the other possible issues that might cause our model to crash.

However, even if you have a working model, the real-world data coming in might not be up to the task. In this section, we will learn how to find out whether you have good data, what to do if you have not been given enough data, and how to test your data.

How to find out whether your data is up to the task

There are two aspects to consider when wanting to know whether your data is up to the task of training a good model:

- Does the data predict what you want it to predict?
- Do you have enough data?

To find out whether your model does contain predicting information, also called a signal, you could ask yourself the question, could a human make a prediction given this data? It's important for your AI to be given data that can be comprehended by humans, because after all, the only reason we know intelligence is possible is because we observe it in humans. Humans are good at understanding written text, but if a human cannot understand a text, then the chances are that your model won't make much sense of it either.

A common pitfall to this test is that humans have context that your model does not have. A human trader does not only consume financial data, but they might have also experienced the product of a company or seen the CEO on TV. This external context flows into the trader's decision but is often forgotten when a model is built. Likewise, humans are also good at focusing on important data. A human trader will not consume all of the financial data out there because most of it is irrelevant.

Adding more inputs to your model won't make it better; on the contrary, it often makes it worse, as the model overfits and gets distracted by all the noise. On the other hand, humans are irrational; they follow peer pressure and have a hard time making decisions in abstract and unfamiliar environments. Humans would struggle to find an optimal traffic light policy, for instance, because the data that traffic lights operate on is not intuitive to us.

This brings us to the second sanity check: a human might not be able to make predictions, but there might be a causal (economic) rationale. There is a causal link between a company's profits and its share price, the traffic on a road and traffic jams, customer complaints and customers leaving your company, and so on. While humans might not have an intuitive grasp of these links, we can discover them through reasoning.

There are some tasks for which a causal link is required. For instance, for a long time, many quantitative trading firms insisted on their data having a causal link to the predicted outcomes of models. Yet nowadays, the industry seems to have slightly moved away from that idea as it gets more confident in testing its algorithms. If humans cannot make a prediction and there is no causal rationale for why your data is predictive, you might want to reconsider whether your project is feasible.

Once you have determined that your data contains enough signal, you need to ask yourself whether you have enough data to train a model to extract the signal. There is no clear answer to the question of how much is enough, but roughly speaking, the amount needed depends on the complexity of the model you hope to create. There are a couple of rules of thumb to follow, however:

- For classification, you should have around 30 independent samples per class.

- You should have 10 times as many samples as there are features, especially for structured data problems.
- Your dataset should get bigger as the number of parameters in your model gets bigger.

Keep in mind these rules are only rules of thumb and might be very different for your specific application. If you can make use of transfer learning, then you can drastically reduce the number of samples you need. This is why most computer vision applications use transfer learning.

If you have any reasonable amount of data, say, a few hundred samples, then you can start building your model. In this case, a sensible suggestion would be to start with a simple model that you can deploy while you collect more data.

What to do if you don't have enough data

Sometimes, you find yourself in a situation where despite starting your project, you simply do not have enough data. For example, the legal team might have changed its mind and decided that you cannot use the data, for instance due to GDPR, even though they greenlit it earlier. In this case, you have multiple options.

Most of the time, one of the best options would be to "augment your data." We've already seen some data augmentation in *Chapter 3, Utilizing Computer Vision*. Of course, you can augment all kinds of data in various ways, including slightly changing some database entries. Taking augmentation a step further, you might be able to *generate your data*, for example, in a simulation. This is effectively how most reinforcement learning researchers gather data, but this can also work in other cases.

The data we used for fraud detection back in *Chapter 2, Applying Machine Learning to Structured Data* was obtained from simulation. The simulation requires you to be able to write down the rules of your environment within a program. Powerful learning algorithms tend to figure out these often over-simplistic rules, so they might not generalize to the real world as well. Yet, simulated data can be a powerful addition to real data.

Likewise, you can often *find external data*. Just because you haven't tracked a certain data point, it does not mean that nobody else has. There is an astonishing amount of data available on the internet. Even if the data was not originally collected for your purpose, you might be able to retool data by either relabeling it or by using it for **transfer learning**. You might be able to train a model on a large dataset for a different task and then use that model as a basis for your task. Equally, you can find a model that someone else has trained for a different task and repurpose it for your task.

Finally, you might be able to create a **simple model**, which does not capture the relationship in the data completely but is enough to ship a product. Random forests and other tree-based methods often require much less data than neural networks.

It's important to remember that for data, quality trumps quantity in the majority of cases. Getting a small, high-quality dataset in and training a weak model is often your best shot to find problems with data early. You can always scale up data collection later. A mistake many practitioners make is that they spend huge amounts of time and money on getting a big dataset, only to find that they have the wrong kind of data for their project.

Unit testing data

If you build a model, you're making assumptions about your data. For example, you assume that the data you feed into your time series model is actually a time series with dates that follow each other in order. You need to test your data to make sure that this assumption is true. This is something that is especially true with live data that you receive once your model is already in production. Bad data might lead to poor model performance, which can be dangerous, especially in a high-stakes environment.

Additionally, you need to test whether your data is clean from things such as personal information. As we'll see in the following section on privacy, personal information is a liability that you want to get rid of, unless you have good reasons and consent from the user to use it.

Since monitoring data quality is important when trading based on many data sources, Two Sigma Investments LP, a New York City-based international hedge fund, has created an open source library for data monitoring. It is called *marbles*, and you can read more about it here: https://github.com/twosigma/marbles. marbles builds on Python's unittest library.

You can install it with the following command:

```
pip install marbles
```

 Note: You can find a Kaggle kernel demonstrating marbles here: https://www.kaggle.com/jannesklaas/marbles-test.

The following code sample shows a simple marbles unit test. Imagine you are gathering data about the unemployment rate in Ireland. For your models to work, you need to ensure that you actually get the data for consecutive months, and don't count one month twice, for instance.

We can ensure this happens by running the following code:

```
import marbles.core                                    #1
from marbles.mixins import mixins

import pandas as pd                                    #2
import numpy as np
from datetime import datetime, timedelta

class TimeSeriesTestCase(marbles.core.TestCase,
mixins.MonotonicMixins):                               #3
    def setUp(self):                                   #4

        self.df = pd.DataFrame({'dates':[datetime(2018,1,1),
                                datetime(2018,2,1),
                                datetime(2018,2,1)],
                    'ireland_unemployment':[6.2,6.1,6.0]})  #5


    def tearDown(self):
        self.df = None                                 #6

    def test_date_order(self):                         #7

        self.assertMonotonicIncreasing(sequence=self.df.dates,
                            note = 'Dates need to increase
monotonically')                                        #8
```

Don't worry if you don't fully understand the code. We're now going to go through each stage of the code:

1. Marbles features two main components. The `core` module does the actual testing, while the `mixins` module provides a number of useful tests for different types of data. This simplifies your test writing and gives you more readable and semantically interpretable tests.

2. You can use all the libraries, like pandas, that you would usually use to handle and process data for testing.

3. Now it is time to define our test class. A new test class must inherit marbles' `TestCase` class. This way, our test class is automatically set up to run as a marbles test. If you want to use a mixin, you also need to inherit the corresponding mixin class.

   In this example, we are working with a series of dates that should be increasing monotonically. The `MonotonicMixins` class provides a range of tools that allow you to test for a monotonically increasing series automatically.

If you are coming from Java programming, the concept of multiple inheritances might strike you as weird, but in Python, classes can easily inherit multiple other classes. This is useful if you want your class to inherit two different capabilities, such as running a test and testing time-related concepts.

4. The `setUp` function is a standard test function in which we can load the data and prepare for the test. In this case, we just need to define a pandas DataFrame by hand. Alternatively, you could also load a CSV file, load a web resource, or pursue any other way in order to get your data.

5. In our DataFrame, we have the Irish unemployment rate for two months. As you can see, the last month has been counted twice. As this should not happen, it will cause an error.

6. The `tearDown` method is a standard test method that allows us to cleanup after our test is done. In this case, we just free RAM, but you can also choose to delete files or databases that were just created for testing.

7. Methods describing actual tests should start with `test_`. marbles will automatically run all of the test methods after setting up.

8. We assert that the time indicator of our data strictly increases. If our assertion had required intermediate variables, such as a maximum value, marbles will display it in the error report. To make our error more readable, we can attach a handy note.

To run a unit test in a Jupyter Notebook, we need to tell marbles to ignore the first argument; we achieve this by running the following:

```
if __name__ == '__main__':
    marbles.core.main(argv=['first-arg-is-ignored'], exit=False)
```

It's more common to run unit tests directly from the command line. So, if you saved the preceding code in the command line, you could run it with this command:

```
python -m marbles marbles_test.py
```

Of course, there are problems with our data. Luckily for us, our test ensures that this error does not get passed on to our model, where it would cause a silent failure in the form of a bad prediction. Instead, the test will fail with the following error output:

[**Note:** This code will not run and will fail.]

```
F                                                          #1
============================================================
FAIL: test_date_order (__main__.TimeSeriesTestCase)    #2
------------------------------------------------------------
marbles.core.marbles.ContextualAssertionError: Elements in 0
2018-01-01
1    2018-02-01
2    2018-02-01                                         #3
Name: dates, dtype: datetime64[ns] are not strictly monotonically
increasing

Source (<ipython-input-1-ebdbd8f0d69f>):               #4
      19
  >   20 self.assertMonotonicIncreasing(sequence=self.df.dates,
      21                     note = 'Dates need to increase
monotonically')
      22
Locals:                                                  #5


Note:                                                    #6
      Dates need to increase monotonically




------------------------------------------------------------
```

Ran 1 test in 0.007s

FAILED (failures=1)

So, what exactly caused the data to fail? Let's have a look:

1. The top line shows the status of the entire test. In this case, there was only one test method, and it failed. Your test might have multiple different test methods, and marbles would display the progress by showing how tests fail or pass. The next couple of lines describe the failed test method. This line describes that the test_date_order method of the TimeSeriesTestCase class failed.

2. marbles shows precisely how the test failed. The values of the dates tested are shown, together with the cause for failure.

3. In addition to the actual failure, marbles will display a traceback showing the actual code where our test failed.

4. A special feature of marbles is the ability to display local variables. This way, we can ensure that there was no problem with the setup of the test. It also helps us in getting the context as to how exactly the test failed.

5. Finally, marbles will display our note, which helps the test consumer understand what went wrong.

6. As a summary, marbles displays that the test failed with one failure. Sometimes, you may be able to accept data even though it failed some tests, but more often than not you'll want to dig in and see what is going on.

The point of unit testing data is to make the failures loud in order to prevent data issues from giving you bad predictions. A failure with an error message is much better than a failure without one. Often, the failure is caused by your data vendor, and by testing all of the data that you got from all of the vendors, it will allow you to be aware when a vendor makes a mistake.

Unit testing data also helps you to ensure you have no data that you shouldn't have, such as personal data. Vendors need to clean datasets of all personally identifying information, such as social security numbers, but of course, they sometimes forget. Complying with ever stricter data privacy regulation is a big concern for many financial institutions engaging in machine learning.

The next section will therefore discuss how to preserve privacy and comply with regulations while still gaining benefits from machine learning.

Keeping data private and complying with regulations

In recent years, consumers have woken up to the fact that their data is being harvested and analyzed in ways that they cannot control, and that is sometimes against their own interest. Naturally, they are not happy about it and regulators have to come up with some new data regulations.

At the time of writing, the European Union has introduced the **General Data Protection Regulation (GDPR)**, but it's likely that other jurisdictions will develop stricter privacy protections, too.

This text will not go into depth on how to comply with this law specifically. However, if you wish to expand your understanding of the topic, then the UK government's guide to GDPR is a good starting place to learn more about the specifics of the regulation and how to comply with it: `https://www.gov.uk/government/publications/guide-to-the-general-data-protection-regulation`.

This section will outline both the key principles of the recent privacy legislation and some technological solutions that you can utilize in order to comply with these principles.

The overarching rule here is to, "delete what you don't need." For a long time, a large percentage of companies have just stored all of the data that they could get their hands on, but this is a bad idea. Storing personal data is a liability for your business. It's owned by someone else, and you are on the hook for taking care of it. The next time you hear a statement such as, "We have 500,000 records in our database," think of it more along the lines of, "We have 500,000 liabilities on our books." It can be a good idea to take on liabilities, but only if there is an economic value that justifies these liabilities. What happens astonishingly often though is that you might collect personal data by accident. Say you are tracking device usage, but accidentally include the customer ID in your records. You need practices in place that monitor and prevent such accidents, here are four of the key ones:

- **Be transparent and obtain consent**: Customers want good products, and they understand how their data can make your product better for them. Rather than pursuing an adversarial approach in which you wrap all your practices in a very long agreement and then make users agree to it, it is usually more sensible to clearly tell users what you are doing, how their data is used, and how that improves the product. If you need personal data, you need consent. Being transparent will help you down the line as users will trust you more and this can then be used to improve your product through customer feedback.

- **Remember that breaches happen to the best**: No matter how good your security is, there is a chance that you'll get hacked. So, you should design your personal data storage under the assumption that the entire database might be dumped on the internet one day. This assumption will help you to create stronger privacy and help you to avoid disaster once you actually get hacked.

- **Be mindful about what can be inferred from data**: You might not be tracking personally identifying information in your database, but when combined with another database, your customers can still be individually identified.

  Say you went for coffee with a friend, paid by credit card, and posted a picture of the coffee on Instagram. The bank might collect anonymous credit card records, but if someone went to crosscheck the credit card records against the Instagram pictures, there would only be one customer who bought a coffee and posted a picture of coffee at the same time in the same area. This way, all your credit card transactions are no longer anonymous. Consumers expect companies to be mindful of these effects.

- **Encrypt and Obfuscate data**: Apple, for instance, collects phone data but adds random noise to the collected data. The noise renders each individual record incorrect, but in aggregate the records still give a picture of user behavior. There are a few caveats to this approach; for example, you can only collect so many data points from a user before the noise cancels out, and the individual behavior is revealed.

  Noise, as introduced by obfuscation, is random. When averaged over a large sample of data about a single user, the mean of the noise will be zero as it does not present a pattern by itself. The true profile of the user will be revealed. Similarly, recent research has shown that deep learning models can learn on homomorphically encrypted data. Homomorphic encryption is a method of encryption that preserves the underlying algebraic properties of the data. Mathematically, this can be expressed as follows:

$$E(m_1) + E(m_2) = E(m_1 + m_2)$$

$$D(E(m_1 + m_2)) = m_1 + m_2$$

  Here E is an encryption function, m is some plain text data, and D is a decryption function. As you can see, adding the encrypted data is the same as first adding the data and then encrypting it. Adding the data, encrypting it, and then decrypting it is the same as just adding the data.

  This means you can encrypt the data and still train a model on it. Homomorphic encryption is still in its infancy, but through approaches like this, you can ensure that in the case of a data breach, no sensitive individual information is leaked.

- **Train locally, and upload only a few gradients**: One way to avoid uploading user data is to train your model on the user's device. The user accumulates data on the device. You can then download your model on to the device and perform a single forward and backward pass on the device.

  To avoid the possibility of inference of user data from the gradients, you only upload a few gradients at random. You can then apply the gradients to your master model.

To further increase the overall privacy of the system, you do not need to download all the newly update weights from the master model to the user's device, but only a few. This way, you train your model asynchronously without ever accessing any data. If your database gets breached, no user data is lost. However, we need to note that this only works if you have a large enough user base.

Preparing the data for training

In earlier chapters, we have seen the benefits of normalizing and scaling features, we also discussed how you should scale all numerical features. There are four ways of feature scaling; these include *standardization, Min-Max, mean normalization,* and *unit length scaling*. In this section we'll break down each one:

- **Standardization** ensures that all of the data has a mean of zero and a standard deviation of one. It is computed by subtracting the mean and dividing by the standard deviation of the data:

$$x' = \frac{x - \mu}{\sigma}$$

  This is probably the most common way of scaling features. It's especially useful if you suspect that your data contains outliers as it is quite robust. On the flip side, standardization does not ensure that your features are between zero and one, which is the range in which neural networks learn best.

- **Min-Max** rescaling does exactly that. It scales all data between zero and one by first subtracting the minimum value and then dividing by the range of values. We can see this expressed in the formula below:

$$x' = \frac{x - \min(x)}{\max(x) - \min(x)}$$

  If you know for sure that your data contains no outliers, which is the case in images, for instance, Min-Max scaling will give you a nice scaling of values between zero and one.

- Similar to Min-Max, **mean normalization** ensures your data has values between minus one and one with a mean of zero. This is done by subtracting the mean and then dividing by the range of data, which is expressed in the following formula:

$$x' = \frac{x - \mu}{\max(x) - \min(x)}$$

Mean normalization is done less frequently but, depending on your application, might be a good approach.

- For some applications, it is better to not scale individual features, but instead vectors of features. In this case, you would apply **unit length scaling** by dividing each element in the vector by the total length of the vector, as we can see below:

$$x' = \frac{x}{\|x\|}$$

The length of the vector usually means the L2 norm of the vector $\|x\|_2$, that is, the square root of the sum of squares. For some applications, the vector length means the L1 norm of the vector, $\|x\|_1$, which is the sum of vector elements.

However you scale, it is important to only measure the scaling factors, mean, and standard deviation on the test set. These factors include only a select amount of the information about the data. If you measure them over your entire dataset, then the algorithm might perform better on the test set than it will in production, due to this information advantage.

Equally importantly, you should check that your production code has proper feature scaling as well. Over time, you should recalculate your feature distribution and adjust your scaling.

Understanding which inputs led to which predictions

Why did your model make the prediction it made? For complex models, this question is pretty hard to answer. A global explanation for a very complex model might in itself be very complex. The **Local Interpretable Model-Agnostic Explanations (LIME)** is, a popular algorithm for model explanation that focuses on local explanations. Rather than trying to answer; "How does this model make predictions?" LIME tries to answer; "Why did the model make *this* prediction on *this* data?"

Note: The authors of LIME, Ribeiro, Singh, and Guestrin, curated a great GitHub repository around their algorithm with many explanations and tutorials, which you can find here: `https://github.com/marcotcr/lime`.

On Kaggle kernels, LIME is installed by default. However, you can install LIME locally with the following command:

```
pip install lime
```

The LIME algorithm works with any classifier, which is why it is model agnostic. To make an explanation, LIME cuts up the data into several sections, such as areas of an image or utterances in a text. It then creates a new dataset by removing some of these features. It runs this new dataset through the black box classifier and obtains the classifiers predicted probabilities for different classes. LIME then encodes the data as vectors describing what features were present. Finally, it trains a linear model to predict the outcomes of the black box model with different features removed. As linear models are easy to interpret, LIME will use the linear model to determine the most important features.

Let's say that you are using a text classifier, such as TF-IDF, to classify emails such as those in the 20 newsgroup dataset. To get explanations from this classifier, you would use the following snippet:

```
from lime.lime_text import LimeTextExplainer          #1
explainer = LimeTextExplainer(class_names=class_names)  #2
exp = explainer.explain_instance(test_example,          #3
                        classifier.predict_proba,       #4
                        num_features=6)                 #5

exp.show_in_notebook()                                  #6
```

Now, let's understand what's going on in that code snippet:

1. The LIME package has several classes for different types of data.
2. To create a new blank explainer, we need to pass the names of classes of our classifier.
3. We'll provide one text example for which we want an explanation.
4. We provide the prediction function of our classifier. We need to provide a function that provides probabilities. For Keras, this is just `model.predict`; for scikit models, we need to use the `predict_proba` method.
5. LIME shows the maximum number of features. We want to show only the importance of the six most important features in this case.
6. Finally, we can render a visualization of our prediction, which looks like this:

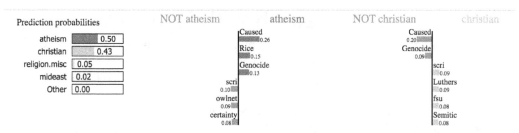

LIME text output

The explanation shows the classes with different features that the text gets classified as most often. It shows the words that most contribute to the classification in the two most frequent classes. Under that, you can see the words that contributed to the classification highlighted in the text.

As you can see, our model picked up on parts of the email address of the sender as distinguishing features, as well as the name of the university, "Rice." It sees "Caused" to be a strong indicator that the text is about atheism. Combined, these are all things we want to know when debugging datasets.

LIME does not perfectly solve the problem of explaining models. It struggles if the interaction of multiple features leads to a certain outcome for instance. However, it does well enough to be a useful data debugging tool. Often, models pick up on things they should not be picking up on. To debug a dataset, we need to remove all these "give-away" features that statistical models like to overfit to.

Looking back at this section, you've now seen a wide range of tools that you can use to debug your dataset. Yet, even with a perfect dataset, there can be issues when it comes to training. The next section is about how to debug your model.

Debugging your model

Complex deep learning models are prone to error. With millions of parameters, there are a number things that can go wrong. Luckily, the field has developed a number of useful tools to improve model performance. In this section, we will introduce the most useful tools that you can use to debug and improve your model.

Hyperparameter search with Hyperas

Manually tuning the hyperparameters of a neural network can be a tedious task. Despite you possibly having some intuition about what works and what does not, there are no hard rules to apply when it comes to tuning hyperparameters. This is why practitioners with lots of computing power on hand use automatic hyperparameter search. After all, hyperparameters form a search space just like the model's parameters do. The difference is that we cannot apply backpropagation to them and cannot take derivatives of them. We can still apply all non-gradient based optimization algorithms to them.

There are a number of different hyperparameter optimization tools, but we will look at Hyperas because of its ease of use. Hyperas is a wrapper for `hyperopt`, a popular optimization library made for working with Keras.

[**Note**: You can find Hyperas on GitHub: `https://github.com/maxpumperla/hyperas`.]

We can install Hyperas with `pip`:

```
pip install hyperas
```

Depending on your setup, you might need to make a few adjustments to the installation. If this is the case, then the Hyperas GitHub page, link above, offers more information.

Hyperas offers two optimization methods, **Random Search** and **Tree of Parzen Estimators**. Within a range of parameters that we think are reasonable, the random search will sample randomly and train a model with random hyperparameters. It will then pick the best-performing model as the solution.

Random search is simple and robust, and it can be scaled easily. It basically makes no assumption about the hyperparameters, their relation, and the loss surface. On the flip side, it is relatively slow.

The **Tree of Parzen (TPE)** algorithm models the relation $P(x \mid y)$, where x represents the hyperparameters and y the associated performance. This is the exact opposite modeling of Gaussian processes, which model $P(y \mid x)$ and are popular with many researchers.

Empirically, it turns out that TPE performs better. For the precise details, see the 2011 paper, *Algorithms for Hyper-Parameter Optimization*, available at: https://papers. nips.cc/paper/4443-algorithms-for-hyper-parameter-optimization -- that was authored by James S. Bergstra and others. TPE is faster than random search but can get stuck in local minima and struggles with some difficult loss surfaces. As a rule of thumb, it makes sense to start with TPE, and if TPE struggles, move to random search.

 Note: The code for this example can be found at: https://www. kaggle.com/jannesklaas/Hyperas.

The following example will show you how to use Hyperas and Hyperopt for an MNIST dataset classifier:

```
from hyperopt import Trials, STATUS_OK, tpe        #1
from hyperas import optim                           #2
from hyperas.distributions import choice, uniform
```

While the code was short, let's explain what it all means:

1. As Hyperas is built on Hyperopt, we need to import some pieces directly from `hyperopt`. The `Trials` class runs the actual trials, `STATUS_OK` helps communicate that a test went well, and `tpe` is an implementation of the TPE algorithm.

2. Hyperas provides a number of handy functions that make working with Hyperopt easier. The `optim` function finds optimal hyperparameters and can be used just like Keras' `fit` function. `choice` and `uniform` can be used to choose between discrete and continuous hyperparameters respectively.

To build on the previous ideas that we've explored, let's now add the following, which we will explain in more detail once the code has been written:

```
def data():                                      #1
    import numpy as np                           #2
    from keras.utils import np_utils

    from keras.models import Sequential
    from keras.layers import Dense, Activation, Dropout
    from keras.optimizers import RMSprop

    path = '../input/mnist.npz'                  #3
    with np.load(path) as f:
        X_train, y_train = f['x_train'], f['y_train']
```

```
        X_test, y_test = f['x_test'], f['y_test']

    X_train = X_train.reshape(60000, 784)          #4
    X_test = X_test.reshape(10000, 784)
    X_train = X_train.astype('float32')
    X_test = X_test.astype('float32')
    X_train /= 255
    X_test /= 255
    nb_classes = 10
    y_train = np_utils.to_categorical(y_train, nb_classes)
    y_test = np_utils.to_categorical(y_test, nb_classes)

    return X_train, y_train, X_test, y_test          #5
```

Let's take a moment to look at the code we've just produced:

1. Hyperas expects a function that loads the data; we cannot just pass on a dataset from memory.

2. To scale the search, Hyperas creates a new runtime in which it does model creation and evaluation. This also means imports that we did in a notebook do not always transfer into the runtime. To be sure that all modules are available, we need to do all imports in the `data` function. This is also true for modules that will only be used for the model.

3. We now load the data. Since Kaggle kernels do not have access to the internet, we need to load the MNIST data from disk. If you have internet, but no local version of the files, you can get the data using following code:

```
from keras.datasets import mnist
(Y_train, y_train), (X_test, y_test) = mnist.load_data()
```
I would still keep the no internet version around because it is the default setting.

4. The `data` function also needs to preprocess the data. We do the standard reshaping and scaling that we did when we worked with MNIST earlier.

5. Finally, we return the data. This data will be passed into the function that builds and evaluates the model:

```
def model(X_train, y_train, X_test, y_test):          #1
    model = Sequential()          #2
    model.add(Dense(512, input_shape=(784,)))

    model.add(Activation('relu'))

    model.add(Dropout({{uniform(0, 0.5)}}))          #3

    model.add(Dense({{choice([256, 512, 1024])}}))          #4
```

```
model.add(Activation({{choice(['relu','tanh'])}}))            #5

model.add(Dropout({{uniform(0, 0.5)}}))

model.add(Dense(10))
model.add(Activation('softmax'))

rms = RMSprop()
model.compile(loss='categorical_crossentropy',
              optimizer=rms,
              metrics=['accuracy'])

model.fit(X_train, y_train,                                   #6
          batch_size={{choice([64, 128])}},
          epochs=1,
          verbose=2,
          validation_data=(X_test, y_test))
score, acc = model.evaluate(X_test, y_test, verbose=0)        #7
print('Test accuracy:', acc)
return {'loss': -acc, 'status': STATUS_OK, 'model': model} #8
```

As you can see, the preceding snippet of code is made up of eight defining pieces. Let's now explore them so that we're able to fully understand the code we've just produced:

1. The `model` function both defines the model and evaluates it. Given a training dataset from the `data` function, it returns a set of quality metrics.

2. When fine-tuning with Hyperas, we can define a Keras model just as we usually would. Here, we only have to replace the hyperparameters we want to tune with Hyperas functions.

3. To tune dropout, for instance, we replace the `Dropout` hyperparameter with `{{uniform(0, 0.5)}}`. Hyperas will automatically sample and evaluate dropout rates between `0` and `0.5`, sampled from a uniform distribution.

4. To sample from discrete distributions, for instance, the size of a hidden layer, we replace the hyperparameter with `{{choice([256, 512, 1024])}}`. Hyperas will choose from a hidden layer size of 256, 512, and 1,024 now.

5. We can do the same to choose activation functions.

6. To evaluate the model, we need to compile and fit it. In this process, we can also choose between different batch sizes. In this case, we only train for one epoch, to keep the time needed for this example short. You could also run a whole training process with Hyperas.

7. To gain insight into how well the model is doing, we evaluate it on test data.

8. Finally, we return the model's score, the model itself, and an indicator that everything went okay. Hyperas tries to minimize a loss function. To maximize accuracy, we set the loss to be the negative accuracy. You could also pass the model loss here, depending on what the best optimization method is for your problem.

Finally, we run the optimization:

```
best_run, best_model = optim.minimize(model=model,
                                      data=data,
                                      algo=tpe.suggest,
                                      max_evals=5,
                                      trials=Trials(),
                    notebook_name='__notebook_source__')
```

We pass the `model` method and the `data` method, and we specify how many trials we want to run and which class should govern the trials. Hyperopt also offers a distributed trials class in which workers communicate via MongoDB.

When working in a Jupyter Notebook, we need to provide the name of the notebook we are working in. Kaggle Notebooks all have the filename `__notebook_source__`, regardless of the name you gave them.

After it's run, Hyperas returns the best-performing model as well as the hyperparameters of the best model. If you print out `best_run`, you should see output similar to this:

```
{'Activation': 1,
 'Dense': 1,
 'Dropout': 0.3462695171578595,
 'Dropout_1': 0.10640021656377913,
 'batch_size': 0}
```

For `choice` selections, Hyperas shows the index. In this case, the activation function `tanh` was chosen.

In this case we ran the hyperparameter search only for a few trials. Usually, you would run a few hundred or thousand trials. To do this we would use automated hyperparameter search, which can be a great tool to improve model performance if you have enough compute power available.

However, it won't get a model that does not work at all to work. When choosing this approach, you need to be sure to have a somewhat-working approach first before investing in hyperparameter search.

Efficient learning rate search

One of the most important hyperparameters is the learning rate. Finding a good learning rate is hard. Too small and your model might train so slowly that you believe it is not training at all, but if it's too large it will overshoot and not reduce the loss as well.

When it comes to finding a learning rate, standard hyperparameter search techniques are not the best choice. For the learning rate, it is better to perform a line search and visualize the loss for different learning rates, as this will give you an understanding of how the loss function behaves.

When doing a line search, it is better to increase the learning rate exponentially. You are more likely to care about the region of smaller learning rates than about very large learning rates.

In our example below, we perform 20 evaluations and double the learning rate in every evaluation. We can run this by executing the following code:

```
init_lr = 1e-6                                              #1
losses = []
lrs = []
for i in range(20):                                         #2
    model = Sequential()
    model.add(Dense(512, input_shape=(784,)))
    model.add(Activation('relu'))
    model.add(Dropout(0.2))
    model.add(Dense(512))
    model.add(Activation('relu'))
    model.add(Dropout(0.2))
    model.add(Dense(10))
    model.add(Activation('softmax'))

    opt = Adam(lr=init_lr*2**i)                             #3
    model.compile(loss='categorical_crossentropy',
                optimizer=opt,
                metrics=['acc'])


    hist = model.fit(X_train, Y_train, batch_size = 128,
epochs=1)                                                   #4

    loss = hist.history['loss'][0]                          #5
    losses.append(loss)
    lrs.append(init_lr*2**i)
```

Let's now take a more detailed look at the preceding featured code:

1. We specify a low, but still reasonable, initial learning rate from which we start our search.

2. We then perform training 20 times with different learning rates. We need to set up the model from scratch each time.

3. We calculate our new learning rate. In our case, we double the learning rate in each evaluation step. You could also use a smaller increase if you want a more fine-grained picture.

4. We then fit the model with our new learning rate.

5. Finally, we keep track of the loss.

If your dataset is very large, you can perform this learning rate search on a subset of the data. The interesting part comes from the visualization of learning rates:

```
fig, ax = plt.subplots(figsize = (10,7))
plt.plot(lrs,losses)
ax.set_xscale('log')
```

When you run this code, it will then output the following chart:

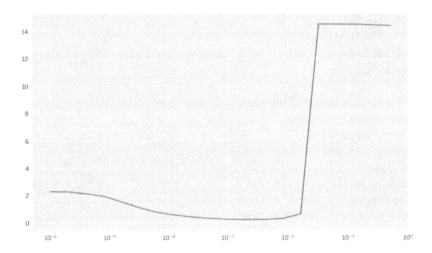

Learning rate finder

As you can see, the loss is optimal between 1e-3 and 1e-2. We can also see that the loss surface is relatively flat in this area. This gives us insight that we should use a learning rate around 1e-3. To avoid overshooting, we select a learning rate somewhat lower than the optimum found by line search.

Learning rate scheduling

Why stop at using one learning rate? In the beginning, your model might be far away from the optimal solution, and so because of that you want to move as fast as possible. As you approach the minimum loss, however, you want to move slower to avoid overshooting. A popular method is to anneal the learning rate so that it represents a cosine function. To this end, we need to the find a learning rate scheduling function, that given a time step, t, in epochs returns a learning rate. The learning rate becomes a function of t:

$$a(t) = \frac{a_0}{2}\left(\cos\left(\frac{\pi \bmod (t-1, l)}{l}\right)\right)$$

Here l is the cycle length and a_0 is the initial learning rate. We modify this function to ensure that t does not become larger than the cycle length:

```
def cosine_anneal_schedule(t):
    lr_init = 1e-2                                  #1
    anneal_len = 5
    if t >= anneal_len: t = anneal_len -1           #2
    cos_inner = np.pi * (t % (anneal_len))          #3
    cos_inner /= anneal_len
    cos_out = np.cos(cos_inner) + 1
    return float(lr_init / 2 * cos_out)
```

The preceding code features three key features:

1. In our function, we need to set up a starting point from which we anneal. This can be a relatively large learning rate. We also need to specify how many epochs we want to anneal.

2. A cosine function does not monotonically decrease; it goes back up after a cycle. We will use this property later; for now, we will just make sure that the learning rate does not go back up.

3. Finally we calculate the new learning rate using the preceding formula. This is the new learning rate.

To get a better understanding of what the learning rate scheduling function does, we can plot the learning rate it would set over 10 epochs:

```
srs = [cosine_anneal_schedule(t) for t in range(10)]
plt.plot(srs)
```

With the output of the code being shown in the following graph:

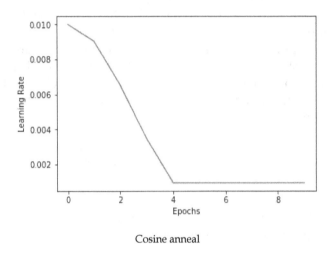

Cosine anneal

We can use this function to schedule learning rates with Keras' LearningRateScheduler callback:

```
from keras.callbacks import LearningRateScheduler
cb = LearningRateScheduler(cosine_anneal_schedule)
```

We now have a callback that Keras will call at the end of each epoch in order to get a new learning rate. We pass this callback to the `fit` method and voilà, our model trains with a decreasing learning rate:

```
model.fit(x_train,y_train,batch_size=128,epochs=5,callbacks=[cb])
```

A version of the learning rate annealing is to add restarts. At the end of an annealing cycle, we move the learning rate back up. This is a method used to avoid overfitting. With a small learning rate, our model might find a very narrow minimum. If the data we want to use our model on is slightly different from the training data, then the loss surface might change a bit, and our model could be out of the narrow minimum for this new loss surface. If we set the learning rate back up, our model will get out of narrow minima. Broad minima, however, are stable enough for the model to stay in them:

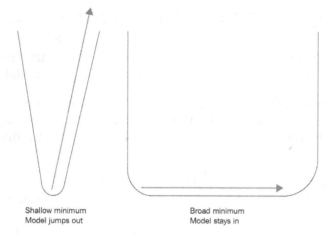

Shallow minimum
Model jumps out

Broad minimum
Model stays in

Shallow broad minima

As the cosine function goes back up by itself, we only have to remove the line to stop it from doing so:

```
def cosine_anneal_schedule(t):
    lr_init = 1e-2
    anneal_len = 10
    cos_inner = np.pi * (t % (anneal_len))
    cos_inner /= anneal_len
    cos_out = np.cos(cos_inner) + 1
    return float(lr_init / 2 * cos_out)
```

The new learning rate schedule now looks like this:

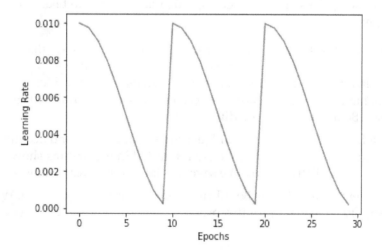

Learning rate restarts

Monitoring training with TensorBoard

An important part of debugging a model is knowing when things go wrong before you have invested significant amounts of time training the model. TensorBoard is a TensorFlow extension that allows you to easily monitor your model in a browser.

To provide an interface from which you can watch your model's progress, TensorBoard also offers some options useful for debugging. For example, you can observe the distributions of the model's weights and gradients during training.

[**Note:** TensorBoard does not run on Kaggle. To try out TensorBoard, install Keras and TensorFlow on your own machine.]

To use TensorBoard with Keras, we set up a new callback. TensorBoard has many options, so let's walk through them step by step:

```
from keras.callbacks import TensorBoard
tb = TensorBoard(log_dir='./logs/test2',              #1
                histogram_freq=1,                     #2
                batch_size=32,                        #3
                write_graph=True,                     #4
                write_grads=True,
                write_images=True,
                embeddings_freq=0,                    #5
                embeddings_layer_names=None,
                embeddings_metadata=None)
```

There are five key pieces of the preceding code that we need to take into consideration:

1. First, we need to specify where Keras should save the data that TensorBoard later visualizes. Generally, it is a good idea to save all logs of your different runs in one `logs` folder and give every run its own subfolder, such as `test2` in this case. This way, you can easily compare different runs within TensorBoard but also keep different runs separate.

2. By default, TensorBoard would just show you the loss and accuracy of your model. In this case, we are interested in histograms showing weights and distributions. We save the data for the histograms every epoch.

3. To generate data, TensorBoard runs batches through the model. We need to specify a batch size for this process.

4. We need to tell TensorBoard what to save. TensorBoard can visualize the model's computational graph, its gradients, and images showing weights. The more we save however, the slower the training.

5. TensorBoard can also visualize trained embeddings nicely. Our model does not have embeddings, so we are not interested in saving them.

Once we have the callback set up, we can pass it to the training process. We will train the MNIST model once again. We multiply the inputs by 255, making training much harder. To achieve all of this we need to run the following code:

```
hist = model.fit(x_train*255,y_train,
                 batch_size=128,
                 epochs=5,
                 callbacks=[tb],
                 validation_data=(x_test*255,y_test))
```

To start TensorBoard, open your console and type in the following:

```
tensorboard --logdir=/full_path_to_your_logs
```

Here `full_path_to_your_logs` is the path you saved your logs in, for example, `logs` in our case. TensorBoard runs on port `6006` by default, so in your browser, go to `http://localhost:6006` to see TensorBoard.

Once the page has loaded, navigate to the **HISTOGRAMS** section; this section should look something like this:

TensorBoard histograms

You can see the distribution of gradients and weights in the first layer. As you can see, the gradients are uniformly distributed and extremely close to zero. The weights hardly change at all over the different epochs. We are dealing with a **vanishing gradient problem**; we will cover this problem in depth later.

Armed with the real-time insight that this problem is happening, we can react faster. If you really want to dig into your model, TensorBoard also offers a visual debugger. In this debugger, you can step through the execution of your TensorFlow model and examine every single value inside it. This is especially useful if you are working on complex models, such as generative adversarial networks, and are trying to understand why something complex goes wrong.

Note: The TensorFlow debugger does not work well with models trained in Jupyter Notebooks. Save your model training code to a Python `.py` script and run that script.

To use the TensorFlow debugger, you have to set your model's runtime to a special debugger runtime. In specifying the debugger runtime, you also need to specify which port you want the debugger to run, in this case, port `2018`:

```
import tensorflow as tf
from tensorflow.python import debug as tf_debug
import keras

keras.backend.set_session(
    tf_debug.TensorBoardDebugWrapperSession(
    tf.Session(), "localhost:2018"))
```

Once Keras begins to work with the debugger runtime, you can debug your model. For the debugger to work, you need to name your Keras model to `model`. However, you do not need to train the model with a TensorBoard callback.

Now, start TensorBoard and activate the debugger by specifying the debugger port as follows:

```
tensorboard --logdir=/full_path_to_your_logs --debugger_port 2018
```

Now you can open TensorBoard as usual in your browser on port `6006`. TensorBoard now has a new section called **DEBUGGER**:

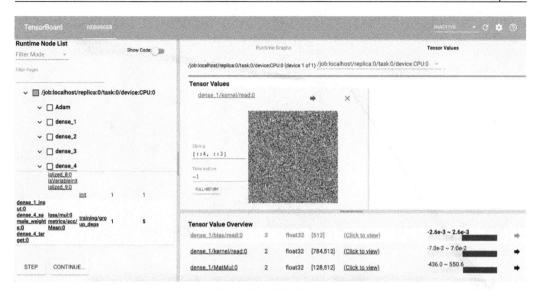

TensorBoard debugger

By clicking **STEP**, you execute the next step in the training process. With **CONTINUE...**, you can train your model for one or more epochs. By navigating the tree on the left side, you can view the components of your model. You can visualize individual elements of your model, to see how different actions affect them. Using the debugger effectively requires a bit of practice, but if you are working with complex models, it is a great tool.

Exploding and vanishing gradients

The vanishing gradient problem describes the issue that sometimes gradients in a deep neural network become very small and as a result, training occurs very slowly. Exploding gradients are the opposite problem; they are gradients that become so large that the network does not converge.

Of the two, the vanishing gradient problem is the more persistent issue. Vanishing gradients are caused by the fact that in deep networks, gradients of earlier layers depend on gradients of layers closer to the output. If the output gradients are small, then the gradients behind them are even smaller. Thus, the deeper the network, the more issues that occur with regard to vanishing gradients.

The key causes of small gradients include sigmoid and `tanh` activation functions. If you look at the following sigmoid function, you'll see that it is very flat toward large values:

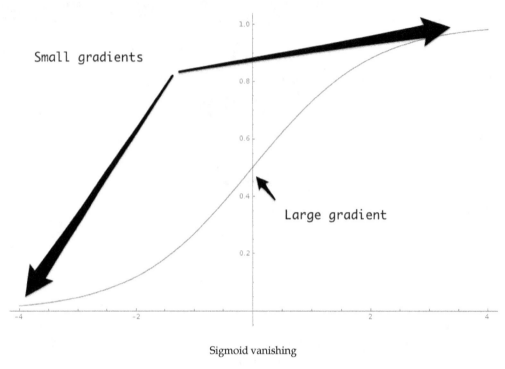

Small gradients

Large gradient

Sigmoid vanishing

The small gradients of the sigmoid function are the reason why the ReLU activation function has become popular for training deep neural networks. Its gradient is equal to one for all positive input values. However, it is zero for all negative input values.

Another cause of vanishing gradients is saddle points in the loss function. Although no minimum was reached, the loss function is very flat in some areas, producing small gradients.

To combat the vanishing gradient problem, you should use ReLU activation. If you see that your model is training slowly, consider increasing the learning rate to move out of a saddle point faster. Finally, you might just want to let the model train longer if it suffers from small gradients.

The exploding gradient problem is usually caused by large absolute weight values. As backpropagation multiplies the later layers' gradients with the layers' weights, large weights amplify gradients. To counteract the exploding gradient problem, you can use weight regularization, which incentivizes smaller weights. Using a method called **gradient clipping**, you can ensure that gradients do not become larger than a certain value. In Keras, you can clip both the norm and the absolute value of gradients:

```
from keras.optimizers import SGD

clip_val_sgd = SGD(lr=0.01, clipvalue=0.5)
clip_norm_sgd = SGD(lr=0.01, clipnorm=1.)
```

Convolutional layers and **long short-term memory (LSTM) networks** are less susceptible to both vanishing and exploding gradients. ReLU and batch normalization generally stabilize the network. Both of these problems might be caused by non-regularized inputs, so you should check your data too. Batch normalization also counteracts exploding gradients.

If exploding gradients are a problem, you can add a batch normalization layer to your model as follows:

```
from keras.layers import BatchNormalization
model.add(BatchNormalization())
```

Batch normalization also reduces the risk of vanishing gradients and has enabled the construction of much deeper networks recently.

You have now seen a wide range of tools that can be used to debug your models. As a final step, we are going to learn some methods to run models in production and speed up the machine learning process.

Deployment

Deployment into production is often seen as separate from the creation of models. At many companies, data scientists create models in isolated development environments on training, validation, and testing data that was collected to create models.

Once the model performs well on the test set, it then gets passed on to deployment engineers, who know little about how and why the model works the way it does. This is a mistake. After all, you are developing models to use them, not for the fun of developing them.

Models tend to perform worse over time for several reasons. The world changes, so the data you trained on might no longer represent the real world. Your model might rely on the outputs of some other systems that are subject to change. There might be unintended side effects and weaknesses of your model that only show with extended usage. Your model might influence the world that it tries to model. **Model decay** describes how models have a lifespan after which performance deteriorates.

Data scientists should have the full life cycle of their models in mind. They need to be aware of how their model works in production in the long run.

In fact, the production environment is the perfect environment to optimize your model. Your datasets are only an approximation for the real world. Live data gives a much fresher and more accurate view of the world. By using online learning or active learning methods, you can drastically reduce the need for training data.

This section describes some best practices for getting your models to work in the real world. The exact method of serving your model can vary depending on your application. See the upcoming section *Performance Tips* for more details on choosing a deployment method.

Launching fast

The process of developing models depends on real-world data as well as an insight into how the performance of the model influences business outcomes. The earlier you can gather data and observe how model behavior influences outcomes, the better. Do not hesitate to launch your product with a simple heuristic.

Take the case of fraud detection, for instance. Not only do you need to gather transaction data together with information about occurring frauds, you also want to know how quick fraudsters are at finding ways around your detection methods. You want to know how customers whose transactions have been falsely flagged as fraud react. All of this information influences your model design and your model evaluation metrics. If you can come up with a simple heuristic, deploy the heuristic and then work on the machine learning approach.

When developing a machine learning model, try simple models first. A surprising number of tasks can be modeled with simple, linear models. Not only do you obtain results faster, but you can also quickly identify the features that your model is likely to overfit to. Debugging your dataset before working on a complex model can save you many headaches.

A second advantage of getting a simple approach out of the door quickly is that you can prepare your infrastructure. Your infrastructure team is likely made up of different people from the modeling team. If the infrastructure team does not have to wait for the modeling team but can start optimizing the infrastructure immediately, then you gain a time advantage.

Understanding and monitoring metrics

To ensure that optimizing metrics such as the mean squared error or cross-entropy loss actually lead to a better outcome, you need to be mindful of how your model metrics relate to higher order metrics, which you can see visualized in the following diagram. Imagine you have some consumer-facing app in which you recommend different investment products to retail investors.

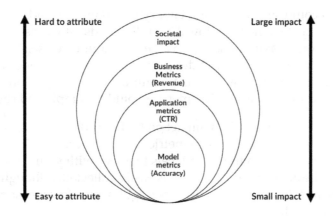

Higher order effects

You might predict whether the user is interested in a given product, measured by the user reading the product description. However, the metric you want to optimize in your application is not your model accuracy, but the click-through rate of users going to the description screen. On a higher order, your business is not designed to maximize the click-through rate, but revenue. If your users only click on low-revenue products, your click-through rate does not help you.

Finally, your business' revenue might be optimized to the detriment of society. In this case, regulators will step in. Higher order effects are influenced by your model. The higher the order of the effect, the harder it is to attribute to a single model. Higher order effects have large impacts, so effectively, higher order effects serve as meta-metrics to lower-order effects. To judge how well your application is doing, you align its metrics, for example, click-through rates, with the metrics relevant for the higher order effect, for example, revenue. Equally, your model metrics need to be aligned with your application metrics.

This alignment is often an emergent feature. Product managers eager to maximize their own metrics pick the model that maximizes their metrics, regardless of what metrics the modelers were optimizing. Product managers that bring home a lot of revenue get promoted. Businesses that are good for society receive subsidies and favorable policy. By making the alignment explicit, you can design a better monitoring process. For instance, if you have two models, you can A/B test them to see which one improves the application metrics.

Often, you will find that to align with a higher order metric, you'll need to combine several metrics, such as accuracy and speed of predictions. In this case, you should craft a formula that combines the metrics into one single number. A single number will allow you to doubtlessly choose between two models and help your engineers to create better models.

For instance, you could set a maximum latency of 200 milliseconds and your metric would be, "Accuracy if latency is below 200 milliseconds, otherwise zero." If you do not wish to set one maximum latency value, you could choose, "Accuracy divided by latency in milliseconds." The exact design of this formula depends on your application. As you observe how your model influences its higher order metric, you can adapt your model metric. The metric should be simple and easy to quantify.

Next, to regularly test your model's impact on higher order metrics, you should regularly test your models own metrics, such as accuracy. To this end, you need a constant stream of ground truth labels together with your data. In some cases, such as detecting fraud, ground truth data is easily collected, although it might come in with some latency. In this case, customers might need a few weeks to find out they have been overcharged.

In other cases, you might not have ground truth labels. Often, you can hand-label data for which you have no ground truth labels coming in. Through good UI design, the process of checking model predictions can be fast. Testers only have to decide whether your model's prediction was correct or not, something they can do through button presses in a web or mobile app. If you have a good review system in place, data scientists who work on the model should regularly check the model's outputs. This way, patterns in failures (our model does poorly on dark images) can be detected quickly, and the model can be improved.

Understanding where your data comes from

More often than not, your data gets collected by some other system that you as the model developer have no control over. Your data might be collected by a data vendor or by a different department in your firm. It might even be collected for different purposes than your model. The collectors of the data might not even know you are using the data for your model.

If, say, the collection method of the data changes, the distribution of your data might change too. This could break your model. Equally, the real world might just change, and with it the data distribution. To avoid changes in the data breaking your model, you first need to be aware of what data you are using and assign an owner to each feature. The job of the feature owner is to investigate where the data is coming from and alert the team if changes in the data are coming. The feature owner should also write down the assumptions underlying the data. In the best case, you test these assumptions for all new data streaming in. If the data does not pass the tests, investigate and eventually modify your model.

Equally, your model outputs might get used as inputs of other models. Help consumers of your data reach you by clearly identifying yourself as the owner of the model.

Alert users of your model of changes to your model. Before deploying a model, compare the new model's predictions to the old model's predictions. Treat models as software and try to identify "breaking changes," that would significantly alter your model's behavior. Often, you might not know who is accessing your model's predictions. Try to avoid this by clear communication and setting access controls if necessary.

Just as software has dependencies, libraries that need to be installed for the software to work, machine learning models have data dependencies. Data dependencies are not as well understood as software dependencies. By investigating your model's dependencies, you can reduce the risk of your model breaking when data changes.

Performance tips

In many financial applications, speed is of the essence. Machine learning, especially deep learning, has a reputation for being slow. However, recently, there have been many advances in hardware and software that enable faster machine learning applications.

Using the right hardware for your problem

A lot of progress in deep learning has been driven by the use of **graphics processing units (GPUs)**. GPUs enable highly parallel computing at the expense of operating frequency. Recently, multiple manufacturers have started working on specialized deep learning hardware. Most of the time, GPUs are a good choice for deep learning models or other parallelizable algorithms such as XGboost gradient-boosted trees. However, not all applications benefit equally.

In **natural language processing (NLP)**, for instance, batch sizes often need to be small, so the parallelization of operations does not work as well since not that many samples are processed at the same time. Additionally, some words appear much more often than others, giving large benefits to caching frequent words. Thus, many NLP tasks run faster on CPUs than GPUs. If you can work with large batches, however, a GPU or even specialized hardware is preferable.

Making use of distributed training with TF estimators

Keras is not only a standalone library that can use TensorFlow, but it is also an integrated part of TensorFlow. TensorFlow features multiple high-level APIs that can be used to create and train models.

From version 1.8 onward, the estimator API's features distribute training on multiple machines, while the Keras API does not feature them yet. Estimators also have a number of other speed-up tricks, so they are usually faster than Keras models.

 You can find information on how to set up your cluster for distributed TensorFlow here: `https://www.tensorflow.org/deploy/distributed`.

By changing the `import` statements, you can easily use Keras as part of TensorFlow and don't have to change your main code:

```
import tensorflow as tf
from tensorflow.python import keras

from tensorflow.python.keras.models import Sequential from tensorflow.
python.keras.layers import Dense,Activation
```

In this section, we will create a model to learn the MNIST problem before training it using the estimator API. First, we load and prepare the dataset as usual. For more efficient dataset loading, see the next section:

```
(x_train, y_train), (x_test, y_test) =
keras.datasets.mnist.load_data()
x_train.shape = (60000, 28 * 28)
x_train = x_train / 255
y_train = keras.utils.to_categorical(y_train)
```

We can create a Keras model as usual:

```
model = Sequential()
model.add(Dense(786, input_dim = 28*28))
model.add(Activation('relu'))
model.add(Dense(256))
model.add(Activation('relu'))
model.add(Dense(160))
model.add(Activation('relu'))
model.add(Dense(10))
model.add(Activation('softmax'))

model.compile(optimizer=keras.optimizers.SGD(lr=0.0001,
              momentum=0.9),
              loss='categorical_crossentropy',
              metric='accuracy')
```

The TensorFlow version of Keras offers a one-line conversion to a TF estimator:

```
estimator = keras.estimator.model_to_estimator(keras_model=model)
```

To set up training, we need to know the name assigned to the model input. We can quickly check this with the following code:

```
model.input_names
['dense_1_input']
```

Estimators get trained with an input function. The input function allows us to specify a whole pipeline, which will be executed efficiently. In this case, we only want an input function that yields our training set:

```
train_input_fn = tf.estimator.inputs.numpy_input_fn(
    x={'dense_1_input': x_train},
    y=y_train,
    num_epochs=1,
    shuffle=False)
```

Finally, we train the estimator on the input. And that is it; you can now utilize distributed TensorFlow with estimators:

```
estimator.train(input_fn=train_input_fn, steps=2000)
```

Using optimized layers such as CuDNNLSTM

You will often find that someone created a special layer optimized to perform certain tasks on certain hardware. Keras' CuDNNLSTM layer, for example, only runs on GPUs supporting CUDA, a programming language specifically for GPUs.

When you lock in your model to specialized hardware, you can often make significant gains in your performance. If you have the resources, it might even make sense to write your own specialized layer in CUDA. If you want to change hardware later, you can usually export weights and import them to a different layer.

Optimizing your pipeline

With the right hardware and optimized software in place, your model often ceases to be the bottleneck. You should check your GPU utilization by entering the following command in your Terminal:

```
nvidia-smi -l 2
```

If your GPU utilization is not at around 80% to 100%, you can gain significantly by optimizing your pipeline. There are several steps you can take to optimize your pipeline:

- **Create a pipeline running parallel to the model**: Otherwise, your GPU will be idle while the data is loading. Keras does this by default. If you have a generator and want to have a larger queue of data to be held ready for preprocessing, change the `max_queue_size` parameter of the `fit_generator` method. If you set the `workers` argument of the `fit_generator` method to zero, the generator will run on the main thread, which slows things down.

- **Preprocess data in parallel**: Even if you have a generator working independently of the model training, it might not keep up with the model. So, it is better to run multiple generators in parallel. In Keras, you can do this by setting `use_multiprocessing` to `true` and setting the number of workers to anything larger than one, preferably to the number of CPUs available. Let's look at an example:

```
model.fit_generator(generator,
                    steps_per_epoch = 40,
                    workers=4,
                    use_multiprocessing=False)
```

You need to make sure your generator is thread safe. You can make any generator thread safe with the following code snippet:

```
import threading

class thread_safe_iter:                          #1
    def __init__(self, it):
        self.it = it
        self.lock = threading.Lock()

    def __iter__(self):
        return self

    def next(self):                              #2
        with self.lock:
            return self.it.next()

def thread_safe_generator(f):                    #3
    def g(*a, **kw):
        return thread_safe_iter(f(*a, **kw))
    return g

@thread_safe_generator
def gen():
```

Let's look at the three key components of the preceding code:

1. The `thread_safe_iter` class makes any iterator thread safe by locking threads when the iterator has to produce the next yield.

2. When `next()` is called on the iterator, the iterators thread is locked. Locking means that no other function, say, another variable, can access variables from the thread while it is locked. Once the thread is locked, it yields the next element.

3. `thread_safe_generator` is a Python decorator that turns any iterator it decorates into a thread-safe iterator. It takes the function, passes it to the thread-safe iterator, and then returns the thread-safe version of the function.

You can also use the `tf.data` API together with an estimator, which does most of the work for you.

- **Combine files into large files**: Reading a file takes time. If you have to read thousands of small files, this can significantly slow you down. TensorFlow offers its own data format called TFRecord. You can also just fuse an entire batch into a single NumPy array and save that array instead of every example.

- **Train with the** `tf.data.Dataset` **API**: If you are using the TensorFlow version of Keras, you can use the `Dataset` API, which optimizes data loading and processing for you. The `Dataset` API is the recommended way to load data into TensorFlow. It offers a wide range of ways to load data, for instance, from a CSV file with `tf.data.TextLineDataset`, or from TFRecord files with `tf.data.TFRecordDataset`.

 Note: For a more comprehensive guide to the `Dataset` API, see `https://www.tensorflow.org/get_started/datasets_quickstart`.

In this example, we will use the dataset API with NumPy arrays that we have already loaded into RAM, such as the MNIST database.

First, we create two plain datasets for data and targets:

```
dxtrain = tf.data.Dataset.from_tensor_slices(x_test)
dytrain = tf.data.Dataset.from_tensor_slices(y_train)
```

The `map` function allows us to perform operations on data before passing it to the model. In this case, we apply one-hot encoding to our targets. However, this could be any function. By setting the `num_parallel_calls` argument, we can specify how many processes we want to run in parallel:

```
def apply_one_hot(z):
    return tf.one_hot(z,10)

dytrain = dytrain.map(apply_one_hot,num_parallel_calls=4)
```

We zip the data and targets into one dataset. We instruct TensorFlow to shuffle the data when loading, keeping 200 instances in memory from which to draw samples. Finally, we make the dataset yield batches of batch size `32`:

```
train_data =
tf.data.Dataset.zip((dxtrain,dytrain)).shuffle(200).batch(32)
```

We can now fit a Keras model on this dataset just as we would fit it to a generator:

```
model.fit(dataset, epochs=10, steps_per_epoch=60000 // 32)
```

If you have truly large datasets, the more you can parallelize, the better. Parallelization does come with overhead costs, however, and not every problem actually features huge datasets. In these cases, refrain from trying to do too much in parallel and focus on slimming down your network, using CPUs and keeping all your data in RAM if possible.

Speeding up your code with Cython

Python is a popular language because developing code in Python is easy and fast. However, Python can be slow, which is why many production applications are written in either C or C++. Cython is Python with C data types, which significantly speeds up execution. Using this language, you can write pretty much normal Python code, and Cython converts it to fast-running C code.

 Note: You can read the full Cython documentation here: `http://cython.readthedocs.io`. This section is a short introduction to Cython. If performance is important to your application, you should consider diving deeper.

Say you have a Python function that prints out the Fibonacci series up to a specified point. This code snippet is taken straight from the Python documentation:

```
from __future__ import print_function
def fib(n):
    a, b = 0, 1
    while b < n:
        print(b, end=' ')
        a, b = b, a + b
    print()
```

Note that we have to import the `print_function` to make sure that `print()` works in the Python 3 style. To use this snippet with Cython, save it as `cython_fib_8_7.pyx`.

Now create a new file called `8_7_cython_setup.py`:

```
from distutils.core import setup          #1
from Cython.Build import cythonize         #2

setup(                                     #3
    ext_modules=cythonize("cython_fib_8_7.pyx"),
)
```

The three main features of the code are these:

1. The `setup` function is a Python function to create modules, such as the ones you install with `pip`.
2. `cythonize` is a function to turn a `pyx` Python file into Cython C code.
3. We create a new model by calling `setup` and passing on our Cythonized code.

To run this, we now run the following command in a Terminal:

```
python 8_7_cython_setup.py build_ext --inplace
```

This will create a C file, a build file, and a compiled module. We can import this module now by running:

```
import cython_fib_8_7
cython_fib_8_7.fib(1000)
```

This will print out the Fibonacci numbers up to 1,000. Cython also comes with a handy debugger that shows where Cython has to fall back onto Python code, which will slow things down. Type the following command into your Terminal:

```
cython -a cython_fib_8_7.pyx
```

This will create an HTML file that looks similar to this when opened in a browser:

```
Generated by Cython 0.27.2

Yellow lines hint at Python interaction.
Click on a line that starts with a "+" to see the C code that Cython generated for it.

Raw output: cython_fib_8_5.c
 1: from __future__ import print_function
 2:
+3: def fib(n):
 4:     """Print the Fibonacci series up to n."""
+5:     a, b = 0, 1
+6:     while b < n:
+7:         print(b, end=' ')
+8:         a, b = b, a + b
+9:     print()
```

Cython profile

As you can see, Cython has to fall back on Python all the time in our script because we did not specify the types of variables. By letting Cython know what data type a variable has, we can speed up the code significantly. To define a variable with a type, we use `cdef`:

```
from __future__ import print_function
def fib(int n):
    cdef int a = 0
    cdef int b = 1
    while b < n:
        print(b, end=' ')
        a, b = b, a + b
    print()
```

This snippet is already better. Further optimization is certainly possible, by first calculating the numbers before printing them, we can reduce the reliance on Python `print` statements. Overall, Cython is a great way to keep the development speed and ease of Python and gain execution speed.

Caching frequent requests

An under-appreciated way to make models run faster is to cache frequent requests in a database. You can go so far as to cache millions of predictions in a database and then look them up. This has the advantage that you can make your model as large as you like and expend a lot of computing power to make predictions.

By using a MapReduce database, looking up requests in a very large pool of possible requests and predictions is entirely possible. Of course, this requires requests to be somewhat discrete. If you have continuous features, you can round them if precision is not as important.

Exercises

Now that we're at the end of this chapter, it's time to put what we've learned into use. Using the knowledge that you've gained in this chapter, why not try the following exercises?

- Try to build any model that features exploding gradients in training. Hint: Do not normalize inputs and play with the initialization of layers.

- Go to any example in this book and try to optimize performance by improving the data pipeline.

Summary

In this chapter, you have learned a number of practical tips for debugging and improving your model. Let's recap all of the things that we have looked at:

- Finding flaws in your data that lead to flaws in your learned model

- Using creative tricks to make your model learn more from less data

- Unit testing data in production or training to make sure standards are met

- Being mindful of privacy

- Preparing data for training and avoiding common pitfalls

- Inspecting the model and peering into the "black box"

- Finding optimal hyperparameters

- Scheduling learning rates in order to reduce overfitting

- Monitoring training progress with TensorBoard

- Deploying machine learning products and iterating on them

- Speeding up training and inference

You now have a substantial number of tools in your toolbox that will help you run actual, practical machine learning projects and deploy them in real-life (for example, trading) applications.

Making sure your model works before deploying it is crucial and failure to properly scrutinize your model can cost you, your employer, or your clients millions of dollars. For these reasons, some firms are reluctant to deploy machine learning models into trading at all. They fear that they will never understand the models and thus won't be able to manage them in a production environment. Hopefully, this chapter alleviates that fear by showcasing some practical tools that can make models understandable, generalizable, and safe to deploy.

In the next chapter, we will look at a special, persistent, and dangerous problem associated with machine learning models: bias. Statistical models tend to fit to and amplify human biases. Financial institutions have to follow strict regulations to prevent them from being racially or gender biased. Our focus will be to see how we can detect and remove biases from our models in order to make them both fair and compliant.

9
Fighting Bias

We like to think that machines are more rational than us: heartless silicon applying cold logic. Thus, when computer science introduced automated decision making into the economy, many hoped that computers would reduce prejudice and discrimination. Yet, as we mentioned earlier when looking at mortgage applications and ethnicity, computers are made and trained by humans, and the data that those machines use stems from an unjust world. Simply put, if we are not careful, our programs will amplify human biases.

In the financial industry, anti-discrimination is not only a matter of morality. Take, for instance, the **Equal Credit Opportunity Act (ECOA)**, which came into force in 1974 in the United States. This law explicitly forbids creditors from discriminating applicants based on race, sex, marital status, and several other attributes. It also requires creditors to inform applicants about the reasons for denial.

The algorithms discussed in this book are discrimination machines. Given an objective, these machines will find the features that it's best to discriminate on. Yet, as we've discussed discrimination is not always okay.

While it's okay to target ads for books from a certain country to people who are also from that country, it's usually not okay, and thanks to the ECOA, often illegal, to deny a loan to people from a certain country. Within the financial domain, there are much stricter rules for discrimination than those seen in book sales. This is because decisions in the financial domain have a much more severe impact on people's lives than those of book sales.

Equally, discrimination in this context is **feature specific**. For example, while it's okay to discriminate against loan applicants based on their history of repaying loans, it's not okay to do so based on their country of origin, unless there are sanctions against that country or similar overarching laws in place.

Throughout this chapter, we'll discuss the following:

- Where bias in machines comes from
- The legal implications of biased **machine learning** (**ML**) models
- How observed unfairness can be reduced
- How models can be inspected for bias and unfairness
- How causal modeling can reduce bias
- How unfairness is a complex systems failure that needs to be addressed in non-technical ways

The algorithms discussed in this book are feature extraction algorithms. Even if regulated features are omitted, an algorithm might infer them from proxy features and then discriminate based on them anyway. As an example of this, ZIP codes can be used to predict race reasonably well in many cities in the United States. Therefore, omitting regulated features is not enough when it comes to combating bias.

Sources of unfairness in machine learning

As we have discussed many times throughout this book, models are a function of the data that they are trained on. Generally speaking, more data will lead to smaller errors. So, by definition, there is less data on minority groups, simply because there are fewer people in those groups.

This **disparate sample size** can lead to worse model performance for the minority group. As a result, this increased error is often known as a **systematic error**. The model might have to overfit the majority group data so that the relationships it found do not apply to the minority group data. Since there is little minority group data, this is not punished as much.

Imagine you are training a credit scoring model, and the clear majority of your data comes from people living in lower Manhattan, and a small minority of it comes from people living in rural areas. Manhattan housing is much more expensive, so the model might learn that you need a very high income to buy an apartment. However, rural housing is much cheaper in comparison. Even so, because the model is largely trained on data from Manhattan, it might deny loan applications to rural applicants because they tend to have lower incomes than their Manhattan peers.

Aside from sample size issues, our data can be biased by itself. For example, "raw data" does not exist. Data does not appear naturally, instead it's measured by humans using human-made measurement protocols, which in themselves can be biased in many different ways.

Biases could include having **sampling biases**, such as in the Manhattan housing example, or having **measurement biases**, which is when your sample might not measure what it is intended to measure, or may even discriminate against one group.

Another bias that's possible is **pre-existing social biases**. These are visible in word vectors, for instance, in Word2Vec, where the mapping from father to doctor in latent space maps from mother to nurse. Likewise, the vector from man to computer programmer maps from woman to homemaker. This is because sexism is encoded within the written language of our sexist society. Until today, typically speaking doctors have usually been men and nurses have usually been women. Likewise, tech companies' diversity statistics reveal that far more men are computer programmers than women, and these biases get encoded into models.

Legal perspectives

There are two doctrines in anti-discrimination law: *disparate treatment*, and *disparate impact*. Let's take a minute to look at each of these:

- **Disparate treatment**: This is one kind of unlawful discrimination. Intentionally discriminating against ZIP codes with the hope of discriminating against race is not legal. Disparate treatment problems have less to do with the algorithm and more to do with the organization running it.

- **Disparate impact**: This can be a problem if an algorithm is deployed that has a different impact on different groups, even without the organization knowing about it. Let's walk through a lending scenario in which disparate impact could be a problem. Firstly, the plaintiff must establish that there is a disparate impact. Assessing if there's a disparate impact is usually done with the **four-fifths rule**, which says that if the selection rate of a group is less than 80% of the group, then it is regarded as evidence of adverse impact. If a lender has 150 loan applicants from group A, of which 100, or 67%, are accepted, and 50 applicants from group B, of which 25 are accepted, the difference in selection is 0.5/0.67 = 0.746, which qualifies as evidence for discrimination against group B. The defendant can counter this by showing that the decision procedure is justified as necessary.

  After this is done, the plaintiff has the opportunity to show that the goal of the procedure could also be achieved with a different procedure that shows a smaller disparity.

Note: For a more in-depth overview of these topics, see Moritz Hardt's 2017 NeurIPS presentation on the topic at `http://mrtz.org/nips17/#/11`.

The disparate treatment doctrine tries to achieve procedural fairness and equal opportunity. The disparate impact doctrine aims for distributive justice and minimized inequality in outcomes.

There is an intrinsic tension between the two doctrines, as illustrated by the Ricci V. DeStefano case from 2009. In this case, 19 white firefighters and 1 Hispanic firefighter sued their employer, the New Haven Fire Department. The firefighters had all passed their test for promotion, yet their black colleagues did not score the mark required for the promotion. Fearing a disparate impact lawsuit, the city invalidated the test results and did not promote the firefighters. Because the evidence for disparate impact was not strong enough, the Supreme Court of the United States eventually ruled that the firefighters should have been promoted.

Given the complex legal and technical situation around fairness in machine learning, we're going to dive into how we can define and quantify fairness, before using this insight to create fairer models.

Observational fairness

Equality is often seen as a purely qualitative issue, and as such, it's often dismissed by quantitative-minded modelers. As this section will show, equality can be seen from a quantitative perspective, too. Consider a classifier, c, with input X, some sensitive input, A, a target, Y and output C. Usually, we would denote the classifier output as $\hat{Y}$, but for readability, we follow CS 294 and name it C.

Let's say that our classifier is being used to decide who gets a loan. When would we consider this classifier to be fair and free of bias? To answer this question, picture two demographics, group A and B, both loan applicants. Given a credit score, our classifier must find a cutoff point. Let's look at the distribution of applicants in this graph:

Note: The data for this example is synthetic; you can find the Excel file used for these calculations in the GitHub repository of this book, `https://github.com/PacktPublishing/Machine-Learning-for-Finance/blob/master/9.1_parity.xlsx`.

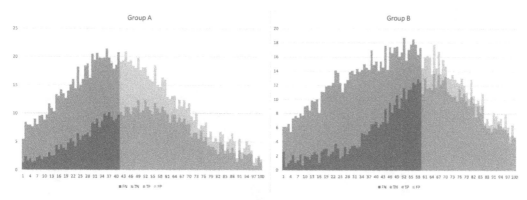

Max profits

For this exercise, we assume that a successful applicant yields a profit of $300, while a defaulting successful applicant costs $700. The cutoff point here has been chosen to maximize profits:

So, what can we see? We can see the following:

- In orange are applicants who would not have repaid the loan and did not get accepted: **true negatives (TNs)**.
- In blue are applicants who would have repaid the loan but did not get accepted: **false negatives (FNs)**.
- In yellow are applicants who did get the loan but did not pay it back: **false positives (FPs)**.
- In gray are applicants who did receive the loan and paid it back: **true positives (TPs)**.

As you can see, there are several issues with this choice of cutoff point. **Group B** applicants need to have a better score to get a loan than **Group A** applicants, indicating disparate treatment. At the same time, only around 51% of **Group A** applicants get a loan but only 37% of **Group B** applicants do, indicating disparate impact.

A *group unaware threshold*, which we can see below, would give both groups the same minimum score:

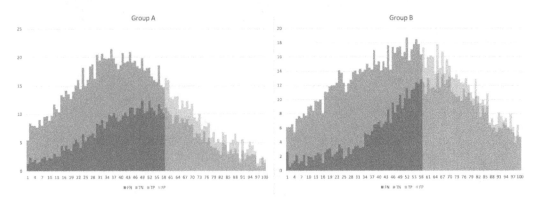

Equal cutoff

In the preceding graph, while both groups have the same cutoff rate, **Group A** has been given fewer loans. At the same time, predictions for **Group A** have a lower accuracy than the predictions given for **Group B**. It seems that although both groups face the same score threshold, **Group A** is at a disadvantage.

Demographic parity aims to achieve fairness by ensuring that both groups have the same chance of receiving the loan. This method aims to achieve the same selection rate for both groups, which is what impact disparity is measured by. Mathematically, this process can be expressed as follows:

$$P(C=1|A=1) = P(C=1|A=0)$$

If we apply this rule to the same context as we used previously, we'll arrive at the following cutoff points:

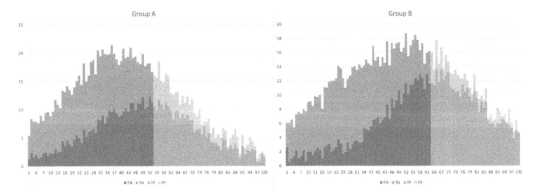

Equal pick rate

While this method cannot be blamed for statistical discrimination and disparate impact, it can be blamed for disparate treatment. In the equal pick rate graphic we can see how **Group A** is given a lower threshold score; meanwhile, there are more successful **Group A** applicants who default on their loans. In fact, **Group A** is not profitable and gets subsidized by **Group B**. Accepting a worse economic outcome to favor a certain group is also known as taste-based discrimination. It could be said that the higher thresholds for **Group B** are unfair, as they have a lower FP rate.

TP parity, which is also called equal opportunity, means that both demographics have the same TP rate. For people who can pay back the loan, the same chance of getting a loan should exist. Mathematically, this can be expressed as follows:

$$P(C=1 \mid Y=1, A=1) = P(C=1 \mid Y=1, A=0)$$

Applied to our data, this policy looks similar to demographic parity, except that the group cutoff point is even lower:

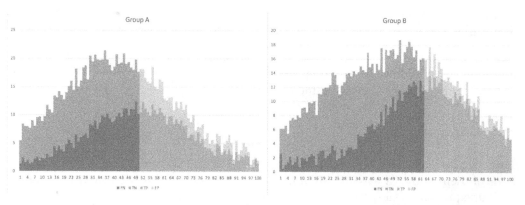

Equal opportunity

Equal opportunity can address many of the problems of demographic parity, as most people believe that everyone should be given the same opportunities. Still, our classifier is less accurate for **Group A**, and there is a form of disparate treatment in place.

Accuracy parity tells us that the accuracy of predictions should be the same for both groups. Mathematically, this can be expressed as follows:

$$P(C=Y \mid A=1) = P(C=Y \mid A=0)$$

The probability that the classifier is correct should be the same for the two possible values of the sensitive variable A. When we apply this criteria to our data, we arrive at the following output:

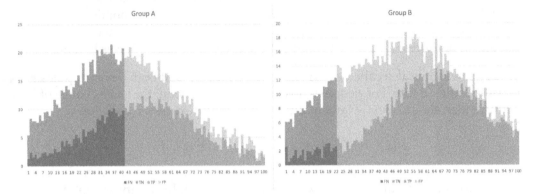

Equal accuracy

From the preceding diagram, the downside becomes apparent. In order to satisfy the accuracy constraint, members of **Group B** are given much easier access to loans.

Therefore to solve this, trade-offs are necessary because no classifier can have precision parity, TP parity, and FP parity unless the classifier is perfect. C = Y, or both demographics have the same base rates:

$$P(Y=1\,|\,A=1) = P(Y=1\,|\,A=0)$$

There are many more ways to express fairness. The key takeaway, however, is that none of them perfectly satisfies all of the fairness criteria. For any two populations with unequal base rates, and unequal chances of repaying their loan, establishing statistical parity requires the introduction of a treatment disparity.

This fact has led to a number of debates, with the best practice to express and eliminate discrimination having not been agreed on yet. With that being said, even if the perfect mathematical expression of fairness was found, it would not immediately lead to perfectly fair systems.

Any machine learning algorithm is part of a bigger system. Inputs X are often not as clearly defined as a different algorithm in the same system that might use different inputs. Demographic groups A are often not clearly defined or inferred. Even the output, C, of the classifier can often not be clearly distinguished, as many algorithms together might perform the classification task while each algorithm is predicting a different output, such as a credit score or a profitability estimate.

Good technology is not a substitute for good policy. Blindly following an algorithm without the opportunity for individual consideration or appeal will always lead to unfairness. With that being said, while mathematical fairness criteria cannot solve all the fairness issues that we face, it is surely worth trying to make machine learning algorithms fairer, which is what the next section is about.

Training to be fair

There are multiple ways to train models to be fairer. A simple approach could be using the different fairness measures that we have listed in the previous section as an additional loss. However, in practice, this approach has turned out to have several issues, such as having poor performance on the actual classification task.

An alternative approach is to use an adversarial network. Back in 2016, Louppe, Kagan, and Cranmer published the paper *Learning to Pivot with Adversarial Networks*, available at `https://arxiv.org/abs/1611.01046`. This paper showed how to use an adversarial network to train a classifier to ignore a nuisance parameter, such as a sensitive feature.

In this example, we will train a classifier to predict whether an adult makes over $50,000 in annual income. The challenge here is to make our classifier unbiased from the influences of race and gender, with it only focusing on features that we can discriminate on, including their occupation and the gains they make from their capital.

To this end, we must train a classifier and an adversarial network. The adversarial network aims to classify the sensitive attributes, a, gender and race, from the predictions of the classifier:

Making an unbiased classifier to detect the income of an adult

The classifier aims to classify by income but also aims to fool the adversarial network. The classifier's minimization objective formula is as follows:

$$\min\left[L_y - \lambda L_A\right]$$

Within that formula, L_y is a binary cross-entropy loss of the classification, while L_A is the adversarial loss. λ represents a hyperparameter that we can use to amplify or reduce the impact of the adversarial loss.

Note: This implementation of the adversarial fairness method follows an implementation by Stijn Tonk and Henk Griffioen. You can find the code to this chapter on Kaggle at `https://www.kaggle.com/jannesklaas/learning-how-to-be-fair`.

Stijn's and Henk's original blogpost can be found here: `https://blog.godatadriven.com/fairness-in-ml`.

To train this model fairly, we not only need data X and targets y, but also data about the sensitive attributes, A. In the example we're going to work on, we'll be taking data from the 1994 US census provided by the UCI repository: `https://archive.ics.uci.edu/ml/datasets/Adult`.

To make loading the data easier, it has been transformed into a CSV file with column headers. As a side note, please refer to the online version to see the data as viewing the data would be difficult in the format of the book.

First, we load the data. The dataset contains data about people from a number of different races, but for the simplicity of this task, we will only be focusing on white and black people for the `race` attribute. To do this, we need to run the following code:

```
path = '../input/adult.csv'
input_data = pd.read_csv(path, na_values="?")
input_data = input_data[input_data['race'].isin(['White',
'Black'])]
```

Next, we select the sensitive attributes, in this case we're focusing on race and gender, into our sensitive dataset, A. We one-hot encode the data so that "Male" equals one for the `gender` attribute and `White` equals one for the `race` attribute. We can achieve this by running the following code:

```
sensitive_attribs = ['race', 'gender']
A = input_data[sensitive_attribs]
A = pd.get_dummies(A, drop_first=True)
A.columns = sensitive_attribs
```

Our target is the `income` attribute. Therefore, we need to encode `>50K` as 1 and everything else as zero, which is achieved by writing this code:

```
y = (input_data['income'] == '>50K').astype(int)
```

To get our training data, we firstly remove the sensitive and target attributes. Then we fill all of the missing values and one-hot encode all of the data, as you can see in the following code:

```
X = input_data.drop(labels=['income', 'race', 'gender'],axis=1)

X = X.fillna('Unknown')

X = pd.get_dummies(X, drop_first=True)
```

Finally, we split the data into train and test sets. As seen in the following code, we then stratify the data to ensure that the same number of high earners are in both the test and training data:

```
X_train, X_test, y_train, y_test, A_train, A_test = \
train_test_split(X, y, A, test_size=0.5,
                 stratify=y, random_state=7)
```

To ensure the data works nicely with the neural network, we're now going to scale the data using scikit-learn's `StandardScaler`:

```
scaler = StandardScaler().fit(X_train)

X_train = pd.DataFrame(scaler.transform(X_train),
                  columns=X_train.columns,
                  index=X_train.index)

X_test = pd.DataFrame(scaler.transform(X_test),
                  columns=X_test.columns,
                  index=X_test.index)
```

We need a metric of how fair our model is. We are using the disparate impact selection rule. The `p_rule` method calculates the share of people classified to have over $50,000 income from both groups and then returns the ratio of selections in the disadvantaged demographic over the ratio of selections in the advantaged group.

The goal is for the `p_rule` method to return at least 80% in order to meet the four-fifths rule for both race and gender. The following code shows how this function is only used for monitoring, and not as a loss function:

```
def p_rule(y_pred, a_values, threshold=0.5):
    y_a_1 = y_pred[a_values == 1] > threshold if threshold else
y_pred[a_values == 1]                                              #1
    y_a_0 = y_pred[a_values == 0] > threshold if threshold else
y_pred[a_values == 0]
    odds = y_a_1.mean() / y_a_0.mean()                             #2
    return np.min([odds, 1/odds]) * 100
```

Let's explore this code in some more detail. As you can see from the preceding code block, it's created with two key features, which are as follows:

1. Firstly, we select who is given a selected threshold. Here, we classify everyone whom the model assigns a chance of over 50% of making $50,000 or more as a high earner.

2. Secondly, we calculate the selection ratio of both demographics. We divide the ratio of the one group by the ratio of the other group. By returning the minimum of either the odds or one divided by the odds, we ensure the return of a value below one.

To make the model setup a bit easier, we need to define the number of input features and the number of sensitive features. This is something that is simply done by running these two lines:

```
n_features=X_train.shape[1]
n_sensitive=A_train.shape[1]
```

Now we set up our classifier. Note how this classifier is a standard classification neural network. It features three hidden layers, some dropout, and a final output layer with a sigmoid activation, which occurs since this is a binary classification task. This classifier is written in the Keras functional API.

To make sure you understand how the API works, go through the following code example and ensure you understand why the steps are taken:

```
clf_inputs = Input(shape=(n_features,))
x = Dense(32, activation='relu')(clf_inputs)
x = Dropout(0.2)(x)
x = Dense(32, activation='relu')(x)
x = Dropout(0.2)(x)
x = Dense(32, activation='relu')(x)
x = Dropout(0.2)(x)
outputs = Dense(1, activation='sigmoid', name='y')(x)
clf_net = Model(inputs=[clf_inputs], outputs=[outputs])
```

The adversarial network is a classifier with two heads: one to predict the applicant's race from the model output, and one to predict the applicant's gender:

```
adv_inputs = Input(shape=(1,))
x = Dense(32, activation='relu')(adv_inputs)
x = Dense(32, activation='relu')(x)
x = Dense(32, activation='relu')(x)
out_race = Dense(1, activation='sigmoid')(x)
out_gender = Dense(1, activation='sigmoid')(x)
```

```
adv_net = Model(inputs=[adv_inputs],
outputs=[out_race,out_gender])
```

As with generative adversarial networks, we have to make the networks trainable and untrainable multiple times. To make this easier, the following function will create a function that makes a network and all its layers either trainable or untrainable:

```
def make_trainable_fn(net):              #1
    def make_trainable(flag):            #2
        net.trainable = flag             #3
        for layer in net.layers:
            layer.trainable = flag
    return make_trainable                #4
```

From the preceding code, there are four key features that we should take a moment to explore:

1. The function accepts a Keras neural network, for which the train switch function will be created.

2. Inside the function, a second function is created. This second function accepts a Boolean flag (True/False).

3. When called, the second function sets the network's trainability to the flag. If False is passed, the network is not trainable. Since the layers of the network can also be used in other networks, we ensure that each individual layer is not trainable, too.

4. Finally, we return the function.

Using a function to create another function might seem convoluted at first, but this allows us to create "switches" for the neural network easily. The following code snippet shows us how to create switch functions for the classifier and the adversarial network:

```
trainable_clf_net = make_trainable_fn(clf_net)
trainable_adv_net = make_trainable_fn(adv_net)
```

To make the classifier trainable, we can use the function with the True flag:

```
trainable_clf_net(True)
```

Now we can compile our classifier. As you will see later on in this chapter, it is useful to keep the classifier network as a separate variable from the compiled classifier with which we make predictions:

```
clf = clf_net
clf.compile(loss='binary_crossentropy', optimizer='adam')
```

Remember that to train our classifier, we need to run its predictions through the adversary as well as obtaining the adversary loss and applying the negative adversary loss to the classifier. This is best done by packing the classifier and adversary into one network.

To do this, we must first create a new model that maps from the classifier inputs to the classifier and adversary outputs. We define the adversary output to be a nested function of the adversarial network and the classifier network. This way, the predictions of the classifier get immediately passed on to the adversary:

```
adv_out = adv_net(clf_net(clf_inputs))
```

We then define the classifier output to be the output of the classifier network, just as we would for classification:

```
clf_out = clf_net(clf_inputs)
```

Then, we define the combined model to map from the classifier input, that is, the data about an applicant, to the classifier output and adversary output:

```
clf_w_adv = Model(inputs=[clf_inputs],
                  outputs=[clf_out]+adv_out)
```

When training the combined model, we only want to update the weights of the classifier, as we will train the adversary separately. We can use our switch functions to make the classifier network trainable and the adversarial network untrainable:

```
trainable_clf_net(True)
trainable_adv_net(False)
```

Remember the hyperparameter, λ, from the preceding minimization objective. We need to set this parameter manually for both sensitive attributes. As it turns out, the networks train best if lambda for race is set much higher than lambda for gender.

With the lambda values in hand, we can create the weighted loss:

```
loss_weights = [1.]+[-lambda_param for lambda_param in lambdas]
```

The preceding expression leads to loss weights of [1.,-130,-30]. This means the classification error has a weight of 1, the race prediction error of the adversary has a weight of -130, and the gender prediction error of the adversary has a weight of -30. Since the losses of the adversarial's prediction have negative weights, gradient descent will optimize the parameters of the classifier to *increase* these losses.

Finally, we can compile the combined network:

```
clf_w_adv.compile(loss='binary_crossentropy'),
                  loss_weights=loss_weights,
                  optimizer='adam')
```

With the classifier and combined classifier-adversarial model in place, the only thing missing is a compiled adversarial model. To get this, we'll first define the adversarial model to map from the classifier inputs to the outputs of the nested adversarial-classifier model:

```
adv = Model(inputs=[clf_inputs],
    outputs=adv_net(clf_net(clf_inputs)))
```

Then, when training the adversarial model, we want to optimize the weights of the adversarial network and not of the classifier network, so we use our switch functions to make the adversarial trainable and the classifier not trainable:

```
trainable_clf_net(False)
trainable_adv_net(True)
```

Finally, we compile the adversarial model just like we would with a regular Keras model:

```
adv.compile(loss='binary_crossentropy', optimizer='adam')
```

With all the pieces in hand, we can now pretrain the classifier. This means we train the classifier without any special fairness considerations:

```
trainable_clf_net(True)
clf.fit(X_train.values, y_train.values, epochs=10)
```

After we have trained the model, we can make predictions on the validation set to evaluate both the model's fairness and accuracy:

```
y_pred = clf.predict(X_test)
```

Now we'll calculate the model's accuracy and `p_rule` for both gender and race. In all calculations, we're going to use a cutoff point of 0.5:

```
acc = accuracy_score(y_test,(y_pred>0.5))* 100
print('Clf acc: {:.2f}'.format(acc))

for sens in A_test.columns:
    pr = p_rule(y_pred,A_test[sens])
    print('{}: {:.2f}%'.format(sens,pr))
```

```
out:
Clf acc: 85.44
race: 41.71%
gender: 29.41%
```

As you can see, the classifier achieves a respectable accuracy, 85.44%, in predicting incomes. However, it is deeply unfair. It gives women only a 29.4% chance to make over $50,000 than it does men.

Equally, it discriminates strongly on race. If we used this classifier to judge loan applications, for instance, we would be vulnerable to discrimination lawsuits.

 Note: Neither gender or race was included in the features of the classifier. Yet, the classifier discriminates strongly on them. If the features can be inferred, dropping sensitive columns is not enough.

To get out of this mess, we will pretrain the adversarial network before training both networks to make fair predictions. Once again, we use our switch functions to make the classifier untrainable and the adversarial trainable:

```
trainable_clf_net(False)
trainable_adv_net(True)
```

As the distributions for race and gender in the data might be skewed, we're going to use weighted classes to adjust for this:

```
class_weight_adv = compute_class_weights(A_train)
```

We then train the adversary to predict race and gender from the training data through the predictions of the classifier:

```
adv.fit(X_train.values,
        np.hsplit(A_train.values, A_train.shape[1]),
        class_weight=class_weight_adv, epochs=10)
```

NumPy's `hsplit` function splits the 2D `A_train` matrix into two vectors that are then used to train the two model heads.

With the classifier and adversary pretrained, we will now train the classifier to fool the adversary in order to get better at spotting the classifier's discrimination. Before we start, we need to do some setup. We want to train for 250 epochs, with a batch size of 128, with two sensitive attributes:

```
n_iter=250
batch_size=128
n_sensitive = A_train.shape[1]
```

The combined network of the classifier and adversarial also needs some class weights. The weights for the income predictions, less/more than $50,000, are both one. For the adversarial heads of the combined model, we use the preceding computed adversarial class weights:

```
class_weight_clf_w_adv = [{0:1., 1:1.}]+class_weight_adv
```

To keep track of metrics, we set up one DataFrame for validation metrics, accuracy, and area under the curve, as well as for the fairness metrics. The fairness metrics are the `p_rule` values for race and gender:

```
val_metrics = pd.DataFrame()
fairness_metrics = pd.DataFrame()
```

Inside the main training loop, three steps are performed: training the adversarial network, training the classifier to be fair, and printing out validation metrics. For better explanations, all three are printed separately here.

Within the code, you will find them in the same loop, where `idx` is the current iteration:

```
for idx in range(n_iter):
```

The first step is to train the adversarial network. To this end, we're going to make the classifier untrainable, the adversarial network trainable, and then train the adversarial network just as we did before. To do this, we need to run the following code block:

```
trainable_clf_net(False)
trainable_adv_net(True)
adv.fit(X_train.values,
        np.hsplit(A_train.values, A_train.shape[1]),
        batch_size=batch_size,
        class_weight=class_weight_adv,
        epochs=1, verbose=0)
```

Training the classifier to be a good classifier but also to fool the adversary and be fair involves three steps. Firstly, we make the adversary untrainable and the classifier trainable:

```
trainable_clf_net(True)
trainable_adv_net(False)
```

Then we sample a batch from X, y, and A:

```
indices = np.random.permutation(len(X_train))[:batch_size]
X_batch = X_train.values[indices]
y_batch = y_train.values[indices]
A_batch = A_train.values[indices]
```

Finally, we train the combined adversary and classifier. Since the adversarial network is set to not be trainable, only the classifier network will be trained. However, the loss from the adversarial network's predictions of race and gender gets backpropagated through the entire network, so that the classifier learns to fool the adversarial network:

```
clf_w_adv.train_on_batch(X_batch,
```

```
                              [y_batch]+\
                              np.hsplit(A_batch, n_sensitive),
                              class_weight=class_weight_clf_w_adv)
```

Finally, we want to keep track of progress by first making predictions on the test:

```
y_pred = pd.Series(clf.predict(X_test).ravel(),
index=y_test.index)
```

We then calculate the area under the curve (ROC AUC) and the accuracy of the predictions, and save them in the `val_metrics` DataFrame:

```
roc_auc = roc_auc_score(y_test, y_pred)
acc = accuracy_score(y_test, (y_pred>0.5))*100

val_metrics.loc[idx, 'ROC AUC'] = roc_auc
val_metrics.loc[idx, 'Accuracy'] = acc
```

Next up, we calculate `p_rule` for both race and gender and save those values in the fairness metrics:

```
for sensitive_attr :n A_test.columns:
    fairness_metrics.loc[idx, sensitive_attr] =\
    p_rule(y_pred,A_test[sensitive_attr])
```

If we plot both the fairness and validation metrics, we'll arrive at the following plot:

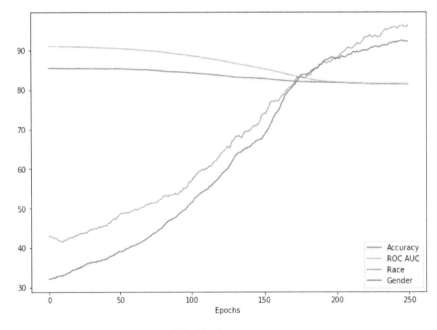

Pivot train progress

As you can see, the fairness scores of the classifier steadily increase with training. After about 150 epochs, the classifier satisfies the four-fifths rule. At the same time, the p-values are well over 90%. This increase in fairness comes at only a small decrease in accuracy and area under the curve. The classifier trained in this manner is clearly a fairer classifier with similar performance, and is thus preferred over a classifier trained without fairness criteria.

The pivot approach to fair machine learning has a number of advantages. Yet, it cannot rule out unfairness entirely. What if, for example, there was a group that the classifier discriminates against that we did not think of yet? What if it discriminates on treatment, instead of impact? To make sure our models are not biased, we need more technical and social tools, namely *interpretability*, *causality*, and *diverse development teams*.

In the next section, we'll discuss how to train machine learning models that learn causal relationships, instead of just statistical associations.

Causal learning

This book is by and large a book about statistical learning. Given data X and targets Y, we aim to estimate $p(y|x)$, the distribution of target values given certain data points. Statistical learning allows us to create a number of great models with useful applications, but it doesn't allow us to claim that X being x caused Y to be y.

This statement is critical if we intend to manipulate X. For instance, if we want to know whether giving insurance to someone leads to them behaving recklessly, we are not going to be satisfied with the statistical relationship that people with insurance behave more reckless than those without. For instance, there could be a self-selection bias present about the number of reckless people getting insurance, while those who are not marked as reckless don't.

Judea Pearl, a famous computer scientist, invented a notation for causal models called do-calculus; we are interested in $p(y|do(p))$, which is the probability of someone behaving recklessly after we manipulated P to be p. In a causal notation, X usually stands for observed features, while P stands for the policy features that we can manipulate. This notation can be a bit confusing, as p now expresses both a probability and a policy. Yet, it is important to distinguish between observed and influenced features. So, if you see $do(p)$, p is a feature that is influenced, and if you see $p(..)$, p is a probability function.

So, the formula $p(y|x)$ expresses the statistical relationship that insurance holders are more reckless on average. This is what supervised models learn. $p(y|do(p),x)$ expresses the causal relationship that people who get insurance become more reckless because they are insured.

Causal models are a great tool for fair learning. If we only build our models in a causal way, then we'll avoid most of the statistical discrimination that occurs in statistical models. Do females statistically earn less than males? Yes. Do females earn less because they are females and females are somehow undeserving of high salaries? No. Instead, the earnings difference is caused by other factors, such as different jobs being offered to males and females, discrimination in the workplace, cultural stereotypes, and so on.

That does not mean we have to throw statistical models out of the window. They are great for the many cases where causality is not as much of an important factor and where we do not intend to set the values of X. For instance, if we are creating a natural language model, then we are not interested in whether the occurrence of a word caused the sentence to be about a certain topic. Knowing that the topic and the word are related is enough to make predictions about the content of the text.

Obtaining causal models

The golden route to obtaining information about $do(p)$ is to actually go and manipulate the policy, P, in a randomized control trial. Many websites, for instance, measure the impact of different ads by showing different ads to different customers, a process known as A/B testing. Equally, a trader might choose different routes to market to figure out which one is the best. Yet, it's not always possible or even ethical to do an A/B test. For instance, in our focus on finance, a bank cannot deny a loan with the explanation, "Sorry, but you are the control group."

Yet, often causal inference can be made without the need for an A/B test. Using do-calculus, we can infer the effect of our policy on our outcome. Take the example of us wondering whether giving people insurance makes them reckless; the applicant's moral hazard, if you will. Given features X and a policy, P, we want to predict the outcome distribution, $p(y|do(p),x)$.

In this case, given observed information about the applicant, such as their age or history of risky behavior, we want to predict the probability of the applicant behaving recklessly, $p(y)$, given that we manipulate the policy, P, of granting insurance. The observed features often end up influencing both the policy and the response. An applicant with a high-risk appetite might, for example, not be given insurance, but might also be more likely to behave recklessly.

Additionally, we have to deal with unobserved, confounding variables, e, which often influence both policy and response. A prominent media article titled *Freestyle skiing is safe, and you should not get insurance*, for example, would reduce the number of people taking insurance as well as the number of reckless skiers.

Instrument variables

To distinguish the influence on policy and response, we need access to an **instrument, Z**. An instrument is a variable that influences the policy, but nothing else. The reinsurance cost, for example, could prompt the insurance company to give out fewer insurance policies. This relationship can be seen in the flowchart below, where the relationship has been mapped:

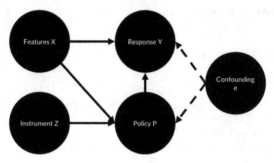

Causal flowchart

The field of econometrics already has a built a method to work with these kinds of situations called **instrumental variables two-stage least squares (IV2SLS,** or just **2SLS).** In a nutshell, 2SLS first fits a linear regression model between the instrument, z, and the policy, p, which in econometrics called the endogenous or treatment variable.

From this linear regression, it then estimates an "adjusted treatment variable," which is the treatment variable as it can be explained by the instrument. The idea is that this adjustment removes the influence of all other factors on the treatment. A second linear regression model then creates a linear model mapping from the features, x, and the adjusted treatment variable, $\hat{p}$, to the outcome, y.

In the following diagram, you can see an overview of how 2SLS works:

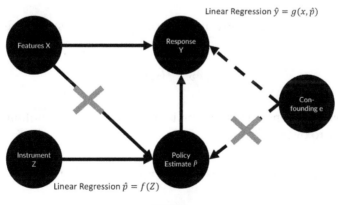

IV2SLS

2SLS is probably what the insurance company in our case would use since it is an established method. We won't go into details here, beyond giving you a brief overview of how to use 2SLS in Python. The `linear model` package in Python features an easy way to run 2SLS.

 Note: You can find the package on GitHub at `https://github.com/bashtage/linearmodels`.

You can install the package by running:

```
pip install linearmodels
```

If you have data X, y, P, and z, you can run a 2SLS regression as follows:

```
from linearmodels.iv import IV2SLS
iv = IV2SLS(dependent=y,
            exog=X,
            endog=P],
            instruments=Z).fit(cov_type='unadjusted')
```

Non-linear causal models

What if the relationships between features, the treatment, and the outcome are complex and non-linear? In this case, we need to perform a process similar to 2SLS, but with a non-linear model, such as a neural network, instead of linear regression.

Ignoring the confounding variables for a minute, function g determines the recklessness of behavior y given insurance policy p and a set of applicant's features, x:

$$y = g(p, x)$$

Function f determines policy p given the applicant's features, x, as well as the instrument, z:

$$p = f(x, z)$$

Given these two functions, the following identity holds, if the confounding variable has a mean of zero overall features:

$$\mathbb{E}[y \mid x, z] = \mathbb{E}[g(p, x) \mid x, z] = \int g(p, x) dF(p \mid x, z)$$

This means that if we can reliably estimate the function, g, and distribution, F, we can make causal statements about the effects of policy p. If we have data about the actual outcome, y, features x, policy p, and instrument z, we can optimize the following:

$$\min_{g \in G} \sum_{t=1}^{n} \left(y_t - \int g(p, x_t) \, dF(p \mid x, z) \right)^2$$

The preceding function is the squared error between the predicted outcome using the prediction function, g, and the actual outcome, y.

Notice the similarity to 2SLS. In 2SLS, we estimated F and g with two separate linear regressions. For the more complex functions, we can also estimate them with two separate neural networks. Back in 2017, Jason Hartfort and others presented just such an approach with their paper, *Deep IV: A Flexible Approach for Counterfactual Prediction*, - available at: `http://proceedings.mlr.press/v70/hartford17a/hartford17a.pdf` - the overview of which you can see in the following diagram:

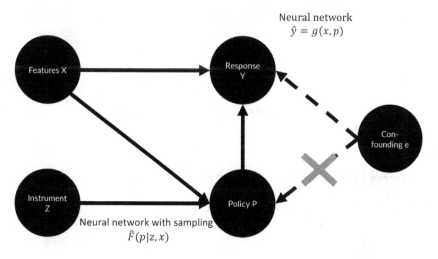

Deep IV

The idea of Deep IV is to first train a neural network to express a distribution, $F(z,x)$, which describes the distribution of policies given certain features, x, and instrument values, z. A second neural network is predicting the response, y, from the estimated policy distribution and features. Deep IV's advantage is that it can learn complex, non-linear relationships from complex data, such as text.

The authors of the *Deep IV* paper have also published a custom Keras model which is used for handling sampling and learning from a distribution part, which you can find on GitHub: `https://github.com/jhartford/DeepIV`.

While their code is too long to be discussed in depth here, it is interesting to think about what the source of our causal claim is, both in Deep IV and IV2SLS. In our insurance case, we assumed that either having or not having an insurance would influence behavior, not the other way around. We never showed or tested the truth behind this direction of causality.

In our case, assuming that insurance influences behavior is justified because the insurance contract is signed before the behavior is observed. However, the direction of causality is not always as straightforward. There is no way to establish the direction of causality other than logical reasoning or experiments. In the absence of experiments, we have to assume and logically reason, for example, through the sequence of events. Another important assumption that we make is that the instrument is actually an independent instrument. If it is not independent, our estimation of the policy will break down.

With these two limitations in mind, causal inference becomes a great tool and an active area of research from which we can hope to see great results in the future. In the best case, your discrimination-sensitive models would only contain causal variables. In practice, this is usually not possible. However, keeping the difference between statistical correlation in mind, as expressed by standard statistical models and causation, can help you avoid statistical biases and wrong associations.

A final, more technical, method to reduce unfairness is to peek inside the model to ensure it is fair. We already looked at interpretability in the last chapter, mostly to debug data and spot overfitting, but now, we will give it another look, this time to justify the model's predictions.

Interpreting models to ensure fairness

In *Chapter 8, Privacy, Debugging, and Launching Your Products,* we discussed model interpretability as a debugging method. We used LIME to spot the features that the model is overfitting to.

In this section, we will use a slightly more sophisticated method called **SHAP (SHapley Additive exPlanation)**. SHAP combines several different explanation approaches into one neat method. This method lets us generate explanations for individual predictions as well as for entire datasets in order to understand the model better.

You can find SHAP on GitHub at `https://github.com/slundberg/shap` and install it locally with `pip install shap`. Kaggle kernels have SHAP preinstalled.

Tip: The example code given here is from the SHAP example notebooks. You can find a slightly extended version of the notebook on Kaggle:

```
https://www.kaggle.com/jannesklaas/explaining-income-
classification-with-keras
```

SHAP combines seven model interpretation methods, those being LIME, Shapley sampling values, DeepLIFT, **Quantitative Input Influence (QII)**, layer-wise relevance propagation, Shapley regression values, and a tree interpreter that has two modules: a model-agnostic `KernelExplainer` and a `TreeExplainer` module specifically for tree-based methods such as `XGBoost`.

The mathematics of how and when the interpreters are used is not terribly relevant for using SHAP. In a nutshell, given a function, f, expressed through a neural network, for instance, and a data point, x, SHAP compares $f(x)$ to $f(z)$ where $E[f(z)]$ is the "expected normal output" generated for a larger sample. SHAP will then create smaller models, similar to LIME, to see which features explain the difference between $f(x)$ and $E[f(z)]$.

In our loan example, this corresponds to having an applicant, x, and a distribution of many applicants, z, and trying to explain why the chance of getting a loan for applicant x is different from the expected chance for the other applicants, z.

SHAP does not only compare $f(x)$ and $p(y)$, but also compares $f(x)$ to $E\left[f(z) \mid z_{1,2,...} = x_{1,2,...}\right]$.

This means it compares the importance of certain features that are held constant, which allows it to better estimate the interactions between features.

Explaining a single prediction can very important, especially in the world of finance. Your customers might ask you, "Why did you deny me a loan?" You'll remember from earlier on that the ECOA act stipulates that you must give the customer a valid reason, and if you have no good explanation, you might find yourself in a tough situation. In this example, we are once again working with the income prediction dataset, with the objective of explaining why our model made a single decision. This process works in three steps.

Firstly, we need to define the explainer and provide it with a prediction method and values, z, to estimate a "normal outcome." Here we are using a wrapper, f, for Keras' prediction function, which makes working with SHAP much easier. We provide 100 rows of the dataset as values for z:

```
explainer = shap.KernelExplainer(f, X.iloc[:100,:])
```

Next, we need to calculate the SHAP values indicating the importance of different features for a single example. We let SHAP create 500 permutations of each sample from z so that SHAP has a total of 50,000 examples to compare the one example to:

```
shap_values = explainer.shap_values(X.iloc[350,:], nsamples=500)
```

Finally, we can plot the influence of the features with SHAP's own plotting tool. This time, we provide a row from `X_display`, not `X`. `X_display`, which contains the unscaled values and is only used for annotation of the plot to make it easier to read:

```
shap.force_plot(explainer.expected_value, shap_values)
```

We can see the output of the code in the following graph:

The influence of features with the SHAP plotting tool

If you look at the preceding plot, the predictions of the model seem, by and large, reasonable. The model gives the applicant a high chance of having a high income because they have a master's degree, and because they're an executive manager who works 65 hours a week. The applicant could have an even higher expected income score were it not for a capital loss. Likewise, the model seems to take the fact that the applicant is married as a big factor of a high income. In fact, in our example, it seems that marriage is more important than either the long hours or the job title.

Our model also has some problems that become clear once we calculate and plot the SHAP values of another applicant:

```
shap_values = explainer.shap_values(X.iloc[167,:], nsamples=500)
shap.force_plot(explainer.expected_value, shap_values)
```

The following outputted graph is then shown. This also shows some of the problems that we've encountered:

The SHAP values showing some of the problems we can encounter

In this example, the applicant also has a good education, and works 48 hours a week in the technology industry, but the model gives her a much lower chance of having a high income because of the fact that she's a female, an Asian-Pacific islander who has never been married and has no other family relationship. A loan rejection on these grounds is a lawsuit waiting to happen as per the ECOA act.

The two individual cases that we just looked at might have been unfortunate glitches by the model. It might have overfitted to some strange combination that gave an undue importance to marriage. To investigate whether our model is biased, we should investigate a number of different predictions. Fortunately for us, the SHAP library has a number of tools that can do just that.

We can use the SHAP value calculations for multiple rows:

```
shap_values = explainer.shap_values(X.iloc[100:330,:],
nsamples=500)
```

Then, we can plot a forced plot for all of these values as well:

```
shap.force_plot(explainer.expected_value, shap_values)
```

Again, this code produces a SHAP dataset graph, which we can see in the following graphic:

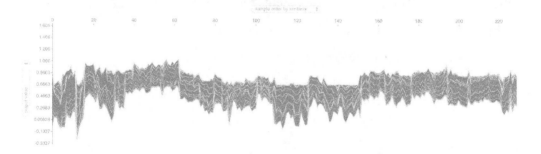

SHAP dataset

The preceding plot shows 230 rows of the dataset, grouped by similarity with the forces of each feature that matter to them. In your live version, if you move the mouse over the graph, you'll be able to read the features and their values.

By exploring this graph, you can get an idea of what kind of people the model classifies as either high or low earners. On the very left, for example, you'll see most people with low education who work as cleaners. The big red block between 40 and 60 are mostly highly educated people who work a high number of hours.

To further examine the impact of marital status, you can change what SHAP displays on the y-axis. Let's look at the impact of marriage:

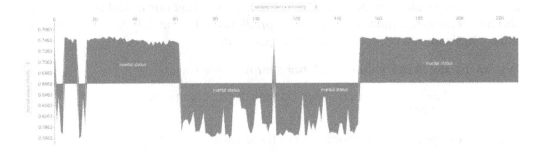

SHAP marriage outcome

As you can see in this chart, marriage status either strongly positively or negatively impacts people from different groups. If you move your mouse over the chart, you can see that the positive influences all stem from civic marriages.

Using a summary plot, we can see which features matter the most to our model:

```
shap.summary_plot(shap_values, X.iloc[100:330,:])
```

This code then outputs the final summary plot graph, which we can see below:

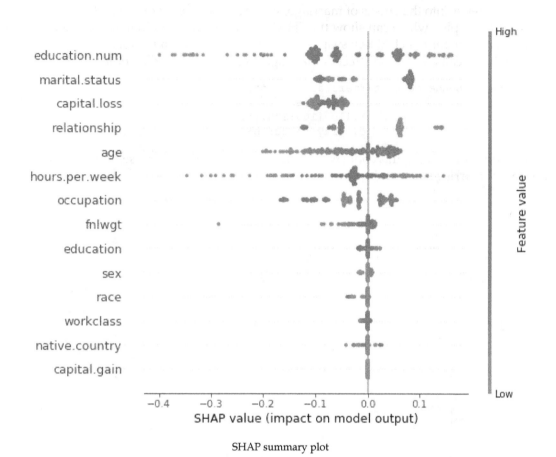

SHAP summary plot

As you can see, education is the most important influence on our model. It also has the widest spread of influence. Low education levels really drag predictions down, while strong education levels really boost predictions up. Marital status is the second most important predictor. Interestingly, though, capital losses are important to the model, but capital gains are not.

To dig deeper into the effects of marriage, we have one more tool at our disposal, a dependence plot, which can show the SHAP values of an individual feature together with a feature for which SHAP suspects high interaction. With the following code snippet, we can inspect the effect of marriage on our model's predictions:

```
shap.dependence_plot("marital-status",
                    shap_values,
                    X.iloc[100:330,:],
                    display_features=X_display.iloc[100:330,:])
```

As a result of running this code, we can now see a visualized representation of the effect of marriage in the following graph:

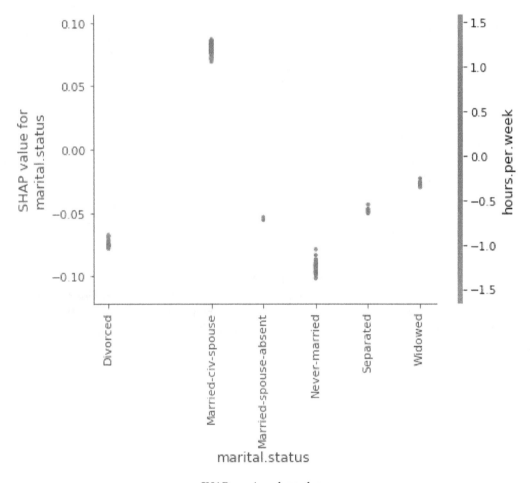

SHAP marriage dependence

As you can see, **Married-civ-spouse**, the census code for a civilian marriage with no partner in the armed forces, stands out with a positive influence on model outcomes. Meanwhile, every other type of arrangement has slightly negative scores, especially never married.

Statistically, rich people tend to stay married for longer, and younger people are more likely to have never been married. Our model correctly correlated that marriage goes hand in hand with high income, but not because marriage causes high income. The model is correct in making the correlation, but it would be false to make decisions based on the model. By selecting, we effectively manipulate the features on which we select. We are no longer interested in just $p(y|x)$, but in $p(y|do(p))$.

Unfairness as complex system failure

In this chapter, you have been equipped with an arsenal of technical tools to make machine learning models fairer. However, a model does not operate in a vacuum. Models are embedded in complex socio-technical systems. There are humans developing and monitoring the model, sourcing the data and creating the rules for what to do with the model output. There are also other machines in place, producing data or using outputs from the model. Different players might try to game the system in different ways.

Unfairness is equally complex. We've already discussed the two general definitions of unfairness, *disparate impact* and *disparate treatment*. Disparate treatment can occur against any combination of features (age, gender, race, nationality, income, and so on), often in complex and non-linear ways. This section examines Richard Cook's 1998 paper, *How complex systems fail* - available at `https://web.mit.edu/2.75/ resources/random/How%20Complex%20Systems%20Fail.pdf` - which looks at how complex machine learning-driven systems fail to be fair. Cook lists 18 points, some of which will be discussed in the following sections.

Complex systems are intrinsically hazardous systems

Systems are usually complex because they are hazardous, and many safeguards have been created because of that fact. The financial system is a hazardous system; if it goes off the rails, it can break the economy or ruin people's lives. Thus, many regulations have been created and many players in the market work to make the system safer.

Since the financial system is so hazardous, it is important to make sure it is safe against unfairness, too. Luckily, there are a number of safeguards in place to keep the system fair. Naturally, these safeguards can break, and they do so constantly in a number of small ways.

Catastrophes are caused by multiple failures

In a complex system, no single point of failure can cause catastrophes since there are many safeguards in place. Failure usually results from multiple points of failure. In the financial crises, banks created risky products, but regulators didn't stop them.

For widespread discrimination to happen, not only does the model have to make unfair predictions, but employees must blindly follow the model and criticism must be suppressed. On the flip side, just fixing your model will not magically keep all unfairness away. The procedures and culture inside and outside the firm can also cause discrimination, even with a fair model.

Complex systems run in degraded mode

In most accident reports, there is a section that lists "proto-accidents," which are instances in the past where the same accident nearly happened but did not happen. The model might have made erratic predictions before, but a human operator stepped in, for example.

It is important to know that in a complex system, failures that nearly lead to catastrophe always occur. The complexity of the system makes it prone to error, but the heavy safeguards against catastrophe keep them from happening. However, once these safeguards fail, catastrophe is right around the corner. Even if your system seems to run smoothly, check for proto-accidents and strange behavior before it is too late.

Human operators both cause and prevent accidents

Once things have gone wrong, blame is often put at the human operators who "must have known" that their behavior would "inevitably" lead to an accident. On the other hand, it is usually humans who step in at the last minute to prevent accidents from happening. Counterintuitively, it is rarely one human and one action that causes the accident, but the behavior of many humans over many actions. For models to be fair, the entire team has to work to keep it fair.

Accident-free operation requires experience with failure

In fairness, the single biggest problem is often that the designers of a system do not experience the system discriminating against them. It is thus important to get the insights of a diverse group of people into the development process. Since your system constantly fails, you should capture the learning from these small failures before bigger accidents happen.

A checklist for developing fair models

With the preceding information, we can create a short checklist that can be used when creating fair models. Each issue comes with several sub-issues.

What is the goal of the model developers?

- Is fairness an explicit goal?
- Is the model evaluation metric chosen to reflect the fairness of the model?
- How do model developers get promoted and rewarded?
- How does the model influence business results?
- Would the model discriminate against the developer's demographic?
- How diverse is the development team?
- Who is responsible when things go wrong?

Is the data biased?

- How was the data collected?
- Are there statistical misrepresentations in the sample?
- Are sample sizes for minorities adequate?
- Are sensitive variables included?
- Can sensitive variables be inferred from the data?
- Are there interactions between features that might only affect subgroups?

Are errors biased?

- What are the error rates for different subgroups?
- What is the error rate of a simple, rule-based alternative?
- How do the errors in the model lead to different outcomes?

How is feedback incorporated?

- Is there an appeals/reporting process?
- Can mistakes be attributed back to a model?
- Do model developers get insight into what happens with their model's predictions?
- Can the model be audited?
- Is the model open source?
- Do people know which features are used to make predictions about them?

Can the model be interpreted?

- Is a model interpretation, for example, individual results, in place?
- Can the interpretation be understood by those it matters to?
- Can findings from the interpretation lead to changes in the model?

What happens to models after deployment?

- Is there a central repository to keep track of all the models deployed?
- Are input assumptions checked continuously?
- Are accuracy and fairness metrics monitored continuously?

Exercises

In this chapter, you have learned a lot about both the technical and non-technical considerations of fairness in machine learning. These exercises will help you think much more deeply about the topic:

- Think about the organization you work for. How is fairness incorporated in your organization? What works well and what could be improved?
- Revisit any of the models developed in this book. Are they fair? How would you test them for fairness?
- Fairness is only one of the many complex issues large models can have. Can you think of an issue in your area of work that could be tackled with the tools discussed in this chapter?

Summary

In this chapter, you have learned about fairness in machine learning in different aspects. First, we discussed legal definitions of fairness and quantitative ways to measure these definitions. We then discussed technical methods to train models to meet fairness criteria. We also discussed causal models. We learned about SHAP as a powerful tool to interpret models and find unfairness in a model. Finally, we learned how fairness is a complex systems issue and how lessons from complex systems management can be applied to make models fair.

There is no guarantee that following all the steps outlined here will make your model fair, but these tools vastly increase your chances of creating a fair model. Remember that models in finance operate in high-stakes environments and need to meet many regulatory demands. If you fail to do so, damage could be severe.

In the next, and final, chapter of this book, we will be looking at probabilistic programming and Bayesian inference.

10
Bayesian Inference and Probabilistic Programming

Mathematics is a big space of which humans so far have only charted a small amount. We know of countless areas in mathematics that we would like to visit, but that are not tractable computationally.

A prime reason Newtonian physics, as well as much of quantitative finance, is built around elegant but oversimplified models is that these models are easy to compute. For centuries, mathematicians have mapped small paths in the mathematical universe that they could travel down with a pen and paper. However, this all changed with the advent of modern high-performance computing. It unlocked the ability for us to explore wider spaces of mathematics and thus gain more accurate models.

In the final chapter of this book, you'll learn about the following:

- The empirical derivation of the Bayes formula
- How and why the Markov Chain Monte Carlo works
- How to use PyMC3 for Bayesian inference and probabilistic programming
- How various methods get applied in stochastic volatility models

This book has largely covered deep learning and its applications in the finance industry. As we've witnessed, deep learning has been made practical through modern computing power, but it is not the only technique benefiting from this large increase in power.

Both Bayesian inference and probabilistic programming are two up and coming techniques whose recent progress is powered by the increase in computing power. While the advances in the field have received significantly less press coverage than deep learning, they might be even more useful to the financial practitioner.

Bayesian models are interpretable and can express uncertainty naturally. They are less "black box," instead making the modeler's assumptions more explicit.

An intuitive guide to Bayesian inference

Before starting, we need to import `numpy` and `matplotlib`, which we can do by running the following code:

```
import numpy as np
import matplotlib.pyplot as plt
% matplotlib inline
```

This example is similar to the one given in the 2015 book, *Bayesian Methods for Hackers: Probabilistic Programming and Bayesian Inference*, written by Cameron Davidson-Pilon. However, in our case, this is adapted to a financial context and rewritten so that the mathematical concepts intuitively arise from the code.

Note: You can view the example at the following link: `http://camdavidsonpilon.github.io/Probabilistic-Programming-and-Bayesian-Methods-for-Hackers/`.

Let's imagine that you have a security that can either pay $1 or, alternatively, nothing. The payoff depends on a two-step process. With a 50% probability, the payoff is random, with a 50% chance of getting $1 and a 50% chance of making nothing. The 50% chance of getting the dollar is the **true payoff probability** (TPP), x.

This payoff scheme is visualized in the following diagram:

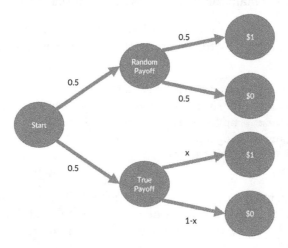

Payoff scheme

You are interested in finding out what the true payoff ratio is, as it will inform your trading strategy. In our case, your boss allows you to buy 100 units of securities. You do, and 54 of the 100 securities pay you a dollar.

But what is the actual TPP? In this case, there is an analytical solution to calculate the most likely TPP, but we will be using a computational method that also works for more complicated cases.

In the next section we will simulate the securities payoff process.

Flat prior

The variable x represents the TPP. We randomly sample 100 truth values, which are 1 if you had gotten the dollar under the true payoff, and 0 if otherwise. We also sample the two random choices at **Start** and **Random Payoff** in the preceding scheme. It is computationally more efficient to sample the random outcomes in one go for all trials, even though they are not all needed.

Finally, we sum up the payoffs and divide them by the number of securities in our simulation in order to obtain the share of payoffs in the simulation.

The following code snippet runs one simulation. It's important, though, to make sure that you understand how the computations follow from our securities structure:

```
def run_sim(x):
    truth = np.random.uniform(size=100) < x
    first_random = np.random.randint(2,size=100)
    second_random = np.random.randint(2,size=100)
    res = np.sum(first_random*truth +
(1-first_random)*second_random)/100
    return res
```

Next, we would like to try out a number of possible TPPs. So, in our case, we'll sample a candidate TPP and run the simulation with the candidate probability. If the simulation outputs the same payoff as we observed in real life, then our candidate is a real possibility.

The following sample method returns real possibilities, or None if the candidate it tried out was not suitable:

```
def sample(data = 0.54):
    x = np.random.uniform()
    if run_sim(x) == data:
        return x
```

As we have to sample a number of possible TPPs, it's only natural that we want to speed this process up. To do this, we can use a library called JobLib, which will help with parallel execution.

 Note: JobLib is preinstalled on Kaggle kernels. For more information, you can visit https://joblib.readthedocs.io/en/latest/.

To do this, we need to import the Parallel class, which will help to run loops in parallel, and the delayed method, which helps to execute functions in order inside the parallel loop. We can import them by running the following:

```
from JobLib import Parallel, delayed
```

The details are not relevant for this example, but the `Parallel(n_jobs=-1)` method makes the job run with as many parallel executions as there are CPUs on the machine. For example, `delayed(sample)()` `for i in range(100000)` runs the sample method 100,000 times.

We obtain a Python list, `t`, which we turn into a NumPy array. As you can see in the following code snippet, about 98% of the array are `None` values. That means that 98% of the values the sampler tried out for *x* did not yield results matching our data:

```
t = Parallel(n_jobs=-1)(delayed(sample)() for i in range(100000))
t = np.array(t,dtype=float)
share = np.sum(np.isnan(t))/len(t)*100
print(f'{share:.2f}% are throwaways')
```

98.01% are throwaways

Therefore, we'll now throw away all of the `None` values, leaving us with the possible values for *x*:

```
t_flat = t[~np.isnan(t)]
plt.hist(t_flat, bins=30,density=True)
plt.title('Distribution of possible TPPs')
plt.xlim(0,1);
```

As a result of running this code, we'll get the following output:

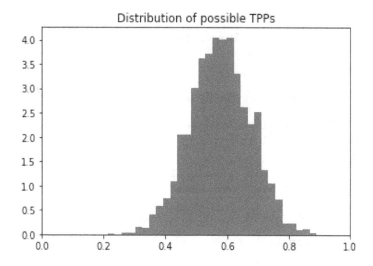

Distribution of possible true payoff probabilities as found by our naïve sampler

As you can see, there is a *distribution* of possible TPPs. What this graph shows us is that the most likely TPP is somewhere around 50% to 60%; though other values are possible, they are somewhat less likely.

What you've just seen is one of the big advantages of Bayesian methods. All of the estimates come in distributions, for which we can then calculate confidence intervals, or credibility intervals, as they are known in Bayesian terminology.

This allows us to be more precise about how sure we are about things and what other values parameters in our model could have. Relating it back to our interest in finance, with financial applications, where millions are staked on the outputs of models, it becomes very advantageous to quantify such uncertainty.

<50% prior

At this point, you are able to take your results to your boss, who is a domain expert on the securities that you are trading. He looks at your analysis and shakes his head saying, "*The TPP cannot be more than 0.5.*" He explains, "*From the underlying business, it's physically impossible to do more than that.*"

So, how can you incorporate this fact into your simulation analysis? Well, the straightforward solution is to only try out candidate TPPs from 0 to 0.5. All you have to do is to limit the space you sample the candidate value of x, which can be achieved by running the following code:

```
def sample(data = 0.54):
    x = np.random.uniform(low=0,high=0.5)
    if run_sim(x) == data:
        return x
```

Now you can run the simulations exactly as before:

```
t = Parallel(n_jobs=-1)(delayed(sample)() for i in range(100000))
t = np.array(t,dtype=float)
# Optional
share = np.sum(np.isnan(t))/len(t)*100
print(f'{share:.2f}% are throwaways')
```

```
99.10% are throwaways
```

```
t_cut = t[~np.isnan(t)]
plt.hist(t_cut, bins=15,density=True)
plt.title('Distribution of possible TPPs')
plt.xlim(0,1);
```

Which, just like before, will give us the following output:

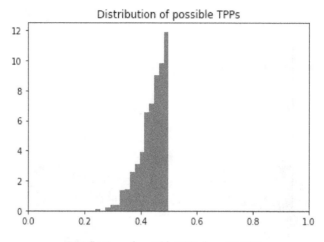

Distribution of possible TPPs from 0 to 0.5

Prior and posterior

Clearly, your choice of values to try influenced the outcome of your simulation analysis; it also reflected your beliefs about the possible values of x.

The first time around, you believed that all TPPs between 0 and 100% were equally likely before seeing any data. This is called a flat prior, as the distribution of values is the same for all values and is therefore flat. The second time, you believed that the TPPs had to be below 50%.

The distribution expressing your beliefs about x before seeing the data is called the prior distribution, $P(TPP)$, or just prior. The distribution of the possible values of x that we obtained from simulation, that is, after seeing data D, is called the posterior distribution, $P(TPP|D)$, or just posterior.

The following plots show samples from prior and posterior for the first and second rounds. The first plot shows the results with a `flat` posterior:

```
flat_prior = np.random.uniform(size=1000000)
plt.hist(flat_prior,bins=10,density=True, label='Prior')
plt.hist(t_flat, bins=30,density=True, label='Posterior')
plt.title('Distribution of $x$ with no assumptions')
plt.legend()
plt.xlim(0,1);
```

This produces the following chart:

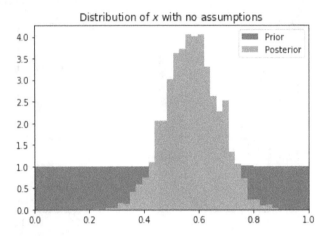

The results of our sampler with a flat prior

The next plot shows the output of our sampler with a <50% prior:

```
cut_prior = np.random.uniform(low=0,high=0.5,size=1000000)
plt.hist(cut_prior,bins=10,density=True, label='Prior')
plt.hist(t_cut, bins=15,density=True, label='Posterior')
plt.title('Distribution of $x$ assuming TPP <50%')
plt.legend()
plt.xlim(0,1);
```

While it's still the same sampler, you can see that the outcome is quite different:

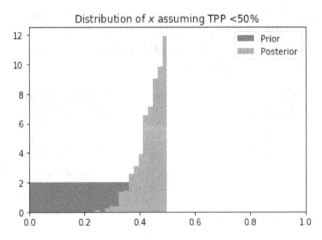

The results of our sampler with a <50% prior

Have you noticed anything curious? The posterior values of the second round are roughly equal to the posterior values of the first round, but here they are cut off at 0.5. This is because the second round prior is 0 for values above 0.5 and 1 for everywhere else.

As we only keep simulation results that match the data, the number of kept simulation results shown in the histogram reflects the probability of running a simulation that yields the observed data D for a given TPP, C, $P(D|TPP)$.

The posterior probabilities, $P(C|D)$, that we obtain from our simulations are equal to the probability that we observe the data when trying out a given TPP, $P(D|TPP)$, times the probability, $P(TPP)$.

Mathematically, this is represented as follows:

$$P(TPP|D) = P(D|TPP)P(TPP)$$

When the data is naturally obtained, such as through a face-to-face meeting, then we might need to account for biases in our data collection method. Most of the time, we do not have to worry about this and can simply leave it out, but sometimes the measurement can amplify certain outcomes.

To mitigate this, we'll divide by the data distribution, $P(D)$, as a final addon to our posterior formula and arrive at the following formula:

$$P(TPP|D) = \frac{P(D|TPP)P(TPP)}{P(D)}$$

As you can see, it's the Bayes formula! When running our simulation, we are sampling from the posterior. So, why can't we just use the Bayes formula to calculate the posterior? The simple answer is because evaluating $P(D|TPP)$ requires integrating over TPP, which is intractable. Our simulation method is, as an alternative, a simple and convenient workaround.

> **Note**: The first round prior (all TPPs are equally likely) is called a "flat prior" because we make no assumptions about the distributions of values. In this case, the Bayesian posterior is equal to the maximum likelihood estimate.

Markov Chain Monte Carlo

In the previous section, we approximated the posterior distribution by randomly sampling from our prior and then trying out the sampled value. This kind of random trying works fine if our model only has one parameter, for example, the TPP. Yet, as our model grows in complexity and we add many more parameters, the random search method will become even slower.

Eventually, there will be too many possible parameter combinations that have no chance of generating our data. Therefore, we need to guide our search and sample parameters with higher posterior probabilities more often.

The approach of a guided, but still random, sampling is called the "Markov Chain Monte Carlo algorithm". The "Monte Carlo" component means that randomness and simulation are involved, whereas the "Markov Chain" means that we move over the parameter space under certain probabilities.

In the specific algorithm covered here, we will move to a different parameter value with a probability that is the ratio of the posterior probability of the parameter value. Here, we'll think of going to the posterior probability of the parameter value. As probabilities cannot be larger than one, we cap the ratio at one, but that is just a mathematical finite that does not matter much for the algorithm.

The following diagram shows the basic workings of the Markov Chain Monte Carlo algorithm:

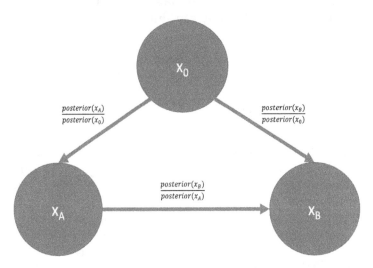

The Markov Chain Monte Carlo algorithm

What the image shows is that we are on a "random walk" in which we more or less randomly go over different parameter values. However, we don't move *entirely* randomly, but instead prefer parameter values that have high posterior probabilities.

To execute this algorithm, we need to do four things:

1. Propose a new parameter value, x_{cand}, from our current parameter value, x.
2. Estimate the posterior probability of x_{cand}, $\pi(x_{cand})$. We can use the Bayes rule for this.

3. Calculate the probability, α, of moving to that new parameter value, x_{cand} (remember that probabilities have to be smaller than one):

$$\alpha = \min\left[1, \frac{\pi\left(x_{cand}\right)}{\pi\left(x\right)}\right]$$

4. Move to the new parameter value with probability α.

The next step is to build up these components step by step:

```
# REPETITION FROM FIRST SECTION
def run_sim(x):
    truth = np.random.uniform(size=100) < x
    first_random = np.random.randint(2,size=100)
    second_random = np.random.randint(2,size=100)
    res = np.sum(first_random*truth +
(1-first_random)*second_random)/100
    return res
# REPETITION FROM FIRST SECTION
def sample(x,data = 0.54):
    if run_sim(x) == data:
        return x
```

First, we need to propose a new X_c. This has to be dependent on the previous value of x since we do not want a blind random search, but a more refined random walk. In this case, we will sample x_{cand} from a normal distribution with mean x and a standard deviation of 0.1.

It's also possible to sample from other distributions or with other standard deviations, as long as x_{cand} is related to x:

```
def propose(x):
    return np.random.randn() * 0.1 + x
```

In the first section, by sampling from the prior and then running the simulation, we sampled directly from the posterior. As we are now sampling through our proposed method, we are no longer sampling from the posterior directly. Therefore, to calculate the posterior probability, we'll use the Bayes rule.

Remember that we usually don't need to divide by $P(D)$ as we don't assume biased measurements. The Bayes rule simplifies to $P\left(TPP|D\right) = P\left(D|TPP\right)P\left(C\right)$, where $P\left(TPP|D\right)$ is the posterior, $P(TPP)$ is the prior, and $P\left(D|TPP\right)$ is the likelihood. So, to estimate the likelihood for a parameter value, x, we run a number of simulations with that parameter.

The likelihood is the share of simulations that match our data:

```
def likelihood(x):
    t = Parallel(n_jobs=-1)(delayed(sample)(x) for i in
range(10000))
    t = np.array(t,dtype=float)
    return (1 - np.sum(np.isnan(t))/len(t))
```

For starters, we will use a flat prior again; each TPP is equally likely:

```
def prior(x):
    return 1 #Flat prior
```

The posterior probability of a parameter value, x, is the likelihood times the prior:

```
def posterior(x):
    return likelihood(x) * prior(x)
```

Now we are ready to put it all together into the Metropolis-Hastings MCMC algorithm!

First, we need to set some initial value for x. To make the algorithm find likely values quickly, it is sensible to initialize it at the maximum likelihood value or some estimate that we deem likely. We also need to compute the posterior probability of this initial value, which we can do by running the following code:

```
x = 0.5
pi_x = posterior(x)
```

Likewise, we need to keep track of all of the values sampled in a trace. Purely for exhibition purposes, we will also keep track of the posterior probabilities. To do this, we're going to run the following:

```
trace = [x]
pi_trace = [pi_x]
```

Now we get to the main loop. However, before we do, it's important to remember that the algorithm consists of four steps:

1. Propose a new candidate x_{cand}

2. Compute the posterior probability of $\pi\left(x_{cand}\right)$

3. Compute the acceptance probability:

$$\alpha = \min\left[1, \frac{\pi\left(x_{cand}\right)}{\pi\left(x\right)}\right]$$

4. Set x to X_C and with a probability, α:

```
for i in range(1000): #Main Loop

    x_cand = propose(x)

    pi_x_cand = posterior(x_cand)

    alpha = np.min([1,pi_x_cand/(pi_x + 0.00001)]) # Save division

    u = np.random.uniform()

    (x, pi_x) = (x_cand,pi_x_cand) if u<alpha else (x,pi_x)
    trace.append(x)
    pi_trace.append(pi_x)

    if i % 10 == 0:
        print(f'Epoch {i}, X = {x:.2f}, pi = {pi_x:.2f}')
```

Epoch 0, X = 0.50, pi = 0.00
Epoch 10, X = 0.46, pi = 0.04...
Epoch 990, X = 0.50, pi = 0.06g

After running this algorithm for a number of epochs, we end up with a distribution of possible cheater shares with payoffs. As we've done before, we can simply run the following code to visualize this:

```
plt.hist(trace,bins=30)
plt.title('Metropolis Hastings Outcome')
plt.xlim(0,1);
```

Once we've run the previous code, we'll receive this graph as the output:

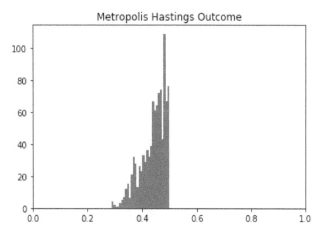

The outcome of the Metropolis Hastings sampler

By viewing the trace over time, it shows how the algorithm moves randomly but centers around highly likely values:

```
plt.plot(trace)
plt.title('MH Trace');
```

We will then get an output, in the form of a chart, which shows us the trace of the **Metropolis Hasings (MH)** sampler:

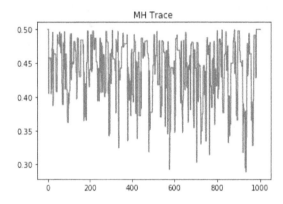

Trace of the Metropolis Hastings sampler

For a better understanding, we can plot the posterior probabilities over the tried out values:

```
plt.scatter(x=trace,y=pi_trace)
plt.xlabel('Proposed X')
plt.ylabel('Posterior Probability')
plt.title('X vs Pi');
```

After successful executing the code, we'll then get the following chart as an output:

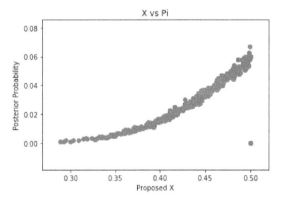

The proposed value versus posterior probability

Metropolis-Hastings MCMC

To demonstrate the power and flexibility of PyMC3, we are going to use it for a classic econometrics task, but we will put a Bayesian spin on it.

 Note: This example is a straight adaptation of an example from the PyMC3 documentation: `https://docs.pymc.io/notebooks/stochastic_volatility.html`. This, in turn, is an adaptation of an example from Hoffman's 2011 paper, *No-U-Turn Sampler*, available at: `https://arxiv.org/abs/1111.4246`.

Stock prices and other financial asset prices fluctuate, and the variance of daily returns is called volatility. Volatility is a commonly used risk measure, so it's quite important to measure it accurately.

The easy solution here would be to compute a backward-looking variance of return. However, there is a benefit to expressing uncertainty about the actual volatility. Similar to the payoff example we looked at earlier on, there is a distribution of "actual" values from which the realized values are drawn. This is also called "stochastic volatility" because there is a distribution of possible volatility values from which the observed volatility is a realized sample.

In this case we are interested in building a model of stochastic volatility of the S&P 500, the American stock market index. To do this, we must first load the data. You can either download them from Yahoo finance directly or find it on Kaggle, at `https://www.kaggle.com/crescenzo/sp500`.

To load the data, run the following code:

```
df = pd.read_csv('../input/S&P.csv')
df['Date'] = pd.to_datetime(df['Date'])
```

In the example we're looking at, we are interested in the closing prices, so we need to extract the closing prices from the dataset. The dataset shows new data first, so we need to invert it, which we achieve with the following code:

```
close = pd.Series(df.Close.values, index=pd.DatetimeIndex(df.Date))
close = close[::-1]
```

When plotting the closing prices, which we do in the following code, we see, through the outputted graphic, a familiar plot:

```
close.plot(title='S&P 500 From Inception');
```

SP500

As a result, we'll then get the following chart as an output:

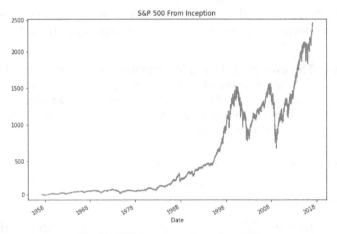

The S&P 500 from inception to late 2018

The dataset contains the S&P since its inception, which for us is a bit too much, so in our case, we're going to cut it off at 1990. We can specify this date by running the following:

```
close = close['1990-01-01':]
```

As we are interested in the returns, we need to compute the price differences. We can use `np.diff` to get daily price differences. We are going to package the whole thing into a pandas series for easier plotting:

```
returns = pd.Series(np.diff(close.values),index=close.index[1:])
returns.plot();
```

This will give us the following chart:

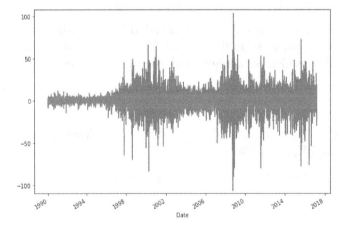

The returns of the S&P 500 from 1990 to late 2018

Now the fun with PyMC3 begins. PyMC3 includes some special distributions for dealing with time series, such as a random walk. This is exactly the right thing to use when we want to model stock prices.

Firstly, we need to import PyMC3 and its tool for time series, the random walk class:

```
import pymc3 as pm
from pymc3.distributions.timeseries import GaussianRandomWalk
```

Then lastly, we need to set up the model. We can achieve this by running the following code:

```
with pm.Model() as model:
    step_size = pm.Exponential('sigma', 50.)       #1
    s = GaussianRandomWalk('s', sd=step_size,       #2
                        shape=len(returns))

    nu = pm.Exponential('nu', .1)                   #3

    r = pm.StudentT('r', nu=nu,                     #4
                lam=pm.math.exp(-2*s),
                observed=returns.values)
```

Let's now look at the commands we just executed in order to set up the model. As you can see, it consists of four key elements:

1. The volatility, s, is modeled as a random walk with an underlying step size, step_size. Our prior for the step size is an exponential distribution with $\lambda = 50$ (once again, understanding the details of every distribution used is not necessary for the demonstration).

2. We then model the stochastic volatility itself. Note how we plug in the step size, which is itself a random variable. The random walk should have the same length as the observed return values.

3. We model the actual stock returns to be drawn from a StudentT distribution with nu degrees of freedom. Our prior for nu is an exponential distribution as well.

4. Finally, we get to model the actual returns. We model them to be drawn from a StudentT distribution with a scaling factor λ (or lam in code) produced by our stochastic volatile model. To condition the model on observed data, we pass on the observed return values.

The standard sampler for PyMC3 is not Metropolis Hastings, but the **No-U-Turn Sampler (NUTS)**. PyMC3 will default to NUTS if we specify no sampler and just call sample.

To make the sampling run smoothly here, we need to specify a relatively high amount of `tune` samples. Those are samples that the sampler will draw from in order to find a good starting point, and that will not be part of the posterior, similar to the burned samples before.

We also need to tell NUTS to be lenient when accepting values by setting a high `target_accept` value. We can achieve this by running the following:

```
with model:
    trace = pm.sample(tune=2000,
nuts_kwargs=dict(target_accept=.9))
```

PyMC3 has a nice utility that we can use to visualize the outcomes of sampling. We are interested in the standard deviation of the volatility random walk, σ, as well as the degrees of freedom of the `StudentT` distribution from which the actual returns are drawn.

As we ran two chains in parallel, you can see that we obtained two different output distributions. If we had run the sampler for longer, those two outcomes would converge. We can obtain a better estimate by averaging them, which is what PyMC3 does for predictions. For instance, let's now try that with the following code:

```
pm.traceplot(trace, varnames=['sigma', 'nu']);
TracePlot
```

With the result of that code being shown in the following charts:

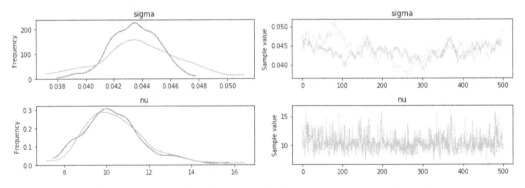

Results overview of the PyMC3 sampler. On the left, you can see the distributions produced by the two sampler chains. On the right, you can see their traces.

In the final step, we can show how stochastic volatility has behaved over time. You can see how it nicely aligns with volatile periods such as the 2008 financial crisis. You can also see that there are periods when the model is more or less certain about volatility:

```
plt.plot(returns.values)
plt.plot(np.exp(trace[s].T), 'r', alpha=.03);
plt.xlabel('time')
plt.ylabel('returns')
plt.legend(['S&P500', 'Stochastic Vol.']);
```

As we can see, the output of that code will return the chart that we see below:

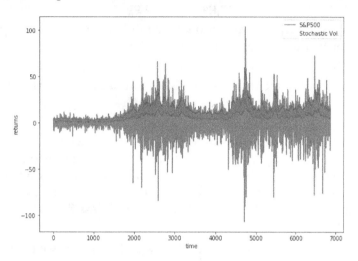

Inferred stochastic volatility from 1990 to late 2018

There are a large number of applications that can be modeled well with such relatively small Bayesian models. The main advantage is that the models are easy to interpret and can express uncertainty well. Probabilistic programming aligns well with the "storytelling" approach to data science, as the story is clearly expressed in the model.

In the next section, we will move from shallow probabilistic programming to deep probabilistic programming.

From probabilistic programming to deep probabilistic programming

The Bayesian models that we've developed so far are all quite shallow. So, let's ask ourselves whether we can combine the predictive power of deep networks with the advantages of Bayesian models. This is an active field of research and a fitting way to close this book.

Deep networks have a number of parameters; this makes searching through the parameter space a hard problem. In traditional supervised deep learning, we would use backpropagation to solve this problem. Backpropagation can also be used for Bayesian models. However, it's not the only, or even necessarily the best, way to do Bayesian deep learning.

By and large, there are four ways to do Bayesian deep learning:

- Use **Automatic Differentiation Variational Inference (AVI)**. This means approximating the posterior with a guide model and then optimizing model parameters using gradient descent. PyMC3 can do this using the AVI optimizer. See the paper, *Automatic Differentiation Variational Inference*, by Alp Kucukelbir and others, 2016 paper at `https://arxiv.org/abs/1603.00788`.

  Alternatively, you can use, Pyro which implements fast, GPU-optimized AVI, which you can view here: `http://pyro.ai/`.

  While it would be too much to give an extensive tutorial on this approach here, the PyMC3 documentation has a good tutorial on this: `https://docs.pymc.io/ notebooks/bayesian_neural_network_advi.html`.

- Assume posterior values are normally distributed, then use a standard neural network library such as Keras and learn a mean and standard deviation for every parameter. Remember how we sampled the z value from a parameterized normal distribution when working on variational autoencoders? We can do this for every layer. This trains faster and takes less computing power and memory than AVI but is less flexible and has twice the parameters of a non-Bayesian neural network.

- Use the dropout trick. When working with time series, we turned dropout on at test time and ran inference multiple times to obtain confidence intervals. This is a form of Bayesian learning that is very easy to achieve, with no more parameters than a regular neural network. However, it's slower at inference time, and does not come with all the flexibility of AVI, either.

- Pick and mix. To train a neural network, we need a gradient signal, which we can obtain from AVI. We can train the socket of a neural network, sometimes called the feature extractor, in a regular fashion and the head of the network in a Bayesian manner. This way, we obtain uncertainty estimates while not having to pay the whole cost of Bayesian methods.

Summary

In this chapter, you got a brief overview of modern Bayesian machine learning and its applications in finance. We've only touched upon this as it is a very active field of research from which we can expect many breakthroughs in the near future. It will be exciting to observe its development and bring its applications into production.

Looking back at this chapter, we should feel confident in understanding the following:

- The empirical derivation of Bayes formula
- How and why the Markov Chain Monte Carlo works

- How to use PyMC3 for Bayesian inference and probabilistic programming
- How these methods get applied in stochastic volatility models

Notice how everything you have learned here transfers to bigger models as well, such as the deep neural networks that we've discussed throughout the entirety of the book. The sampling process is still a bit slow for very large models, but researchers are actively working on making it faster, and what you've learned is a great foundation for the future.

Farewell

And thus, we close the last chapter of our journey, and I say goodbye to you, dear reader. Let's look back at the table of contents that we were met with at the start of our journey.

Over the past 10 chapters, we've covered a whole lot, including the following:

- Gradient descent-based optimization
- Feature engineering
- Tree-based methods
- Computer vision
- Time series models
- Natural language processing
- Generative models
- Debugging machine learning systems
- Ethics in machine learning
- Bayesian inference

In each chapter, we created a large bag of practical tips and tricks that you can use. This will allow you to build state-of-the-art systems that will change the financial industry.

Yet, in many ways we have only scratched the surface. Each of the chapter topics merit their own book, and even that would not adequately cover everything that could be said about machine learning in finance.

I leave you with this thought: Machine learning in finance is an exciting field in which there is still much to uncover, so onward dear reader; there are models to be trained, data to be analyzed, and inferences to be made!

Further reading

You made it to the end of the book! What are you going to do now? Read more books! Machine learning, and in particular, deep learning, is a fast-moving field, so any reading list risks being outdated by the time you read it. However, the following list aims to show you the most relevant books that have a safety net of remaining relevant over the coming years.

General data analysis

Wes McKinney, *Python for Data Analysis*, http://wesmckinney.com/pages/book.html.

Wes is the original creator of pandas, a popular Python data-handling tool that we saw in *Chapter 2, Applying Machine Learning to Structured Data*. pandas is a core component of any data science workflow in Python and will remain so for the foreseeable future. Investing in sound knowledge of the tools he presents is definitely worth your time.

Sound science in machine learning

Marcos Lopez de Prado, *Advances in Financial Machine Learning*, https://www.wiley.com/en-us/Advances+in+Financial+Machine+Learning-p-9781119482086.

Marcos is an expert at applying machine learning in finance. His book is largely focused on the danger of overfitting and how careful researchers have to be when doing proper science. While focused more on high-frequency trading, Marcos writes very clearly and makes potential issues and solutions very understandable.

General machine learning

Trevor Hastie, Robert Tibshirani, and Jerome Friedman, *Elements of Statistical Learning*, https://web.stanford.edu/~hastie/ElemStatLearn/.

The "bible" of statistical machine learning, containing good explanations of all the important concepts of statistical learning. This book is best used as a lookup book whenever you need some in-depth information on one concept.

Gareth James, Daniela Witten, Trevor Hastie, and Robert Tibshirani, *Introduction to Statistical Learning*, https://www-bcf.usc.edu/~gareth/ISL/.

Introduction to Statistical Learning is a bit like a companion to *Elements of Statistical Learning*. Written by some of the same authors, it introduces the most important concepts in statistical learning in a rigorous manner. It's ideal if you are new to statistical learning.

General deep learning

Ian Goodfellow, Yoshua Bengio, and Aaron Courville, *Deep Learning*, `https://www.deeplearningbook.org/`.

While this book is very praxis-oriented, *Deep Learning* is more focused on the theory behind deep learning. It covers a broad range of topics and derives practical applications from theoretical concepts.

Reinforcement learning

Richard S. Sutton and Andrew G. Barto, *Reinforcement Learning: An Introduction*, `http://incompleteideas.net/book/the-book-2nd.html`.

The standard work of reinforcement learning discusses all major algorithms in depth. The focus is less on flashy results and more on the reasoning behind and derivation of reinforcement learning algorithms.

Bayesian machine learning

Kevin P. Murphy, *Machine Learning: a Probabilistic Perspective*, `https://www.cs.ubc.ca/~murphyk/MLbook/`.

This book covers machine learning techniques from a probabilistic and much more Bayesian perspective. It's a very good guide if you want to think about machine learning differently.

Cameron Davidson-Pilon, *Probabilistic Programming and Bayesian Methods for Hackers*, `http://camdavidsonpilon.github.io/Probabilistic-Programming-and-Bayesian-Methods-for-Hackers/`.

This is probably the only probabilistic programming book that focuses on practical applications. Not only is it free and open source, it also gets frequent updates with new libraries and tools so that it always stays relevant.

Other Books You May Enjoy

If you enjoyed this book, you may be interested in these other books by Packt:

Tokenomics

Sean Au, Thomas Power

ISBN: 978-1-78913-632-6

- The background of ICOs and how they came to be
- The difference between a coin and a token, a utility and a security, and all the other
- acronyms you're likely to ever encounter
- How these ICOs raised enormous sums of money
- Tokenomics: structuring the token with creativity
- Why it's important to play nicely with the regulators
- A sneak peak into the future of ICOs from leaders in the industry

Mastering Blockchain - Second Edition

Imran Bashir

ISBN: 978-1-78883-904-4

- Master the theoretical and technical foundations of the blockchain technology
- Understand the concept of decentralization, its impact, and its relationship with blockchain technology
- Master how cryptography is used to secure data - with practical examples
- Grasp the inner workings of blockchain and the mechanisms behind bitcoin and alternative cryptocurrencies
- Understand the theoretical foundations of smart contracts
- Learn how Ethereum blockchain works and how to develop decentralized applications using Solidity and relevant development frameworks
- Identify and examine applications of the blockchain technology - beyond currencies
- Investigate alternative blockchain solutions including Hyperledger, Corda, and many more
- Explore research topics and the future scope of blockchain technology

Python Machine Learning - Second Edition

Sebastian Raschka, Vahid Mirjalili

ISBN: 978-1-78712-593-3

- Understand the key frameworks in data science, machine learning, and deep learning
- Harness the power of the latest Python open source libraries in machine learning
- Explore machine learning techniques using challenging real-world data
- Master deep neural network implementation using the TensorFlow library
- Learn the mechanics of classification algorithms to implement the best tool for the job
- Predict continuous target outcomes using regression analysis
- Uncover hidden patterns and structures in data with clustering
- Delve deeper into textual and social media data using sentiment analysis

Leave a review - let other readers know what you think

Please share your thoughts on this book with others by leaving a review on the site that you bought it from. If you purchased the book from Amazon, please leave us an honest review on this book's Amazon page. This is vital so that other potential readers can see and use your unbiased opinion to make purchasing decisions, we can understand what our customers think about our products, and our authors can see your feedback on the title that they have worked with Packt to create. It will only take a few minutes of your time, but is valuable to other potential customers, our authors, and Packt. Thank you!

Index

www.ingramcontent.com/pod-product-compliance
Lightning Source LLC
Chambersburg PA
CBHW060645060326
40690CB00020B/4527

9 781789 136364